War Crimes

IISS Studies in International Security

Mats Berdal, SERIES EDITOR

Strategic Thinking: An Introduction and Farewell
Philip Windsor, edited by Mats Berdal and Spyros Economides

Waging War Without Warriors:
The Changing Culture of Military Conflict
Christopher Coker

War Crimes: Confronting Atrocity in the Modern World
David Chuter

WAR CRIMES

Confronting Atrocity in the Modern World

David Chuter

LYNNE
RIENNER
PUBLISHERS

BOULDER
LONDON

Published in the United States of America in 2003 by
Lynne Rienner Publishers, Inc.
1800 30th Street, Boulder, Colorado 80301
www.rienner.com

and in the United Kingdom by
Lynne Rienner Publishers, Inc.
3 Henrietta Street, Covent Garden, London WC2E 8LU

Library of Congress Cataloging-in-Publication Data
Chuter, David
    War crimes : confronting atrocity in the modern world / David Chuter.
      p. cm. — (IISS studies in international security)
    Includes bibliographical references and index.
    ISBN 1-58826-209-X (alk. paper)
    1. War crimes.   2. Crimes against humanity.   I. Title.   II. Series.
  K5301.C485   2003
  341.6'9—dc21

                               2003046722

British Cataloguing in Publication Data
A Cataloguing in Publication record for this book
is available from the British Library.

Printed and bound in the United States of America

The paper used in this publication meets the requirements
of the American National Standard for Permanence of
Paper for Printed Library Materials Z39.48-1992.

5   4   3   2   1

Contents

Acknowledgments

This book could not have been written without the advice and assistance of a large number of individuals in governments and international organizations in different parts of the world who helped me to locate information, clarified points of difficulty, discussed the underlying issues, and in some cases read and commented on parts of the text. To all of them I am grateful, even if they must be covered by an agreed general cloak of anonymity.

Among the named, I should first thank the British Ministry of Defence, my employers, who suggested unbidden that I should write this book and paid my salary and expenses while I did so. I would particularly like to thank Simon Webb, then director general of operational policy, and Andrew Mathewson, then head of the Balkans directorate, for encouraging me in this direction.

Mats Berdal, director of studies at the International Institute for Strategic Studies (IISS) at the time, suggested that I might find a temporary home at IISS, and I am grateful to him, to the director, Dr. John Chipman, and to all their colleagues for making my stay so pleasant. In the general atmosphere of intellectual stimulation that prevailed, I would like to single out Nomi Bar-Yaacov and Spyros Economides for their personal kindness as well as their intellectual input. Over the road, at the Department of War Studies at King's College, University of London, Beatrice Heuser once again read a manuscript of mine with care and attention and made many suggestions for improvement. I also benefited very much—as I have in the past—from the knowledge and insights of James Gow and Jan Willem Honig, two of that very small group of individuals who combine a sound academic foundation in these issues with practical experience of them.

Adam Roberts of the University of Oxford was kind enough to read the text in its final form and to comment on it in some detail. He thereby saved me from a number of serious errors, especially in the area—the development of the laws of war—in which he is an acknowledged expert.

Johan Pottier and Nigel Eltringham of the School of Oriental and African Studies did their best to guide me through the complex and sensitive issue of group identity in Rwanda. Pottier's excellent book on the Rwandan crisis and its aftermath was published just before my manuscript was completed, and I was not able to take as much account of it as I would have liked. Eltringham kindly allowed me to read parts of his forthcoming book on postgenocide debates in Rwanda.

I presumed upon the time of several busy individuals who had occupied eminent positions in the general effort to investigate war crimes in the past, several of whom I had had the privilege of working with previously. Richard Goldstone, whom I had not met before, nonetheless kindly made time for me in his busy schedule as a judge of the Supreme Court in Johannesburg, and he provided me with many insights, not only as prosecutor of the two ad hoc tribunals but also as an investigator of his own country's troubled past. Louise Arbour put aside a remarkable amount of time for me from her duties as a justice of the Canadian Supreme Court to talk about her own time as prosecutor, and she also very kindly read and commented on parts of the text. John Ralston, former chief investigator of the International Criminal Tribunal for the Former Yugoslavia (ICTY), and now of the New South Wales Crime Commission, spent time helping me to understand the investigative process and its frustrations; and David Scheffer, President Bill Clinton's ambassador-at-large for war crimes issues, gave me many useful pointers, as well as offering to read parts of the text.

I was new to the operations of nongovernmental human rights organizations, and I am grateful to a number of their officials who received me with hospitality and helped me to understand their particular perspective on these issues. I would especially like to thank Richard Dicker of Human Rights Watch, Piers Pigou and Candida Earnest of the Centre for the Study of Violence and Reconciliation in Johannesburg, and Priscilla Hayner and Marieke Werda of the International Centre for Transitional Justice in New York.

In South Africa, my old friends Rocky Williams and Gavin Cawthra not only gave me their own perspectives from their days in the struggle in South Africa but also facilitated discussions with others from different backgrounds. I would especially like to thank Major General (Rtd.) Roland de Vries, Major General (Rtd.) Len LeRoux, Abbobaker "Rashid Patel" Ismail, and Howard Varney. In Australia, Mark Aarons, scourge of successive Australian governments on war crimes issues, debated some of the political issues surrounding them with great gusto and several bottles of wine. Richard Wright of the University of Sydney introduced me over dinner to a subject—forensic anthropology—of which I knew nothing and explained its importance to the preparation of war crimes prosecutions. In Sierra Leone, I was very grateful to the prosecutor of the special court, David Crane, and the registrar, Robin Vincent, for taking time away from establishing the court to come and talk to me. I was also very grateful to Bishop Joseph Humper and his colleagues from the Sierra Leone Truth and Reconciliation Commission for a fascinating and stimulating afternoon discussing their own approach to investigating Sierra Leone's past troubles.

In this book I have made much use of the trials that have taken place at The Hague; this includes not only transcripts of the proceedings (which are easily available) but also documents introduced in evidence (which are generally not). I am most grateful to the registrar of the ICTY and his staff for allowing me access to this material and making copies of some of it for me.

Finally, the advent of genuinely lightweight and high-powered laptop computers has made a huge difference to the writing of academic texts of all types, and I should record that without my trusty Samsung Q10 laptop, production of this book would have taken far longer. But I alone am responsible for any imperfections that the final text may contain.

—David Chuter

War Crimes

Introduction:
A Grave in the Air

Black milk of daybreak we drink you at night
we drink you at noon death is a master from Germany
we drink you at sundown and in the morning we drink and we drink you
death is a master from Germany his eyes are blue
he strikes you with leaden bullets his aim is true
a man lives in the house your golden hair Margarete
he sets his pack on to us he grants us a grave in the air
he plays with the serpents and daydreams death is a master from Germany
　　　　　　　　　　　　　　　　—Paul Celan, "Todesfuge" (1944)

Since this is a slightly unusual kind of book, it is probably sensible for me to give an explanation at the very beginning of what kind of book it is and what it is intended to do.

The main focus is a discussion of the possibilities and difficulties of establishing organizations to address war crimes issues, to investigate alleged offenses, and to arrest, try, and convict those thought responsible. In writing these chapters I have drawn on my personal experience, as well as the experiences of colleagues in the United Kingdom, in other countries, and in international organizations. I have tried to paint a picture that is as fair and authoritative as possible. When I was first considering the shape of the book and discussing it with others, however, it rapidly became clear that discussing these issues in the abstract would not always be useful or informative and that some context was required to explain to the reader

"Death Fugue" from *Poems of Paul Celan,* translated by Michael Hamburger. Translation copyright © 1972, 1980, 1988, 1994, 2002 by Michael Hamburger. Reprinted by permission of Persea Books, Inc. (New York) and Anvil Press Poetry (London, 1988).

something of what these crimes are and the circumstances under which they are committed. Chapters 1 and 2 try to address these issues. In doing this, I am conscious that I am trespassing on several different disciplines and half a dozen contentious issues, all of which have generated large volumes of commentary. I am not intending to provide a full account of all of these debates, still less to try to reach conclusions on them: to do so would add massively to the length of the book and unbalance the structure as well. I have therefore concentrated on trying to isolate, from this large corpus of work, conclusions and findings that seem to be useful as background to the narrower issues I proceed to address. In particular, I have tried to shed some light on why atrocities happen and to outline some conclusions on how, and by whom, they are committed. I have added a chapter on the law (Chapter 3), which is not intended as a comprehensive survey (again for reasons of size and balance), but does try to focus on the practical problems that arise when we try to turn abstract law into prosecutions of individuals. (I have also passed lightly over such issues as the evolution of just war tradition, except where such thinking continues to influence practices today.) Finally, I have added a chapter on the politics of war crimes (Chapter 4), which is essential for an understanding of what follows and is informed not only by practical experience of that particular subject (my own and that of others) but also by my quarter-century of experience as a bureaucrat in the defense and security areas.

This, then, is a book about how and why atrocities occur, what can be done to investigate and bring the perpetrators to justice, and what the prospects are for preventing atrocities in the future. It is partly informed by my experiences between 1997 and 2001 dealing with Balkans war crimes issues and the International Criminal Tribunal for the Former Yugoslavia in The Hague, but it is not a history of that period. So anyone expecting revelations and scandals, or sensitive details of military operations, has opened the wrong book, and should put it back now. There is, of course, no shortage of books on war crimes issues, but they tend to be either technical works of jurisprudence or sensational populist treatments that obscure the issues behind a welter of special pleading. Here, in trying to situate war crimes in their historical and cultural backgrounds, I cover issues and describe incidents that may initially seem to belong to another field entirely but that are nonetheless relevant.

I make no pretense to being a legal expert, or a military or intelligence expert, for that matter, but I have tried to ensure, by speaking to those who are and having them read portions of the text, that what I say about these issues is as accurate as possible. From the beginning, the concept behind this book was that it should represent the collective wisdom of those who have worked in the war crimes area over recent years. I have already thanked a number of people in the Acknowledgements, but there are many others whom it would not be fair or appropriate to name; they have given me the benefit of their comments and advice not only while this book was being written but also over a number of years of common endeavor as well.

I have already used the expression *war crimes* several times: it is probably inescapable, but it needs to be used with great care. Neither The Hague nor the Rwanda tribunals punish war crimes—they punish serious violations of international humanitarian law. Confusingly, the Statute of the International Criminal Court (ICC) *does* refer to war crimes, but in a context that is describing what was called Violations of the Laws or Customs of War or Grave Breaches of the Geneva Conventions in the past. It is a mistake to assume that war crimes are a conceptual category all their own. The crimes actually prosecuted, for all that they may be described in a vocabulary different from that used in a local police court, are fundamentally the same, and so this book contains accounts of murder, torture, rape, and theft. Even such crimes as ill-treatment of prisoners protected by the Geneva Conventions are, in practice, crimes that under another name are prosecuted every week in local courts. This is important, since the Nuremberg and Tokyo trials—unhelpful in this as elsewhere—have led to the popular perception that war crimes are a special category of crime that takes place only in war. Indeed, while many of the most terrible crimes that have been prosecuted recently may take place *during* war, since the chaos and confusion of the time makes them possible, they are not crimes *of* war in any meaningful sense. It is true that some of the crimes charged at Nuremberg—waging an aggressive war, for example—are truly crimes of war, but that experience was not generally seen as helpful and has not been continued. Although the ICC Statute foresees aggression as a separate crime, at the time of writing no progress has been made on defining it to the satisfaction of all. So we are probably stuck with the phrase *war crimes*, and it will be used in this book with a mental footnote, along the lines of the paragraph above, at each occurrence.

This book deals with subjects that some may find distressing but that others (like those who collect medical videos about the treatment of wounds) may find oddly fascinating. So I have chosen to describe, in plain language, what atrocities are all about in the knowledge that it may upset some and excite an unhappy few. But then I remember a few years ago receiving an e-mail from the Defence Intelligence staffs forwarding some material on atrocities in Bosnia for which we had asked. "If this is what you have to deal with every day," wrote the sender in a postscript, "then you're welcome to it." It is important—indeed essential—never to forget the reality of death and suffering that lies behind the tepid phrases lawyers inevitably use; but it is also important not to allow ourselves to be overwhelmed by that reality so that we take refuge in bitter cynicism or adolescent desires for undifferentiated revenge.

I have made extensive use in what follows of the work of the International Criminal Tribunal for the Former Yugoslavia in The Hague. But I have also referred frequently to the experiences of its sister organization, the International Criminal Tribunal for Rwanda (ICTR), in Arusha, Tanzania. I have naturally referred back from time to time to the Third Reich, since it is a point of departure for much thinking about war crimes. Finally, I have also made a number of references to the experiences of South Africa under the apartheid regime, especially from 1961 to 1990. I have done this for several reasons. First, although the violence and the killing was on a much smaller scale than in Rwanda and the former Yugoslavia, there are many points of similarity. Moreover, the regime that organized the violence fancied itself to be a democracy and an outpost of civilized Christian values. Second, a vast mass of material about these years is now available, especially through the work of the South African Truth and Reconciliation Commission (TRC), which itself is important as an alternative model to the model of investigation and punishment this book addresses. Scattered references are also made to the experiences of the French in Algeria, the Americans in Vietnam, and various incidents from World War II, all of which seem to me to be relevant and useful.

Many of these episodes are still very controversial, and even today most writing about the humanitarian disasters of the 1990s contains as much sanctimoniousness and emotionalism as it does rational analysis. I have tried to steer clear of this, except where some kind of judgment is required for the argument I am making. Then, I have relied either on recent scholarly work (with conclusions that often differ substantially from the polemical productions of the time), or on what has emerged in The Hague and Arusha, which probably represents the closest approximation to the truth that we are likely to get. There are, therefore, a number of things in this book that will not please the ideological police who patrol the borders of these subjects, but there is nothing I can do about that.

1

The Basics

In war people get killed. They also get wounded and mutilated, some-times horribly. They may be held in confinement against their will and forcibly prevented from escaping. Even as civilians, they may be killed in an attack on a legitimate target. And all of this is perfectly legitimate. While there are strict controls on what may be legally done in war, it inevitably entails violence and suffering. We can seek to reduce this aspect, but we can never turn war into a video game, and it is dangerous and self-deluding to imagine that we can. Thus, the consideration of war crimes raises issues of proportionality and balance. Moreover, many illegal acts of war have a sound military justification behind them and, if practiced, might well end a war or battle more quickly, and with fewer casualties, than would otherwise have been the case. When we add to this the fact that many acts of war that are illegal today were thought acceptable, if not praiseworthy, in the past, then the moral and ethical—as well as the legal and practical—issues raised by the notion of war crimes are complex, rela-tive, and murky.

Partly this is because of the curious fashion in which the laws of war have been elaborated, in two distinct ways and according to two distinct traditions. On the one hand, the military has always recognized the need for limitation. Notwithstanding the tendency to see war as just episodes of mindless slaughter and wanton destruction, military professionals have, in fact, often tried to limit the amount of violence used for practical reasons. The military, after all, is about *controlled* violence. To continue fighting after an enemy seeks to surrender, or after a peace treaty has been signed, for example, could involve unnecessary casualties and frustrate political aims. Economy of force is generally a good military principle, and profes-sionals will respect a general who wins a cheap victory more than one who wins a titanic battle of attrition. One never knows, after all, how soon one might fight again and whether there will be any more soldiers. This in turn produces a general agreement among military professionals that they must establish rules for their mutual protection. Although for much of human history "prisoners could count themselves lucky if they were only enslaved," treating prisoners well may be in one's own best interests if it influences an enemy to behave likewise.[1] The same applies to the use of prisoners for forced labor, as well as to the use of weapons that cause unnecessary suffering. These rules certainly helped to civilize warfare; but if taken to the extreme, as in Renaissance Italy, they could produce endless polite battles that settled nothing.

There has been more controversy about treatment of the civilian population. Some commanders (e.g., the Duke of Wellington and Frederick the Great) thought that it was pointless to antagonize locals, since they were a source of food and other necessities and a possible source of information about the enemy. At the very least, treating locals badly would simply cause more problems later. Not all commanders took this enlightened view, however, and some continued to allow the ancient practice of robbery and plunder as a way of compensating for late or nonexistent pay. It was generally accepted, though, that the civilian population would lose whatever rights it had if it were to try to take up arms against an enemy force. The practice of taking and executing civilian hostages lasted until at least the Franco-Prussian War, without causing much comment. These principles were prompted less by moral fervor (although pronouncements by religious leaders did have some practical influence) than by a recognition that professionals had the most to gain if they treated each other in a civilized fashion and if civilians simply stayed out of the way. There have, therefore, always been powerful *practical* arguments for moderation in warfare.

Superimposed on this pragmatic scheme are some idealistic proposals for limiting war whose origins are somewhat different. Many treaties (e.g., on the environment or arms control) owe part of their inspiration to lobbying by outsiders, but such lobbies are perhaps more powerful in the international humanitarian law arena than elsewhere, partly because there are far more international lawyers and humanitarian lawyers outside government than inside. So international humanitarian law tends to reflect the proposals of some theologians, philosophers, and lawyers who have never themselves been in uniform and whose proposals are intended to limit war and to make it, in a few cases, impossible to perform. This idealist tendency has recently been influential and has had a considerable effect on the four Geneva Conventions and the two Additional Protocols, which are the basis of current international law. For example, the International Committee of the Red Cross (ICRC) was for some years obsessed with the so-called Geneva Zones in which all military activity—even in war—would be forbidden.

This proposal was "open to so many objections on the grounds of military realism that it got nowhere" in preparatory discussions, but the ICRC eventually managed to place an attenuated form into the final 1949 texts.[2] More organized states try so far as they can to ensure that issues of practicality (and not just military ones) do play a part in the negotiations that produce these texts. But practical issues—which can be very complex and even counterintuitive—have to struggle for precedence with the demands of the negotiating process itself, the views of other states (especially allies), the requirement to reach a compromise text, and the needs of states to strike acceptable moral poses in public.

Larger states try to ensure that delegations to law-producing conferences also include practical experts from other disciplines, but for smaller states this is often impossible. Many small states do not have the capacity to analyze and develop proposals within government in such a complex area, and their negotiating position will therefore be entirely political. As a result, the laws of war are disproportionately influenced by rather ethereal individuals, remote in every way from their subject matter. (Certainly, when I was in Rome for part of the 1998 Diplomatic Conference which led to the establishment of the International Criminal Court there were plenty of representatives from ministries of justice and foreign affairs, but, so far as I could see, few who had ever put on a uniform in anger). This is probably inevitable and not necessarily a bad thing, because few would think that committees of frontline commanders would do the job better, but it does give rise to certain practical problems.

In Chapter 3, I set out the main provisions of current international humanitarian law in terms of the legal distinctions and definitions. But nobody sets out to violate an article of the International Criminal Court (ICC) Statute or the Geneva Conventions; rather, they set out to commit an act that seems to them necessary or attractive or even fun. A commander makes a decision to burn a village and drive out the inhabitants not to commit a crime against humanity. He or she makes a decision to use prisoners for forced labor not to violate the laws or customs of war. And so on. So here I shall concentrate on a typological, rather than a legal, analysis of wrongdoing. In taking this approach, I recognize that there is relativism in the way in which various actions are defined as crimes. The current state of international humanitarian law—represented by the Geneva Conventions/Protocols and the ICC Statute—is essentially the result of a series of political compromises made during negotiations. Had the balance of negotiating forces been slightly different, certain acts that are now thought criminal might not have been and vice versa. The law of war is accordingly not based on revealed truth but on bureaucratic and political compromises. It is wrong to take a one-dimensional, moral, absolutist approach to what is a compromise collection of different texts that could themselves have turned out differently. Moreover, such texts are not necessarily logically consistent within themselves, and many of the offenses they describe are, in fact, relatively minor. I shall therefore concentrate on gross violations of international humanitarian law, focusing on the kind of crimes that have always been thought most serious.

There are five broad categories of war crimes, corresponding to the rhythm of events on and off the battlefield. First, there are illegal actions committed by military personnel during the fighting itself. These can include the use of illegal weapons or tactics (such as disguising combat personnel as medical personnel), firing on assets that, although military, are protected (such as medical facilities), and announcing an intention not to take any prisoners. The second category is the conduct of illegal actions by military personnel and against other military personnel once the fighting is over. Obvious examples include the execution or ill-treatment of prisoners who have surrendered, or, for example, their use as forced labor in digging trenches. Although this is forbidden, and armies will always try to prevent it, it is also very common. It may require a superhuman degree of self-control to treat in a civilized fashion an enemy soldier who has tried to kill you, and perhaps killed your best friend. Moreover, there are certain understood customs at the end of a battle, which mean that mercenaries, snipers, and operators of unpopular weapons such as flamethrowers are not treated with as much kindness as others who have surrendered or been captured.

The third category includes illegal acts committed against civilians or civilian objects during the fighting itself. Examples include the use of civilians as human shields and the deliberate targeting of civilian facilities (e.g., to encourage the population to flee and so to assist the capture of a town). A related phenomenon is the use of children in combat, which is becoming increasingly common, especially in societies where family and social structures have been destroyed by violence. Some military forces (like the Kosovo Liberation Army in 1998–1999) have not only made use of children as young as twelve directly in combat but also used younger children as couriers, making the judgment that they are less likely to be targeted by the opposition but, if killed, will be of propaganda value nonetheless.

The fourth category includes illegal acts committed against civilians when the fighting is over. The most obvious examples are destruction and theft of property. This occurs when discipline in the attacking force is lacking or when loot itself is one of the major reasons for the fighting. It is common in parts of Africa for armies to be poorly paid, if at all; stealing becomes a matter of deliberate policy. For much of the fighting in the former Yugoslavia, the distinction between war and armed robbery was not always clear. Often paramilitary forces (especially Serbs) were asked to destroy homes and murder their inhabitants, or force them to flee, in return for being able to keep what they could loot. Also, there are random killings, rapes, and other forms of ill-treatment of civilians after a town has been captured. Some of this is traditional. Soldiers who expect to die but are suddenly reprieved by the end of the fighting will respond in various ways. Some may simply want to rest or sleep, but others, overflowing perhaps with testosterone, will seek an outlet for their aggression—and perhaps also their desire for revenge. One of the themes of this book is that revenge is often symbolic and compensatory, and it is often taken against those who are available rather than those who actually committed the acts for which revenge is sought.

The fifth category is the use of military or paramilitary forces for purposes that are entirely political and have no military objective. Often, these operations are conducted against groups that are unarmed or incapable of any meaningful resistance. At this point, it becomes increasingly difficult to describe these offenses as war crimes. Some may indeed take place *during* wars—as did the use of the German armed forces and the SS to murder Jews and other groups in World War II—but they are not crimes *of* war in any real sense. More commonly, these acts amount to the use of military force to destroy or evict groups incapable of any serious resistance in the absence of any armed conflict at all. Obvious examples here include the exterminations of the Hereros in German Southwest Africa, and the indigenous people of Tasmania. In all the examples here, the possession of an organized and trained military force gave governments exterminatory options that they were ruthless enough to take and that would not have existed had the target group been seriously armed.

The fourth and fifth categories are conceptually different from the first three because attacks on civilians, rather than being incidental or even cynically connived at, become the main purpose of the operation. Sometimes the purpose is the physical destruction of an ethnic or other group; sometimes it is to drive a group out of a place intended for occupation; sometimes it is simply for reasons of terror and intimidation. In the 1980s, for example, the South African state used *askaris*—former supporters of the African National Congress (ANC) who had been induced to change sides—to entice teenagers from the townships into going off with them under the pretence of recruiting them for the ANC's military wing. Inevitably, the children would be ambushed and murdered. This tactic was intended to make potential recruits fear genuine recruiters and to be less likely to join up.[3]

All of these examples assume a deliberate attack by one party on another, leading to atrocities being committed. But it can also be politically valuable to *provoke* attacks and atrocities in certain circumstances. Many guerrilla groups have recognized that the support of the civilian population is often best gained by encouraging the opposition to commit atrocities against them. Groups such as the Kosovo Liberation Army, which had a Maoist intellectual pedigree, sought to provoke Serbian forces into attacking the civilian population in 1998–1999 in order to radicalize locals. But there is a long tradition of such activity in the Balkans; it was a Partisan tactic in World War II, and such tactics linger in the consciousness. These days, however, provoking (or even inventing) atrocities against one's own people may also gain sympathy from others, as in the former Yugoslavia. Thus, there is evidence that snipers were placed on the city walls of Dubrovnik to draw fire from the attacking Yugoslav forces, and mortars and artillery pieces were placed within hospital grounds in Sarajevo, Osijek, and Gorazde for much the same purpose.[4] We can expect to see more of such activities in the future, as the struggle for international support becomes an even more important factor in conflicts.

As for moral relativism, there are few, if any, war crimes (as listed in the above categories) that were not at some time regarded as permissible, if not actually praiseworthy, in various civilizations. The God of the Old Testament, for example, commanded the Israelites that

> if a city will make war against thee, then thou shalt besiege it: . . . and when the LORD thy God hath delivered it into thine hands, thou shalt smite every male thereof with the edge of the sword. But the women, and the little ones, and the cattle, and all that is in the city, even all the spoil thereof, shalt thou take unto thyself. . . . But of the cities of these people, which the LORD thy God doth give thee for an inheritance, thou shalt save alive nothing that breatheth. But thou shalt utterly destroy them; namely, the Hittites, and the Amorites, the Canaanites, and the Perizzites, the Hivites, and the Jebusites; as the LORD thy God hath commanded thee. (Deuteronomy 20:12–18)

Texts such as these, of course, gave Christian societies of a later era a justification for their own exterminatory practices.

Accepting that this relativism certainly exists, it would be ridiculous to assume that acts that were once acceptable are acceptable today, or, alternatively, that we should not condemn certain actions until a legal provision is enacted to prevent them. Laws do not make things bad; they merely indicate that those with the power to pass laws *think* they are bad. The real issue here is a moral and not a legal one. I will therefore take the Geneva Conventions/Protocols and the ICC Statute as a point of departure for the rest of this book. Without worrying too much about exact phraseology, I assume that they represent a convenient summary of acts that we now think should not be committed. In the remainder of this chapter, and Chapter 2, I shall examine why and how human beings nonetheless commit them.

A Useful Act

Before continuing, keep in mind that many gross violations of human rights, in battle and elsewhere, are planned and perpetrated, or sometimes adopted on the spur of the moment, because they are thought to be *useful*. The administrative and logistic burden of complying fully with current international humanitarian law provisions is considerable, and this may detract substantially from one's fighting capability. As a young British paratroop officer, Eric Carlton recalled being told by veterans of the Arnhem campaign during World War II that few German prisoners were taken during the many small skirmishes because it was impossible to take, let alone keep, prisoners in such a situation.[5] Many similar examples could be given from all eras. Guerrilla and other irregular forces, in particular, often do not have the capability to hold prisoners and so often do not take them. The use of human shields, or the ability to bombard a town where the enemy is hiding, even at the cost of heavy civilian casualties, may help win a battle more quickly and cheaply. Targeting civilian political leaders, despite seeming legally dubious to some, may bring a war to an early conclusion with lower casualties on both sides. It is important to be clear about this to help dispel the idea that war crimes are simply outbursts of meaningless barbarity. There are some incidents of that type, but in most cases there is a logic to what is done, even if the objective itself may not seem very acceptable to anyone else.

Here, for example, is Pietro Loredan, a Venetian commander fighting the Turks in 1416, informing the authorities about what followed the battle: "Aboard the captured vessels we found Genoese, Catalans, Sicilians, Provencals and Cretans, of whom those who had not perished in battle I caused to be hanged—together with all the pilots and navigators, so the Turks have no more of these at present." As one modern historian commented on the same situation, "There is no indication that the . . . savagery, reported here with such nonchalance, . . . caused any adverse comment in the Republic [Venice] or elsewhere."[6] The point, however, is that Loredan saw clearly that pilots and navigators were a scarce and expensive resource for the Turks and took a long time to train. Executing them gave the Venetians a considerable temporary military advantage. The same arguments may well apply to the use of military force against defenseless civilians. Many recent intrastate conflicts, notably those in parts of Africa and in the former Yugoslavia, are essentially contests for the control of territory. The best way to ensure control over territory is to persuade representatives of other groups to leave it, and the best way to do that is to kill a few of them and threaten the rest with similar treatment unless they leave. The various factions in the Bosnian fighting used this technique extensively as a way of gaining new territory or holding the territory they already had.

Sometimes, however, atrocities are a good way of intimidating and disciplining populations when your forces are too weak to expel them. In Africa, the technique seems to have been pioneered by the Renamo (Resistencia National Mocambicana) opposition forces in Mozambique, initially under Rhodesian guidance, then under that of South Africa. When it first began operations in the late 1970s, Renamo amounted to only a few hundred men, with little military capability. The atrocities (notably mutilations) were intended to destabilize local society and to emphasize that the Frelimo (Frente de Liberacao de Mocambique) government could not protect its citizens. They were used particularly when Renamo was very weak as an efficient way of controlling territory. Similar tactics have been used more recently in Liberia and Sierra Leone. Though brutal, these tactics are by no means senseless.[7] Likewise, during the civil war in Liberia Prince Johnson circulated a tape he had made of the torture and execution of the former president, Samuel Doe, thus making the political point that his rival, Charles Taylor, by no means had complete control of the country. Both of these cases involve the deliberate use of atrocity for considered political ends rather than the manipulation of ethnic hostility.

In most of these cases there is little effective distinction between the military and civilians. Where the fighting is basically between militias, every male of military age is a potential soldier and in some cases (as in the former Yugoslavia) may have had military training anyway. Taken to its ultimate, this type of action can result in the mass killing of males of military age just because they might some day become soldiers. This, in turn, is a tactic with a long history. In the ancient world, the destruction of cities by the execution of males and the sale into slavery of women and children was routine. Even in the Greek world, with its rules for the conduct of internecine warfare, it has been estimated that "about two dozen Greek city-states suffered the extreme form of annihilation" during the classical period.[8] Again, the motive was not mindless violence. One of the principal purposes, indeed, was discipline: during the long struggle with Sparta, the Athenians used such tactics, and the threat of their repetition elsewhere, to discourage their allies from leaving the Delian League. The Romans did the same thing during the contest with Carthage. Moreover, annihilation of this kind probably represented the only way in which a political entity could ever win a decisive battle over another. Until recently, the standard measure of military power was the trained human being. Even a massively one-sided battle, therefore, like Cannae, would not be finally decisive because, in a few years, the losing side would train more human beings to fight and, perhaps, win. This is why the Romans eventually decided to destroy Carthage—not because it was then a threat but because it might become a threat later (rather in the same spirit as Cold War strategists targeting the recovery capability of an enemy).

"The Man in the House"

Although plans for war crimes can have a grisly logic, they also have a tendency to spiral out of control when implemented on the ground. Whether prompted by the exploitation of difference or the desire for gain, the actual killing must be carried out by ordinary human beings prone to all kinds of failings. So the perpetration of these crimes often has elements of chaos, stupidity, and sick farce to it. The confessions of various killers and dirty tricksters employed by governments often read like unusually violent episodes from the Keystone Kops. Thus, accounts given by killers from the apartheid regime reveal not a group of iron-nerved Rambos but rather a bunch of overweight men whose weapons often did not work, who failed to destroy the bodies of those they did manage to kill, who were so excited about breaking into the ANC's London offices that they forgot to bring a bomb with them, and were drunk for most of the time anyway.[9]

"Todesfuge," the famous poem by Paul Celan, with its musical title, jaunty rhythms, and bitter humor, provides an unforgettable synthesis of the mixture of farce and horror that war crimes tend to involve. The poem is supposedly spoken by the inmates of a concentration camp, describing the processes by which they live and die. But the central figure of the poem is actually "the man" who "lives in the house"—the camp commander—who

> whistles his pack out
> He whistles his Jews out in earth has them dig for a grave
> he commands us strike up for the dance . . .
> jab deeper you lot with your spades you others play on for the dance . . .
> He calls out more sweetly play death death is a master from Germany . . .
> his eyes are blue
> he strikes you with leaden bullets his aim is true.[10]

There are several historical incidents—including some at Auschwitz—on which this poem might loosely be based.[11] But what it primarily reflects, in fact, is more the absurd situations that result when individuals are given total power over others without having to worry about the consequences of their actions. Psychotics, sadists, people with violent childhoods, and those simply without scruples will tend to gravitate toward situations of this kind.

For example, there was Goran Jelisic, a Bosnian Serb from Bijelina. Jelisic was sent to a concentration camp for non-Serbs at Luka, in Brcko, a strategically vital town in Bosnia, in 1992. Jelisic frequently referred to himself (even in court) as the "Serb Adolf" who came to Brcko to kill Muslims, which he did in large numbers, with his pride and joy, a Skorpion machine-pistol, usually forcing them to lie over an open grate so that the blood would drain away quickly. Jelisic had the habit of killing twenty to thirty Muslims before he had his morning coffee. Eventually, his behavior became so extreme that whoever originally sent him to Brcko had him reassigned elsewhere. Jelisic is an obvious psychopath, the prototype baby-faced killer who still looked about eighteen when he went on trial in The Hague. Somebody had sent Jelisic to Brcko for a purpose, but like most psychopaths he turned out ultimately to be uncontrollable. The "madness of war" is a cliché, and not always an accurate one, but it does remind us that war frequently produces extreme and bizarre situations in which disturbed and often frightening people come to the fore, sometimes because the situation demands unorthodox actions, and sometimes because such people muscle in anyway, taking advantage of the confusion that seems endemic in war. Just as the gangsters who mostly ran the Third Reich, for example, could only have come to power in a time of severe national crisis, so their atrocities could only have been committed during the chaos of wartime, when normal rules tend to be suspended.

There is, in fact, a sick, surreal side to most wars, which is not emphasized in official histories, but of which the participants themselves have always been conscious. Modern writing about war at the tactical level often presents it as a phantasmagoric nightmare, full of absurdity and chaos.[12] A contemporary emblematic figure from the fighting in Sierra Leone, who mixes farce and horror in equal proportions, is Liberia's General Butt Naked (Joshua Milton Blahi), who was renowned for his supposed "magical" powers, which he claimed to have acquired through regular human sacrifice. He led a rag-tag militia of men who would enter battle naked or wearing dresses and wigs and who then engaged in barbaric acts, ranging from the disembowelment of pregnant women to settle arguments over the probable sex of the fetus to ritual cannibalism. This kind of behavior is especially common in civil wars between factions, where there may be no real front lines or uniforms, where friends and neighbors wind up killing each other, and where the sides are confused and change frequently.[13] A simple recital of the facts of the fighting in Bosnia, for example, makes Joseph Heller's novel *Catch-22* read less like a satire on war and more like documentary reporting. Captain Milo Milenbinder, taking money from the Germans to bomb his own comrades, would be absolutely at home in Bosnia between 1992 and 1995, with its business relations between bitter enemies, factionlets changing sides in the middle of a battle, sieges continuing for mutual profit, and enemies selling and renting each other weapons.

In this atmosphere of moral chaos, those responsible for atrocities at ground level frequently respond to the freedom they have been given by adopting a surreally vicious attitude toward those who have been put in their power. It is not enough for enemies to be killed or even beaten; they must be humiliated and destroyed psychologically while providing entertainment for their captors. The persistent comparisons between life in a concentration camp and the punishments of hell are particularly under-standable if we remember, say, the paintings of Hieronymous Bosch, with their never-ending but endlessly inventive tortures of the damned. (Indeed, accounts of many of the atrocities in Bosnia read like nothing so much as a Bosch painting dramatized by the Marx Brothers.) All factions in Bosnia in 1992 were quick to set up concentration camps in which shifting coalitions of jailers kept shifting sets of victims. Conditions in these camps were generally made deliberately vile, and killings, beatings, and rapes were commonplace, as much for the enjoyment of the jailers as for any effect they might have on the inmates. What stands out from the weeks of testimony by the victims in various trials at The Hague is the sheer pointless, gratuitous savagery of their treatment, which often seemed to be aimed at humiliation above all.

In the baking heat of a Bosnian summer, Muslim and Croat inmates of the notorious Omarska camp, near Prijedor, were forced to sing Serb nationalist songs before being given any water. When the guard was eventually satisfied with the quality of the singing, water was thrown through a window to the prisoners; most of it was spilled. Likewise, inmates who asked to use the toilet were allowed to do so but savagely beaten when they did. Unable to tolerate this, they were reduced to soiling themselves or urinating and defecating in public.[14] Almost no form of humiliation seemed to have been overlooked during the chaos of the time. According to witness statements by inmates of a Croat-run concentration camp at Stolac, near Mostar, the camp guards fed the prisoners only once a day, with boiling soup. The prisoners were given thirty seconds to run to the soup tureen, swallow what they could, and then run back. If they exceeded the time limit they were savagely beaten.[15] Guards at the Celebici concentration camp, run by Muslims and Croats for Serbs, regularly forced male prisoners to commit fellatio on each other, and at least one Serb prisoner was killed by having a badge of the Muslim Party of Democratic Action nailed to his forehead.[16] The point about these atrocities is precisely that they have no point. They are what happen when vicious individuals of moderate intelligence are put in a position of power over others, with no external controls over their behavior.

This accounts, perhaps, for the typical pattern of war crimes, which we shall see in the course of this book: a high-level political objective put into action in a brutal, incompetent, and unnecessarily (and sometimes self-defeatingly) violent fashion. Some infamous war crimes episodes, indeed, seem to have been conceived, or at least executed, with absolutely no thought as to what they were supposed to achieve. The Bosnian Serb concentration camps around Prijedor seem to have been designed, according to documents used in evidence at The Hague, as temporary holding areas for individuals suspected of participating, or having participated, in military actions against Serbs. Yet as the Trial Chamber in the Keraterm camp case noted, prisoners did not seem to have been selected on any rational basis: they included butchers, taxi drivers, and café owners as well as people of greater standing in the community. Likewise, the small percentage of inmates in comparison to the non-Serb population of the municipality, and the haphazard nature of the way they were treated, meant that if the plan was to destroy the non-Serb population in the area, or even to terrify it, then the plan was incompetently devised and very poorly executed. Yet the political damage to the Bosnian Serb cause that coverage of the camps brought about was immense, and this lost them whatever international sympathy they may have retained until that point.[17]

The same is true of the Ahmici massacre in April 1993, when Bosnian Croat forces killed more than a hundred Muslims in a mixed Croat-Muslim village in Central Bosnia. Ahmici was important for Croat lines of communication, and its seizure would have been a legitimate act of war. But Croat forces staged a heavy military attack on the village at dawn on April 16, although it was effectively undefended. They used grenades, antiaircraft weapons, and heavy machine-guns against an unarmed populace, most of whom were still asleep. Whole families, including old people and children, were butchered; many were burned alive. The violence and savagery of the attack bore no relationship to the resistance encountered (there was none), or to any conceivable wider objective. What it did do was lose the Bosnian Croat cause much sympathy after the massacres were discovered by British troops under the United Nations (UN).[18] Again, one witness in the *Celebici* trial recalled that he asked why he, still a schoolboy, and who could never have been a threat, was being beaten and incarcerated. "Because you're Serbs" was his answer, which, with variations by ethnicity, could have been the response from all over Bosnia in 1992.[19] But perhaps the ultimate answer to the question of why these horrific things were done is that given to the young Primo Levi by an SS guard in a concentration camp in 1944: *Hier ist kein warum* (There are no why's here).[20]

Meno's Idea of Virtue

The commission of large-scale atrocities, with their mixture of cynical policy, viciously farcical execution, and gratuitous cruelty, are common, but they are by no means universal, nor do they happen all the time. Some societies seem to avoid these atrocities entirely and others at least to avoid them for long periods of time. A common pattern is that of the former Yugoslavia: a few episodes of frightening violence separated by long periods of relative tranquility. So what are the factors that produce these outbreaks, and why do they occur when they occur? I can provide only a partial answer because there is, of course, no model, no factor or groups of factors, that will inevitably produce mass atrocities as a result. There is a series of contributory circumstances, varying combinations of which are important in different cases. And there is an important category of atrocities in recent years, such as those in Sierra Leone, where ethnic or other differences do not seem to be a major factor and where explanations of conduct must therefore be different.

Let us begin with the case of the Other. In one of Plato's dialogues, Socrates and Meno discuss the question of what virtue is and whether it can be taught. Meno believes that he can define virtue without difficulty. Masculine virtue, he argues, is "managing the city's affairs capably, and so that he will help his friends and injure his foes while taking care to come to no harm himself."[21] Meno's definition (which suggests that depressingly little has changed in Balkan politics in the past two-and-a-half millennia) is challenged by Socrates on several grounds, one of which is that virtue requires temperance and justice, although since these two terms are not defined, the argument is essentially circular. But Meno has a point, of course, and his view of virtue—of what is just, and how we should live—is, in practice, the one that most of us hold and practically all of us revert to under pressure. The fundamental distinction in human relations is, surely, what Tzvetan Todorov has called "We and Others."[22] In early societies, laws were primarily for the internal regulation of the group. The biblical injunction against killing, for example, the cause of so much heart-searching in the Christian era, applied only to members of the in-group: the Israelites. Killing non-Israelites, by contrast, was actively encouraged. Most, if not all, early societies seem to have had similar rules. While there often were, and are, rules of hospitality dictating how guests should be treated, and cooperation between groups was common, there was no sense that the internal rules of the tribe of other group applied to nonmembers. Killings, wife-stealing (the basic story in Homer's *Iliad*), cattle-rustling, and the spoiling of crops were among the staples of intergroup relationships in earlier times, and there was no sense that any of these acts was wrong, provided it was directed at a member of the out-group. Indeed, most heroic poetry (see Homer) praises deeds that today would be thought illegal as well as immoral. There are still societies today (including some in the Balkans) where cheating, robbing, or murdering members of an out-group are regarded as honorable and even praiseworthy.

It follows that the limitations we place on our personal conduct within the group are not necessarily valid outside it. Care of women and children, for example, is a priority within the group, but not necessarily beyond. The harsher the conditions of life, the more the survival of the group takes priority over all other considerations, including abstract moral ones. As states became more sophisticated and more centralized, they sought to universalize these internal values and to promote the revolutionary idea that members of out-groups should be treated in the same way as members of the in-group provided they were all part of the same state. The feud and the reprisal were to be replaced with disinterested justice administered from a central authority. Even today, there is a strong correlation between a breakdown in central authority and the commission of atrocities. When faith in an overarching system of justice fails, people tend to fall back on the protection of their own group and to see other groups as threats. Sitting in the courtroom at The Hague I heard as succession of thuggish-looking Balkan males insist that "we were only protecting our people." This has rhetorical value, of course, but somewhere beyond that, perhaps, was a genuine conviction, first that the survival of their group *was* threatened, and second that its survival took precedence over all other considerations. With a few trivial exceptions, none of the accused at The Hague has expressed sorrow or repentance; rather, they have sought to justify their conduct, especially through the argument that "the other side started it." (Below I discuss just how the murders of innocent women and children can be regarded as essential for survival.)

In fact, the universalization of internal values was always problematic, and this remains so today. Most of us feel instinctively that our own group's interests are more important than the interests of other groups, and this applies especially when violence is involved. For example, when British soldiers have been convicted and imprisoned for the murder of Irish civilians, in circumstances where it is clear that they have not only broken the law but also disobeyed orders, public anger in Britain, and demands for their release, have been intense. The message is clear: the lives of Irish people are less important than British lives. This kind of reaction, in fact, is the norm, even in developed democracies with strong traditions of the rule of law.

Take the public reaction to the 1968 My Lai massacre. On the face of it, reactions should have been unproblematic. After all, the U.S. Army was well-trained, its officers educated professionals who had been taught the laws of war, the country itself a liberal democracy with a strong humanitarian tradition; not least, a large part of the population disapproved of the war itself. But after Lieutenant William Calley's conviction, no less than 79 percent of a telephone sample said they disapproved of that outcome, and only 9 percent approved. Two American sociologists designed a survey to test public opinion more widely: the results are striking. A total of 36 percent of respondents thought that Calley's actions (in effect, the deliberate murder of women and children) were morally right without qualification. Forty-five percent thought that Calley's actions were justified "if the people he shot were communists," and 58 percent thought that it was "better to kill some [South] Vietnamese civilians than risk lives of American soldiers."[23]

It is further interesting that most of those questioned said they would have acted as Calley had done, if ordered to commit a massacre, and thought that most other people would, too. Those who disapproved of Calley being put on trial were then asked for their reasons. Among the most common were that "it is unfair to send a man to fight in Vietnam and then put him on trial for doing his duty" (83 percent), and "the trial is an insult to our fighting men and weakens the morale of the [U.S.] Army" (67 percent).[24] Effectively, therefore, the deaths of large numbers of "Oriental human beings," as the U.S. authorities unfortunately put it, was less important than the maintenance of the Army's morale. But it would be unfair to single out the United States for special criticism: the same sentiments seem to be found everywhere. When Svetlana Alexievich began to publish the accounts of the Afghanistan fighting from the mouths of Russian soldiers, full of atrocity, incompetence, and corruption, she received a number of furious complaints. "How dare you cover our boys' graves with such dirt? They did their duty by the Motherland," complained one mother.[25] It requires uncommon courage for a public figure—still more a politician—to make an issue of alleged atrocities by one's own troops against an enemy.

Calley never expressed any remorse for his actions and always claimed to be unable to understand why he had been punished. Fellow veterans from Vietnam told very similar stories (there seem to have been many such incidents). One marine sergeant explained: "It wasn't like they were humans. We were conditioned to believe that this was for the good of the nation, the good of the country, and anything we did was okay. And when you shot at someone you didn't think you were shooting at a human. They were a gook or a Commie and it was okay."[26]

A Russian Afghan veteran agreed: "The Afghans weren't people to us, and vice versa. We couldn't afford to see each other as human beings."[27] Should we, then, see atrocities as a result of dehumanization resulting from the stress of combat and forcible indoctrination? It is clearly more than that, because the same sentiments are found frequently among noncombatants and political leaders. A few months before My Lai, the U.S. Army had conducted an investigation into allegations of excessive violence in search-and-destroy operations carried out in Quang Ngai Province, where some 70 percent of the estimated 450 hamlets had been destroyed. Estimates of civilian dead and wounded ranged from 33,000–50,000 per year over a period of several years. The Army accepted these estimates but reassured Washington that it was okay because "the population is totally hostile towards the [Saigon] government and is probably nearly in complete sympathy with the [Vietcong]. . . . For the [Vietcong] there isn't any distinction: the [Vietcong] *are* the people."[28] The journalist Neil Sheehan tackled General William Westmoreland, the American commander in Vietnam, about "whether he was worried about the large number of civilian casualties from the airstrikes and the shelling. He looked at me carefully. 'Yes, Neil, it is a problem,' he said, 'but it does deprive the enemy of the populations, doesn't it?'"[29]

Collective Punishment

We tend to regard the killing of women, children, and the elderly as especially iniquitous, at least as long as they are part of a political entity that we support. This relies on the assumption that we can distinguish in our minds between combatants and others and carry out actions only against the former. At the tactical level, where men with guns actually shoot and kill, this distinction has often broken down, partly because of the dehumanizing effects described above. But another reason is that this distinction, close as it is to the heart of international humanitarian law, has *actually* broken down and "may not correspond with the moral and political realities of societies in armed conflict."[30] One might add that it does not necessarily correspond with *military* realities either, as civilians are increasingly taking a direct part in combat. The U.S. Army report referred to above, although dishonest in intent, is correct in the sense that the Vietcong saw less of a distinction between civilians and combatants than did the Americans, at least in theory. In Afghanistan, much of the population was mobilized against the Russians. One veteran recalled how a Russian patrol encountered an abandoned baby lying by the side of the road, freezing to death. After a debate, it was decided that the lieutenant would take the baby to a nearby village. When the lieutenant and his driver failed to return, a search was instituted, which led to the discovery that the women of the village had beaten them to death with their hoes.[31] God knows what happened to the village. Some decades before, Algerian nationalists, in their struggle with the French, had resorted to using civilians—including women—to plant bombs in French areas of Algiers.

It is much easier for troops and their commanders to justify acting in violent ways if the enemy can be characterized as an abstraction rather than a set of individuals. That is why, in general, wars fought against abstractions—heresy, communism, terrorism—are always the most brutal. In Vietnam, the United States believed itself to be fighting communism. In this context, civilian political workers—or just people sympathetic to the Vietcong—were probably a greater threat to U.S. objectives than was the Vietcong. The problem is that, while it is just about possible to fight *for* an abstraction, it is effectively impossible to fight *against* one, because military activities require a concrete target of some sort. By a common progression of logic, therefore, the target you can engage comes to stand for the target you wish to engage. Thus, the villagers were believed sympathetic to the Vietcong, and killing them amounted to fighting communism. The same thought process evidently was behind French actions in Algeria, where again the Western power considered itself to be fighting communism. The French army had studied its defeat in Indochina and taken to heart the words of General Vo Nguyen Giap that French leaders had not paid enough attention to the political dimension.[32] They had also studied the writings of Mao and concluded, correctly, that the armed element of the Algerian nationalists, the Armée de Libération National (ALN), was politically subservient to the Front de Libération National (FLN) leadership. Moreover, the threat to French control came more from the terror attacks in Algiers than from military operations in the desert. So with remorseless Gallic logic, the French identified the political leadership as the main effort. According to one recent account, some 3,000 Algerian civilians believed linked to the FLN were kidnapped, tortured, and murdered in the space of about two years in the fight against communism.[33] And finally, as if the Bosnian fighting had any need to be more vicious, the fight against abstractions played a part also. Much Serb behavior, and some Croat behavior also, was conditioned by a fear of Islamic fundamentalism. By the kind of logic set out above, it is then possible to turn on your neighbors and even your friends and slaughter them in unspeakable ways. For their part, most of the vicious atrocities carried out by the Muslims seem to have been concentrated in the 7th Muslim Brigade of III Corps, where the mujahideen were generally to be found.

But the distinction between combatants and noncombatants is one that governments and their populations always forget easily during times of stress. There are a number of reasons for this. For example, collective punishment remains a feature of many societies—in most schools, for example, or in the treatment of sports-team supporters or certain immigrants as a group deserving punishment or harsher control because of the misdeeds of a few. The same applies at the international level, where distinctions between combatants and noncombatants, or even just the innocent and the guilty, are often not made. Economic sanctions, always a useful political standby, are a classic example of collective punishment. In early societies, where the distinction between We and Others was still very strong, punishment could take the form of retributive murder of an individual or individuals from the group held responsible. One explanation for the culture of massacre and countermassacre of civilians that has so distinguished the Balkans, for example, may be that

> Peasant communities had regulated life both officially and informally in terms of collective responsibility and sanctions since Byzantine times, if not earlier. Punishment, even by the state, long reflected the popular view

that families were responsible for the misdeeds of their individual members. . . . Anti-brigandage laws often deported or levied fines not only on the brigand but on his relatives too.[34]

This in turn reflected the Ottoman practice of ruling subjects by ethnic or religious groups, which bargained with the authorities as a group. This is a system whose influence was still strong in Yugoslavia under Marshal Tito and then later, when politics was organized along very similar lines. And even in societies in which the principle of individual criminal responsibility had long been accepted, the underlying urge toward collective punishment remains strong. After all, if the actual target is unavailable for any reason, then collective punishment is the only satisfaction you are likely to get.

The most interesting example of collective punishment and complete failure to distinguish between combatants and civilians is the Allied bombing offensive against Germany and Japan during World War II. I am not going to get involved in pointless and anachronistic polemics about the legality of incidents in the past. It is enough to say that *by current standards* the strategy would have been illegal and therefore falls within the criteria for examination that I set out earlier. The fundamental point about strategic bombing (i.e., bombardment from the air to achieve strategic goals) is that from the very beginning it was conceived as a strategy directed at civilians. Its earliest advocates took note of the panic of civilians on the few occasions when bombing had actually been carried out during World War I and hypothesized that future wars could be won by bombarding the cities of the enemy so that civilian morale collapsed and the populations rose up against the government. At that point, the war would conclude without any need for huge land battles between soldiers. Although this policy was aimed directly at civilians, its advocates actually defended it on the grounds that it was more humane: General Giulio Douhet, the most famous (if not the most influential) airpower advocate argued that precisely *because* the targets were civilians, least able to sustain the shock of war, such conflicts might be "more humane than wars in the past" because "they may in the long run shed less blood."[35] Lord Trenchard, fairly regarded as the founder of the Royal Air Force (RAF), agreed strongly with this view, and his view was influential.

The British did not immediately implement this policy in World War II, partly out of moral queasiness, partly out of fear of German retaliation. In any case, aircraft capable of taking a worthwhile bomb load to Germany were not immediately available. By February 1942, however, the RAF's Bomber Command was directed to employ its forces "without restriction" against "the morale of the enemy civilian population, and, in particular, the industrial workers."[36] But this policy was never formally acknowledged, which is why it is hard to measure either official or popular reaction to it. In public, the government maintained stoutly that only military targets were being attacked, and aircrews, until the very end of the war, were given only military objectives (in the widest sense) in their briefings, although the crews must have known that current technology was too primitive to allow this. If the British government lied to others, it also lied, to an extent, to itself. Lord Cherwell, British prime minister Winston Churchill's scientific adviser and a great advocate of bombing, in March 1942 proposed a strategy described as "dehousing," calculating that one-third of the German people could be made homeless within a year, which would "break the spirit of the people." The idea that bombs would destroy buildings but not kill people must have seemed as extraordinary at the time as it does today.[37]

But why would the British, a civilized people who had earlier had moral qualms, now approve of what Churchill in an injudicious moment at the end of the war was to call "acts of mere terror and wanton destruction" disguised "under other pretexts"?[38] In essence, it was a way of justifying the only policy that, for political, military, and technical reasons, was actually available: indiscriminate area, or saturation, bombing. Since that was the only policy there was, all the hopes of the nation had therefore to rest on an "absolutely devastating, exterminating attack . . . on the Nazi homeland," as Churchill described it as early as 1940.[39] Since the inaccuracy of the weapons meant that large urban centers were the only possible targets, attacking them had to be seen as morally justified. For that reason, both publicly and privately, the key to victory was judged to be the morale of the German people, since, as a propaganda leaflet dropped in 1939 put it, they could "insist on peace at any time."[40] Since the German people were choosing not to insist on peace, the responsibility for the continuation of the war rested with them as individuals, and they were thus a legitimate target. Everyone in the British government must have known this was rubbish (the German people had no influence whatever on the conduct of the war), but it served its bureaucratic purpose at the time.

Defenders of the strategic bombing campaign (both at the time and since) have generally used four arguments in its support. They are relevant to the wider question of justifications advanced in all ages for causing widespread destruction of civilian life. (I leave out the charge that criticism of the bombing campaign is "an insult" to the aircrew who died: that is not an argument.) The first argument is that the underlying cause (the defeat of Nazi Germany) was just and therefore any means to achieve it was justified. This description of the cause, of course, is a statement of value, not a statement of fact, although most people would agree with it. Traditional theories of the just war required a number of tests to be met for a war to be lawful. The two that have remained influential into modern times are that the cause itself is just (*ius ad bellum)* and that the means used are lawful (*ius in bello)*. This argument says in effect that the first test makes the second unnecessary. There are several problems with this argument, which amounts to saying that a higher moral standard is expected of the guilty party. First, it is not clear whether it is an absolute or a relative one. Does the intrinsic justice of the cause mean that *all* methods are acceptable? Would a threat to murder all German women and children in Allied-controlled areas in February 1945, unless the Germans surrendered, have been acceptable? And what if it were carried out? Or is the argument a relative one, in which the degree of justice makes certain things acceptable on a sliding scale? Moreover, few entities have gone to war for consciously evil reasons: the Nazis considered that they were fighting a just war as well. In the absence of an agreed objective standard of measurement, we are forced into subjective judgments of the worth of various causes. For most groups, their survival and safety represents a just cause against which there is no argument.

Second, it is argued that the Germans "started it," and this is true in a limited sense, although strategic bombing as such was never part of German thinking. But we run immediately into the same question: Does the fact that they started it justify *any* level of response? If so, we are in the world of the defenders of the Ahmici massacre, who argued that Muslims had previously been killing Croats, and the defenders of the Srebrenica massacre, who argued that Muslims had previously killed Serbs. Both of these assertions are true, but courts and others have held that the fact that someone else started it is not a defense, especially when the revenge is so disproportionate. It is not clear why the British situation is different.

Third, it is argued that Britain was fighting for its national survival at the time, and so all means were acceptable. (Again, we might query whether *all* means were acceptable.) The problem, of course, is once again the lack of any independent way of evaluating this assertion. The Nazis in World War II, the Hutu in Rwanda, the Serbs and, to some extent, the Croats in the former Yugoslavia all believed that their very existence was threatened, and all argued that they were therefore entitled to use extreme measures. It would surely be very dangerous to have a principle that if the survival of a group is threatened (or believed to be threatened) then it is allowed to use any means to defend itself. The apartheid regime in South Africa, for example, genuinely believed itself to be threatened by a vast total assault, orchestrated from Moscow, which represented the "powers of chaos, Marxism and destruction," according to then–President P. W. Botha.[41] In such circumstances, who could argue with the use of the most extreme measures?

Finally, it is argued that strategic bombing resulted—or was at least intended to result—in a shortening of the war and a lower level of suffering overall, the argument that Douhet had used. Again, of course, this argument can be used to justify virtually anything. The Nazis believed that they were the victims of a vast international conspiracy directed by the Jews that had plunged the world into war; the extermination of the Jews was therefore the quickest way to end it. Similarly, the Bosnian Serbs in 1992 judged that, with Bosnian independence certain and fighting inevitable, their best tactic would be a quick grab for the areas they wanted to control before anyone else could get organized. Had this tactic succeeded, ironically, there would have been far less suffering in Bosnia than there actually was.

In practice, all of these arguments, whoever may use them, are one and the same. The argument is about We and Others, and it says that Our interests are fundamentally more moral and more important than Theirs, that Our cause is inherently just and Theirs is not, and, ultimately, that We deserve to survive and They don't. These arguments seem to touch something very basic in the collective human psyche and will no doubt continue to be used to justify extreme actions.

Conclusion

In concluding this chapter, I want to briefly compare the justifications above with the justifications given by the U.S. government for the bombing of Hiroshima. That episode was unusual in that, unlike the British raids, it evoked a considered public defense and explanation in the form of a radio broadcast by President Harry Truman on August 9. There was no attempt to present Hiroshima as a military target (there were scarcely any by that stage of the war). The selection of the target, according to those involved, was from those that would "most adversely affect the will of the Japanese people to continue the war."[42] This strains belief even more than the German example: the Japanese people had never been consulted about issues of war and peace and had not the slightest influence on the policy of their government. But the idea was a necessary fiction, as with the Germans, if an attack on civilians was to seem morally acceptable. Truman's justification, meanwhile, mixed two themes that his advisers no doubt felt would strike a chord with listeners: revenge, and the saving of American lives. The bomb was used "against those who attacked us at Pearl Harbor" and against "those who have starved and beaten and executed American prisoners of war."[43] Now it is unlikely that Truman, or his speechwriter, genuinely thought that the inhabitants of Hiroshima had done these things *themselves* or in most cases knew, let alone approved, of them. Once again, the argument is for collective punishment and (rather like the Balkan examples above) for the families of the men on the front line to be punished for their crimes. The other justification was to "shorten the agony of war" and save

American lives.[44] This requires, of course, a belief that American lives are more important than Japanese lives, but that is a commonplace thought when nations are at war with each other.[45]

Running through the discussion of these two bombing cases, and several of the other incidents as well, has been the theme of revenge. I shall deal with this at greater length later, but here I wish only to remark that human beings have a strong tendency to believe that not just revenge but disproportionate revenge is justified when their own group is in some way wounded. Since Our lives are more important than Theirs, we can contemplate the most appalling revenge while still feeling morally superior. I have given examples from the Balkans already, but in fact such violent emotions appear to be universal. Telford Taylor recalled how, while in Washington briefly for leave in early 1945, he attended a dinner party at which "the almost unanimous view of the guests (mostly libertarian New Dealers) was that all members of the SS"—a couple of million men, at a conservative estimate—"should be put to death." Taylor was attacked as "soft on Germany" for opposing this gruesome suggestion.[46] Firsthand reports of the Nazi death camps had started to emerge by then, but probably a greater source of concern was the stories (subsequently proved to be correct) of the murder of some sixty U.S. soldiers by the SS after they had surrendered in the Battle of the Bulge. Taylor's dinner companions would no doubt have been pleased to learn that, not long before, senior U.S. officials seriously discussed the logistics of shooting out of hand some 2,500 senior Nazis, even to the point of worrying whether the superior-orders doctrine would protect the soldiers who did the executions.[47]

Next I consider some of the deeper political and psychological origins of this distressing willingness to consider the mass extermination of others.

Notes

1. Geoffrey Best, *War and Law Since 1945*, p. 136.
2. Ibid., pp. 116–117.
3. One such case is described by Martin Meredith, *Coming to Terms*, pp. 60–62.
4. See Susan L Woodward, *Balkan Tragedy,* p. 236; Misha Glenny, *The Fall of Yugoslavia*, p. 136.
5. Eric Carlton, *Massacres*, p. 107.
6. John Julius Norwich, *A History of Venice*, p. 294.
7. See Alex de Waal, "Contemporary Warfare in Africa," in Mary Kaldor and Basker Vashee, eds., *New Wars*, p. 315, and Alex de Waal, ed., *Who Fights? Who Cares?* For the rationality of much recent conflict in Africa, see William Reno, *Warlord Politics and African States*, and Paul Richards, *Fighting for the Rain Forest*.
8. Hans van Wees, "War and Peace in Ancient Greece," in Anja V. Hartmann

and Beatrice Heuser, eds., *War, Peace, and World Orders in European History*, p. 34.

9. See, for example, Eugene de Kock, *A Long Night's Damage*; Jacques Pauw, *Into the Heart of Darkness*.

10. Paul Celan, "Todesfuge," from *Poems of Paul Celan*. Reprinted by permission of Persea Books and Anvil Press Poetry.

11. John Felsteiner, *Paul Celan*, gives some examples and prints a photograph (p. 30) of a Jewish orchestra playing the so-called "Death Tango" to accompany the murder of prisoners at the Janowska Road Camp in Lvov. When the killings were over the orchestra was shot in turn.

12. See, for example, Michael Herr, *Dispatches*, about the Vietnam War; Svetlana Alexievich, *Zinky Boys*, about the fighting in Afghanistan; Anthony Lloyd, *My War Gone By I Miss It So*, about Bosnia and Chechenya.

13. On Liberia, see Stephen Ellis, *The Mask of Anarchy.*

14. *Kvocka and Others* (IT-98–30/1), Judgement of November 2, 2001.

15. Statements from the Stolac camp were made available to me through the course of my work for the British Ministry of Defence; these documents have not been released publicly.

16. *Delalic and Others* (IT-96–21), Judgement of November 16, 1998.

17. *Sikirica and Others* (IT-95–8–3), Judgement on Defense Motions to Acquit, September 3, 2001.

18. *Kupreskic and Others* (IT-95–16), Judgement of January 14, 2000.

19. *Celebici* case, Transcript, p. 1617 (April 2, 1997).

20. Primo Levi, *If This Is a Man*, p. 35.

21. Plato, *Protagoras and Meno*, p. 71E.

22. Tzvetan Todorov, *Nous et les autres.*

23. Herbert C. Kelman and V. Lee Hamilton, *Crimes of Obedience*, pp. 169–179.

24. Ibid., p. 214.

25. Alexievich, *Zinky Boys*, p. 187.

26. Cited by Joanna Bourke, *An Intimate History of Killing*, p. 205.

27. Alexievich, *Zinky Boys*, p. 117.

28. Cited by Neil Sheehan, *A Bright Shining Lie*, p. 689 (emphasis in original).

29. Ibid., p. 621.

30. Best, *War and Law*, p. 259.

31. Alexievich, *Zinky Boys*, p.156.

32. Raoul Girardet, *La Crise militaire francaise.*

33. Général Aussaresses, *Services Spéciaux.*

34. Mark Mazower, *The Balkans*, p. 130.

35. Giulio Douhet, *The Command of the Air*, pp. 57–58. Douhet's arguments were taken up by several prominent British thinkers, notably J. F. C. Fuller, who argued in 1923 that "if a future war can be won at the cost of two or three thousand of the enemy's men, women and children killed, in place of over 1,000,000 men and incidentally several thousands of women and children," then such a war was actually humane. Cited in Beatrice Heuser, *The Bomb*, p. 45.

36. Quoted in Sir Charles Webster and Noble Frankland, *The Strategic Air Offensive Against Germany*, vol. 4, pp. 144–148.

37. Ibid., vol. 1, pp. 331–336.

38. Ibid., vol. 3, p. 112. Churchill's minute was later withdrawn.

39. Cited by Stephen A. Garrett, *Ethics and Air Power*, p. 47.

40. Cited by Norman Longmate, *The Bombers*, p. 75.

41. Cited by Pauw, *Into the Heart of Darkness*, p. 22.

42. Leslie R. Groves, *Now It Can be Told*, p. 267.

43. Ibid.

44. Cited by David McCullough, *Truman*, p. 459.

45. Ironically, the United States had been among the most forward of critics of Japanese bombing of civilians in China, claiming in 1937 that "any general bombing of an extensive area wherein there resides a large population engaged in peaceful pursuits is unwarranted and contrary to principles of law and of humanity." Cited by John Dower, *War Without Mercy*, p. 58.

46. Telford Taylor, *The Anatomy of the Nuremberg Trials,* p. 42. Taylor's doubts were not about the morality of the idea as such but because he had met a few SS men he rather liked.

47. Gary Jonathan Bass, *Stay the Hand of Vengeance,* pp. 157–160.

2

The Origins

In most places, and at most times, people have been able to conceptualize, and in some cases carry out, massive atrocities against others. In doing this, they claim a special status and justification for their own interests and their own well-being and deny the same privileges to others. They make excuses for what they (or a cause with which they sympathize) have done yet seek punishment, and refuse tolerance, of others in similar situations. Yet the fact remains that most human beings get on with each other pretty well most of the time. The world is, generally speaking, not some Hobbesian nightmare of all against all but a place where different groups can coexist for long periods of time without any overt conflict between them. Telford Taylor's dinner partners did not actually go out and massacre millions of Germans, and the U.S. government itself drew back, after some thought, from the idea of mass summary executions. Yet similar dinner parties in Munich and Kigali, and in Belgrade and in Zagreb, led to unspeakable atrocities later. In this chapter, I try to describe the special factors that turn latent horrors into real ones.

The Strange Voyage of Social Darwinism

Most people in the world have a sense of who others are and that they are a little different in language, in color, in customs, or in religion. Under normal circumstances these differences don't matter very much. They matter more, however, when they are subsumed into a developed theory that explains *why* these differences matter and what needs to be done about them. The major ideology that fastened onto these differences and exploited them ruthlessly was what we now describe as Social Darwinism. Like most influential ideas in human history, Social Darwinism was never prop-erly articulated—indeed, it was such an incoherent set of ideas in the first place that that would have been difficult. But it is best understood as a somewhat simple-minded transposition of popular understandings of Darwin's theory of evolution to human relations. The idea that human beings differed was not new, of course—various eighteenth-century writers like Carl von Linné in Switzerland and the famous Comte de Buffon in France divided human beings into racial types and tried to classify them.[1] But Darwin's ideas suggested that it was possible to classify humans as neatly as animals and to do so in a scientific manner. More important, they also suggested that not all human "races" would be equally successful and that there was a scientific rationale—interspecies competition through natu-ral selection—that explained the causes and consequences of this fact.

Until Darwin and the geologist Charles Lyell, it had been assumed that the earth and its living population were fairly static during the few thou-sands of years they had existed. Lyell demonstrated that the earth was thou-sands of times older than had been thought, and Darwin demonstrated that vast numbers of species had lived and perished; he also provided a scientif-ic explanation of how this happened. The temptation to apply this logic to human beings was irresistible. It operated at two levels. First, if there was an inevitable struggle between races (which could be defined as anything from whites versus blacks to French versus Germans), then each "race" had to be as tough and hardy as possible. This meant, thought Herbert Spencer, letting the "sickly, the malformed and the least powerful" die as part of the "purifying process."[2] Misguided liberals who wanted to improve the lot of the poor were simply blinded by their own sentimentality from seeing that these miserable people were beyond help and that attempts to intervene would simply enable the weak to survive artificially and were enfeebling the race overall. In turn, this hardness allowed the race to compete in the life-or-death struggle with others to avoid the fate of the dinosaur and the dodo.

It is curious in some ways that Social Darwinism lasted as long as it did, given that people and nations will generally choose to cooperate if they can, and given that experience suggests that cooperation is a better tactic than conflict anyway. But this longevity is explained partly by the fact that the theory suited the interests of many rich and powerful people. Domestically, it was of use in combating expensive ideas for the relief of the poor, opposing democracy and the emancipation of women, and gener-ally keeping political and financial privileges intact. At the international level, it was even more useful, since every nation either believed that its present exalted position was justified by its natural virtues or that its natu-ral virtues entitled it to a more exalted position than it had, if necessary, through the use of force. In the absence of a nation with a fully worked-out theory of its own insignificance, we can probably assume that it was useful to every ethnic group. It was particularly useful to states with empires, or states that wanted them. Imperialism was justified by what Lord Salisbury, then the British prime minister, described as the division of "the nations of the world into the living and the dying." Weak nations became increasingly weak and strong nations became increasingly strong, Salisbury argued, so that "the living nations will fraudulently encroach on the territory of the dying."[3] The next logical step was made by the German historian Heinrich von Treitschke, who argued that in "the unhappy clash between races . . . the blood-stained savagery of a quick war of annihilation is more humane . . . than the specious clemency of sloth."[4] Indeed, he argued that it was wrong to apply existing standards of warfare to "barbaric people."[5]

This way of thinking turned genocide into something approaching a moral duty in the colonies, and it helped to validate the unspeakable treatment often meted out to "natives" in the Congo and elsewhere. In that country (actually the private possession of the king of the Belgians), rubber was harvested in such a way that literally no account was taken of human life: the natives were just a resource to be used up and thrown away.[6] But much of the same logic applied even between races that were deemed to have some element of parity with each other. The famous struggle for life could only lead to the extermination of a number of European races, for example, because there was so little space and so much competition. ("War is life itself," explained Emile Zola on the twenty-fifth anniversary of the battle of Sedan; "it is necessary to eat or be eaten.")[7] Genocide then becomes a prudent tactic to employ against others, since otherwise it is likely to be employed against you. This extends to the mass killings of women and children: the struggle for existence was, after all, between races, not armies. There was no real distinction to be made between combatants and civilians—the child or the mother was just as much a threat to the survival of your race as the soldier was, and killing pregnant women, for example, could protect you against reprisals.[8] This was all taken very seriously by many educated people, and they would treat critics with the kind of weary asperity now reserved for those who want to subsidize industries in decline: some people will never understand that it's a hard world.

When war actually came, this ideology implied that there was no need—indeed, no point—in treating the enemy as though They were equivalent to Us. The Nazis' dismissal of their enemies on the Eastern Front as subhumans is well known, but that kind of thinking was common whenever there was a specifically racial or ethnic tinge to a conflict. Thus, in early 1943, the Australian general Sir Thomas Blamey told his troops in New Guinea that the Japanese were " a curious race—a cross between the human being and the ape." That being so, "we have to exterminate these vermin if we and our families are to live."[9] His troops appear to have taken the hint.

These days we are inclined to assume that such sentiments are a figurative way of speaking, perhaps brought about by the stress of war. But there is every reason to think that Blamey was entirely serious, reflecting the common view that the Japanese were not human in the sense that whites were and so did not deserve to be treated as white troops would be treated.

It is hardly surprising, in the circumstances, that popular literature of the late nineteenth and early twentieth centuries is full of racial annihilation. The United States seems to have seen a particularly virulent outbreak of this kind of thinking, mostly aimed at the "lower races" in Asia. Stories of Chinese and Japanese invasions were the equivalent of the "invasion scares" of nineteenth-century English fiction but with the added twist that defeat, for one side or the other, usually meant extermination. Jack London's 1906 short story "The Unparalleled Invasion" recounts an invasion of China using germ warfare and the massacre with firearms of any survivors. The Japanese were even more feared, and a whole succession of popular novels depicts traitorous "locust-like" swarms of immigrants combining with invaders from the homeland to attempt to exterminate Americans, only to be exterminated themselves. Not that America's other racial problems were forgotten: in a book published in 1892, northern and southern whites, finally united after the Civil War, combine to dispatch 30 million blacks by war and starvation.[10]

The effect this kind of material had is unclear. Books of this sort certainly coincided with anti-Japanese pogroms in California; it has also been suggested that at least part of the unparalleled viciousness of the Pacific War was due to the racial conditioning of American soldiers. It is certainly interesting that, according to surveys done in the last months of the war, 42 percent of American soldiers in the Pacific wanted the Japanese to be "wiped out altogether." But before we draw any conclusions about combat stress leading to genocidal intentions, it is worth noting that 61 percent of soldiers *in Europe* wanted the Japanese exterminated, and 67 percent who had not left the United States did so as well. Perversely, therefore, actual combat experience against the Japanese decreased exterminatory feelings about them, which must mean that these feelings had been implanted before men put on the uniform.[11] This is, in fact, consistent with what we know of the behavior of soldiers involved in real, as opposed to fantasy, exterminations. Christopher Browning's study of the men of Reserve Police Battalion 101 in occupied Poland suggests that most of the men killed out of a sense of duty and obligation. They did not seem to be greatly affected by the exterminatory anti-Jewish propaganda of the Nazis.[12]

Whereas the practical influence of Social Darwinism in the Anglo-Saxon countries was limited, and is now largely in the past, it proved to be deadly when mixed with the poisonous ethnic nationalism in areas like the Balkans. It revived there in the 1990s, not least because the nationalities policy of the Tito years—like that of the Soviet Union—emphasized national groups and interpreted them as primordial in nature (i.e., membership of them was essentially deterministic, not elective). Unsurprisingly, therefore, words like *annihilation, exterminations,* and *genocide* were frequently used by nationalists as dire warnings of what would happen to their group if they did not mobilize. It was also one explanation of why the apartheid regime in South Africa found it easy to send armed policemen to kill black schoolchildren. The doctrines of Social Darwinism found a ready audience among the Afrikaner extremists. Although the latter never wanted to physically exterminate the nonwhites (someone had to do the work, after all), they effectively abolished them through a rigorous system of residential exclusion, which meant that the average white was scarcely conscious of blacks except as domestic servants. (Likewise, there were no traffic signs to Soweto). Indeed, blacks were increasingly given their own "homelands"—quasi-independent statelets of which they were nominal citizens. In time, therefore, South Africa would have had no blacks in it at all. To this was linked a policy of repression that could be carried out only by those who believed (as many did) that blacks were not human beings.

This abolition of the ethnic Other can be both symbolic and real at the same time, as with the Croatian constitution, for example, which effectively denied the existence of Serbs.[13] Likewise, many Albanians dispossessed by the Serbs in Kosovo in 1999 had their identity papers—their identities, really—taken away. Partly this was to disrupt the social structures that were giving sustenance to the Kosovo Liberation Army, but something deeper was at work as well. Often the abolition was very literal: to make someone "disappear" is a well-known euphemism used all over the world for kidnap-murder. It gave its name to the Disappeared—the political enemies of right-wing regimes in Latin America. It was not enough that their victims should die; they had to physically disappear as well—often pushed out of airplanes over the sea. South Africans used the same technique in Namibia in the 1980s and went even further domestically: their death squads would blow up the bodies of their victims with explosives, continuing until all traces had been eradicated. Misha Glenny has suggested that the long Balkan tradition of facial mutilation of victims may reflect a need to destroy those who superficially are very similar to oneself but who, by one's own ideology, are totally different. Mutilation therefore becomes a way of dehumanizing victims and retrospectively justifying their assault.[14]

The Nation and the People

Most of the time, thankfully, these kinds of problems don't matter very much. Left to themselves, people form their own networks of friends and acquaintances, generally without worrying too much about differences between themselves and others. Indeed, even in the early days of the Third Reich, relations between Jews and their neighbors were often sufficiently cordial that the first nationwide boycott of Jewish businesses, on April 1, 1933, was a very mixed success despite massive government pressure. In Wesel, on the lower Rhine, one Jewish war veteran put on his old uniform and medals to protest the boycott on behalf of the war dead and apparently received considerable support.[15] In general, it seems that there was very little *spontaneous* anti-Semitism at all. Indeed, some brave souls complained to the authorities about the treatment of their neighbors—not because they were Jewish, necessarily, but because they were neighbors. It was only later, under the stress of crisis and war, that the German people came to identify the Jews they actually knew with the monsters of Nazi propaganda, rather like some science-fiction film in which the hero suddenly realizes that his neighbors are in fact aliens coming to destroy the earth.

The same was true elsewhere: in Denmark, Jews received so much assistance from local people that the small Jewish community escaped almost entirely to Sweden. Here one could point to a strong religious and humanitarian tradition, and strong left-wing political parties, but this does not explain why the behavior of the Italians was very similar. Italian military forces in Croatia interned Jews for their own protection and refused to take action against them anywhere they were under Italian control. The answer, perhaps, was that both societies, in their different ways, had a tradition of humanity and concern for others, which three years of occupation or twenty years of fascism hardly dented.[16] It is these elective bonds—which the promoters of hatred and separation have to somehow destroy, to be replaced with bonds exclusively concerned with shared ethnicity or religion—that encourage hatred and fear of anybody outside the group. Who we think we are, in other words, counts for less than which category we were born in; ethnic predestination, substituting, as Michael Ignatieff describes it, ethnic nationalism for the more inclusive civic variety.[17]

One of the saddest aspects of the recent trials at The Hague and Arusha is the way in which perpetrators were often neighbors and friends of victims. It was the culmination—in Yugoslavia, at least—of a process that had begun with the moves toward ethnic policies and republican independence in the late 1980s. By 1991, as Susan Woodward notes, "many who might have been expected to fight against these developments had begun to succumb emotionally. Pro-Yugoslav Slovenes began to 'recall' unpleasant encounters in Belgrade or in the Army. Non-nationalist Croat intellectuals . . . began to reassess their own contacts with Serb friends and the stereotypes of ordinary people."[18] In its extreme form, this alienation from experience led directly to the commission of atrocities as ideas of primordial ethnic determinism reasserted themselves. Tihomir Blaskic, for example, a former captain in the Yugoslav People's Army (Jugoslavenska Narodna Armija, JNA), had left Yugoslavia and married an Austrian woman, only to be summoned back to Bosnia when the fighting started: "Come back! You cannot escape your destiny as a Croat!" It earned him forty-five years in prison. Part of his defense—that he had had many non-Croat friends and neighbors all his life—revealed how far things had disintegrated when such elective bonds between people were destroyed and replaced by ones based on ethnic determinism.

In this work of destruction, political leaders were and are greatly helped by the uncontrolled rise of the nation-state. A successful nation-state is very difficult to achieve, since it relies for its success on a fairly exact match between territory and ethnic-religious affiliation, of a kind that is actually very uncommon. There are, indeed, very few successful nation-states, and many entities called "nation-states" are actually wracked by ethnic, separatist, or religious tensions. Moreover, nation-states do not usually arise spontaneously and are usually the progeny of educated political leaders, often of extremist tendencies. This is as true today as it ever was: Slobodan Milosevic was a lawyer and a banker; Radovan Karadzic was a poet and psychiatrist; Biljana Plavisc was a biologist (a dangerous profession for a nationalist); Franjo Tudjman was a historian (another dangerous profession); even Alija Izetbegovic was an intellectual who had written a book on an Islamic state.

But extremist ideas have often been attractive to intellectuals: the Nazis may have been generally fairly stupid, but they were popular in the universities. Likewise with the old South Africa: some years ago, before one of my earlier visits to South Africa, I mentioned to a colleague that I was reading Alistair Sparks's book *The Mind of South Africa*. "Must be a short book then," came the response, quick as a flash. This is understandable, but unfair: the Boer leaders may have seemed like porcine farmer-politicians, slow of speech and even slower of thought, but they were educated men. Indeed, apartheid was a complex and thoroughly worked out design. It foundered because it was too intellectually complex for the real world. And the Afrikaner identity itself, in its modern form, was a carefully calculated, elite-sponsored mobilization strategy aimed at displacing English speakers as the political elite in South Africa, something essentially achieved after 1948.

So in the nineteenth-century Balkans, for example, even after groups of illiterate Greek-speaking peasants got used to the idea of being Greeks, "'Romania' and 'Bulgaria' were notions which . . . animated only a handful of intellectuals and activists, 'Albania' and 'Macedonia' next to none."[19] Little had changed a century later: the moves toward independence in Slovenia and Croatia just before the collapse, while responding to well-established traditions of nationalism within the Slovene and Croat communities, were ultimately elite political maneuvers designed to protect the positions of those in power there.[20] Much of what passes for national tradition and timeless custom in such societies, seized on and exploited by elite nationalists, was actually invented, or at least popularized, in the nineteenth century. Artists created largely mythical pasts from which a new national identity could be constructed. Among such figures as Sir Walter Scott, Victor Hugo, and Bedrich Smetana was, unfortunately, Vuk Karadzic (1787–1864), whose collections of ancient Serb songs provided the new Serbian state with a definitive (although highly colored) account of the battle of Kosovo Polje in 1389. Karadzic, typically, was an extreme nationalist who argued that most of the inhabitants in regions surrounding the new Serbia were, in fact, Serbs, even if they were unaware of this because of their own tiresome adherence to Catholicism or Islam. Serbia thus had a claim on all these territories. And in 1847, Prince-Bishop Petar II of Montenegro published *The Mountain Wreath,* an epic poem that "was to inspire generations of young Serbs and Montenegrins with its glorification of Milos Obilic, the legendary hero of Kosovo who was said to have killed the Sultan."[21]

It inspired them, one might add, with hatred and the desire for revenge, as well as an atavistic urge to conquer the long-lost lands of Kosovo. The same process happened in almost every new state, with the complication that minorities in such states tended to have their own equally bloody and compelling myths that could also be used as a spur to action. Now in principle, there is no reason why a nation-state cannot be constructed on inclusive principles, and indeed that was the reality of revolutionary France—a nation that all could join, a *réferendum de tous les jours*. Traces of this survive even today, for example, in the offer of French citizenship to anyone who serves in the Foreign Legion for five years. But constructing a national identity out of tolerance and variety is very difficult, whereas conducting one out of intolerance and exclusivity is very easy. Indeed, many of the new Balkan states defined themselves by insisting that they were different from their neighbors. In this concept, *demos* the state is replaced by *ethnos* the group as the unit of account. This is especially dangerous when—as in some Slavic and African languages, for example—there is no distinction between those two words.

It is at this point that minorities start to become a problem. The creation of a national identity in a previously multiethnic area tends to lead to the dominance of the largest faction. If there is another large group, or a group that occupies a strong economic or social position, then the construction of a national identity is threatened by the alternative discourse that that group offers. Thus, the elite group who founded modern Turkey believed that "the Turks are a people who speak Turkish and live in Turkey"; one of the most influential of them "defined 'nation' in such a way as to exclude the possibility of pluralism and diversity. One language, one culture and one religion were essential to a nation."[22] From that point onward, it became effectively essential to get rid of the Armenians in some—probably violent—fashion. There is evidence that much the same happened in Rwanda, where Hutu extremists resurrected old racial theories holding that the Tutsi were actually the descendants of invaders from Ethiopia and so did not belong in Rwanda at all.[23] These theories, it is not surprising to learn, were especially popular with educated Hutu—teachers, lecturers, government officials, and others.

This, of course, is only stage one. There is then the unhappy recognition that some of the *ethnos* are outside the bounds of the *demos* and are, indeed, minorities within a larger group themselves. This is what happened in modern Yugoslavia. Although the borders between the republics were not as arbitrary as the Serbs claimed, they "were never meant to be ethnic boundaries. They left some 650,000 to 700,000 Serbs in Croatia and roughly twice as many in Bosnia; they left almost 800,000 Croats in Bosnia, 200,000 in Serbia and some in Montenegro," and Albanians all over the place.[24] The urge then comes to rescue these unfortunates by moving into (nationalists would say *back* into) the areas that they occupy. This urge arises partly because fear seems to be a natural concomitant of a newly created nation-state. The majority fears the disruptive influence of the minority, whereas the minority's own numerical status makes them afraid. Very often aggressive nationalism on the part of the majority leads to equal intransigence on the minority's part, demanding greater autonomy and perhaps even independence. A large group can suddenly find itself a minority in several contiguous states: a small group that had been socially or ethnically dominant in a multinational entity can suddenly be dangerously scattered. In these dangerous circumstances, much depends on what leaders of various groups decide to do. Too many of them, unfortunately, play the nationalist card, to make use of the so-called instrumental conception of nationalism, which looks back into the past to find—or rather to construct—versions of history and popular memory that can then be used to mobilize political support for them.[25] Very often, too, these are the people with the power—including military and political power. There are always voices in favor of civilization and tolerance, and any book on recent crises can produce heartwarming examples, but they are usually marginalized. There were certainly many thousands of people from all communities in Yugoslavia in 1991–1992 who did not want to fight; they had nobility, perhaps, but they did not have power. Nor, in general, do such groups have a joint ideology to offer that can compete with the seductive simplicities of nationalism. As a result, relative moderates tend to be elbowed aside by extremists peddling simple solutions based on fear and aggression. This happened widely in Bosnia in 1990–1992. In the case of Srebrenica, which has been studied in detail, there was a power struggle between the moderate and extreme wings of the Stranka Demokratske Ackije (SDA, Party of Democratic Action), leading to victory for the latter, and a de facto alliance with Muslim military forces that had begun to form in the summer of 1991. As a result, Serbs were forced out of their jobs and replaced by SDA extremists.[26] Subsequently, under the stress of war, the SDA itself was disbanded, and Naser Oric effectively ran the enclave as a military-criminal dictatorship, not an uncommon result in various parts of Bosnia at the time.

Part of the strength of the extremists can lie in their control of the media (although the connection between propaganda and atrocity is often overstated). Sometimes this is blatant and obvious, as with the exterminatory rhetoric of Radio Milles Collines in Rwanda. But there is also a more subtle use, as when control of the media is used to alienate populations from each other and so make the violence more acceptable. The Serbs were particularly good at this, using historical documentaries and reconstructions to remind their people of the appalling suffering of the Serbs in World War II, with the clear message that such events would be repeated unless the Serbs stood together now. Because the Yugoslav crisis resulted, in effect, in the attempted replacement of a totalitarian communist state with a series of totalitarian nationalist ones, control of the media simply changed hands from one political group to another, and the new nationalist parties used their control of the media to pump out a nationalist message. In Bosnia before the fighting started, the existence of a formally multiethnic government did not lead to the state-controlled media promoting tolerance. If anything, it produced the opposite, as the three nationalist parties divided the media between them and used it not so much to fight each other but rather the moderates in their respective Serb, Croat, and Muslim communities. Once the fighting started, of course, things got worse. The UN Human Rights Commissioner noted that Serbs in Tuzla in 1993 were being persecuted partly because of the influence of the party magazine of Izetbegovic's SDA, *Zmaj od Bosne* (Dragon of Bosnia), one of whose editorials argued that "instinctively every Muslim would wish to save his Serb neighbour instead of the reverse, however, every Muslim must name a Serb and take an oath to kill him."[27] I quote this example because it is unusually honest in recognizing that nationalist politicians have to overcome the normal human bonds that form in any society if they are to succeed in their aims. In the Yugoslav case, there was also another target for nationalist agitation: the apparatus of the communist state, including the army, which represented perhaps the last hope of an alternative nonnationalist future. The nationalists were able to use their control of the media—especially in Croatia—to attack the old apparatus in the name of democracy (of a individual kind) as well as nationalism. President Tudjman's office issued instructions in 1991 that the army was henceforth to be called the "Serbo-Communist occupation army" in the media.[28] This was odd, since two of the three most senior commanders at the time were Croats, and the vast majority of the officer corps was from Bosnia.[29]

The Tendency to Extremes

I have suggested that the nationalist agenda was attractive to certain politicians because it provided them with a convenient and easy means of mobilizing popular support. But in many ages politicians have espoused other agendas, and even in Rwanda and Yugoslavia there were some major figures preaching compromise. So what makes politicians take up the nationalist agenda?

Politics is inherently divisive. Even in one-party or authoritarian states there will be different tendencies of thought, as well as jockeying for position by individuals with different power bases. Sometimes these may be institutional, like the police or the army, but sometimes they may be regional or ethnic. In a democracy, these trends are greatly intensified. Politicians mark themselves out by emphasizing what differentiates them from others and rejecting the views of others as dangerous or simply stupid. There are few states where support for political parties is not based, at least in part, on the representation of demographic, ethnic, or religious groups. Where a country is already divided along ethnic or religious lines, democracy generally increases the tendency toward disintegration by forcing politicians into ever more extreme positions to avoid being outflanked by a more radical party that will claim that all others are selling out the interests of that group. So in the case of Bosnia, elections become rather a series of miniature referenda within various groups, and each party will claim that "only we can represent your interests properly."

However, there does seem to be a loose connection between complexity of ethnic and religious divisions and the risk of atrocities being carried out. In Uganda, for example, which in the 1970s and 1980s saw atrocities of Rwandan proportions (although over a much longer timescale), it cannot be a coincidence that the British legacy was a state with twenty-one *major* ethnic groups, four major language families, tensions between the Buganda, the traditional regional power and their rivals from the north, and significant tensions between the smaller but dominant Protestant group and the Catholic majority. Politics in countries like Uganda feeds upon and requires a local political power base and generates an assumption that politicians from wherever will reward their supporters and benefit the local economy. A broad-based coalition government in these circumstances is next to impossible.

In this kind of situation, democracy can be a threat. The Western habit of forcing elections on people whether they are ready or not is one point I will return to. But here it is enough to say that, in ethnically divided societies, where people vote along ethnic lines, it is easy for a majority, quite democratically, to dominate and exploit a minority, as happened in Northern Ireland before 1969. In the former Yugoslavia, it had been traditional to base politics on the interaction and collective rights of ethnic groups as groups, irrespective of how large they were. The move to democratic head-counting meant that control of any political unit would inevitably go to the larger ethnic group, and this in turn would mean control of the police, the media, and the allocation of jobs in the public service. If you are a small minority—say, the Croats in Bosnia—then your only hope, in a democratic environment, is to join with a larger political unit in which you predominate ethnically, or to try to control an area ethnically so that you can dominate it politically. Thus, the fighting in Yugoslavia was essentially about carving out or joining up enclaves that could be dominated by one ethnic group on a head-count basis, so that it would automatically win the upcoming democratic elections, then expelling those who would vote for another ethnic party.

Much of the time, such political tendencies can be kept under control. In the generation that followed World War II, inclusive politics was in fashion, itself prompted by a recollection of what the politics of division had earlier accomplished. At the domestic level this meant the promotion of internal stability through high levels of employment, the abolition of poverty, and the pursuit of egalitarian social policies—all designed to ensure that extremists never again had a fertile ground in which to recruit. To those who whined about high taxation there was a simple response: if you think peace is expensive, then try war. At the international level, the emphasis was on multinational consensual structures: the United Nations, the European Community, and the Organisation of African Unity all date from this time, as do the ideologies of pan-Africanism and pan-Europeanism.

But nothing lasts forever, and a generation of politicians in the 1970s began to find this all a bit tedious (and perhaps took it for granted) and to revert to earlier modes of exclusive politics. This process began—inevitably, perhaps—in the United States under President Richard Nixon. A young speechwriter named Patrick Buchanan advised Nixon in 1971 to provoke a confrontation over issues such as race in order to "cut the Democratic Party and the country in half; my view is that we would have far the larger half."[30] From this beginning, the politics of division spread through most of the Western world, at both the domestic and the international levels, and extremist political groups flourished as mainstream political parties found themselves becoming more extreme in order to keep up. These groups also benefited from the dislocation caused by the much higher levels of poverty and social insecurity that the accompanying economic policies produced; indeed, the social and economic collapse that followed the abandonment of communism in the East produced violent political extremism almost overnight. In many societies, the resulting damage was kept within manageable bounds, simply because the underlying ethnic or religious tensions were not that serious, and also because (e.g., in Western Europe) there were powerful countervailing political and institutional forces. In Yugoslavia, ethnic tensions (which were very real) were kept under control by a combination of careful political appeasement at all levels and a ruthless and efficient secret police force.

Democracy, in a very real sense, was the undoing of Yugoslavia, not because the majority of the people wanted war, by any means, but because the only way in which mass political parties could be organized quickly in a society where politics had been *about* nationalism was on nationalist lines. (Indeed, when political parties were permitted in Bosnia, in periods before and after World War I, they were almost always nationalist ones.) It would have taken much longer for cross-nationalist parties to have organized themselves properly and differentiated themselves from each other. It is also clear that the rise of nationalism in Yugoslavia paralleled, and was probably inspired and certainly assisted by, the similar rise of nationalism in many Western societies. Politicians are very much creatures of fashion, and the prevailing fashion in the West at the time of the fall of communism was for aggressive nationalism and a distrust of consensual and supranational structures.

Although the Serb paranoid allegation that the West deliberately destroyed the old Yugoslavia as part of an anticommunist crusade is not true, it is true that the nationalist "dissidents" who replaced the communists were very much the kind of people that right-wing Western politicians wanted to see at the head of the new republics (unlike Milosevic, who represented "old guard" communism to them; ironically, he had earlier been identified with reformist economic policies). What the leaders of the new nationalist parties had in common with their Western counterparts (but not with the Hutu extremists in Rwanda) was a willingness to flirt with extreme nationalist ideas for political advantage. None of them actually sought the conflagration that resulted when they started playing with nationalism like children playing with matches in a fireworks factory.[31] Indeed, they typified a type of political leaders who welcome political instability because they increase their power and enable them to mobilize the population against a real or imagined enemy.

Poverty and Extremism

One of the greatest pieces of wisdom that the leaders of the post–World War II world possessed was the understanding that political extremism flourishes best in conditions of hardship and insecurity and is dispelled by security and plenty. They recalled, of course, that the Nazis rose from being a maverick fringe party of lunatics who liked dressing up, with only 2 percent of the vote in 1928, to 37 percent in 1932. Although the inadequacy of the Weimar parties, and the exasperation thus caused, are part of the explanation, the main reason is the direct and indirect effects of unemployment, which, it has been estimated, impacted some 23 million people.[32] Unemployment was not just a matter of dire poverty; it also destroyed communities and their values, destroyed bonds of solidarity that had been forged at work, and undermined the trades unions and left-wing parties that were a force for moderation. Moreover, the mainstream parties—even the Social Democrats—had no idea what to do about the problem. In this age of avant-Keynes, the best they could manage was spending cuts and wage restraint, which of course made the situation worse. The Nazis—and to a lesser extent the communists—by contrast, offered a completely untried and radical alternative, and the former therefore benefited from the world's most disastrous protest vote.

It is always annoying to political scientists to discover that the reasons why electorates vote as they do generally have little to do with the programs of the competing parties. Huge amounts of research have gone into trying to analyze the Nazis' electoral base between 1928 and 1933, and much of this is wasted, because it seems clear that voters had only the vaguest idea of what the Nazis actually stood for. People from many classes voted for the Nazis because they were different, untainted by government, and had a modern, thrusting image and promised a return to traditional values. Anti-Semitism was a trivial factor in all this, if it was a factor at all. Much the same was true in the last days of Yugoslavia, where voting was largely along ethnic lines, not because people wanted war but because in a crisis people look around for something familiar and fall back on what they know. Even in Serbia, Milosevic was perceived, if anything, as a moderate continuity candidate, popular with those worried at the pace of change, and much less worrying than the terrible twins of Serb extremism, Vojislav Seselj, the self-proclaimed Chetnik leader, and Vuk Draskovic, who modeled his personal appearance on that of Jesus Christ. It is not surprising, therefore, that the slogan of Milosevic's atavistically named Socialist Party of Serbia was *Sa nama nema neizvesnosti*—"With us, there is no insecurity."[33]

Because insecurity there certainly was at the time—and for reasons not connected with the manipulation of unscrupulous politicians. The Yugoslav economy had grown rapidly after World War II, although the rural areas, where political extremism is always more commonly found, benefited less. Unable to generate all the funds it needed for investment at home, Yugoslavia took to borrowing abroad, only to suffer disastrously from the oil shocks and the financial chaos of the 1970s. Attempts to appease nationalist sentiment through devolution of economic decisionmaking produced conflict as different parts of the country pursued different policies. By the end of the 1980s, living standards had been falling and unemployment rising for some years. Bosnia was particularly hard hit: for strategic reasons much of the nation's defense industry was there and had previously been a big export earner and a provider of jobs. In pursuit of self-sufficiency, 30 percent of the defense industry's output was for export—10 percent of all exports. By 1991, however, with the general collapse of the defense market after the end of the Cold War, the industry was operating at less than half capacity.[34] The Yugoslav state, indeed, collapsed economically before it collapsed politically, and the attempt by the International Monetary Fund (IMF) to tie further loans to free elections simply destroyed what little stability remained. No nationalist politician could have asked for a better inheritance. As before, social and economic bonds broke down, leading to a revival of nationalism simply as a way of understanding what was going wrong with the world and finding someone to blame for it. Much the same happened in Rwanda, where the collapse of the coffee price prompted one of the infamous IMF structural adjustment programs. The dire economic situation enabled Western states to dictate a political settlement giving an extraordinary degree of representation to the invading Rwandan Patriotic Front (RPF) forces, which included "a reform agenda out of a textbook" that was "force-fed" by the donor community in exchange for desperately needed financial assistance.[35] This was at a time when the real wealth of the country had shrunk rapidly and the government was trying to fight a war and reduce its overall budget at the same time to placate the IMF. The consequence for average Rwandans was a massive decline in living standards.

The question remains, however, why—even with these powerful stimuli—people who have lived peacefully together for many years should suddenly be at each other's throats. Manipulation by unscrupulous leaders is an important part of the answer, but only part. Individuals did more than passively support, after all, the great atrocities of the 1990s: they came out to murder in the tens of thousands. To put all this down to the diabolism of a few individuals is not only wrong; it's also insulting, suggesting that various types of foreigners are incapable of logical thought and simply automata in the hands of political leaders. ("Hey, Dusan, there's this bloke Milosevic on TV telling us to go and kill the Muslims." "OK love, soon as I've finished my dinner I'll get my rifle and go and slot the Abramovics next door.") Successful political leaders very seldom attempt to create a public mood; they will generally strive to articulate it. The nationalist leaders of 1991 in Yugoslavia would not have had the success they did if they had not been preaching to many who wished to be converted, or at least were prepared to be so. After all, if popular sentiment had been strongly against nationalism, there would have been little point in using it as a strategy. (It is also true, of course, that the demography of Yugoslavia would have made a peaceful dissolution very difficult, even under ideal circumstances.)

Here—as elsewhere when discussing war crimes—the shadow of the interpretation of the Third Reich looms large. For a long time, the standard explanation of the atrocities performed by that regime amounted to what I would call the Superman of Evil theory: Hitler and a group of fellow extremists brainwashed the German people into supporting them. This theory—which those born in the generation after 1945 grew up with—was instrumentally useful in that it enabled a distinction to be made between Nazis and Germans and so paved the way for German rearmament and membership in the North Atlantic Treaty Organization (NATO). Recent scholarship has painted a far more complex picture and has illuminated the way in which the thought of the Nazis was similar not only to many right-wing political groupings in Germany but also to currents of thought in right-wing European circles generally. Consequently, rather less brainwashing was required than was once thought, but this has yet to fully penetrate the public consciousness. Likewise, far from the extermination of the Jews being conducted according to some great master plan, it proceeded in fits and starts and down blind alleys, driven mostly by the demands of bureaucratic politics.[36] But commentators on the dissolution of Yugoslavia, reaching as always for a handy explanatory model, seized on the Superman of Evil theory because they were familiar with it. This theory (in which Slobodan Milosevic played the main part) is now being modified as historians learn what government officials always knew: that Milosevic's control over the Serbs outside Serbia was far from absolute. A counterfactual example may make all this a little clearer. Assume that an extremist English politician tries to gain political power by playing on the "Scottish menace," claiming that Scottish extremists intend to declare independence and massacre or drive out every ethnic English person north of the border, and urging that the army should be sent in to protect the English. No matter how persuasive the individual, no matter how violent the rhetoric, it is hard to believe that such a campaign would ever get beyond the political curiosity stage, because it would simply seem incredible to anyone in the light of recent history. And history is the key.

History as Nightmare

The idea that history has a role to play as a causative factor in atrocities is extremely—almost violently—controversial, although perhaps a little less so today. Those who pointed to the need to understand why things had happened as they had tended to be caricatured as believing that atrocities were caused by the spontaneous eruption of "ancient ethnic hatreds." And if an author of a recent book on Bosnia has omitted to declare that his book is intended to nail this myth, a reviewer will certainly note that it has done so. Quite why this long-dead horse continues to be so viciously flogged is not clear: from my own experience, few if any of those in a position of knowledge or influence in the West believed anything remotely like this, nor did they act as though it were true. Western governments, indeed, had been watching the rise of nationalist extremism in Yugoslavia for some time. (If they *had* believed this, of course, they would not have sought to put pressure on leaders of the various factions to make peace—a strategy for which, ironically, they were bitterly criticized at the time.) There are, perhaps, three reasons for the existence of this controversy.

First, we should not underestimate the natural human aversion to complexity. The Anglo-Saxon political tradition, in particular, shuns complex explanations, especially if they involve historical or cultural factors, in favor of abstract norms, which generally exist in a contextual vacuum. For journalists and pundits, academics and government officials, who are required to master, and even pontificate upon, a subject at short notice, complexity is an enemy. Far better to express oneself in abstract terms (democracy, human rights, aggression), which can be applied *to* an issue, rather than trying to deduce what to do *from* a careful study of the issue. (In any case, there is a risk you might get the wrong answer.) Second, righteous indignation is among the most attractive of emotional postures. It enables you simultaneously to feel angry and aggressive but also morally superior to the object of your aggression. There is no logical reason why discovering a complex historical background should affect the morality of an atrocity one has seen or read about, but in practice it does tend to do so. The fact that the current villains, for example, suffered the same atrocities from their current victims in the past should not logically make their current crimes any more defensible. In practice, though, and given the irrationality of such emotions, feelings of anger and aggression will be more difficult and embarrassing to express as more of the background becomes clear. Third, and closely related, is the tendency to use atrocities as aids in defending certain political groups and criticizing others. Sometimes, though not always, atrocities go in cycles, and today's victim is yesterday's killer. Those who emotionally identify with a cause can take it as a personal insult if it is sullied by references to a different balance of atrocities in the past. It must be recognized, of course, that history *is* frequently used to justify atrocious behavior in the present day. The Serbs could, and did, point to their unspeakable sufferings in World War II (far worse than anything that happened during the later fighting in Bosnia) not only as an explanation but also as a justification for what happened between 1992 and 1995, and this is obviously quite unacceptable.

This debate is analogous to, and partly depends upon, the furious polemic that has arisen over attempts to examine the Third Reich, and in particular its atrocities, as subjects of ordinary historical inquiry and to look for parallels and antecedents. This thesis, put forward by some conservative German historians in the mid-1980s, led to the *Historikerstreit,* the so-called battle of the historians. The bitterness of the dispute arose partly because of the very clear right-wing political agenda of the revisionists, especially the suggestion by Ernst Nolte that the Nazi death camps might have been constructed not only in emulation of the Soviet gulags but also out of fear: that the Nazis "regarded themselves and their kind as the potential or real victims" of what Nolte describes as an "Asiatic deed."[37] This aside, however, the revisionists had fastened on an important point of general application. There are some things that appear so horrible that we genuinely wonder whether it is right and fair to try to bring the usual tools of analysis to bear on them. The great psychoanalyst Bruno Bettelheim, commenting on a book about Nazi doctors, recalled that he "shied away from trying to understand the psychology of the SS—because of the ever-present danger that understanding fully may come close to forgiving." Some things, he argued, must be prevented, not understood.[38] It is depressing to see a student of the human soul acting like this.

It is true, of course, that, as Hayden White notes, "peculiar to the modern conceptualization of the historian's task [is] to enter sympathetically into the minds or consciousness of human agents long dead . . . and to understand . . . the most bizarre social and cultural practices."[39] But this has its limits: a historian who sympathetically empathized with an SS trooper in Russia in 1943, or with a paramilitary thug in Bosnia fifty years later, would rightly attract suspicion and concern. There is, in fact, little real danger that understanding will lead to forgiving. Those who know most about the atrocities of modern times—investigators, lawyers, intelligence experts, policy types like me—are universally of the view that, if anything, the more we understand, the less sympathetic we become. The alternative view—that we should not inquire into the background of atrocities for fear that we might become more sympathetic to the perpetrators—is a form of intellectual and moral cowardice, not least if we are to have a hope of preventing such things in the future.[40] A good part of the resistance to understanding, of course, comes from an associated fear that, once we understand, intellectually at least, what motivated some of these people, they begin to seem less alien to us and more like normal human beings, subject to enormous stress, to fear and confusion, and to manipulation by political leaders. At that point, we start to wonder, rather uneasily, whether they are such subhuman monsters after all. Could we not imagine ourselves in such circumstances, possibly behaving similarly under similar stresses? And is not the distinction between victim and perpetrator, therefore, at least partly a matter of accident?

But not all experiences of history are the same. Britain and America are as much dominated by their histories as any nations, but the influence tends to be subtle and at a more strategic level. The Anglo-Saxon concept of history, indeed, is cozy: battles (victories, anyway), kings and presidents, color and heraldry; history, in other words, as pageant. For most of the world, the concept of history is absolutely different: invasion, occupation, domestic strife, betrayal, repression; history, in other words, as trauma. (Few English or American readers of James Joyce's *Ulysses*, for example, will ever understand Stephen Daedalus's complaint that Irish "history is a nightmare from which I am trying to awake.") History of this type provides, among other things, a series of normative rules telling you how to behave in future. When the extremists of the Srpska Demokratska Stranka (SDS, Serb Democratic Party) came round the Prijedor area seeking recruits in 1992, we know that they told ordinary Serbs that they had discovered a plan for the Muslims to launch a coup after the declaration of independence, to round up Serbs and put them in concentration camps, and to establish a Muslim theocratic state. For those who expressed disbelief, there was a simple answer: remember what they did to your parents in World War II: *never again!* And it is an established fact that many of the worst atrocities in 1992–1995 happened in places where the worst atrocities of World War II took place also. As you drive down from Zagreb toward the border with Bosnia—passing from the Hapsburg Empire into the Ottoman—you pass a turnoff for Jasenovac, the Auschwitz of the Balkans, where Serbs, Jews, and Gypsies were interned and exterminated by the pro-Nazi forces of the Croatian Ustashe and their Muslim allies (Bosnia was at that time part of the so-called Independent State of Croatia). If you are a Serb, you believe that more than 1 million died in Jasenovac; if you are Croat, it's a few thousand. The best independent estimates put deaths at between 100,000 and 200,000 at that camp alone. The Prijedor area, where some of the worst atrocities of the war took place in 1992, was a major staging point for Jasenovac.

It is almost impossible for Anglo-Saxons to comprehend what it must be like to have this kind of history. But here (with due regard for differences of geography) is an attempt to cast it in a British mold. Assume that there was a successful German invasion of Britain in 1940 and that a collaborationist regime was set up in London. It was opposed by a multiethnic partisan force under the half-Irish half-Welsh leader of the British Communist Party. The partisans, mainly English, fought the Legion of St. George, an extreme nationalist group that murdered Jews and Celts and sometimes cooperated with the Germans. Meanwhile, the latter had recognized the Independent Kingdom of Scotland and the Independent Principality of Wales, whose armed forces collaborated with the Germans to hunt down partisans as well as ethnic English. A Cornish SS division spread terror through the West Country. A transit camp was established outside Berwick through which passed millions of Jews, English, and Gypsies on their way to the infamous extermination camps near Edinburgh, where hundreds of thousands (some say millions) were put to death. When the Germans were driven out, hundreds of thousands of English collaborators and Celts were put to death, often without a trial. Altogether, some 5 million British citizens died during the war. The British Communist Party's rule lasted until the late 1980s, but, with economic recession and political stagnation, separatist tendencies grew, and in the early 1990s armed clashes between different ethnic groups became common. At this point, our English extremist friend appears.

Such a history inevitably produces fear. One side is afraid of a repetition of the past; the other side is afraid of revenge for that past. In both cases, the conclusion is obvious: strike before the other side can strike. There is no doubt that some Serbs in Bosnia were genuinely afraid of being a minority in a state where the leader of the largest party was an intellectual who had written about the Islamic state and been imprisoned as a nationalist extremist and whose party contained a group of radicals who certainly *did* see Bosnia as a Muslim national home from which other nations would be expelled.[41] Few Serbs would have read his *Islamic Declaration* of 1970, or his book *Islam Between East and West*, published in 1984, but it is likely that many of them had heard second- and thirdhand distorted reports of what they contained and theses taken out of context. One such was Alija Izetbegovic's suggestion that an Islamic state should be set up when half the population of a country was Muslim. It appears that he was speaking generically, rather than about Bosnia, and not advocating a practical policy, but such nuances get lost in an atmosphere of political crisis.[42] So it didn't require that much encouragement from Serb nationalists for many ordinary Serbs to conclude that if this was going to happen they were better off in a kind of parastate that they could control. It is also clear that the fear generated by the RPF's invasion of Rwanda in 1990, and the possibilities of renewed Tutsi domination that it implied, was a major factor in turning the Hutu Power extremists from "a fringe preoccupation to the mainstream of respectable politics."[43] The power-sharing regime designed by the West in 1993 gave the RPF five important ministerial portfolios, half the army, and control of the police, and hardly helped to calm the Hutu down. It did not help either that some of the Hutu extremists had themselves escaped Tutsi massacres in Burundi twenty years before, when perhaps 200,000 had died. *Never again!*

Under the stimulus of fear, people seldom think rationally, and they are inclined to operate on the basis of worst-case assumptions. Under the lash of fear, people will do things that in other circumstances they would never contemplate. Fergal Keane aptly entitled his book on the last days of the apartheid regime *Bondage of Fear* because fear of the *swart gevaar,* the "black peril," was a major motive for that regime's murderous policies. The UN representative in Burundi (tipped for some time now as the next Rwanda) commented that what Burundi needed was not peacekeepers but psychiatrists. The politicians were "all frightened of each other. When I shake their hands, they are dripping with sweat."[44] Likewise, we tend to forget just how *frightened* the Nazis were. The leadership itself was largely made up of individuals with domineering, brutal fathers of whom they were generally terrified. But the Nazis were institutionally afraid as well. Take, for example, an extract from Hitler's *Mein Kampf,* which is generally regarded these days as the product of a disordered mind:

> The Jewish doctrine of Marxism . . . would bring about the end of any order intellectually conceivable to man. And as, in this greatest of all recognisable organisms, the result of an application of such a law could only be chaos, on earth it could only be destruction for the inhabitants of this planet. . . . If, with the help of his Marxist creed, the Jew is victorious over the other peoples of the world, his crown will be the funeral wreath of humanity and this planet will, as it did thousands of years ago, move through the ether devoid of men.[45]

Hard as it may be to accept, Hitler meant what he said, as did various Nazi leaders who claimed that the Jews were bent on the extermination of the German "race." If you genuinely believed that the Jews, through their imposed doctrines of Marxism and capitalism, and with their control of the nations and armed forces of most of the world, were bent on the extermination of humanity, and that the Germans were the front-line troops preventing them, then adherence to the normal rules of war would be self-defeating. Certainly, it is clear that ordinary German soldiers had fully internalized these views, and fought for as long and as violently as they did, to protect, as they saw it, their families and communities from the subhuman invaders from the East.[46] The sense of fighting mysterious and sinister forces is always disruptive and leads to violations of the laws of war, because those you are ultimately fighting are not the soldiers on the battlefield. As we have seen, in wars of ideology, where the enemy is heresy, communism, terrorism, and so forth, the distinction between combatants and noncombatants is generally lost. The same is true of contemporary conflict in Africa, where witchcraft is an acknowledged reality and the loss of a battle may be attributed to intervention by local witches: this does something to explain the frequent murders of African women in battle zones. In some African countries, moreover, there is a tradition of ritual murder, as well as the use of human sacrifice to gain magical advantages on the battlefield, since battles—even in the modern world—are often believed to be decided by magical forces.[47]

Much depends, of course, upon the way in which history is interpreted by its custodians, and it is not true that every society with a violent history must be dominated by it. However, there is an unfortunate tendency for societies to cling to their history, especially their defeats and tragedies, with a kind of masochistic determination that utterly defeats most Anglo-Saxons, for whom fifty years is a very long time. Yet most of the societies of the world have a consciousness of history that goes back a great deal farther. Anyone who has been around the Balkans will be wearily familiar with the eagerness of its citizens to offer impromptu history lessons, complete with maps, and usually beginning several hundred years ago if you are lucky. But the past in most countries is a snake that strikes when least expected, and history, in such a context, exists in an eternal present, where the events of a millennium ago are as real, in many ways, as those that occurred last week. In some ways, they are more real, since time and art have polished and simplified them into familiar artifacts. Richard Goldstone, who was the prosecutor for the International Criminal Tribunal for the Former Yugoslavia, recalled being present at a dinner for F. W. de Klerk, the deputy president of South Africa at the time, given by the queen of the Netherlands. When the conversation turned to the queen's forthcoming visit to South Africa, de Klerk became emotional and suggested she should visit the Women's Monument in Blomfontein, commemorating the 25,000 women who died in British concentration camps during the Boer War. She would "see for herself how the British . . . had treated Afrikaners similarly to the way the Nazis had treated their victims." As Goldstone remarked, there had been no Truth and Reconciliation Commission and no war crimes trials after that war, and the bitterness remains.[48] Some would argue, indeed, that the memory of their suffering was a major reason for the ruthlessness the Afrikaners showed toward other groups in their turn.

One final characteristic can be suggested that makes atrocities more likely: *habituation*. Put simply, in some societies violence and cruelty are very common and have historically been so. Put crudely, as in the former Yugoslavia, people know how to do these things: if they have not experienced them personally, they know through folk memory. It is generally a perception of injustice that allows bitter memories to thrive and, in due course, to be acted upon. All over Bosnia in the summer of 1992 nationalist political parties took power, rounded up, tortured, and sometimes murdered those of other ethnic groups and drove them from their homes, following a script written long before. Yet before we become too smug, it is worth recalling that there is nothing that whites did to each other in the twentieth century that they had not done to nonwhites the century before. Whether we should therefore number nineteenth-century imperialism among the causes of the Holocaust is an interesting question.[49]

Prime Evil

The factors reviewed above can, in various combinations, produce circumstances in which atrocities can take place. Absurd racial theories, irresponsible nationalist myths, ruthless politicians, social and economic dislocation, a violent and inescapable history all create the conditions for atrocities, and fear, in particular, makes people capable of carrying them out. But whereas civilized bureaucrats and politicians have found themselves able to contemplate the destruction of whole groups of people in the theoretical sense, the actual killing must be done by real human beings on the ground. How are people capable of such deeds? We need to remember, of course, that Anglo-Saxon societies of the present day are untypical in having largely abandoned violence and cruelty as entertainment and spectacle. Well into the nineteenth century the public torture and execution of traitors and important criminals could be guaranteed to draw a crowd. This could, and did, extend to the deaths of women and young children. Indeed, the purpose of such punishment (and this remains the case in some societies) was to make an example of the consequences of deviance or rebellion and to enforce respect for the law by fear. As late as 1931, an American presidential commission reported that torture, including electric shocks, tear gas, and sexual assault was "widespread throughout the country" to extract confessions. Such methods seem to have persisted into the 1960s in American prisons, not to force confessions but just to punish the inmates.[50] It is also true that advanced Western states have, until relatively recently, used exemplary violence on their own people agitating for greater economic or political rights, without regard to age or sex. The most notorious case is probably that of the Paris Commune in 1871, when French troops murdered some 30,000 of their own citizens, mostly noncombatants, including many women and children. Such treatment of one's own people hardly implies that foreigners will be treated any better.

There are some purely personal factors as well. From what we know of many of the thugs who actually did the killing in the former Yugoslavia, they often came from violent authoritarian backgrounds, and many had convictions for violence before the war. This is consistent with studies of killers in the Nazi SS and the South African apartheid regime, who tended to have violent and overbearing fathers and to have been brought up in a rigid and authoritarian environment. If you are socialized through being beaten at home and at school into the thought that violence is always used against the weak, you will naturally seek those weaker than you on which to practice it yourself. As long as parts of society think it is acceptable for adults to inflict pain and humiliation upon small children who love them helplessly, the world will not lack volunteers for atrocities against the weak. Sometimes, however, the process is institutionalized. In both the German and the Japanese armies in World War II, for example, discipline was extremely brutal for the soldiers, but there were few constraints on their behavior toward the local people. Atrocities then become a kind of safety valve through which otherwise intolerable tensions are released.

In any event, most of the foul deeds of recent times have been carried out not by relatively disciplined armies, for whom the control of violence is a professional skill, but by militias, paramilitary forces, criminals, and police (sometimes together). Police and military police units were responsible for some of the most brutal atrocities of the Yugoslav fighting, and improvised militias, scarcely different from criminal gangs, operate in many parts of Africa. In South Africa, the conventional military forces were relatively uninvolved in the domestic campaign of murder and intimidation, which was left predominantly in the hands of the South African Police, a paramilitary force staffed by Afrikaners of generally limited intellect that was expected to use maximum force to put down threats to white rule.[51] Interestingly, and perhaps symbolically, the only military unit deeply implicated in this campaign—the so-called Civil Cooperation Bureau (CCB)—was an allegedly civilian organization with a "managing director" and "shareholders."[52] Combatants in Sierra Leone and Liberia had scarcely any training before they were let loose with guns to kill and loot. In Rwanda, the idea was taken even further. The Interahamwe militia were described by one commentator as "a lumpenproletariat of street boys, rag-pickers car-washers and the hopeless unemployed."[53] Moreover, many of these ad hoc units, criminals, and political militias simultaneously are made up of young, poorly educated males living out violent fantasies drawn mostly from Hollywood war films of the 1980s, with their limited respect for human rights and exultation of mindless slaughter. In Liberia, for example, most of the militias took their inspiration and their ethos not from the Geneva Conventions but from films like *Rambo*. As a result, "military culture was formed from the bottom upwards . . . by teenagers enthralled by Sylvester Stallone, motivated by dreams of glory and nightmares of revenge."[54] And so combatants in such wars call themselves by noms de guerre designed to emphasize their supposed ruthless bellicosity: General Murder, General Killer III, Colonel Savage, Captain Terminator. They see little distinction, in practice, between war, murder, and robbery and have often revenged themselves on the inhabitants of cities they attack just for being wealthy and having jobs, as they have murdered and intimidated adults they see as oppressing them in paternalistic and hierarchical societies. The paradigm appeared in a similar form in Bosnia, with swaggering paramilitary thugs of all kinds, many of whom had a criminal or psychologically disturbed background. Naser Oric from Potocari near Srebrenica, for example, with his "Airborne" and "Special Forces" shoulder patches, often "created the impression of having seen too many Rambo films."[55]

It was in the former Yugoslavia that the use of criminals for the commission of atrocities was turned into an art form. Under the Communist Party, criminals were often used by the police to carry out illegal acts such as assassination. (Zjelko "Arkan" Raznatovic, the best known, if not the most important or representative of the paramilitary leaders, got started in this way.) The Serbs made extensive use of criminal and paramilitary organizations in Bosnia and Croatia: often they worked on a contract basis and would enter a town after the army had bombarded it, massacring those who had not fled and keeping whatever they could loot as payment. The origins and makeup of these groups remain obscure. They had names like the Wolves and the Eagles and probably represented a merging of two related traditions: the criminal gang and the political party militia. On several occasions, the next logical step was taken, and criminals themselves were let out of prison to fight in the war. Mladen "Tuta" Naletilic was a right-wing Croat Mafioso and paramilitary leader who formed the so-called Convicts Brigade before the Bosnian declaration of independence. He was indicted for the particularly vicious role that the Convicts Brigade played in the attack on Muslims in Mostar.[56] Perhaps the height of surrealism was reached in the early days of the fighting in Bosnia when the criminals *were* the army, or at least part of it. Many of the early Muslim defenders of Sarajevo were criminals. The most notorious was Musan "Caco" Topalovic, who had been one of the organizers of illegal Muslim paramilitary units in 1991 and who was one of those Izetbegovic turned to for support the following year. (The two had met in prison some time before.) Caco was by all accounts a brave fighter but remained a ruthless criminal, exploiting his own people as well as murdering Serbs and Croats. He was eventually murdered by his own side after seizing nine policemen and torturing them to death. Jusuf Prazina, another distinguished gangster, later switched sides and fought for the Croats before fleeing abroad, where he was murdered.[57]

There are many other examples of gangsters being used to commit atrocities by all sides: one would not look to such people for any kind of discipline or restraint at all, given what they had previously been up to, nor any scruples about killing the defenseless. But even when killings are committed by regular forces, they seldom accept that they are doing anything morally wrong. The SS, for example, claimed to be a deeply moral organization, a new order of Teutonic Knights, embodying the finest Aryan traditions. In a speech delivered in October 1943, Heinrich Himmler told the assembled SS that, in spite of the massacres they had committed, they had nonetheless "stayed decent." This was emphasized by the fact that, while they had the "moral right" to destroy "this people that wanted to destroy us . . . we do not have the moral right to enrich ourselves," and anyone caught looting would be shot.[58] Similarly, Eugene "Prime Evil" de Kock, who carried out countless murders on behalf of the apartheid state, beat up any of his men who misbehaved sexually. He "subscribed to a curious set of rules . . . they could murder, torture and cheat the state, but woe betide any of them who made overtures to a married woman."[59]

When noble sentiments failed, they could always fall back on cynicism. Some units (especially the elite, or those who think they are) take a perverse pride in the dirty jobs they do: it is precisely *because* murdering women and children is so repulsive that only the truly tough can do it. Thus, the South African death squads were "not a place for '*sissies*,' but for men who would unflinchingly carry out orders without even knowing why they were pulling the trigger."[60] And when things got too much, there was always the traditional compensation of alcohol and the newer one of hard and soft drugs. Militias in Africa have used various sorts of drugs in their massacres, and some investigators at The Hague will tell you that the war lasted as long as it did only because slivovitz, cocaine, and heroin were so easy to come by.

There are other reasons why people are prepared to behave in this way. Transferred revenge is one: Christopher Browning's policemen murdered Jews in Poland as a way of revenging themselves upon the Jews who, they believed, sent aircraft to bomb German cities and kill civilians.[61] Anger is another: many of the militia killers in Africa are relatively well-educated youths. African armies have turned on civilians they think have betrayed them politically, or paternalistic elders who will not respect them, or do not value the protection they have been given. There is also evidence that young unemployed men with a grudge against society in general were well represented in the various paramilitary units in the former Yugoslavia.

Ultimately, though, it seems that even the most liberal and humanitarian individual will commit atrocities under orders. We have already seen how large numbers of Americans volunteered that they would have done as Lieutenant Calley did at My Lai, but there is experimental evidence that takes the issue farther. In the early 1970s, an American psychologist, Stanley Milgram, conducted a famous series of experiments at Yale University in which an experimental group of mostly males were asked to take part in a fake study into learning and discipline. They were told to administer a learning test to a "student" (actually a member of the research team) and to punish wrong answers with electric shocks. In spite of the apparent pain suffered, and even loss of consciousness by some students, most of the volunteers continued to administer shocks for as long as they were asked to do so. A significant minority even followed orders to forcibly hold the student's hand against the plate that was transmitting the shocks.

The results of the experiments came as a surprise, and the high level of compliance has been attributed to the prestige of the institution, the natural authority of the scientist, the implicit contract deriving from the fact that the volunteers were paid a small sum of money, and the fact that the volunteers were assured that no permanent harm would be caused. Milgram's experiments have been strongly criticized and powerfully defended.[62] And we must be careful not to read across directly to the kind of situations this book addresses. But ordinary people often follow orders, even when they contradict basic notions of decency, if those orders seem to come from authority figures who must have good reasons. Various studies of those who have taken part in murder and torture indicate that this is a powerful factor in obedience, especially when combined with the desire to maintain group solidarity and not to let down your comrades.

There do seem to be some real-life analogues to this experiment. Although some regimes, such as the Uruguayan Junta and the Greek Colonels, tried to make torturers by brutalizing trainees, this seems, in practice, to be unnecessary. Examinations of the psyches of Nazi killers found that, on the whole, they were frighteningly normal. Interrogators in the U.S. Army who regularly tortured Vietcong suspects do not seem to have been specially selected as anything more than intelligence specialists.[63] And Henri Pouillot, an antiwar activist, nonetheless found himself among a group of conscripts torturing and murdering Algerian nationalists without it seeming strange at the time.[64]

Conclusion

Most societies and most individuals can envisage and passively accept violent and exterminatory behavior toward Other and will find excuses for it if it happens. It is also clear that most of these atrocities have been carried out by ordinary people: frightened, disoriented, in some cases brutalized or motivated by hate, but ordinary people nonetheless, and in some cases women or children. It would be unsafe to conclude that any of us are exempt from these feelings or that we could not, if circumstances were different, find ourselves among the perpetrators.

With this depressing conclusion in mind, we turn to what the law has to say about these matters.

Notes

1. See Peter Gay, *The Cultivation of Hatred*, pp. 71–72.
2. Ibid., p. 41.
3. Cited by Sven Lindquist, *Exterminate All the Brutes*, p. 140.
4. Cited by Daniel Pick, *War Machine*, p. 85.

5. Cited by Lindquist, *Exterminate All the Brutes*, p. 157.

6. Recent studies (e.g., Adam Hochschild, *King Leopold's Ghost*) suggest that the picture painted of the Congo in Conrad's *Heart of Darkness*, far from being exaggerated for artistic purposes, was actually sober reportage.

7. Pick, *War Machine*, p. 86.

8. This is a habit of thought that has apparently endured. During the massacres in Beirut in 1980, a young Israeli officer observed the Phalangists killing groups of women and children, and remonstrated with them. He was told that "the pregnant women will give birth to terrorists and children will grow up to be terrorists." The full story is reproduced in the Kahan Commission's report in the section entitled "The Events from the Entry of the Phalangists into the Sabra and Shatilla Camps Until Their Departure." The text, available on the Internet (www.israel. org/mfa/go), has no paragraph or page numbers.

9. Cited by John Dower, *War Without Mercy*, p. 71.

10. These examples are taken from Mike Davis, *Ecology of Fear*. I. F. Clarke's *Voices Prophesying War* and *The Pattern of Expectation* contain as much as anybody needs to know about exterminatory wars in imaginative fiction.

11. Joanna Bourke, *An Intimate History of Killing*, p. 158.

12. Christopher Browning, *Ordinary Men*. This is the revised paperback edition, which contains a powerful rejoinder to the criticism of Browning's book in Daniel Joshua Goldhagen, *Hitler's Willing Executioners*.

13. The extensive historical preamble to the Croatian constitution refers to the "millennial national identity of the Croat nation and the continuity of its statehood," as well as the "inalienable . . . right of the Croatian nation to self-determination and state sovereignty." This means that the new state is "hereby established as *the* national state of the Croatian people and *a* state of the members of other nations and minorities," such as Serbs, Muslims, and Jews. Emphasis added.

14. Misha Glenny, *The Fall of Yugoslavia*, p. 172.

15. Michael Burleigh, *The Third Reich*, p. 283.

16. Jonathan Glover, *Humanity*, pp. 387–391.

17. Michael Ignatieff, *Blood and Belonging* (1994), p. 3.

18. Susan L. Woodward, *Balkan Tragedy*, p. 229.

19. Mark Mazower, *The Balkans*, p. 86.

20. See Woodward, *Balkan Tragedy*, pp. 117–119.

21. Tim Judah, *The Serbs*, p. 86.

22. Peter du Preez, *Genocide*, p. 33.

23. Mahmood Mamndani, *When Victims Become Killers*, esp. pp. 79–87.

24. Bogdan Denitch, *Ethnic Nationalism*, p. 26.

25. See, for example, E. Gellner, *Nations and Nationalism*. A typical example from the British experience would be the instrumental use of the "constructed" myth of World War II.

26. Nederlands Instituut vor Oorlogsdocumentatie, *Srebrenica: A "Safe" Area*, pt. 2, chap. 2, sec. 2.

27. *Periodic Report on the Situation of Human Rights in the Territory of the Former Yugoslavia Submitted by Mr. Tadeusz Mazowiecki, Special Rapporteur of the Commission on Human Rights* (May 5, 1993, para. 72. According to the Sarajevo magazine *Dani* (June 23, 2000), the article was called "There Must Be No More Partisans." In this context "Partisans" equals "Serbs."

28. Woodward, *Balkan Tragedy*, p. 231.

29. Ibid., p. 258.

30. Cited by Jonathan Schell, *The Time of Illusions*, p. 185.

31. Contemporary reports suggest that the various Bosnian factions came extremely close to a settlement during the seventeen-hour parliamentary debate on a referendum in January 1992 and, with a little luck, might have succeeded. Whether the West (and especially the United States, with its obsession with a unitary Bosnia) would have permitted the settlement to go ahead will never be known. See Steven L. Burg and Paul S. Shoup, *The War in Bosnia-Herzegovina,* pp. 105–107.

32. Burleigh, *Third Reich,* p. 122.

33. Glenny, *The Fall of Yugoslavia,* p. 41.

34. Vesna Bojicic and Mary Kaldor, "The Political Economy of the War on Bosnia-Herzegovina" in Mary Kaldor and Basker Vashee, eds., *New Wars.* See also Woodward, *Balkan Tragedy,* pp. 47–81, for the story of the International Monetary Fund's disastrous meddling.

35. Mamdani, *When Victims Become Killers,* p. 214.

36. Technically known as the debate between intentionalists and functionalists. See, for example, Ian Kershaw, *The Nazi Dictatorship,* pp. 69–92. Many of the arguments turn up again, in a watered-down form, in discussions about the collapse of Yugoslavia.

37. Cited by Charles S. Maier, *The Unmasterable Past,* p. 30.

38. Cited by Christopher Browning, "German Memory, Judicial Interrogation, and Historical Reconstruction: Writing Perpetrator History from Post War Testimony" in Saul Friedlander, ed., *Probing the Limits of Representation,* p. 35.

39. Hayden White, "The Politics of Historical Interpretation," in *The Content of the Form,* p. 67.

40. Compare the comment by Ian Kershaw in the preface to the second volume of his biography of Adolf Hitler: "To call Hitler evil may well be both true and morally satisfying. But it explains nothing." Ian Kershaw, *Hitler, 1936–1945,* p. xvii.

41. For example, see Adnan Jahic, the SDA leader in Tuzla, who produced an article entitled "Virtuous Muslim State" in *Zmaj od Bosne* no. 51 (September 17, 1993).

42. The official Dutch report into Srebrenica has useful summaries of the political careers of Izetbegovic and Karadzic and their main lieutenants. See *Srebrenica: A "Safe" Area,* pt. 1, chap. 3, secs. 3–4.

43. Mamdani, *When Victims Become Killers,* p. 189.

44. Ahmed Ould Abdullah, cited by Michael Ignatieff, *The Warrior's Honour.*

45. Cited by Burleigh, *The Third Reich,* p. 92.

46. See, for example, Omer Bartov, *Hitler's Army.*

47. See, for example, Stephen Ellis, *The Mask of Anarchy,* pp. 249–265.

48. Richard J. Goldstone, *For Humanity,* pp. 60–61.

49. See Lindquist, *Exterminate All the Brutes,* p. 161.

50. John Conroy, *Unspeakable Acts,* pp. 31–32.

51. See Gavin Cawthra, *Policing South Africa.*

52. Little of any real substance has emerged about the CCB. See Jacques Pauw, *Into the Heart of Darkness,* pp. 223–226, and Terry Bell and Dumisa Buhle Ntsebeza, *Unfinished Business.*

53. Gerard Prunier, *The Rwanda Crisis,* p. 231.

54. Ellis, *Mask of Anarchy,* p. 111.

55. *Srebrenica: A "Safe" Area,* pt. 2, chap. 6, sec. 6.

56. See ICTY indictment IT-98–34-I dated December 18, 1998.

57. See Burg and Shoup, *The War in Bosnia-Herzegovina,* pp. 68, 138–139. Also Duro Kozar, "100 Witnesses Against the Tenth Mountain Brigade," *Dani*

(February 4, 2000), and Yvonne Badal "From Thug to Hero," *OMRI* (November 12, 1996).

58. Cited by Burleigh, *The Third Reich*, pp. 660–661.

59. Jeremy Gordin's introduction to Eugene de Kock, *A Long Night's Damage*, p. 21.

60. Pauw, *Into the Heart of Darkness,* p. 19.

61. Browning, *Ordinary Men*, p. 2.

62. Herbert C. Kelman and V. Lee Hamilton give a good summary of the experiments and the issues surrounding them in *Crimes of Obedience*, pp. 148–166.

63. Conroy, *Unspeakable Acts,* pp. 84–115, discusses these cases. On the Nazis see also Henry V. Dicks, *Licensed Mass Murder*.

64. Henri Pouillot, *La Villa Sursini*.

3

The Law

This chapter addresses issues of international humanitarian law, or the law of armed conflict. Put simply, this chapter describes what the law says. I begin by explaining the laws and their origins, then how international treaties and statutes yield specific crimes to be investigated and punished. Finally, I address some of the practical problems to which this body of law gives rise.[1]

Essentially, international humanitarian law has a twofold purpose: It is intended to protect noncombatants, or those who are not now, or never were, taking part in the fighting; it also limits the methods and means by which the fighting is carried out. Some international humanitarian law is based on international treaties, and some is based on the customs of war. There are two broad divisions within international humanitarian law, although the distinction is now somewhat blurred. Humanitarian law properly defined seeks to protect military personnel who are not, for whatever reason, now taking part in the fighting, as well as civilian noncombatants; this is sometimes referred to as the *law of Geneva*. In addition, there is the *law of war*, sometimes referred to as the *law of The Hague*, which establishes the rights and duties of those actually doing the fighting and limits the methods that can be employed to harm the enemy. There was always some overlap between the two, and the adoption of the 1977 Additional Protocols to the Geneva Conventions ended any distinction for all practical purposes.

These rules apply to armed conflicts of all kinds. Traditionally, they applied only to so-called international armed conflicts, but today they also apply to noninternational armed conflicts, which are usually taken to be conflicts on the territory of a state between its own armed forces and identifiable armed groups, or between such armed groups fighting each other. The definition and threshold of an *armed conflict* is very important for the investigation and prosecution of war crimes. International humanitarian law is not, of course, the only body of law of treaties that covers what happens between states during peace and war. It is unique, however, in that, while treaties are entered into by *states*, they actually impact *individuals*, who can in theory be prosecuted if they fail to obey the laws. These laws are included in the second category of those described in Chapter 1 (i.e., they are the work of jurists and diplomats, albeit sometimes with specialist military advice, attempting to limit the violence of war). Like all such political treaties, they are essentially reactive in nature, and they had their origin in reactions to the newly destructive nature of warfare in the second half of the nineteenth century, when new technologies and large standing armies began to make war more violent and destructive than in the past. The origins of international humanitarian law are conventionally linked to the 1864 Diplomatic Conference, following the founding of the International Society of the Red Cross in Geneva in 1863; the conference adopted the Geneva Convention for the Amelioration of the Condition of the Wounded in Armies in the Field. This single convention, signed by sixteen nations, laid the foundation for much of what followed. It was a standing convention, rather than a temporary arrangement; it was open to all states, rather than only between immediate combatants; it imposed an obligation to treat the wounded of whatever side; and it enforced the marking of, and respect for, medical personnel and equipment. In 1906 the original Geneva Convention was reviewed and extended; and in 1929 the second Geneva Convention, addressing treatment of prisoners of war, was adopted. This was a reaction to the unprecedented numbers of prisoners taken in World War I, as well as the length of time for which they were held. A Convention covering the wounded and sick was agreed in the same year. In 1949, the Geneva Conventions assumed their final form, with the addition of a new convention covering the protection of civilians in war, a consequence of the immense human suffering in the world war that had just concluded. In 1977, and after difficult negotiations, two Additional Protocols were agreed upon; they strengthen the protection of victims in international conflicts (Protocol I) and noninternational conflicts (Protocol II).

In addition, there were a number of treaties not connected with the Geneva process but that were nonetheless the result of international negotiations. As early as 1868, the St. Petersburg Declaration (technically not a treaty) indicated that the contracting parties would renounce "in case of war among themselves, the employment . . . of any projectile of a weight below 400 grammes, which is either explosive or charged with fulminating or inflammable substances." Two things are of interest in this declaration. First, the text makes it clear that the agreement is not to have universal application: it does not apply to wars against nonsignatories, and certainly not to imperial wars. Second, the preamble sets out, for the first time, the central myth of international humanitarian law—and I do not mean that in a derogatory sense—when it claims that the "only legitimate object which States should endeavour to accomplish during war is to weaken the military forces of the enemy" and so "for this purpose it is sufficient to disable the greatest possible number of men." In turn "this objective would be exceeded by the employment of arms which uselessly aggravate the sufferings of disabled men, or render their death inevitable," and so "the employment of such arms would, therefore, be contrary to the laws of humanity." Even in 1868 it is doubtful whether states actually saw their only legitimate object in war as weakening the enemy's forces. After all, wars are fought (as Clausewitz taught us) ultimately for political reasons. Weakening the forces of the enemy is, at best, a device for furthering our political goals, and by 1868 it was already clear that social and technological changes made war no longer just about two armies fighting each other. Yet this assumption remains at the center of international humanitarian law thinking today, even though it is almost totally irrelevant to how wars are actually conducted.

The St. Petersburg Declaration was followed by more agreements, this time in treaty form. In 1899, the Hague Conference agreed four new conventions. One was for the peaceful settlement of disputes; a second agreed a series of "Regulations Respecting the Laws and Customs of War on Land"; a third extended the 1864 convention to maritime warfare; and the fourth prohibited "Launching of Projectiles and Explosives from Balloons." Again, we see the continuous process of trying to adapt the laws of war to military developments. There is one particular provision of the Second Hague Convention that is of particular interest: responding to the rise of guerrilla and partisan warfare, the convention extended the protection of belligerent status to "the population of a territory which has not been occupied who on the enemy's approach, spontaneously take up arms to resist the invading troops," provided they are properly organized and themselves obey the laws of war. The provision has remained essentially unaltered. The 1907 Hague Conference also added a new convention ("Concerning Bombardment by Naval Forces in Time of War"), reflecting the fact that *Dreadnought*-type battleships could now bombard coastal towns from long range. Article 1 of the convention stipulated sternly that "the bombardment by naval forces of undefended ports, towns, villages, dwellings or buildings is forbidden." Unsurprisingly, an attempt was made after World War I to extend these provisions to air forces as well. The "Rules of Aerial Warfare," drafted in the 1923 Hague Conference, would have prohibited "aerial bombardment for the purpose of terrorising the civilian population," or for "destroying or damaging private property not of a military character, or of injuring non-combatants"; the convention allowed bombardment only against "a military objective, that is to say, an object of which the destruction or injury would constitute a distinct military advantage to the belligerent." Although these rules were never actually put into effect, their underlying logic, and much of the language, has survived in other forms.

At the end of this complex and lengthy process, we are left with a large corpus of legal documents, some overtaken by later texts, others less so. What does all this amount to in practical terms? Some of the provisions—for example, on the right of prisoners of war to elect representatives by secret ballot—are specialized and not relevant here. But the fundamental principles of the laws of war probably amount to less than a page and can be summarized thus:

- Attacks must be confined to military objectives, and neither civilians nor civilian property may be attacked. If there is doubt about whether a target is a civilian or military one, it is assumed to be civilian.
- An enemy who has surrendered or who cannot take part in fighting any longer may not be killed or wounded.
- The wounded and sick must be cared for by whichever party to the conflict has them under its control. Medical personnel and equipment are exempt from attack.
- Prisoners of war and civilians who are in the power of an enemy must have their rights protected.
- There are practical constraints on the methods and means of warfare that are allowed. In particular, those that cause unnecessary losses or suffering are illegal.
- Reprisals are forbidden.
- Unavoidable civilian casualties are acceptable, but every effort should be made to keep them to a minimum, and they should be proportionate to the military advantage expected to be gained.

Of course, these provisions are only normative statements. They merely represent a series of undertakings by states, unless, of course, those states take concrete steps to implement them. The first stage, as with any treaty, is *ratification*, usually by the parliament or legislature of the country whose representatives have signed the treaty. When ratification is delayed (as happened in 2002 with the United States and the treaty establishing the International Criminal Court), a state that has signed the treaty is still bound to act in a way consistent with its philosophy. The next stage is the *incorporation* of the treaty into the rules for behavior of one's own armed forces—usually manuals of military law and disciplinary regulations; indeed, various provisions of the Geneva Conventions require states to do this. Lastly, and most important, states must enforce the rules in practice. If this is not done, then little of the above has any point at all. Thus, the old Yugoslavia was a signatory and promulgated international humanitarian law in its military handbooks. But the tactical instructions it actually issued to troops nonetheless covered such points as how to make use of medical facilities to derive advantages in combat.

Enforcement

The conventions do not contain provisions for supranational or independent enforcement if the state concerned is unwilling to take action against its own nationals. It is depressing to note that very few of the incidents that have been described already led to prosecutions on a national basis. There are a variety of reasons for this. One is simply lack of knowledge and understanding. The provisions of international humanitarian law are very complex and require trained specialists to interpret them and to advise a commander on how to behave. There are many nations in the world whose military forces do not have the capacity to understand and apply the rules properly, even if their foreign ministries had signed up to them for political reasons, and that have received little or no training in them. In parts of Africa, for example, the military seems to believe that civilians being used as human shields by soldiers are a legitimate target. Thus, Sierra Leone helicopter crews accused of killing civilians in attacks on the rebel Revolutionary United Front told journalists that they regretted the deaths, but they "said that the rebels deliberately used civilians as human shields."[2] And wars are increasingly fought between scratch militias who may have had little formal training in anything, let alone the laws of war, led by leaders, rather than officers, who may have had little more.

Another reason for nonprosecution is lack of reciprocity. It is an established fact that fewer atrocities tend to be committed when both sides are playing according to similar rules. Thus, in World War II the Western Front was much less brutal than the Eastern Front, and some of the brutality there was directed against partisans and the resistance. Such groups, because they are generally few in number and militarily weak, have little choice but to conduct operations through bombings, assassinations, and ambushes. Where a resistance group does not itself show any interest in obeying the laws of war and explicitly targets civilians, there is a strong temptation to pay them back in kind and to regard adherence to the laws of war as pointless. After all, few of us would be happy in a situation where we had consistently to treat another group better than they were treating us, especially if they were trying to kill us. (This, of course, is where military discipline comes in.)

Another reason is lack of interest. There is a common view among combat soldiers that, while restraints on war are certainly a good thing in themselves, the laws of war as they now exist are too complex, negotiated by clever lawyers who have never worn a uniform and who have no idea what war is actually like. This attitude is not universal, but in its extreme form it regards international humanitarian law as unrealistic, as well as unnecessarily limiting; this leads some to simply disregard the law. In states where the military has a large degree of autonomy in operational matters, this can be a particular problem, as it can when the battlefield is remote and hard to access. In addition, there have been certain states that have not regarded adherence to international humanitarian law in war as of any importance. Nazi Germany felt itself to be engaged in a war for racial survival, where obedience to the laws of war was for wimps. Likewise, both the Soviet Union and China were heirs to a Marxist tradition of seeing all moral standards as relative, the product of underlying patterns of economic relations.

Inevitably, wider political factors also loom large, as they do in any important prosecution. U.S. authorities were initially unwilling to prosecute Lieutenant Calley for the My Lai massacre and were driven to do so only by a sustained campaign by politicians and the media. Although My Lai was far from an isolated incident, there was no way in which the United States could conceivably have mounted large-scale war crimes trials without splitting the country hopelessly in two and, not least, undermining a Vietnam policy that had wide public support. In general, it is very bad politics to prosecute your own people for war crimes while a war is on, or in its immediate aftermath, and it is seldom done. Although a number of states, including Indonesia and those of the former Yugoslavia, have been criticized for not putting their nationals on trial for alleged human rights violations, the fact is that the records of the critics (mostly in the West) suggest that they would not have behaved any better. It takes uncommon courage for a public figure to say something like "these people were our nationals, there can be no excuse for the crimes they are alleged to have committed, and they must stand trial." Societies where this has started to happen—such as Croatia after Franjo Tudjman—deserve the highest praise. In any event, conducting war crimes trials, especially of more senior officers, is a complex and difficult task. Given that many prosecution witnesses will be from the same military force as the accused, the actual trial will be fraught with practical difficulties. In general, states will not want to hold trials of this kind unless there is an excellent chance for conviction. After all, if there is one political problem worse than putting your own people on trial, it is putting them on trial and having them acquitted.

In most cases, the reluctance to prosecute, as well as the sheer difficulty of staging a trial, have been the end of the matter. In a small number of cases, however, special international courts have been set up, with special procedures, to try the same crimes. It is often said that such courts take an interest when a state is *unable* or *unwilling* to prosecute itself. In some cases this is because the physical infrastructure of justice (or even a sovereign state) is missing. In others it is because the state itself is involved in the events that led to the trial and is either protecting or persecuting the defendant(s). And in some cases it is because a domestic trial may not produce the outcome that the international community demands.

Although international criminal justice is generally reckoned to have begun with the war crimes tribunals set up in Nuremberg and Tokyo after World War II, steps were taken to set up an international court after World War I, and a few trials were actually conducted. The Paris Peace Conference established a special commission to consider "the Responsibility of the Authors of the War and the Enforcement of Penalties." The report of the commission urged prosecution of a number of German military and political leaders for violations of the laws of war. Four articles in the Versailles Treaty (articles 227–230) established procedures "to bring before military tribunals persons accused of having committed acts in violation of the laws and customs of war." The judges were to be nationals of the state against whom the accused was alleged to have committed criminal acts. In February 1920, the former Western allies submitted a list of almost 900 names of people to be extradited, including practically every military and political leader of any substance. The list caused a violent reaction in Germany, and it was eventually whittled down to forty-five, of whom only twelve were eventually tried, with six being convicted. The situation was not helped by the refusal of the Dutch government to extradite Kaiser Wilhelm, in exile in the Netherlands.

This episode was an early and useful sign of the practical difficulties that war crimes trials can produce, especially when the motive is political rather than legal. For propaganda purposes during World War I, the Western allies made allegations of German atrocities and placed the responsibility on Germany for that war in the first place. Public opinion (and elite opinion, for that matter) was so inflamed that those who merely wanted the Kaiser executed were dismissed as liberal faint-of-hearts. The problem, however, was that there was no legal basis on which a trial of the Kaiser could actually be held, since there was nothing to link him, or his senior advisers, with the violations of the laws of war that had in fact taken place. The alternative was to try the Kaiser and his entourage for, in effect, starting the war. This made many people uncomfortable, since it was the first suggestion that starting a war was unlawful, and it amounted to a unilateral ex post facto change in the law. In any event, Germany had scarcely started the war; that honor probably went to Austria-Hungary, which had attacked Serbia.

The next, and best known, of all international criminal courts was the

Nuremberg International Military Tribunal, which sat from November 1945 to October 1946. It was international only in the sense that it was composed of judges and prosecutors from the four victorious states, who signed the enabling charter, although nineteen other states subsequently adhered to the charter. The very existence of the court owed much to U.S. pressure and resources and represented an about-face from the earlier U.S. position that senior Nazis should be shot on sight. Twenty-four individual defendants were indicted, as well as seven organizations, including the Nazi party and the SS. Three were acquitted, and the remainder were sentenced to death or, in a few cases, to imprisonment for long terms. They were charged uder three main headings.

The first was *crimes against peace*, defined as the "planning, preparation, initiation or waging of a war of aggression." The second was *war crimes*, defined as "violations of the laws and customs of war." The third was *crimes against humanity*, defined as "murder, extermination, enslavement, deportation, and other inhumane acts." The crimes against humanity charge was new and reflected the fact that many of the crimes were not directly related to the war or caused by it. Indeed, some had happened before 1939. They could not, therefore, be considered as war crimes, but neither could they be left unaddressed, and so a special category was created. The new allegation also reflected the feeling that the crimes themselves were so appalling that in some senses they were directed at the whole human race as much as against the individuals concerned. Thus, four counts were included in the final indictments: (1) a common plan or conspiracy; (2) crimes against peace; (3) war crimes; and (4) crimes against humanity.

The Nuremberg tribunal has been subjected to much criticism over the years. Most of this has centered around two themes: that it was "victor's justice," and that it charged and convicted the defendants for actions that had not previously been thought of as crimes. Of course, the tribunal *was* victor's justice; it could not be otherwise. There was no functioning system of justice in Germany at the time, and even if there had been, political reality would have prevented it being involved. There was no serious alternative to what was actually done. In the event, the tribunal probably did the best and fairest job it could under the circumstances. If the vast majority of the defendants were found guilty, it was because of the huge amount of evidence against them rather than because the court itself was biased. A more fundamental criticism was the nature of the charges. Ironically, waging an aggressive war was the easiest charge to prove, even if it was among the most contentious. The tribunal argued that Germany was a party to the 1928 Kellog-Briand Pact, under which a total of sixty-three states by 1939 agreed to "condemn recourse to war for the solution of international controversies, and renounce it as an instrument of national policy in their relations with each other." It was argued that this made an aggressive war illegal. But the resort to war was, after all, a sovereign right of states, and there were rules about how it should be done. It was not clear either that violation of an undertaking of this kind should automatically attract a death sentence. The argument was complicated by the fact that Britain and France had declared war on Germany—in the traditional fashion—rather than the other way around (although the charges implied the opposite), and that the Soviet Union had calmly helped itself to half of Poland in 1939. The use of the conspiracy charge has also come in for criticism, both at the time and subsequently. This was basically a tactical device: an organization could be found guilty of conspiracy, then all its members punished without the need for a trial. In practice, there was little evidence of a detailed common plan among the defendants, and none was found guilty on this count alone.

The tribunal demonstrated how inherently complex and unpredictable such trials were. The trial was conducted in four languages, and a huge translation and interpretation staff was required. Much use was made of captured documents, all of which had to be translated, such that a Russian judge could examine a German document while an American witness answered questions in English posed in French by a French judge looking at a French translation of the same German text. There were arguments about the structure and contents of the indictments, rules for the conduct of the trial, about which systems of legal procedure to use, and even what formal clothing the judges would wear. It became clear that there was nowhere near enough historical and military analytical expertise and far too few military and intelligence experts who could read, let alone speak, German. Nor was there enough money: without massive financial support from the Americans, the tribunal would never have finished its work. Nuremberg also set a series of precedents for the future, some good and some bad, many of which were seen again in the work of the two ad hoc tribunals. One was its establishment by a small group of states (acting on behalf of what was just starting to be called the United Nations), rather than through international agreement (which, to be fair, would have taken far too long). Similarly, the Germans themselves were not consulted about the need for it or its jurisdiction over them. It developed a hybrid legal system: closer to the Anglo-Saxon adversarial model, but with elements of the continental system grafted on. It also demonstrated the enormous value of documentation in establishing basic facts and lines of control, provided the effort was available to read and understand it.

Nuremberg also had some longer-term political consequences, which still resonate. It was clear from the beginning that there were long-term dangers in conducting a trial according to abstract ideological criteria about aggression. Robert Jackson, the U.S. judge arguing against Soviet suggestions that the tribunal statute should refer only to crimes of aggression carried out by the European Axis, asserted that "if certain acts of violations of treaties are crimes, they are crimes whether the United States does them or whether Germany does them, and we are not prepared to lay down a rule of criminal conduct against others which we would not be willing to have invoked against us."[3] Jackson's idealism—and his naiveté in believing that the United States would be prepared to have the same rule invoked against itself—are a good example of the doctrine of unintended consequences: the United States was pilloried for various alleged crimes in later years, including Vietnam. A similar situation arose with respect to the NATO attack on Yugoslavia in 1999.

Another problem arose with the argument that lawyers call *tu quoque*—"you're another." The tribunal was, of course, concerned with the misdeeds of only the Axis, although the defense was quick to find counterexamples of allegedly similar behavior by the Allies. For example, one of the charges was aggression against Norway, although it was a matter of record that the British and French had been planning their own invasion and were preempted. (The judges decided that that did not matter.) More serious was the allegation that the German navy had practiced unrestricted submarine warfare and, in particular, left the crews of torpedoed merchant ships to drown. This charge was eventually dropped once it was officially admitted that the British and Americans had done the same, although whether the two examples were equally bad or equally acceptable was never fully clear. The most awkward case, however, was the tribunal's indictments for the bombing of civilians, in Rotterdam and elsewhere. Perhaps out of embarrassment, these were not pressed too hard.[4]

The Ad Hoc Tribunals

I now want to say a few words about the two tribunals created by the UN Security Council in the 1990s: the International Criminal Tribunal for the Former Yugoslavia, and the International Criminal Tribunal for Rwanda. I will not go through the documentation in detail but will highlight some important elements as well as differences. I will then go on to make a few remarks about the International Criminal Court before discussing some of the main issues raised in all the various documents. These tribunals represent yet another model, in the sense that they were set up as an executive act by a simple vote of the UN Security Council. Members of the United Nations who were not on the Security Council were thus not involved (although they have to contribute to costs), and the states of the former Yugoslavia were not consulted, although the Tutsi-led government of Rwanda was. For this reason, the two tribunals were set up by a formal resolution of the Security Council, and in both cases the council acted under chapter VII of the United Nations Charter, so that the cooperation of states was mandatory: it was not a treaty to which they had to accede. This has been criticized, but it was the only way in which either of the tribunals could have been set up promptly. There are a number of significant points in the resolutions and the statute: I will use ICTY as a model, then indicate where the ICTR differs.

UN Security Council Resolution (UNSCR) 827 (1993), setting up the ICTY, has a preamble suggesting that the situation in the former Yugoslavia "continues to constitute a threat to international peace and security," thus enabling the provisions of chapter VII (Enforcement) of the UN Charter to be invoked. UNSCR 995 (1994) for the ICTR has a similar formula. Likewise both preambles indicate that the council determined "to put an end to such crimes and to take effective measures to bring to justice the persons who are responsible for them." Thus, the council defined both of these initiatives as essentially operational in nature, designed to achieve specific policy goals. In both cases, one of the operational paragraphs of the resolution "decides that all States shall co-operate fully" with the tribunals and "take any measures necessary under their domestic law" to implement the provisions of the resolutions. The jurisdiction of the tribunals is also set out in the resolutions. There are two elements to jurisdiction: geography and time. The ICTY's jurisdiction is limited to "the territory of the former Yugoslavia," that of ICTR to "the territory of Rwanda," but "Rwandan citizens responsible for genocide and other such violations committed in the territory of neighbouring states" are included also. The ICTY's jurisdiction began on January 1, 1991 (i.e., before the first serious atrocities), and lasts until "a date to be determined by the Security Council upon the restoration of peace." In practice, ICTY jurisdiction still does not have an ending date, and it became, a little unexpectedly, involved in the crises in Kosovo and Macedonia as a result.

The statutes set out the offenses that may be prosecuted by the tribunal: grave breaches of the Geneva Conventions of 1949 (i.e., not the Additional Protocols); violations of the laws or customs of war; genocide; and crimes against humanity. Reflecting the different nature of the fighting in Rwanda, that tribunal's statute covers genocide, crimes against humanity, and violations of the common article III of the Geneva Conventions and Additional Protocol II. Both tribunals have concurrent jurisdiction with national courts (i.e., they do not have to wait until the national courts have deliberated) but have primacy over national courts if they choose to exert it. In each case, the tribunal is divided into three parts: the prosecutor, responsible for investigation and prosecution; the president and other judges of the trial chambers and appeals chamber; and the registrar, responsible for administration. Finally, an article of each statute sets out the types of assistance that states must supply if asked: they include but are not limited to identification and location; testimony and evidence; serving documents; arrest and detention; and surrender and transfer of the accused.

There are a number of significant differences from the Nuremberg model. Unlike Nuremberg, the ad hoc tribunals have not attempted to prosecute crimes against peace; nor do they sit in judgment against organizations, only individuals. A common appeals chamber has been added and has already overruled a number of decisions by the trial chambers. For the first time, too, an attempt has been made to make the judges and the staff truly international—although this is subject to practical constraints. There are also many similarities to the Nuremberg model. The main one is the desire to be seen as addressing a political problem that is not addressable otherwise. Western governments were extremely frustrated by their inability to influence events on the ground during the fighting in the former Yugoslavia. Immense efforts were made to stop the killing and reach a political agreement, but the West's ability to enforce any kind of settlement was practically nonexistent. Public opinion, fed on intervention fantasies and impatient with mundane reality, demanded action, and establishing the ICTY was almost the only initiative within the power of the wider international community. Nor should we overlook the very real sense of helplessness that Western decisionmakers felt toward the fighting as well as their obligation to do everything to stop it. The Rwanda tribunal in some senses benefited from the Hague model: it is not obvious that it would have been established if the earlier example had not been there.

Finally, some words on the differences between these earlier examples and the International Criminal Court.[5] First, the ICC was not established, unlike the other examples, because of a specific incident; it had first been mooted after World War II, but it took until the 1990s for the constellation of political forces to come together to make it possible. This is an advantage in the sense that it is not limited by geography and time, but it is a disadvantage inasmuch as it has no obvious body of work with which to begin. It is also a treaty-based organization, not an organ of the Security Council, although it had its original inspiration in a General Assembly resolution of December 1996, and the negotiations have taken place under UN auspices. It is therefore necessary for states to sign and ratify the treaty before they are bound by it. On the face of it, this is a crippling handicap, because states that are most likely to commit the "most serious crimes of concern to the international community as a whole," in the words of the ICC Statute, are evidently the least likely to be bound by a statute that could be used against them. A state also has to accept that the ICC has jurisdiction over particular crimes. The position is, however, eased by the stipulation that the ICC has jurisdiction when the state with custody of a suspect and the state on whose territory the crime occurred agree to accept the ICC's jurisdiction. The court does, however, have inherent jurisdiction in the case of genocide. It is foreseen that the ICC will have jurisdiction over crimes of aggression (a reversion to Nuremberg), but no progress has been made on this to date. It also has jurisdiction over crimes against humanity and war crimes, which are basically violations of the laws or customs of war.

Although the ICC, like the ad hoc tribunals, does have an independent prosecutor, that role is more constrained (this was one of the most bitterly contested parts of the ICC Statute). The prosecutor will be able to bring charges of aggression only once the UN Security Council has determined that there is an aggressor, and no charges may be brought if the Security Council is itself dealing with the issue under Chapter VII. The original draft of the ICC Statute put forward by the International Law Commission denied the prosecutor any independent initiative at all. During the negotiations, the so-called like-minded group, including the United Kingdom, were successful in introducing the concept of an investigation on the prosecutor's initiative, against the opposition of some powerful states who thought that it might be used against them. The eventual compromise included this right, but it also requires the prosecutor to persuade a pretrial chamber of judges that there is a "reasonable" case for an investigation.

This does not exhaust the list of tribunals being planned or under discussion. A Special Court for Sierra Leone has been set up, and others for Cambodia, Indonesia, and Iraq are being discussed. And though the organizational and funding arrangements for each may be very different, all the organizations spend much of their time grappling with a fairly small range of issues of principle; it is to these that I now want to turn.

Giving and Receiving Orders

Almost all of the cases dealt with by the various courts and tribunals described above involve some element of hierarchical control. Most war crimes are committed by members of a group of some kind, whether formally structured with uniforms or just a gang of semicriminals. There will therefore be a commander and probably others in positions of authority. In turn, this group is likely to be part of a larger formal or informal group, perhaps with links to political parties or similar organizations. So it is very unlikely that a single atrocious act will take place in a complete vacuum, with no prior orders and no bureaucratic consequences. Moreover, it is generally accepted that the person with his finger on the trigger is, in some ways, less guilty than the person who gave the orders for the killing. For that reason, all aspects and stages of the crime will normally be investigated, even though charges may be brought, for reasons of resources, against only the most senior figures.

Let us start with the immediate perpetrators, that is, the ones who kill and the ones who command the killers on the ground. In many cases, detailed evidence of their complicity is available, including witness statements, visual identification, and captured documents that reveal that their unit was involved. So what kind of a defense could a soldier or a junior commander offer in such circumstances? In general, it will be: "I was only following orders." This defense has become, through decades of use in war films and media commentaries, little more than a joke. But the issue of obedience to orders goes to the heart of the way the military functions, and deciding when it does and does not constitute a defense is one of the most serious issues in war crimes trials. In principle, any military force runs on obedience to orders; indeed, discipline breeds coherence, and the force with the greatest coherence will generally win a battle. The problem surfaces when the orders given—or taken as being received—raise problems of legality. The principle laid down by the Nuremberg trials, and continued by the ad hoc tribunals, is that the "fact that the Defendant acted pursuant to order of his Government or of a superior shall not free him from responsibility, but may be considered in mitigation."[6] This seems—and probably is—reasonable enough, but it represents a change from the way in which military obedience was considered in the past. The absolute defense of superior orders was effectively that offered by Lieutenant Calley in the My Lai trial.[7] Calley told the court-martial that he understood that "all orders were to be assumed legal, that the soldier's job was to carry out any order given him to the best of his ability." Calley conceded that he had been instructed in the Geneva Conventions but claimed that he remembered nothing of the classes and that he had received no instruction on the "laws and rules of warfare." Calley was not the sharpest tool in the box, and his background—not very bright and not trained to think for himself—probably means that he did think these things. But the same excuses can be, and are, used all the way up the command hierarchy. For example, writing after World War II about the destruction of Dresden, the former deputy commander in chief of Bomber Command, Air Vice Marshal Robert Saundby, claimed that he

> was not in any way responsible for the decision to make a full-scale air attack on Dresden. Nor was my Commander. . . . Our part was to carry out, to the best of our ability, the instructions we received from the Air Ministry. And, in this case, the Air Ministry was merely passing on instructions received from those responsible for the higher direction of the war.[8]

The defense of ignorance of the law and deference to superior orders is one that has not been much used in the Hague or Rwanda tribunals and may well not feature very greatly in trials before the ICC. Modern combat is much less between organized and trained groups than was once the case, and so formal patterns of command and control are less important. One defense that has already been offered is that of coercion, where the defendant insists that, if he had not carried out the crime, he would himself have been punished, probably by death. This kind of situation is likely to increase in the future, as militias tend to have rough and brutal ways of enforcing discipline. A good example is the case of Drazen Erdemovic, who helped carry out the mass killings at Srebrenica. Erdemovic, in an example of the insanity of the Bosnia fighting, was actually a Bosnian Croat, who was conscripted into the VRS (Vojska Republike Srpske, the army of the Bosnian Serb Republic). Hoping for a life away from combat, he found himself in the 10th Sabotage Detachment, one of the numerous special units that proliferated during the fighting. Erdemovic admitted his part in the killings but argued that, had he not participated, he would have been killed himself. Moreover, since there were plenty of other soldiers available to do the killing, his sacrifice would have been completely in vain. Eventually, the Appeals Chamber of the ICTY decided by a 3-2 majority verdict that duress "does not afford a complete defence to a soldier charged with a crime against humanity and/or a war crime involving the killing of innocent human beings." Erdemovic was therefore found guilty, although the lenient sentence he received reflected the situation he found himself in, as well as the help he gave to the prosecution in other cases.[9] The defense of duress is also recognized in the ICC Statute, but this is a difficult area, and defendants who want to use it will have to show that the sanctions threatened against them were both real and terminal. In the past, such evidence has often not been persuasive: many, if not most, German commanders on the Eastern Front apparently gave their men the right to opt out of mass executions.

A much more significant issue is the responsibility of senior military and civilian commanders for the conduct of their subordinates. In a sense, this is an outgrowth of the responsibility that a commander has for the good order and discipline of his unit anyway. As a distinguished British general testified at the *Krstic* trial, "Command is a very personal thing, in that every Commander is given orders from above and he is responsible for carrying out those orders and achieving the mission. . . . He is personally liable for the success or failure of the actions of all under his command" so that "he must ensure that all those under his command are doing what he wants in the way he wants done . . . if something goes wrong, then he has to take responsibility in a personal way for it."[10] The most succinct statement of what this means in the criminal context is article 7 of the ICTY Statute (article 6 of the ICTR Statute), which says in part:

> A person who planned, instigated, ordered, committed or otherwise aided
> and abetted in the planning, preparation or execution of a crime . . . shall
> be individually responsible for the crime.
>   The fact that any of the acts . . . was committed by a subordinate does
> not relieve his superior of criminal responsibility if he knew or had reason
> to know that the subordinate was about to commit such acts or had done
> so, and the superior failed to take the necessary and reasonable measures
> to prevent such acts or to punish the perpetrators thereof.[11]

This has several implications. First, a number of trials in The Hague
have made it clear that the "individual" mentioned here can be a civilian as
well as a military commander. For example, Dario Kordic, the Bosnian
Croat political leader in central Bosnia, was convicted on several counts in
February 2001 because the judges found that he "played his part as surely
as the men who fired the guns." Indeed, "the fact that he was a leader
aggravates the Offences."[12] The situation was even clearer in Rwanda,
where there was no longer any serious armed conflict to speak of by 1994,
and many of those responsible for planning and directing the killings were
civilians anyway. Second, a commander is accountable not merely for the
acts of others but also for scrutinizing the behavior of his subordinates,
demanding to be kept informed about their activities. Courts have accepted,
however, that a commander cannot spend his entire time suspiciously cross-
examining his subordinates about everything, or he would have no time to
do his main job. The postwar Tokyo trials introduced the concept of *ordinary diligence*, which is the level of interest that a commander should take
in the actions of his subordinates to ensure that they behave properly. It
would be accepted, for example, that if a group of subordinates conspire to
commit violations of the laws of war in the absence of the commander, and
then successfully cover up what they have done, it would be unreasonable
to hold the commander responsible. The problem, as always, lies in the
subjective nature of the tests that a court must apply.

Direct responsibility is fairly easy, although it cannot be assumed that
position in a command hierarchy, or membership of a committee, *necessarily* implies a direct role in planning or committing an atrocity: it is possible
that in certain types of political systems power and command will be so
personalized that the command system as it appears on paper actually does
not represent reality. Thus, a defense minister might attend cabinet meetings where defense issues were discussed, but the president might instead
have taken all of the major decisions with the chief of defense.

More difficult to establish are the duties to prevent and punish. In some
cases the issue will be fairly straightforward, if it can be shown that *no*
attempts were made to do either of these things. Much more difficult, and
more common, will be a situation in which a defendant clearly made at
least some effort to carry out these duties, but the prosecution will argue

that not enough was done. The trial of Tihomir Blaskic partly revolved around this issue. Blaskic's lawyers produced a number of orders that he had issued in 1993 requiring units under his command to observe the laws of war and to treat noncombatants with respect. The authenticity of these documents has been challenged, but even if they were genuine they would not, in and of themselves, discharge the responsibility of the commander unless steps were actually taken to follow them up and ensure compliance. Indeed, it "is now well established that operational commanders must exercise the full potential of their authority to avert war crimes. They will not be exonerated in cases of non-assertive orders or failure to supervise their implementation."[13]

Likewise, the former Bosnian Serb president, Radovan Karadzic, wrote a very strange letter to the spiritual leader of Orthodox Serbs, Patriach Pavle, which was published in the Belgrade magazine *Nedeljni Telegraf* in May 2001. With the letter, Karadzic enclosed several hundred documents that, he claimed, showed the "enormous efforts made by the Serb side . . . to prevent the misdeeds which typically occur in any civil war." The documents—some of which the magazine also published— include orders signed by Karadzic requiring the Bosnian Serb forces to respect the laws of war and to investigate alleged atrocities. These documents, claims the magazine, show "what kind of orders Radovan Karadzic really issued" and "reveal a different truth about the war." What a court would make of such documents remains to be seen, but a commander, or political leader, cannot simply issue orders and then assume that the job is done. In other cases, however, there will be some evidence that a commander has actually tried to prevent or punish atrocities, but a prosecution will argue that these efforts were insufficient. A court would then have to decide whether a busy and harassed commander under stress actually met the "necessary and reasonable" standard. One panel of judges might decide that, on balance, he did just about meet the criteria and acquit him. Another might decide that the same commander narrowly failed to make the standard and sentence him to twenty-five years in prison on the same set of facts.

The position is further complicated because the commander's responsibility extends to forces that are not narrowly in the written command structure. Thus, paramilitary forces, forces nominally under the command of other leaders, militias, territorial defense forces, and even police units may be within the responsibility of a commander, even if they are not formally subordinated. The test is *effective control*: If the commander gives an order, is it then followed, and what are the mechanisms available to ensure compliance? The fact that no written orders exist to subordinate the unit in question is not a defense. It is not necessary, of course, to show that a command relationship existed for every moment of every day and for every order. If, for example, international monitors complained about cease-fire violations by paramilitary forces, and the local commander promised to stop them and did so, then a pattern of effective control would have been established. Command responsibility can extend even to other nations' troops. The most obvious example of this is multinational forces, where a commander can be responsible for the activities of a unit with whom there may be no common language of communication and may thus be required to work through liaison officers and interpreters. In peacekeeping operations the position will be complicated further by the frequent existence of parallel command chains from national capitals. Because of different national laws about the use of lethal force, commanders could, in theory, find themselves giving an order that would be illegal under (say) UK law but legal under the law of the contingent that was performing it.

An interesting—if slightly extreme—example of the lengths to which a commander's responsibility could extend is provided by the massacre at the Sabra and Shatila refugee camps in Beirut in 1982. The massacres were carried out by units of Lebanese Christian paramilitaries loyal to the Phalangist organization in the confusion surrounding the Israeli invasion of Lebanon that year and the advance into Beirut. The Phalangist militias were under the direct control of the Israeli Defense Force, which made the decision, approved by the then–defense minister Ariel Sharon, to send the militia into the two camps to flush out the Palestinian fighters who remained there. The official estimate of the death toll is some 700–800, including many women and children, although unofficial estimates put the figure higher. As a result of the outcry when the massacres were discovered, the Israeli government set up the Kahan Commission, which produced a magisterial report based on official documents. Senior Israeli military and civilian leaders claimed that the massacres had taken them completely by surprise, and they had not expected anything similar to happen. The report did not accept this, not least because the popular Phalangist leader Bashir Jemayel had been murdered, allegedly by Palestinians, only a few days before, and it required no great intellectual penetration to deduce that revenge might be taken. The report found Sharon "personally responsible" for the killings and recommended that he resign. Depressing as it may be to learn, recent moves to indict Sharon in a Belgian court were condemned by some on the basis that no parallel moves were taking place to apprehend "the Arabs who did order those murders" (they were Maronite Christians) and that no Israelis had actually pulled the triggers. It was also argued that, since Sharon was democratically elected, he could not be a war criminal.[14]

However this may be—and it is not clear yet whether any legal proceedings will actually be brought—the Kahan Commission itself dealt with the point about foreign personnel in a magisterial fashion. Although the commission was not a legal body, it concluded with a description of command responsibility that perhaps sums up the position best:

> If it indeed becomes clear that those who decided on the entry of the Phalangists into the camps should have foreseen—from the information at their disposal and things which were common knowledge—that there was a danger of massacre, and no steps were taken which might have prevented this danger or at least greatly reduced the possibility . . . then those who made the decisions and those who implemented them are indirectly responsible for what ultimately occurred, even if they did not intend this to happen.[15]

Command responsibility is the only way in which those who give the orders can themselves ever be addressed. But it is a doctrine that, understandably, makes many modern commanders rather apprehensive, confronted as they are with the twin complexities of modern war, on the one hand, and the modern law of war on the other. It is perhaps also the only example in the law of war where the accused is effectively required to prove their innocence: to explain, in other words, why the normal pattern of command and control that would have allocated responsibility to them did apply in a certain case.

Armed Conflict

Self-evidently, violations of the laws or customs of war, as well as grave breaches of the Geneva Conventions, require an armed conflict of some kind if they are to be charged. (The phrase *armed conflict* is preferred to *war* in current use because of the awkward issues raised by the latter expression and because much current fighting, though serious, does not resemble the traditional model of war.) Until recently, it was not thought necessary to define an armed conflict, because everybody knew what it was: Nuremberg took for granted that an armed conflict had been taking place between September 1939 and May 1945, and few would have disagreed. Before the Geneva Conventions, indeed, international humanitarian law protected noncombatants in time of war only—a situation covered by precise definitions. But as the nature of war changed, the same conflict could be described by one party as an "internal security problem" and by the other as a "war of national liberation"; it was obvious that an agreed definition would be necessary. This was provided by the trial of Dusko Tadic, an official at one of the Bosnian Serb–run camps in Prijedor. In the *Tadic* trial, the first to be conducted by ICTY, the judgment of the court stated that an armed conflict "exists whenever there is a resort to armed force between States or protracted armed violence between governmental authorities and organized armed groups or between such groups within a State."[16] This definition was extremely important for the ICTY, since its statute requires it to prove the existence of an armed conflict first before crimes against humanity can be charged. (This stipulation is not found in the statute for the Rwanda tribunal or in the ICC Statute.) Assessing the existence of an armed conflict between states is relatively easy but somewhat more difficult in an internal armed conflict where it is necessary to avoid confusion with "banditry, unorganized and short-lived insurrections, or terrorist activities, which are not subject to international humanitarian law."[17]

The *Tadic* case was relatively straightforward, in that there was both a recognized state (Bosnia-Herzegovina) and an organized entity (the Republika Srpska) that wished to secede from it. Moreover, after the attempt by the JNA to put an end to Bosnian independence, and the violent secession of the Serbs from Bosnia that followed, it was clear that the level of violence amounted to an armed conflict. In other cases, things have been far less clear-cut. In the case of the Kosovo indictment against Milosevic and others, for example, almost all of the charges relate to the events following the start of the NATO bombing in March 1999. This is because the level of violence was low during most of 1998, equating roughly to a counterinsurgency or counterterrorist campaign. The violence fell off further after the introduction of international monitors in October 1998, although the Kosovo Liberation Army was making strenuous efforts to provoke the Federal Republic of Yugoslavia (FRY) authorities into overreaction and thereby trigger Western intervention. Thus, it would be far more difficult to prove the existence of an armed conflict before the NATO bombing started.

Moreover, since the armed conflict ended for all practical purposes with the entry of KFOR into Kosovo in June 1999, Albanian attacks on Serbs after that date are not within the ICTY's jurisdiction. This is the kind of outcome that lawyers find reasonable, but it brings politicians close to despair. It was effectively impossible to explain to Serbs why Serbs were being punished for attacks on Albanians, but not the other way around, although this problem has now partly been addressed by the establishment of UN-sponsored courts in Kosovo.

The qualification that armed groups should be organized is also important. In effect, an armed conflict requires enough organization on both sides to differentiate the fighting from either ad hoc skirmishing by improvised groups or counterinsurgency-type operations. This is why, for example, ICTY investigators were interested in the structure and organization of the Kosovo Liberation Army in 1998–1999: if it was not an organized armed group, then there was no armed conflict, and the tribunal would not have been able to bring charges against Milosevic and others. It will be interesting to see how the Kosovo trials turn out. If the ICTY decides that there was an armed conflict in Kosovo at any point before March 1999, then it will establish an important principle. The level of violence in Kosovo at that time was so low that, in the future, almost any antiterrorist or counterinsurgency campaign will count as an armed conflict.

Civilians Are Irrelevant

The law of war requires combatants to "at all times distinguish between the civilian population and combatants and between civilian objects and military objectives" and to direct their operations "only against military objectives." These objectives are "those objects which by their nature, location, purpose or use make an effective contribution to military action and whose total or partial destruction, capture or neutralization, in the circumstances ruling at the time, offers a definite military advantage."[18] And if there is doubt about whether a target is military or not, it should be assumed not to be. This formula is not unproblematic, however. Some inanimate things are clearly military, such as units themselves and their equipment, command-and-control centers, and military headquarters. Some are clearly off-limits, like military medical units and the barracks and equipment of paramilitary units like the French gendarmerie or the Yugoslav Ministry of Internal Affairs, unless they have been formally and publicly incorporated into the armed forces. Some things are more equivocal, however, and their status can change depending on whether or not they are actually being used for military purposes. Thus, a hospital, school, or even church that is evacuated and used for military purposes is a legitimate target, provided it is not being used to treat or shelter noncombatants. Medical facilities or equipment being used for combat purposes forfeit their normal protection. (A colleague traced his political awakening in the Balkans to walking down a street in Zagreb in 1991 and seeing weapons piled in the back of an ambulance: that would have been a legitimate target.) A normal bridge can be a legitimate target provided that it is used by military traffic. Civilians themselves, however, and facilities that are unambiguously civilian are protected.

The laws of war are realistic enough to accept that there will be civilian casualties if weapons are used, and this is accepted provided every effort is made to minimize such casualties and the casualties that do result are not disproportionate to the military benefit gained. (Many campaigners seem not quite to understand that there is no legal difference between being killed with a cluster bomb and being killed with an ordinary bomb: the legality depends on how you use it, not what it is). Thus, civilians are protected not because they are civilians but because they are noncombatants, and they can lose their protected status if they join the fighting. Legally, this means that children and women who engage in combat are legitimate targets, although this conclusion would be difficult politically.

In some ways, the assumption behind the laws of war that civilians and other noncombatants are irrelevant is strange, and it underlines the fact that the laws of war, as they stand today, express the reality of the forces and command structures in 1914 quite well but are less applicable to more modern times. Back then, fighting was largely between organized uniformed contingents with good discipline and command and control. Even in World War I, however, it was clear that a nation's military potential was partly measured by what went on at the home front—a phrase coined at that time—especially in the munitions factories, where many of the workers were women. This tendency increased after 1939, when civilian scientists, engineers, cryptographers, intelligence analysts, and industrialists played a major role in the total war effort; this has increased further since then. The laws of war assume, however, that civilians, unless they group themselves into combat formations, have no effect on military operations, and this is probably because the laws themselves have always been tactically focused on events on the battlefield, lifting their eyes only reluctantly to higher levels. It cannot seriously be maintained that civilians have no such effect, especially at the level of strategic direction: a well-placed bomb on London in 1940, for example, might have dispatched Winston Churchill and led to a negotiated settlement with Germany. (It still seems peculiar that the Pentagon, for example, is considered a legitimate target whereas the White House is not).

Likewise, the laws of war do not provide much help in deciding how to deal with situations where a conventional army is opposed by a significant part of a civilian population, some of which may be armed, but some of which may also plant bombs, gather intelligence, or provide logistic support. Indeed, conventional armies can find themselves traumatized when they are attacked by women and children. What does one actually *do*, after all, when a twelve-year-old combat veteran points a gun in anger? Any troops sent into Rwanda in 1994 to "stop the genocide" would have found themselves firing on women and children, who made up a substantial proportion of the Hutu killers.[19] Increasingly, in the view of many lawyers involved with these issues, the only real distinction is between combatants and others, whether or not those combatants are organized in traditional ways.

As always, there is a degree of subjectivity in these definitions, and much depends on the intent of the attacker and the thought that is given to the consequences of an attack. Contrary to what is sometimes suggested in the media, the mere fact that civilians have died does not make any given attack a war crime. If a civilian target was bombed because of faulty intelligence, or because its use had changed in the preceding hours, then there would be no crime because there was no intent. But if an attack was launched without regard for civilian casualties, or if no serious intelligence preparation was carried out, then a crime may have been committed. To complicate things further, variations of these rules may apply depending on the importance of the objective and the situation on the ground at the time. The concept of *military necessity* applies when an attack on a legitimate target is expected to have grave consequences for civilians and civilian targets but where the practical requirements of the situation faced by the commander make such an attack imperative. Military necessity is not an excuse for breaking the law, and it does not mean that anything at all is allowed. It slightly changes the calculus of what is permitted.

In certain very limited cases, international humanitarian law does provide explicit recognition of the need to adapt general rules to situations of crisis. Thus, article 54 of Protocol I permits the adoption of scorched-earth policies in "the vital requirements of any Party to the conflict in the defence of its national territory against invasion." Likewise, article 17 of Protocol II allows the displacement of the civilian population ("ethnic cleansing," as it is sometimes called) if "the security of the civilians involved or imperative military reasons so demand." Military necessity has to take account of the rule of proportionality. As formulated in Protocol I (article 51), it is forbidden to make an attack "which may be expected to cause incidental loss of civilian life, injury to civilians, damage to civilian objects, or a combination thereof, *which would be excessive in relation to the concrete and direct military advantage to be gained*" (emphasis added). Such judgments will always be very difficult to make and will depend on not just the situation at the time but the commander's own perception of it. For this reason, it is likely that only the most egregious cases would ever be prosecuted.

The Crime of Crimes

The defendants at Nuremberg in 1945 were not charged with genocide. This was not because charges did not include incidents of what we would now describe as genocide—they did—but because the word itself did not then exist. Instead, in those parts of the indictments that covered mass murder, deportation, and other acts against the civil population, the defendants were charged with crimes against humanity. The concept of genocide was originated by jurist Raphael Lemkin when describing the German treatment of populations in occupied Europe. He described it as "a coordinated plan aimed at the destruction of the essential foundations of the life of national groups so that these groups wither and die like plants that have suffered a blight." Killing was only one way in which this might be done: others included the destruction of political and social institutions or the culture and personal security of the group.[20] Lemkin's advocacy, and his coinage of the word itself, were influential in the 1946 decision of the UN General Assembly to encourage the drafting of the Convention Against Genocide, which was eventually adopted in 1948. Inevitably, the text of the convention was subject to the usual process of consensus drafting, and the eventual product was much more complex and nuanced than Lemkin's original proposal. The definition adopted in 1948 as article II of the Genocide Convention has three basic requirements, which are cumulative.

First, there is a list of crimes: killing, causing serious harm, trying to destroy a group by indirect means, trying to prevent births, and transferring children to another group. (This list is exhaustive, not indicative.) Second, the crimes must be committed against a defined "national, ethnical, racial or religious group." Thus, killings of members of a political group would not be genocide, nor would acts of violence against isolated members of different groups. Third, and most important, these crimes must be carried out against these groups with the "intent to destroy . . . in whole or in part" a group "as such." In effect, therefore, it is the *intention* that differentiates genocide from crimes against humanity, and a court has to decide what the individual's actual motives were. This is a complex, technical definition and one that is, to a degree, counterintuitive. The main thing people remember about Nazi crimes in World War II is how extensive they were; that, indeed, is part of the horror. But the convention has no threshold provisions in it, and so a government that undertook a campaign to destroy its political opponents and killed thousands of them might not be accused of genocide, but another regime that outlawed the use of a minority language and conducted a campaign of forced sterilizations could be so accused, even if no deaths were caused as a result. The situation is complicated by the fact that some groups can be considered political *and* ethnic-religious, and a court would have to decide how the group was perceived by the defendant.

The Genocide Convention is a good example of an international treaty that was prompted as a response to world events. Although there was nothing in the charges brought against the Nazis for their mass murders that would not already have been a crime, there was a sense that what had happened under the Nazis was somehow new and unprecedented, at least in scope if not in motivation. Whether or not this is true (the thesis has aroused much controversy), at the political level there was probably no choice but to crown the defeat of the Nazis, the holding of Nuremberg trials, and the foundation of the United Nations by some kind of a post hoc justification emphasizing that the evil that had been fought against was, in fact, unprecedented in history. Like most international law treaties, therefore, the Genocide Convention was more about interpreting the past and justifying the present than it was about looking to the future.[21] Indeed, it is not clear that any of the major signatories ever genuinely expected the Genocide Convention to become operational or trials to be conducted at any stage in the future. In 1946 it was possible to believe that the new dispensation symbolized by the five permanent members of the Security Council would prevent such things from happening again, or punish them promptly if they did occur. Moreover, the only paradigm for genocide was the Nazi one, and it was assumed that questions of definition and proof would be fairly simple. In any event, the Genocide Convention was never operationalized, and to this day nobody really knows what the signatories' commitment to "prevent and punish" genocide (article I) is supposed to mean. What it clearly does *not* mean is that at a whisper of the word *genocide* the world is obliged to charge in with guns blazing to rescue the presumed victims. As an international agreement, the Genocide Convention cannot override customary international law or the UN Charter, which prohibits the use of force except in self-defense or if authorized by the Security Council. Thus, any action to prevent or punish genocide would have to be agreed by the Security Council under chapter VII procedures (as indeed is foreseen in article VIII). And since the Security Council can take any action it likes if it perceives a threat to international peace and security, the existence or otherwise of genocide is essentially irrelevant.

Clearly, then, there never can be any kind of effective operational arrangements for preventing genocide, because genocide is fundamentally an *interpretation* of an action, decided after the event by a court. In practical terms, it is impossible to ever be sure that genocide is under way or being planned except in the most extraordinary circumstances. It would be bizarre, after all, to have large military forces on standby while a committee of psychologists and jurists agonized over whether a particular incident constituted genocide or not, based on its assessment of the mental state of the alleged perpetrators. In any event, deciding what to do about genocide is ultimately a political issue rather than a legal one, since somebody has to take a practical decision about a course of action. In 1999, the FRY accused NATO states of planning genocide in their attack on it, but there was no rush of countries volunteering to put an end to NATO's actions. Likewise, a UN General Assembly resolution of December 16, 1982, accusing Israel of responsibility for genocide in Lebanon (ironically, quite a strong case in view of the Kahan Commission report) led to no practical results whatever. In effect, genocide has become little more than a term of abuse, to be invoked by any state that has a grievance against any other, often in the most cynical fashion. Indeed, it is arguable that the Genocide Convention has outlived whatever practical usefulness it may have had, because public understanding of genocide, and the political use of the term, bear effectively no relationship to the legal definition. Genocide is assumed to mean large-scale killing, and popular, or even educated, opinion is impatient of the need to prove the complex chain of evidence required. Indeed, the fixation with the word is positively unhelpful: if large-scale human rights violations are indeed taking place, then their extent and gravity matter far more, in terms of a response, than the exact state of mind of the perpetrator, assuming that can be known.

These difficulties are reflected in the problems encountered in actually convicting those accused of genocide in court. To some extent, the Rwanda examples are atypical, since the killings there were of such a scale, and incorporated at least some degree of organization, that there are some similarities with the kind of horrors that the drafters of the Genocide Convention had in mind. Yet as many commentators have noted, there was no ethnic, racial, or religious differences between Hutu and Tutsi, which logically implies that the killings in Rwanda could not have been genocide (and evidently the large-scale killings of Hutu by other Hutu could not have been genocide, or the Hutu would have been trying to wipe themselves out).[22] The Trial Chamber in the *Akayesu* case (Akayesu was the first genocide indictee to be convicted in Arusha) based its guilty verdict on the genocide charge on the supposition that the victims had been from the "Tutsi ethnic group."[23] Yet the distinction between Hutu and Tutsi was essentially a political and social one, and by no means immutable, since, for example, children took the group of the father in the event of mixed marriages. The killings were a consequence of an internal power struggle among the Hutu, decided in favor of those who also believed that the Tutsi were a danger that should this time be eliminated; these killings are perhaps best understood as a "degenerated class conflict."[24]

Yet so deeply ingrained had the idea become that genocide had been committed in Rwanda that the ICTR probably felt it had little choice but to go along with the perception for political reasons. Anything else would have provoked a furious reaction, probably extending to demands for the sacking of the judges and the winding-up of the ICTR. Judgments from Arusha indicate that the judges themselves were confused about this issue. In one case, the judges accepted that ethnic difference was not involved but resolved the problem by arguing, in effect, that issues of ethnicity were essentially subjective and that, contrary to what the drafters of the Genocide Convention had supposed, it was enough that the Hutu mistakenly *considered* the Tutsi to be a separate ethnic group for them actually to be one.[25] The problem with this line of argument, as William Schabas notes, is that in theory it allows "genocide to be committed against a group that does not have any real objective existence." As he argues, this is the equivalent of arguing that a person who kills another under the mistaken impression that the victim is his or her father would be guilty of parricide rather than just murder.[26]

It is not hard to see why commentators cling to the notion of genocide in Rwanda with such ferocity. Genocide has become in recent times a vague term, meaning "something terrible," and serving to establish a hierarchy in the fiercely competitive area of the ranking of human rights violations around the world. Those who would argue that genocide took place in Rwanda, therefore, essentially make a political point about the importance the episode should be given in comparison with others that might seem equally terrible. By contrast, denying the genocide is to demote the episode into the second division of atrocities, with the depredations of the Khmer Rouge or the Stalinist treason trials and exterminations of the 1930s, which is where it logically belongs. In theory this should not matter, because the horror of Rwanda does not become greater or less depending on the label stuck upon it, but for political reasons (including the satisfaction to be gained from the furious belaboring of Western states) it matters a lot. In some cases, indeed, the argument that genocide was committed there is not actually based on legal arguments at all. Helen M. Hintjens, for example, argues that the killings amounted to genocide because they were "planned well before April 1994," and because "we can define genocide as 'a form of one-sided mass killing in which the state or another authority intends to destroy a group, as that group and membership in it are defined by the perpetrator.'"[27] We *can* define genocide like that if we wish, of course, provided we understand that the definition actually used by the courts, and which must be proved before them, is completely different. (Hintjens speculates that denial of the existence of genocide in Rwanda might be made a criminal offense.)[28] This points the way ultimately to some postmodernist situation where anyone can be guilty of genocide because the crime itself can be defined in any way you like.

For the sake of balance, it should be added that attempts to argue that genocide did *not* occur in Rwanda are often just as unconnected to legal definitions. In spite of what the defense counsel argued in Arusha, and indeed what apologists for the Hutu extremists have themselves claimed, the fact that Hutu were also killed by Tutsi, or that there was conflict between the two groups, or that the Hutu might have felt genuinely threatened, have nothing whatever to do with the existence of genocide at that time. The Vatican, for example (the *Osservatore Romano* anyway*)*, has consistently argued that there was a "double genocide" in Rwanda, since the Tutsi were attempting to exterminate the Hutu in the years before 1994.[29] Even if this were objectively true (and it is not, whatever some Hutu extremists might have thought), it is not a defense. Similarly, the Belgian lawyer Luc de Temmerman, who appears to have exceptionally close contacts with the Hutu extremists, has argued rather incoherently that there was "no genocide. It was a situation of mass killings in a state of war where everyone was killing their enemies."[30] What matters is whether the events that actually occurred correspond, beyond a reasonable doubt, to the definition of genocide in the Genocide Convention, and there are logical reasons to doubt this.

It has proved much more difficult to get a genocide conviction in The Hague, primarily because the judges were not convinced, in several cases, that the motivation of the accused had actually been demonstrated and that the objective facts supported the genocidal interpretation. In the *Jelisic* case (see Chapter 1), for example, Jelisic—the "Serb Adolf"—pleaded guilty to every factual count in the indictment but argued that his motives had not been genocidal, and the ICTY agreed with him. The ICTY has also (thus far) declined to convict the organizers of the Bosnian Serb concentration camps in Prijedor of genocide, concluding that the intent had not been demonstrated. The solitary success of the tribunal so far has been the *Krstic* case, where General Radislav Krstic was convicted of genocide as a result of the killings at Srebrenica. At first sight, this decision might seem strange, since the killings were all of males of military age and thus could not, by definition, have been aimed at the destruction of the Muslim population of Srebrenica. The court, however, appears to have accepted the prosecution's argument that the sum total of the executions together with the removal of the women and children "would inevitably result in the physical disappearance of the Bosnian Muslim population of Srebrenica," and so the intent to commit genocide was, in the court's view, established.[31] The fact that it took the court some twenty-five pages of dense legal argument to reach that conclusion is perhaps an indication of the complexities involved. This kind of judgment also provokes some rather counterintuitive speculation. For example, it is clear that the women, children, and elderly left in Srebrenica and Potocari when the men had escaped genuinely *wanted* to leave and gladly boarded the coaches provided by the Bosnian Serbs. But had the Serbs in fact forcibly insisted that these people stay behind in the heat of a Bosnian summer with little food and water, then presumably genocide would not have been committed, which is a perverse conclusion. Likewise, if all the men had escaped, then the treatment of the women and children would no longer be relevant.

The problem here is that, even more than in Rwanda, the use of the word *genocide* in the context of Bosnia (and encouraged by the Sarajevo government from the beginning) has come to dominate people's understanding of the conflict that it is regarded as a proven fact, from a political point of view, if not necessarily a legal one. So sure is the public mind that genocide was committed that not accusing defendants of genocide (Serbs, anyway) arouses comment and criticism. Likewise, acquittals on genocide charges (there have already been some, with doubtless more to come) tend to be interpreted as failures by the prosecution, or incompetence by the judges, rather than lack of actual evidence. In these circumstances it is likely that, in the ICTY and later in the ICC, courts will adjust the definition of "genocide" to suit the facts of the case before them. This will be particularly so with cases involving ethnic cleansing, where populations have been forcibly expelled from an area to facilitate its control by another group. Increasingly, forced deportation, as it is more properly called, is being reinterpreted by both lay and learned commentators as genocide (the Milosevic Bosnia indictment is constructed along these lines). Yet this is not what the drafters of the Genocide Convention had in mind, and in spite of many attempts to link the two crimes it is clear that "displacing a population in order to change the ethnic composition of a given territory . . . is not the same thing as genocide, which is directed at the destruction of the group."[32]

Part of the problem is that, as the ICTR judges in the *Bagilishema* case observed in clearing him of the charge of genocide, "national, ethnical, racial, and religious groups enjoy no generally or internationally accepted definition."[33] In the period when the Genocide Convention was drafted, this was less of a problem. It was doubtful, after all, that trials would ever be conducted, and so it was not worth the immense, and probably nugatory, effort that would be required to agree on a series of definitions. It is clear that in Lemkin's original conception all of the four categories in practice amounted to the same thing to the "national minorities," whose alleged persecution by the Soviet Union was a major topic of the day. Moreover, as late as the 1940s, educated individuals could still talk about "races" without blushing, and before the discovery of DNA it was generally assumed that "nations" were genetically different from each other. Thus, it was popularly reckoned that there were actual genetic differences not only between (say) blacks and whites in Africa or the United States but even between Russians and Poles, and therefore distinguishing between different national or racial groups would be easy. (Recall that the words *genetic* and *genocide* share the same root.) These were also the days when ethnic groups were supposed to be primordial entities rigidly and permanently distinguished from each other. More recently, as the debates about ethnicity have grown more complex, it is becoming clear that it is a variable concept, constructed often by elites for their own benefit. It is also clear that individuals can have multiple, and overlapping, ethnic or group identities. The simplicity of views in the 1940s must have meant that Lemkin and his followers imagined that it would be very easy to tell whether or not a given case constituted genocide. Yet guilty verdicts have come, and probably will in the future, only by strained interpretations of evidence and law and long, dense legal arguments sometimes upheld only on a majority basis. This is not at all what the "crime of crimes" was supposed to be like.

The real problem, then, is that the Genocide Convention is based on a series of outdated racial and sociological assumptions. The actual practical task of securing convictions is therefore always going to be extremely difficult, as the experiences in Arusha and The Hague have shown. We can react to this in one of two ways. We could simply decide not to level charges of genocide in the future—a position that a surprising number of practicing prosecutors in Arusha and The Hague would favor. But this would be politically impossible. Genocide as a concept is exceptionally useful politically. It is the nuclear weapon of the human rights and international humanitarian law lobbies, a priceless piece of ammunition for states to fire at each other in their political conflicts. Since in the media and public mind "genocide" means "murder," there is probably no episode of mass killing in the last century to which the label has not been applied. It can be assumed that in every armed conflict in the future the various parties will play the genocide card at the earliest opportunity, since the political upside can be immense. So it is likely that charges will continue to be brought based ever more tentatively on the legal definition. Guilty verdicts will thus require ever more creative interpretation of the Genocide Convention, which will increasingly come to seem a meaningless document as a result.

Almost as soon as the Genocide Convention was agreed, in 1948, it was assailed for the exclusion of groups that critics sympathized with. Socioeconomic groups, such as the Hutu and Tutsi, were proposed for protection, as were political and ideological tendencies, speakers of minority languages, political parties, aborted fetuses, and even the Buddhist monks persecuted by the Khmer Rouge. Some indeed have argued that the Genocide Convention should include these groups in the definitions because it nowhere explicitly *excludes* them. These attempts to stretch the definition of protected groups, as William Schabas notes, often go "beyond all reason."[34] This trend will no doubt continue in the future, and it will be an obscure and friendless group indeed that cannot allege that genocide is being conducted against it and find some supporters.

Yet all this is rather pointless. One wonders how survivors of the Rwandan killings would view ideological struggles between educated whites to pin one or another label on their suffering, as though these things actually mattered. Ironically, the definition of crimes against humanity (which genocide is coming increasingly to resemble) suffers from none of these problems. As codified by the ICC Statute, it includes, among many other offenses, persecution "against any identifiable group or collectivity on political, racial, national, ethnic, cultural, religious, gender [grounds, as well as] any grounds that are universally recognised as impermissible under international law."[35] Anyone believed to be committing these offenses can be charged under this heading, with a far greater chance of being convicted than if they are charged with genocide, and the penalties will, on recent evidence, be little different. It is even arguable from a purely political perspective that it is better for a defendant to be convicted of crimes against humanity than to be acquitted of genocide.

Conclusion

In this chapter, I have deliberately tried to outline not only what various International Humanitarian Law texts say but also how (if at all) they have been applied and misapplied, as well as the practical problems that arise in using them. We are moving into a world where the laws of war as they have been elaborated are increasingly irrelevant, partly because the situations they were intended to cope with no longer exist, but mainly because modern armed conflict is increasingly between groups fighting for economic and/or territorial objectives such as the assortment of rebel groups and militias now fighting in the Democratic Republic of the Congo (DRC) who will probably know little and care less about these laws. In turn, these militias may be opposed by forces from the developed world, burdened by exaggerated expectations of what they can accomplish, and limited in the force they can apply by complex rules requiring specialist interpretation. The reported comment made by Jean Pictet, the senior representative of the International Committee of the Red Cross, after the Additional Protocols had been negotiated ("If we cannot outlaw war, we will make it too complex for the commander to fight") is stupid as well as naive. It is hard to imagine any of the combatants in Sierra Leone, for example, agreeing to suspend the war to hold seminars on the Geneva Conventions. As Mark Osiel comments in discussing the Pictet episode, the actual result is likely to be to "give comfort to officers already inclined to reject rules restricting the use of force as legalistic intermeddling."[36]

It can be argued, as Eugene Davidson has, that nations cannot and should not rely on these legal instruments to eliminate conflict but use traditional methods instead.[37] For reasons that will become apparent, I do not fully share this view, but it is likely that current and future courts will be largely ineffective in preventing and punishing war crimes, partly because they are addressing some of the wrong questions, and partly because the practical obstacles to successful prosecutions are enormous. But as those of us involved in these issues have always replied: What's the alternative? Even given the practical problems involved (including the political ones reviewed in Chapter 4), there are some things that can and should be done. The alternative—shrugging your shoulders and walking away—is not politically feasible, even if it were ethically acceptable. We are condemned to try to make these processes work; eventually I will explain how this can best be done. Before doing so, however, I examine the politics of war crimes.

Notes

1. This is necessarily a rapid and superficial overview, and I have not attempted to cover the evolution of the law of war in detail. Books that do this

include Geoffrey Best, *War and Law Since 1945*, and Ingrid Detter, *The Law of War*. The main documents are collected in Adam Roberts and Richard Guelff, eds., *Documents on the Laws of War*. A good general presentation of these issues, intended for a nonspecialist audience, is on the International Committee of the Red Cross website (www.icrc.org).

2. BBC News, July 12, 2000.

3. Cited by Telford Taylor, *The Anatomy of the Nuremberg Trials*, p. 66.

4. "There is a sense that Nuremberg tells us that Nagasaki was not a war crime and that the Soviet invasion of Finland in 1941 was not aggression." Garry J. Simpson, "War Crimes: A Critical Introduction," in Timothy L.H. McCormack and Gerry J. Simpson, eds., *The Law of War Crimes*.

5. For an excellent introduction to the ICC, with full texts of the major documents, see William A. Schabas, *An Introduction to the International Criminal Court*.

6. *Charter of the International Military Tribunal,* art. 8.

7. There is a good collection of transcripts and other documents on the University of Missouri School of Law website (www.law.umkc.edu).

8. Foreword to David Irving, *The Destruction of Dresden*.

9. *Erdemovic* (IT-96–22), Appeals Chamber Judgment of October 7, 1997.

10. *Krstic* (IT-98–33), testimony of Major General Richard Dannatt, July 24, 2000, p. 5581.

11. See also article 28 of the ICC Statute, "Responsibility of Commanders and Other Superiors."

12. *Kordic and Cerkez* (IT-94–14–2) Trial Chamber Judgment, February 2001, para. 853.

13. Ilias Bantekas, "The Contemporary Law of Superior Responsibility," *American Journal of International Law* 93, no. 3 (July 1999).

14. See "The Simon Wiesenthal Centre Condemns *Human Rights Watch*'s Call for Criminal Investigation of Israel Prime Minister Sharon on Eve of Bush Meeting," Simon Wiesenthal Centre, press release, June 26, 2001.

15. Kahan Commission Report, available on the Internet (www.israel.org/mfa/go).

16. *Tadic* (IT-94–1), Judgment of May 7, 1997, para. 561.

17. Ibid., para. 562.

18. Additional Geneva Protocol I (1977), art. 48.

19. See, for example, Africa Rights, *Not so Innocent: When Women Become Killers*, August 1995; "Front Line of UN Effort to Take the Guns from Children," *New York Times*, July 15, 2001, p.4. The UN commander in Rwanda estimated that most of the more than 300,000 children who died in 1994 were murdered by other children.

20. Raphael Lemkin, "Genocide: A Modern Crime," in *Free World* (April 1945).

21. Although Peter Novick, *The Holocaust and Collective Memory*, pp. 100–101, points out that Lemkin argued for the ratification of the convention in an essentially Cold War context. His strongest supporters were from anticommunist Soviet minority groups.

22. Most of the early killings were of Hutu; see, for example, Africa Rights: *Rwanda: Death, Despair, and Defiance*, rev. ed. (1995), pp. 178–198.

23. *Akayesu*, September 2, 1998, Judgment, para. 124.

24. Johan Pottier, *Re-imagining Rwanda*, p. 9.

25. See *Kayishema and Ruzindana* (ITCR-95–1), Judgment of May 21, 1999, para. 98.

26. William Schabas, *Genocide in International Law,* p. 110.

27. Helen M. Hintjens, "Explaining the 1994 Genocide in Rwanda," *Journal of Modern Africa Studies* 37, no. 2 (1999): 241–286, esp. 246.

28. Ibid., p.282.

29. See, for example, "Vatican Newspaper Defends Jailed Rwandan Bishop," Associated Press, May 18, 1999.

30. "Rwandan International Tribunal: First trial 'On Hold,'" *The Guardian,* September 28, 1996.

31. *Krstic,* Trial Chamber Judgment, August 2, 2001, para. 595.

32. Schabas, *Genocide in International Law,* p. 201.

33. *Bagilishema* (ICTR-95–1A-T), Trial Chamber Judgment, June 7, 2001, para. 65.

34. Schabas, *Genocide in International Law*, p. 102; see generally pp. 102–150 for a thorough discussion of the "groups" issue.

35. *Statute of the International Criminal Court,* art. 7(1)(h).

36. Mark Osiel, *Obeying Orders,* p. 100.

37. Eugene Davidson, *The Nuremberg Fallacy.*

4

The Politics

I n this chapter, I examine the politics of the treatment of war crimes and their investigation and how this complicates the work of governments and international courts. I am not (except incidentally) concerned with the narrower issues of the way in which decisions to establish courts were arrived at in particular cases; I am more concerned with the wider political issues, as well as the link to various other fashionable subjects at the moment, including humanitarian intervention.

Courts and Politics

The idea of establishing special international courts to try alleged war criminals is unusual. As we have seen, states have been reluctant, except under extraordinary pressure, to put their own nationals on trial for such alleged offenses, and they resist with even greater ferocity the idea that anyone *else* should do so. Yet special courts are complex and expensive bodies, and they are not set up lightly. Indeed, while the two current ad hoc tribunals certainly deserve to exist, it is unclear what differentiates the sufferings in Yugoslavia—or even Rwanda—from many other incidents that took place in the decades that followed World War II: slaughter in colonial wars in Algeria and Vietnam, a half-million dead in Uganda, 1 million dead in Mozambique—mostly civilians. It is hard to disagree with the cynical view current in some non-Western circles that all that differentiates the Yugoslav experience, in particular, is that both victims and perpetrators were white. And so it is that all the countries of the United Nations pay money every year toward the $100 million it costs to keep the court at The Hague going, and it must seem strange to the inhabitants of, say, Benin that their government does so, if, indeed, they even know where The Hague is. The simple answer, of course, is that a correlation of political forces now exists that did not before. That is true, but there is more to it than that.

Politics is about choices, and every choice that is taken implicitly precludes the taking of other choices, especially where money and other resources are concerned. Thus, the establishment of the two ad hoc tribunals, and the Sierra Leone Special Court, has effectively preempted resources that might have been devoted to other options, since the amount of money, personnel, and even political interest are all limited. The issue, of course, is who makes the decisions about which atrocities to address. All such decisions will be made by perhaps eight or ten states, depending on the context, and almost all of them are white. This is because decisions in any area of international politics do not happen by majority vote, except in the most superficial of fashions; they depend on the support, or at least the passive acquiescence, of this small number of states. Thus, a proposal by Andorra, Myanmar, and Zimbabwe to set up a court of some kind would be most unlikely to succeed. Indeed, unless it attracted support from key states, it would probably not even be discussed, no matter how much wider support it received. As a result, all the legal mechanisms for addressing war crimes that have ever been established have either been suggested by white Western states or, at a minimum, tolerated by them. Moreover, without the diplomatic, financial, and intelligence support of the world's wealthiest and most powerful states, such institutions can do little, and states will, of course, exact what they see as a reasonable price for this support. This can include an effective veto on senior appointments, satisfactory arrangements for safeguarding the positions of powerful states, and influence in the general policy of the institution. This kind of thing is inevitable (and the above is not offered as a value judgment), but the result is that international criminal justice has a heavily Western, white, Anglo-Saxon character, and for the foreseeable future this will continue to be the case. It is thus not surprising that, at a special session of the UN Commission on Human Rights in September 1999, an expected resolution to establish a court of some kind was blocked by Asian opposition. This was less a judgment on the morality of what happened in 1999 than a protest about white Western states once more dominating the agenda and threatening to dominate the process.[1]

Put simply, international criminal law's vocabulary and concepts are not neutral. They are culturally specific, constructed and manipulated by a very small number of countries, most of which have English as their native or second language. Some would argue that this does not greatly matter, since Western values are effectively universal ones, or ought to be. One interpretation, indeed, of this process is that liberal Western states, seeking to extend to others the rights and protections that they hold dear, are engaged in a selfless exercise to bring justice and human rights to the rest of the world.[2] But this is too rosy a view. None of the major players in the international humanitarian law game can dictate to others from a position of complete moral superiority: all have done things comparable to some of the atrocities in Rwanda and Yugoslavia in modern times, or they have excused similar behavior on the part of their allies. Likewise, all have blocked, or attempted to block, investigations by international authorities into their own conduct more recently. As one Serb journalist said to me at a meeting in 2001: "We do understand that the [ICTY] tries to be objective, and we try to explain this to our readers. But they will not believe us so long as the [ICTY] fails to even begin an investigation of NATO for its attacks on Yugoslavia in 1999." In general, until the West is actually ready to accept enforcement on itself of the same standards and procedures it recommends to others, wider support for international criminal justice is likely at most to be grudging and reluctant.

How Universal?

Moreover, the values that international courts embody are, of course, normative, which is to say that they are not so much the values the West holds as the values that the West *ought* to hold, at least by the standards of those who are influential in the international humanitarian law debate. They are not values that Western public opinion as a whole holds; nor does that opinion necessarily support a wide extension of international criminal justice, especially when it costs money. And, of course, Western public opinion is in general adamantly opposed to investigations of alleged atrocities by its own nationals, even by national authorities. Elite opinion, on the whole, takes much the same view: liberal principles have a habit of breaking down once they are no longer being applied to other nations but to one's own. Even human rights activists have found it a challenge (especially during the Kosovo crisis of 1999) to apply these principles consistently, especially when they lead to a conclusion that is politically displeasing.

So the idea that the international humanitarian law agenda embodies values collectively arrived at and universally respected is clearly not convincing. Rather, there is a respectable argument that the international humanitarian law agenda is in part a form of neocolonialism, in the sense that it gives the West practical leverage to achieve political objectives such as the replacement of rulers or regimes. This would not matter if it were clear that these values were in fact universal, or at least very common, and attempts to determine whether this is true have generated huge controversy, most of it pointless. One view is that, once a group of dictators and authoritarian rulers (generally nonwhite) are removed from power, it will become clear that, in fact, notions of rights are universal, and they happen to be, by coincidence, exactly those notions that are generally held by educated liberal Western opinion in the early twenty-first century. It is true, of course, that cultural relativism can be used as an excuse for denying rights, and this has happened. But there is no way of knowing whether these values *are* actually universal, since there is no practical way of finding out without asking billions of people.[3] So it is commonly assumed that the values embodied in the Geneva Conventions are universal and are reflected in codes of military law the world over. But in practice we have no idea whether or not this is true, since few if any attempts have ever been made to analyze military codes to see whether, for example, they all see command responsibility in the same way. These values are simply assumed to be common in the absence of any evidence either way.

It is true, at the most mundane level, that the kind of crimes punished in the ICC Statute are against the laws of most, if not all, states, at least in present times (though rape, for example, is treated very differently in different societies). But that is not the point: it is the way that such crimes and positive rights are contextualized in a society that differs greatly. Take the issue of individual rather than collective rights, for example. British and American concepts of rights are, as one would expect, individualist and often aggressive in nature. I may exert my rights as far as possible, and so do others, with the result that one day our rights will come into conflict with each other. At that point, we turn to lawyers and wait to see whose rights will eventually prevail. Usually, it will depend on who can afford the better lawyer, and so the degree to which people in the West can exercise their theoretical rights tends in practice to depend on how wealthy or powerful one is. This is, in truth, a very unsophisticated concept of rights, particularly when placed beside concepts found in parts of Africa and Asia, which have a strong emphasis on collective benefits—rather than rights—and parallel obligations.[4]

Unlike in the West, where we all seek to extend our rights and reduce our obligations, more sophisticated societies recognize that rights and obligations increase proportionately with each other. This difference has a particular relevance for attempts to find legal means of addressing atrocities. The Anglo-Saxon approach suggests that responsibility for crimes should lie with the individual, and this is sound in principle. But in many parts of the world it would be considered hopelessly naive to examine what an individual actually *did* without reference to his ethnic background and religious affiliation, and to the collective rights of the groups, of which he and his victims form a part. Those who follow trials in The Hague closely have noticed that in most cases the prosecution and the defense adopt completely different approaches to this issue. As one tribunal officer put it: the prosecution wants to talk about the individual, whereas the defense wants to talk about the group. Thus, critics of the conviction and sentence of Tihomir

Blaskic argued not merely that the verdict was factually wrong but that Blaskic, as a Bosnian Croat in a particular time and place, was *automatically* innocent because the Croats were defending themselves against Muslim aggression. Yet a Muslim who had carried out exactly the same acts would be automatically guilty. In arguing this, of course, they were faithfully reproducing the philosophy that guided the former Yugoslav justice system when it had to deal with politically sensitive issues.

Before we are too dismissive of this type of argument, we might reflect that it is not unknown in the West. Some Americans made up their mind about whether O. J. Simpson was guilty of murder based on his skin color, just as the Irish victims of miscarriages of justice in England in the 1970s were assumed to be guilty because they were Irish. And there has always been a flavor of this kind of approach in official Western thinking as well, as when President Harry Truman effectively accused the Japanese of collective responsibility for the sufferings of U.S. servicemen. More recently, the lynch-mob mentality often demonstrated by the media in war crimes issues often assumes that ethnic affiliation implies criminal guilt. Nonetheless, the formal Anglo-Saxon position, and thus the logic of various international courts, continues to stress individual responsibility alone, and this means that such approaches will in the end be unconvincing to many different societies.

A second area of uncertainty is the whole issue of command responsibility and superior orders. Even if codes of military law in various countries have been brought into line textually with the Geneva Conventions, it is not at all clear that attitudes, both within the military and in society more generally, have necessarily kept pace with these changes. There are many societies in which hierarchy is still a major organizing principle, and in some Asian armies a positive duty to disobey unlawful orders would have little meaning in practice, irrespective of what a manual said. Likewise, the current doctrine of command responsibility, complex and subtle as it has become, is hard enough for the Western states that originated it to accept. Doing so will be much more difficult for others, especially in parts of the world where the formal training of officers and the sophistication of command structures are well below Western norms.

Nor are all philosophies of law and its application the same. The difference between states that have abandoned judicial killing and those few that have retained it, for example, is not only a technical issue of legal policy but also a fundamental cleavage between different views of the function of punishment and the role and powers of the state. Discussions between representatives of opposing systems will always be partly dialogues of the deaf. Likewise, some Asian societies have had thousands of years to ponder the arguments of Confucius that a son's duty to a father extends to covering up for him if he has committed a crime. While this implied conflict may not be a normal occurrence today, it is a mistake to think that it no longer has any influence. It leads, indeed, to the whole question of whether a single-minded determination that the law should take its course is always the best way to proceed, irrespective of the amount of disruption and even suffering that it might bring, and in turn to how this judgment is made in various societies.

Most societies have drawn back from the full rigor of law enforcement, in some cases, because they believed that other, more important objectives were thereby better secured. These objectives may seem to us now dubious, such as the decision by successive Australian governments to allow former Nazis into the country because of their strong anticommunist sympathies.[5] One can also point to the decision by U.S. authorities not to try their military personnel for crimes in Vietnam. Others evoke much more sympathy, such as the decision by postwar French governments to draw a line quickly under attempts to punish collaboration with the German occupiers and to substitute a myth of national resistance instead. Something analogous has recently taken place in South Africa, and it is hard to believe that the rigid and unbending attitude typical of Anglo-Saxon thinking—that "justice" must be done *whatever* the consequences—would have produced a better result.

Yet in discussing the politics of war crimes, at least in the abstract, the assumption that justice (as a process and an objective, if not always an outcome) trumps all other considerations, and so must always be done, is generally allowed to go unchallenged, especially in Britain and the United States. At bottom, though, it is only an assumption, and so it cannot be proved. It therefore remains essentially an ideological issue. Although most people would agree that it is desirable that justice should generally be done, there are, of course, lots of other objectives that societies should pursue, and it is not clear that justice inevitably takes priority over everything else, whatever the consequences. It is true, of course, that those professionally involved with international humanitarian law, especially if they are advocates for it, will take this extreme view, since they assist their political and career objectives by doing so. But this is an attitude typical of any single-issue lobbying group and does not entitle those who hold it to any special moral status.

Justice and Revenge

Much depends on what we mean by "justice." Although in theory justice and law should go together, in practice, at least where war crimes are concerned, they are often opposed. Popular ideas of justice—those that are politically influential—have little to do with the bureaucratic business of applying legal codes and ensuring due process but are much more based on atavistic emotions, notably the desire for revenge. They are also subjective. (When incidents as various as the bombing of Hiroshima in 1945, the invasion of Afghanistan in 2001, or the killings at Srebrenica in 1995 can all be defended as justice, we might reasonably ask whether the concept actually retains any value at all.) At bottom, the establishment of war crimes courts to pursue justice incorporates an attempt to provide a rational outlet for feelings of revenge. Sometimes this is obvious (Nuremberg and especially Tokyo), but it is always possible to discern in the background. Thus, the decision to investigate Tutsi as well as Hutu perpetrators during the Rwandan killings was controversial not because there were no killings by Tutsi but because of the widespread assumption that the ICTR was an internationally sanctioned mechanism for revenge against the Hutu. Likewise, prosecution of Croat and Muslim offenders in The Hague was criticized— not simply by those communities but by Western commentators who should have known better—on the basis that they were "victims" and so presumably entitled to do these things, whereas the court existed to take revenge on the Serbs.

The desire for revenge and punishment is, of course, natural when we consider the appalling nature of the crimes. Those of us who deal with such crimes on a professional basis perhaps become a little blasé, but in fact a sober recitation of the facts of even a fairly mundane modern atrocity, from Rwanda or Yugoslavia, is usually enough to provoke immense anger and the desire to see justice—or at least revenge—done. Most of us in the protected West have probably never seen a murdered person, and if we encounter an act of violence it may disturb us for hours or days afterward. Even in societies where violence is more common, human beings seem to find it difficult to actually contemplate it on a large scale. If one death is a shock and five is horrifying, we rapidly run out of emotions by the time the death toll reaches twenty or thirty. It is probably impossible even for the most hardened among us to have a rational response to something like the killings at Srebrenica, much less the larger-scale atrocities that took place earlier in the twentieth century.

The most common reaction, in fact, is a type of helpless rage, which demands satisfaction in some form and is often impatient of legal process and the requirements of proof. The problem, of course, is that this approach leads very easily to miscarriages of justice, such as those perpetrated against Irish citizens in Britain in the 1970s. Taken to extremes, the desire—or at least the call—for justice can degenerate into little more than an unfocused urge for retaliation and revenge. The vocabulary of international humanitarian law is actually well suited to disguising hostility and hatred in more judicious terms. Victims in Yugoslavia and other conflicts have learned by now to express their hatred in a palatable form: to ask for justice rather than revenge. But in most cases revenge is exactly what it is, and it is often legitimated and even stoked by an irresponsible media.

Our feelings about revenge, and whether it can be seen as justice, are very complex and contradictory, as one would expect. In the end, it is probably true that we feel that revenge is a kind of justice if we sympathize with the victims of the original hurt, but not otherwise. There are many stories about Allied troops killing SS personnel at liberated concentration camps out of hand, or standing by as inmates did so. These are crimes and should be punished, but it would be hard from a political—and even perhaps a moral—standpoint to judge the perpetrators too harshly. But as time passes and the original focus is lost, the argument changes subtly. What do we think of the ethics of the revenge killing of several hundred Nazis after the war by undercover members of the British army's Jewish Brigade? And what of serious plans discussed in 1946 to poison the water supplies of major German cities in an attempt to kill as many Germans as they had killed Jews?[6] Objective criteria do not apply here. The Soviet Union—the greatest victim of the Nazis—was never allowed its revenge. Indeed, conservative historians competed with each other to describe the horror of the Soviet capture of Germany in 1945, without conceding that the Soviets might perhaps have been a little upset by their previous experiences. Ironically, it seems that there is less sympathy for victims who fought back than for the truly weak who could not.

But governments and international courts, of course, must try not to be driven by the desire for revenge, and they have to take account of boring things like the need for proof beyond a reasonable doubt and evidence that crimes actually took place. One consequence of this: it is common for governments and courts to be publicly criticized, even by lawyers, for following the legal norms of a democratic society. It seemed that many people wanted to indict Slobodan Milosevic for being president of Serbia, if nothing else would do it—a grievous crime, to be sure, but not actually one punishable by the ICTY. Nothing, indeed, has done more damage to the cause of international criminal justice than politically inspired campaigns to indict this or that unpopular person, since such campaigns can be conducted only on the basis that indictments should be issued for political reasons, whether or not they are legally justified. Convincing people in the former Yugoslavia that the ICTY pursues justice objectively has been hard enough without some idiot publicly calling for it to pursue justice as a subset of politics.

Yet it is likely that governments and courts will come under increasing pressure to behave this way in the future. Because human tolerance for suffering is so low, the amount of visible suffering required to produce political pressure on governments to act is small. Partly it is a function of media technology: had the fighting in Yugoslavia occurred a decade before it did, it is possible that pressure on governments to do *something*, no matter what, would have been less intense. Even today, the international human rights agenda is driven far more by the availability of pictures than by the amount of actual suffering involved. Thus, when the Yugoslav army attacked Dubrovnik in 1991, the episode received far more coverage than the much more horrifying attack on Vukovar, which was farther away, harder to get to, and less photogenic. As the journalist Nik Gowing has commented, "Often no dish means no coverage. On the other hand, the presence of a dish creates news coverage because of a TV news manager's corporate obligation to justify its costly deployment."[7] The advent of mass use of the Internet will make things worse. With modern image manipulation software, atrocity photographs can be prepared on demand and circulated around the world in hours. The International Criminal Court is likely to see a grim form of competitive bidding by political groupings wishing to publicize their sufferings, whether real or exaggerated. The politics of disgust and revenge are very easy to mobilize, and journalists themselves can make things worse by being credulous or by actually stoking up the fires of revenge themselves. The format is by now familiar: sorrowful ethnic music, widows tending graves, black-and-white slow-motion photography, relatives and survivors asking in a dignified fashion for justice, and TV footage of the alleged perpetrators, perhaps caught in a jocular moment in the company of Western politicians or diplomats. This, of course, is no more than a series of techniques that any journalist can use for any purpose, but it tends to strengthen the demand for revenge or retaliation in some form while simultaneously closing off rational debate about the alleged incidents and how they should be addressed.

The situation is further complicated by the conviction of a number of journalists that they should not necessarily be under any obligation to tell the truth. Sophisticated arguments have been produced questioning the concept of objectivity and suggesting that journalists should suppress or invent information if they feel that a sympathetic cause would be advanced.[8] Journalists are free to do this, of course, provided that they do not then expect to be seen as observers whose views are worthy of respect but rather as propagandists for one political cause or other. Martin Bell has described what he calls the "journalism of attachment" as "a tendency to take the side of the victims against the aggressors."[9] This implies that the two are easily distinguishable and that it is for journalists to make that assessment anyway. Even when a journalist acts with integrity, those who control the way his or her story is disseminated may have agendas of their own. One distinguished Dutch journalist, who tried to report what he saw in Bosnia as objectively as possible, commented bitterly that his editors urged "adopting a position and gave credence to the horror stories that emerged from the combatants' propaganda machines, suggesting that by not adopting a position he was 'on the wrong side' in this war."[10] Yet even if journalists and their editors are conscientious, there must be some practical limitations on what the most objective journalism can accomplish. In the context of Rwanda, for example, the anthropologist and Great Lakes expert Johan Pottier has worried about the coverage of that region by journalists and aid workers, whose work is "regularly conditioned by scant background information, tight deadlines, the demand for simplified commentary, and sometimes powerful manipulations" and so "must not be taken at face value."[11] Yet it is precisely these early writings, with their moral certainties and tidy separations into victims and perpetrators, that set the political context in which demands for revenge or justice (if they can be differentiated) are first heard.

Victims

Most modern-day reporting on wars concentrates on the victims. It was not always thus. Until the end of World War II, reports of war largely stressed heroism and victory, as well as how many casualties the enemy had suffered. "Saul has slain his thousands, but David his ten thousands," exulted the First Book of Kings, without feeling a need to interview the relatives of the slain. Today, however, with the need to produce human-interest stories (and the difficulty of representing actual combat in an interesting fashion), dwelling on victims has become the norm. As Michael Ignatieff notes, there has arisen "an anti-ideological and antipolitical ethic of siding with the victim," exacerbated "by television's visual insistence on consequences rather than intentions."[12] Since there are innocent victims in any war, this can mean that sympathy, and consequently the desire for punishment, can depend on which pictures are shown first. It is fascinating to speculate, for example, what would have happened to Western policy in the Balkans had news teams followed a different deployment plan. The main reason the Ahmici massacre received such coverage was because a BBC team was following the British battalion (1st Battalion, Cheshire Regiment) that happened to be deployed in the Lasva Valley. Now we must not, of course, fall into the trap of assuming that media reporting drives government policy in any mechanistic sense. Where brute reality prevents more being done—as in Bosnia—the media can produce a bitter and even hysterical trend in public opinion, but they cannot actually dictate policy, especially when more than one government is involved. But the media can have a powerful effect in more focused situations. The treatment of the breakup of Yugoslavia by the right-wing German media, with its ready support for the Catholic Croats—and its frankly racialist treatment of the Orthodox Serbs—had a definite effect on the fateful and ultimately disastrous decision by the

German government to ram through recognition of Croatia's independence by the European Union.

One of the principal arguments in Germany for recognition of Croatia was that it was, as a Catholic country, a victim of aggression by a non-Catholic state. There has always been sympathy for small states attacked by larger ones, especially if their people put up a heroic defense (Belgium and Serbia in World War I come to mind), but what is new is the phenomenon of victimism: the earnest search for victims and the accompanying desire to present oneself as a helpless victim too weak to fight at all. Like many similar ideas, this one seems to have begun in the United States, where competition for victim status is profound and often bitter, essentially because it makes one powerful: it entitles one to financial and practical recompense, and it excuses any violence one may later commit against others. One American critic has even described modern politics in the United States as "a competition for enshrining grievances. National public life becomes the settlement of a collective malpractice suit in which all citizens are patients and physicians simultaneously."[13]

Victims have rights and are excused duties; suffering empowers. British soldiers who surrendered to a Japanese force one-third their size in 1942, for example, in one of the most humiliating defeats suffered by a British army in modern history, demand, because of their subsequent suffering, the right to influence government policy on relations with Japan. Contrarily, survivors of the atomic bomb in Hiroshima in 1945 were asked for their views on the nuclear confrontation between India and Pakistan. And an interesting, if extreme, example of assertions about the rights of victims is the series of trials held in Los Angeles of the Menendez brothers, Lyle and Erik, for the alleged premeditated murder of their parents in August 1989. The two boys admitted the act but claimed that they had suffered years of physical abuse at the hands of their parents. Their defense at the trial was not that this suffering (for which no evidence was ever provided) constituted mitigating circumstances, but rather that it meant that they were *innocent*, because as victims they were not responsible for their acts. They argued, in an interesting variant of some of the defenses in The Hague, that the years of abuse they had suffered led them to conclude that their parents were going to kill them—and so they struck first. (This defense confused one jury, although they were finally convicted by another.)

The ultimate victims of modern times are, of course, the Jews of Europe. To what extent the suffering of the Jews in World War II was unique and unprecedented is a serious historical question, but it is also an issue of brute practical politics, since attenuation of it might allow other groups to contest what is an effective monopoly on major-victim status.

One Jewish writer, Jacob Neusner, has argued that the "unique evil of the Holocaust" gives Jews "a claim on others."[14] The Jews were a gentle, civilized, pacific group of people who threatened no one and were unable to put up any large-scale resistance against their appalling treatment. They were persecuted, moreover, by a German regime, along with its collaborationist allies, that was among the most unspeakable in history. To be a true victim is to aspire to a status something like this, and it is hardly surprising, seeing the way in which that suffering has been so successfully manipulated for political gain, that others wish to follow the example. Because we would all like to have a claim on others, there have naturally been attempts by non-Jewish victim groups of the Nazis to stress their own Holocaust suffering. They include women, gays, and the deaf.[15]

Others would dispute the centrality of the Nazi depredations compared to other historical incidents. There is the so-called African American Holocaust, with the Black Holocaust Museum in Milwaukee, Wisconsin. An Armenian genocide museum is being built in Washington, D.C. A book on the misdeeds of the United States around the world in modern times is alleged to recount the American Holocaust.[16] There is an online Native American Holocaust Museum and an online Waco Holocaust Museum.[17] There are attempts to use the discourse of the Holocaust to leverage political and financial advantage, as has been done with the suffering of the Jews. The Chinese American novelist Iris Chang has admitted that she wrote her gruesome book *The Rape of Nanking: The Forgotten Holocaust of World War II* in the hope that the Japanese would pay money and apologize to the people of Nanking.[18] Sometimes polemical writings make use of the discourse in a submerged fashion. The blurb for one book on France and Rwanda claims that "since the 1960s France's African policy has cost more than six million lives," although the text makes no attempt to substantiate this.[19] And finally, even serious academic studies will often use Holocaust terminology as a means of calibrating the importance they feel the story they tell should have. Thus, a book on interethnic violence in Poland in the first half of the twentieth century is called *Poland's Holocaust*.[20] Similarly, David Stannard's book on the destruction of the American Indians after Columbus, which argues that their sufferings were as great as those of the Jews, is entitled *American Holocaust*.[21] The Internet provides more examples. The Jewish political community has reacted angrily to this extension of the focus, even suggesting that to feature non-Jewish suffering is to deny the reality of the Holocaust. Sometimes this gets out of control, as when media mogul Ted Turner denounced his fellow mogul Rupert Murdoch as a "fuehrer" and the Jewish Anti-Defamation League demanded that he apologize for having "demeaned the holocaust."[22]

These are not trivial arguments, because victim status, especially if one can claim to have been betrayed, can lead to substantial political benefits. The Tutsi-led government that has ruled Rwanda since 1994 has been well aware of this. After Tutsi soldiers of the Rwandan Patrotic Army (RPA) massacred between 2,000 and 8,000 Hutu at a camp for internally displaced persons at Kibeho in 1995, the Rwandan government effectively dared the rest of the world to criticize it, arguing that it had no moral right to do so. The same argument was made when the RPA invaded Zaire in 1996: the invasion (allegedly in defense of the tiny Tutsi community there) was not criticized, and many who argued for intervention by the United Nations in 1994 argued against it two years later, in spite of the attendant bloodshed.[23] And the government has also refused to cooperate with the Rwanda tribunal in investigations of Tutsi, claiming that the prosecutor is not "qualified to venture into this area when she hasn't even brought the perpetrators of genocide to justice" without exciting much adverse comment.[24]

In part, this fixation with the victim—indeed, the perfect victim—is a question of demand as well as supply. We like to feel that there are pure and blameless victims to identify with. Moreover, a victim implies a clearly guilty perpetrator against whom it is permissible to discharge our feelings of aggression and hatred—and from a position of moral superiority at that. When the "search for blameless victims becomes a fruitless task," it may be, as Michael Ignatieff suggests, that the reaction is a sour universal misanthropy.[25] But just as often it can be a disinclination to face up to the truth, as well as a perverse desire to retain the purity of the victim one has adopted by denying or decrying evidence that suggests the victim is not wholly pure after all (what one former war correspondent has called the "tyranny of victimology").[26]

There are, of course, plenty of situations in history where right and wrong are apparently easy to differentiate. But such judgments are seldom universal, and they are always subject to qualification: outside children's books and Hollywood movies, it's often a matter of more wrong and more right. This desire in turn dictates a bipolar view of any issue where there is only space for two sides: one good, one evil. This is not a useful paradigm through which to consider the world: even leaving moral issues to one side, few conflicts in the world have only two sides, and in many (such as the conflicts in the Democratic Republic of Congo and Somalia) the number of mutually hostile factions is enormous. It is for this reason that so much confusion was caused by the fighting in Bosnia; unlike in Croatia, there were at least three sides, as well as fragments that fought each other. If the Muslims could be considered as victims, and the Serbs as perpetrators, where did this leave the Croats, who seemed to be simultaneously both and neither? Thus, an experienced British journalist, reviewing the BBC-TV drama *Warriors* about British soldiers and their experiences of the 1993 Ahmici massacre, does not mention that the massacre was carried out by

Bosnian Croats. Indeed, the surrounding context implies that the perpetrators were Serbs. This is unlikely to be bias, especially on the part of a knowledgeable journalist, but is rather an unconscious result of what happens when a paradigm takes over and retrospectively simplifies a complex situation.[27] Most commentators have agreed that the effect of the Ahmici publicity dissipated quickly, not because it failed to horrify but because it represented an unneeded complexity and a disruptive element in what was otherwise a tidily simple moral duality.

It follows from all this that no group seeking to attract Western support is now likely to overlook the opportunity to present itself as a helpless victim while important sections of Western society are on the lookout for helpless victims to adopt. The apotheosis of the innocent victim is, of course, to be in the camp, and this is a good example of the way in which the history of war crimes and atrocities is vulgarized and simplified. Concentration camps as such were used by the Americans in the Philippines, and the British a little later in the Boer War, as places to *concentrate* noncombatants, mainly women and children, to deprive the combatants themselves of support. They were also employed by Croats and Slovenes (then part of the Hapsburg army) in World War I to incarcerate Serbs and Bosnians. Many thousands died in each case, but this was not the main purpose and probably not specifically wished anyway. After the Nazi seizure of power in 1933, the new German regime promptly began to put its opponents—communists, socialists, trade unionists—in what were also described as concentration camps, like Dachau, near Munich. After 1938, Jews were also incarcerated there, although, like other inmates, they tended to be released after a period of "punishment." After the beginning of the war, and the move into Poland, new camps were created—Auschwitz being the most famous—and Jews, Soviet prisoners of war, resistance fighters, and others were sent to them. The frail majority was exterminated, the rest worked to death as slave labor. The *extermination* camps, by contrast, were in more obscure parts of Poland, at Belzec, Sobibor, and Treblinka. Here, an almost entirely Jewish set of victims, probably more than 2 million, were murdered by SS and Ukrainian troops in 1942 and 1943, using poison gas. Much less is known about this episode because there were few survivors (most Jews were dead within two hours of arrival), and the camps themselves were destroyed by the Germans afterward. But the iconography of the camp, with its photographs of skeletal survivors, is overwhelmingly from the Auschwitz model, and even the name of that camp has become emblematic.

So when the Serbs began to collect Croats and Muslims in 1992 and put them into camps a historical nerve was suddenly touched. It would be fair to describe these institutions as *concentration* camps, in the sense that a rather random group of those the Serbs regarded as enemies were concentrated there. (Muslims and Croats did the same in other areas, although on a smaller scale.) It seems, though, that the Muslims, on the advice of New York public relations firm Ruder and Finn, decided to deliberately encourage the use of the term (with its Nazi, rather than British-American, associations), and the name stuck.[28] Once the Bosnian Serbs decided to invite the world media to see the camps, in a cynical attempt to pressure the United Nations into evacuating non-Serbs from the area, it took only a few photographs of emaciated men and barbed wire for the historical archetype to be confirmed and an immediate identification made between Serbs and Nazis. (Some otherwise sensible people made some extremely stupid remarks at this time and speculated that hundreds of thousands of Muslims may already have been murdered.) At this point, the comparisons seem to have escaped from the confines of common sense and to have taken on a life of their own. For example, a right-wing German member of parliament claimed in early 1993 that the Bosnian Serbs were deliberately implanting Muslim women with dog fetuses in an apparent reminiscence of Nazi concentration camp experiments. He later claimed to have been the victim of a translation error.[29]

While these pictures could not of themselves change Western policy—which was still subject to the same constraints of practicality—that policy arguably never recovered its equilibrium thereafter. Yet the whole episode of media coverage of the camps was a matter of happenstance and interpretation. The American journalist Roy Gutman published accounts of them in the summer of 1992, although he was scrupulous enough to acknowledge that he had not witnessed any of the events himself, and was reporting second- or third-hand testimony.[30] Yet Gutman's free comparisons between the reported atrocities in Bosnia and the deeds of the Nazis struck a chord and were taken up by U.S. presidential candidate Bill Clinton as a useful stick with which to beat up the George H.W. Bush administration for its perceived lack of interest in foreign affairs. A TV news report from the Trjnopole camp with a few frames showing Muslim prisoners, one of whom was clearly emaciated, standing behind a wire fence then proceeded—to the surprise of the reporters themselves—to open the historical floodgates. At once, a complex and difficult subject was reduced to a simple historical archetype, which told even the casual viewer who the good guys and bad guys were.[31] Moreover, the effect of this episode, by resurrecting an archetype, was to set up an expectation that international justice could never fulfill. If the Bosnian Serbs were just like the Nazis, then trials in The Hague were the equivalent of Nuremberg. The real story of the camps has come out in those trials, as the main perpetrators have been progressively rounded up by British soldiers in Bosnia. It is sick and sadistic and brutal, but it is not, of course, the story presented in the media at the time. Indeed, by definition it could not be, because that story was not based on reality but rather on the mechanical application of a historical paradigm. So the story, the verdicts against the culprits, and the absence (so far, anyway) of any legal support for the frequent political charges that genocide was performed or planned in 1992 are bound to disappoint.[32]

The conceptualization of the sufferings of the Muslims in 1992 as a repetition of the extermination of the Jews is not unprecedented. Throughout the Cold War, the political right attempted to paint the Soviet Union as a new Nazi Germany, and the same vocabulary was used about Soviet behavior in Eastern Europe in the late 1940s as was used about the Serbs in Bosnia.[33] Soviet anti-Semitism—real enough as it was—became an excellent issue with which to beat up Moscow during the Cold War. Comparisons were made, by President Jimmy Carter and others, between the atrocities of the Khmer Rouge and the extermination of the Jews. The same analogy was wheeled out to criticize the Soviet invasion of Afghanistan. Subsequently, President George H.W. Bush was to describe Iraqi leader Saddam Hussein as "worse than Hitler," and the Simon Wiesenthal Center enterprisingly alleged that German companies had been building gas chambers for Iraq, though no proof of this was ever offered.[34]

By the time of the breakup of Yugoslavia, therefore, there was clear precedent for the polemical use of Holocaust comparisons for political ends, although the mantle of victim could relatively easily have fallen on any of the communities. The Serbs, after all, were viewed as among the greatest victims of World War II, and relationships between Jews and Serbs were often close. Israel and the old Yugoslavia were on good terms, and Serb nationalists were often also pro-Zionist. And for its part the state of Israel was generally supportive of the Serbs at the beginning of the crisis. The Croats, by contrast, seemed worryingly keen to resurrect the memory of the wartime Ustasha state, which exterminated Jews and Serbs with indifferent savagery, and their cause was backed especially strongly by Germany and Austria, which might itself have had uncomfortable echoes for some. And Muslim eagerness to embrace such regimes as Iraq and Libya might have given pause to their backers. But while it is likely that world sympathy would have turned away from the Bosnian Serbs eventually, the rather hysterical comparisons with the Nazis were largely the result of some freak media coverage that could have gone differently and that happened to plug exactly into a conceptual and moral void demanding to be filled. It is likely, moreover, that if the camps had been reported differently, there would have been much less interest in setting up a court to try the perpetrators—a thought perhaps to store away for the future.

But why should that particular historical incident, terrible as it may have been, be so powerful that it obstructed rational thought and rational policymaking when applied to recent incidents that had virtually nothing in common? There are two answers to this question, one particular, one general. First, the particular answer has to do with the controversy over whether anything could have been done to prevent, or at least reduce, the destruction of European Jewry. This controversy is a new one: during World War II, and for a generation afterward, it was accepted, by Jews as much as gentiles, that a victory by the Allies was always the only way in which the Jews could have been saved and that those who were, indeed, saved were saved for that reason. At that time, "probably no historical work on the Holocaust criticised the actions of the Allies or suggested that much more could have been done than was done."[35] But from the 1960s, a new orthodoxy began to develop in various (largely unspecified) ways: more could and should have been done to save the Jews of Europe, and the actual inaction resulted from anti-Semitic sentiments on the part of British and American leaders and government officials. Quite why this new orthodoxy arose then is unclear. It has been plausibly linked to the need to garner support for the state of Israel after the 1967 Six Day War, but it also probably illustrates the Oedipal trend in historical studies generally, where any orthodoxy must be overthrown and replaced by another, every generation or so, as a younger group of historians begins publishing. (The 1960s was a time when revisionist treatments of various incidents in World War II had already begun to appear.) Finally, of course, writing hostile history, attacking individuals of an older generation, especially if they cannot answer back, is much more fun than sober attempts at justification will ever be, and it is an understandably popular mode of historical writing.

The new interpretations were accompanied by much accusation and self-righteous anger—as they continue to be. They promulgate a myth of universal exterminatory anti-Semitism to explain what happened. As Cynthia Ozick has argued, "The world wants to wipe out the Jews . . . the world has always wanted to wipe out the Jews."[36] This is untrue, of course, even for the war period itself. Genteel anti-Semitism was very common among Western leaders at the time, but it was largely theoretical. Confronted with the actuality of the killings of Jews, Western leaders were overwhelmingly horrified, as well as frustrated by their inability to help. Publicity was given to the incidents, and threats of retribution made, which represented pretty much all that could be done at the time. But *exterminatory* anti-Semitism was always confined to small groups of extremists who became influential in Germany because of the way the Nazis wriggled into power in 1933 and were influential elsewhere because of German conquests. Studies of ordinary members of German SS and police units responsible for the killings have suggested that anti-Semitism, as such, was not a particularly important motivation. Nonetheless, the stereotype of passive acquiescence, if not active malevolence, by Western leaders has endured and has been enormously influential. For example, in Michael Marrus's masterly summary of the issues, there is a section entitled "Bystanders," which, albeit in moderate terms, concludes that more might have been done.[37] (The use of the word *bystanders* is an almost infallible sign that, in commenting on contemporary atrocities, a writer has the Holocaust unconsciously in mind.)

The next logical step is the argument by some radical historians that Allied leaders—or some of them, at least—actually *wanted* the Jews to be exterminated and so they (and, for that matter, Jewish leaders who had not tried hard enough to persuade Allied governments to act) were somehow as guilty as the Nazis.[38] The link with recent events will now be clear enough. The allegations that the West "stood by" in Bosnia and Rwanda, and "failed to rescue" the Tutsi and "Bosnians" (an interesting constructed category), are not simply a rerun of a historical paradigm; they also represent despair at a failed opportunity to exculpate fancied guilt. (It's worth recalling that Steven Spielberg's harrowing film *Schindler's List* was released in 1993, at the height of the "intervention" controversy in Bosnia, and was fresh in people's minds as the first stories from Rwanda came in.) If we could not help the Jews, runs the argument, then we can at least look for a situation that vaguely resembles that of the 1930s and 1940s and find a victim we can "save" and a perpetrator we can bomb. That might not help the Jews— and it may not actually address current problems—but it would make us feel better about the Holocaust and help to assuage any guilt. Failure to "save" Bosnians, Rwandans, and others can also be seen as the continuation of a historical tendency. The Netherlands, for all its current liberal internationalism, actually "handed over" (another coded phrase) a greater percentage of its Jewish population (some 75 percent) to the Nazis than any other European country. When we read bizarre allegations of Dutch soldiers "handing over" thousands of Muslim males to be slaughtered by the Serbs at Srebrenica, it is clear that Dutch commentators are not talking about that sorry episode but about events fifty years before. The poor Dutch troops—who were nowhere near the massacres and could not have stopped them—have attracted the transferred aggression and hysteria that a younger generation feels about the behavior of the Dutch government in the 1940s.

The selection of modern-day analogues to the Jews is not wholly random, of course. As well as the reality of large-scale suffering by the Muslims, and even more the Tutsi, there was also the perception of each as more cosmopolitan, urbanized, educated, and refined (the Tutsi were the old aristocratic caste). Hutu and Serbs (the Croats lost over the side, as usual), by contrast, were the thuggish rural idiots. While this is not a particular good analogy to the destruction of Central European Jewish culture by the Nazis, it does have enough apparent points of commonality to be serviceable. It is cheering that the modern image of the Jews, especially in the United States, has improved to the point that they are seen as full, and in some ways ideal, members of society. This was exemplified by the 1978

TV series *Holocaust*, portraying an urbanized, professional, intellectual, German (and therefore untypical on several counts) family of victims, with whom American viewers could identify. They were called Weiss (i.e., White) as a signal that they were really Anglo-Saxons. We tend most easily to accept people as victims if they are like us and correspond to positive images that we have of our own society. So the Bosnian Muslims, sensibly, fielded urbane, educated, professional English-speakers to advance their case. A group that seeks victim status would be well advised to find some telegenic doctors, lawyers, or priests and start teaching them English now.

To some extent, the Tutsi were also able to benefit from this comparison with the Jews, initially by outsiders, and later by the new Tutsi-dominated government in Kigali. Thus, one journalist described Rwanda as "Africa's Israel," which, if it meant anything at all, presumably meant that the Tutsi were the dominant community, oppressing the marginalized Hutu, which may not have been what the writer intended. And a U.S. government source similarly claimed that the Tutsi "are the Israelis of Africa. . . . They are a minority, they suffered genocide," which, since the Jews (with whom the comparison is presumably to be made) are a massive *majority* in Israel, is close to meaningless logically, even if it has political force.[39] Such are the perils of reasoning by half-digested analogy.

The archetype of the clash between moral fervor and reality has also been continued. The reasons why more Jews could not be saved may be briefly stated. Before 1939, the world put massive efforts into saving the Jews of Germany. No less than 72 percent of all German Jews had been rescued by September 1939, and no less than 83 percent of children and young people. Had the war been delayed a little longer, virtually everyone who wanted to leave would have been saved.[40] After 1939, with the wholly unanticipated German occupation of Europe, there was no chance of saving the remaining Jews, whom the Nazis firmly intended to exterminate, except by military victory. Ideas were floated for bombing the camp at Auschwitz or the railway lines leading to it in the brief period when the capability existed to bomb it and before the killing stopped. But there was no chance of destroying the camp's facilities without killing most of the inmates, given the inaccuracy of bombing technology at that date, and bombing railway lines proved totally ineffective throughout the war (and, indeed, since). The most that might have been achieved was mild inconvenience to the plans of the Nazis, who had many other ways to do their killing anyway.[41]

The situation in Bosnia was not analogous, but it reflected the same basic contrast between fervor and reality: no international agreement on a political objective and strategy to pursue, no chance, therefore, of a sensible military plan, and not enough troops even if there had been a plan. But in many ways this is beside the point. In many of the self-deluding plans for "rescue" of the Jews that William Rubenstein reviews, and in much of the writing since that time, there is a clear feeling that, even if the scheme failed totally, it should still somehow have been tried because, as one historian rather desperately urges, "even if few or no lives had been saved, the moral obligation would have been fulfilled."[42] This is perhaps the origin of the something-must-be-done school of the 1990s, and, of course, the bombing of the Bosnian Serbs (and the Serbs themselves in Kosovo) was the conceptual descendent (what biblical scholars call the *antitypos*) of the nonbombing of Auschwitz. So the advocates of bombing assorted Serbs in the 1990s seldom had any clear idea either of the purpose it would serve or what would happen later, because it was an essentially symbolic act to make them feel better about the past. Unsurprisingly, therefore, when in 1993 General Colin Powell asked what would happen if bombing Serb targets did not bring them to the conference table, the question "proved impossible to answer."[43]

As with the Holocaust, so with Bosnia and Rwanda: the idea that something *ought* to have been possible shades quickly into the belief that something *was* possible, and therefore the fact that nothing could be done becomes a moral issue rather than a practical one. In the historiography of Bosnia and Rwanda, we are seeing a high-speed reprise of the historiography of the Holocaust. Already, books are appearing with titles like *Unfinest Hour: Britain and the Destruction of Bosnia*; *A People Betrayed: The Role of the West in Rwanda's Genocide*; and *Complicité de génocide? La politique de la France au Rwanda* from which the unwary might conclude that Western troops were actually *involved* in the killings.[44] And it is not far, then, to the allegation that the "British secret service MI6" (sic) actually *organized* the killings at Ahmici, to discredit the Croats and strengthen the pro-Serb policy of the British, by proving "that the war in Bosnia-Herzegovina was a 'civil war' rather than a 'Serb aggression.'"[45] (For what it's worth, the allegations of a "pro-Serb" or "anti-Muslim" policy allegedly pursued by some Western governments are, as one might expect, as much a figment of the historical imagination as the anti-Jewish accusations described above, which are their historical *typos*.) Likewise, an enterprising French writer has come up with the suggestion that it was the French themselves who were responsible for shooting down the plane carrying President Juvenal Habyarimana, the relatively moderate Hutu leader, the incident that is generally credited with having sparked the killings. What purpose would have been served thereby heaven only knows.[46]

This kind of writing, of course, is inimical to any attempt to run an honest system of justice, because it blurs the issue of personal responsibility and substitutes collective guilt for the guilt of individuals. It is also morally dangerous, because with a little determination anyone can be dragged into the morass of guilt. After all, smirked a commentator on

Croatian Radio after the *Blaskic* verdict was announced in The Hague, British forces were in the area when the Ahmici massacres took place. Weren't they at least as guilty as Blaskic of failure to stop the killings?[47] In the end, of course, if everyone is guilty, then no one is guilty, and any form of criminal justice is simply pointless.

Why Did the Heavens Not Darken?

It is reasonable to ask at this point: Why the obsession with intervention, and where it came from? After all, practical experience is scarcely very encouraging: the results of intervention have ranged in recent years from making the situation fractionally better to disasters of Somalian proportions. Yet we do not seem to be able to kick the habit. Why is this? There are, of course, powerful practical arguments for intervention in specific cases, and there are certainly isolated situations where intervention has had some positive effects. But I am concerned here not with rational debates about intervention but with the separate issue of the urge to intervene as a compelling moral duty, usually uncomplicated by any understanding of the local situation or any rational assessment of whether it might succeed.

These days, we associate "intervention" with "humanitarian," an odd choice, perhaps, since the compound noun usually implies fighting your way into someone else's country and killing them until they do what you want. But until about a century ago, intervention usually meant *divine* intervention: God was understood to intervene routinely in the world to punish the wicked and reward the virtuous. The "special providence in the fall of a sparrow" that Hamlet mentioned was a commonplace thought at the time, especially in Protestant societies like England, where the doctrine of predestination implied that God had already intervened in the life of each individual to save or to damn him or her. From the beginning, this idea posed problems, given that the wicked clearly flourished in the world and the good often did not. It also produced the famous Problem of Evil: How could a benevolent and omnipotent God allow evil and suffering in the world? From time to time incidents occurred that shook the faith in the idea of a benevolent God with the capacity to intervene in the world; the terrible death toll in the 1755 Lisbon earthquake (which claimed 60,000 lives and prompted Voltaire to write *Candide*) was one. But it was the two wars of the twentieth century that made it impossible for most thinking people to believe in the idea of a God who was *both* omnipotent and good. How, it was asked, could the suffering of innocent civilians contribute to *any* divine plan, however abstruse and complex? Why, in the words of one book on the Holocaust, did the heavens not darken?[48]

The decay in religious faith in the West did not remove the urge to believe in an all-wise, all-powerful, and perfectly just entity; it simply meant that that urge had to be projected elsewhere. States have carried some of the burden, but most of it has inevitably fallen on that curious thing, the international community, especially in the guise of the United Nations, which has its own temples, its own priesthood, its own liturgy (the UN Charter), and its own commandments, principally international humanitarian law. (It is interesting that one of the best-known early books about the United Nations, by Connor Cruise O'Brien, was entitled *Sacred Drama*.)[49] But, of course, a divine being has attributes that no human institution can hope to posses, and so humans will always turn in a relatively disappointing performance. Divine intervention was never stymied by logistic problems or lack of trained personnel; divine omniscience was never compromised by intelligence failures; and divine justice was swift and decisive and not a hostage to confused witnesses or higher courts that could overturn a verdict. So the bitter criticisms of the international community and the United Nations during the 1990s were essentially a reprise of the Lisbon earthquake argument: How *could* they have allowed these things to happen and not intervene to prevent them? It was not, in other words, a complaint about real options that were available in the real world to real people but rather a protest that the international community, which had divine expectations reposed in it, was failing to act in a suitably omnipotent manner.

In turn, these attitudes—both religious and secular—probably have their origins with our experience as small children. Then, we see the world as a frightening and inexplicable place, and we put infinite trust in our parents, who tell us, in turn, that everything is for the best and that good will always triumph. As a result, we invest our parents with what are basically divine attributes of power and knowledge, and adolescence is partly the cruel realization that our parents are mere mortals; more than that, they have lied to us about the essential benevolence of the world. Those who do not come to terms with these disappointments (most of us) project these disappointments, as we grow older, on figures of authority, and ultimately government, which in many ways fills the role of collective parent of society. Like parents, governments must be realistic and practical and have to look to the longer term. Sometimes governments have to tell their people that they cannot have tax cuts today, just as parents told them they could not have sweets all the time. Sometimes governments have to tell their people that intervention is impossible, just as parents have to tell their children that there isn't enough money to go to Disneyland. Children are bad at recognizing practical obstacles ("*Please* can we go to Disneyland?"). They blame their parents for things that are beyond control and believe that tantrums, emotional blackmail, and sulking can somehow alter reality.

As we get older, we project all of these feelings onto governments. Indeed, one of the most curious things about working for government is the realization that the public actually holds government responsible for just about everything—literally, even the weather. We seek and expect justice in the world, and when we do not get it, we turn on the nearest target to vent our anger.

The Lessons of History

I suggested earlier that there was a general, as well as a particular, reason for the urge to intervene all over the place. On top of the myth of Western inactivity over the Holocaust is the myth of Munich. I have written about this at length elsewhere.[50] In brief, it is charged that the democracies failed to "stand up to aggression" in the late 1930s, when war might have been averted, but through spinelessness gave way to Hitler, thus encouraging further adventures. The reality is, and was, different: Hitler was intent on war with Czechoslovakia and was furious at the way in which he had been maneuvered into a peaceful resolution of the crisis. Moreover, the dynamics of the Nazi state (as well as its own policy goals) absolutely required war before too long. All Munich did was to start the war before the Germans were fully ready. But the myth is more powerful than the reality, and in their attempt to atone for the imagined sin, Western governments have spent the last sixty-odd years seeking out aggression and standing up to bullies in the most unlikely places—and often with disastrous results. At different times, Joseph Stalin, Gamal Abdul Nasser, Ho Chi Minh, Muammar Qaddafi, Saddam Hussein, Fidel Castro, Ayatollah Khomeini, General Mohammed Aideed of Somalia, Slobodan Milosevic, and a number of others have been confidently identified as the "new Hitler," bent on expansionist territorial acquisition. The urge to atone, of course, is a never-ending process, since by definition the past can never be undone, and new opportunities for expiation must be sought all the time. This is why there are so many examples of new Hitlers and why few if any of them are the least bit convincing. Proponents of the use of violence in international crises nonetheless refer to Munich (the code is "aggression") in justifying their acts. In each case, the assumption is that inaction will result in further aggression and ultimately a general war. Likewise, any concession, any consideration, no matter how small and fleeting, of the opponent's point of view is stigmatized as "appeasement." So the only policy is utter intransigence, leading to overwhelming victory and the fundamental reconstruction of a society, if necessary, at gunpoint. And, of course, precisely because the past cannot be undone, the "shame" of Munich will never die, and this process must be repeated again and again. Moreover, when the requisite hard line is not taken, the analogy requires that as a result we have to find someone whom we have "betrayed" as the Czechs were betrayed at Munich. So in the 1990s unconvincing attempts were made to substitute "Bosnians" and "Rwandans" for the Czechs to whom we had allegedly behaved so badly.

The Munich myth has underlain the handling of practically every international crisis since 1945. It is a constructed myth, in the sense that it is not based on serious analysis, and it is not, for the most part, held by people with any real knowledge of history. Thus, one of President Lyndon Johnson's biographers remarks that he was "like so many people who do not read history . . . peculiarly a creature of it, and perhaps a prisoner of one particular interpretation of it," and that this explained much of the way in which he approached international crises.[51] Yet the Munich myth is a very portable way of thinking, a tent that can be erected in a matter of minutes to cover virtually any episode, and that provides an easily assimilated set of norms and judgments that do not require any actual firsthand knowledge of the crisis. It turns current events into a Disney-like progression of bland look-alike episodes where the correct behavior is never in doubt and the good guys always win. It turns up in the most surprising contexts. In the Cuban missile crisis, for example, those who argued for anything less than outright war were stigmatized as favoring a "Caribbean Munich."[52] The choice of naval quarantine rather than massive attack was apparently criticized as "almost as bad as the appeasement at Munich" by General Curtis LeMay.[53] "The principal lesson I learned from World War II was that if aggression is allowed to gather momentum it can continue to build and lead to general war," intoned the secretary of state. Those who "advocate retreat or appeasement," warned the president, have "the blotch of Munich" still on their faces.[54] This was not Madeleine Albright and Bill Clinton speaking about Bosnia (though they used similar words) but Dean Rusk and Lyndon Johnson speaking about Vietnam. Indeed, the parallels between the two episodes, in the American context, anyway, are unnervingly close. In both cases, a Soviet-equipped nationalist-communist dictatorship was seen as bent on conquest and aggression, and the stability of the region depended on the United States stopping it. Just as the Johnson administration refused to believe that the Vietcong and the National Liberation Front had significant support in South Vietnam, and thought they were in fact invaders, so the Clinton administration could not believe that many "Bosnians" supported the policies of Belgrade and Zagreb. In each case, it was hoped that the enemy could be bombed to the conference table. In this model of things, Slobodan Milosevic is Mao Tse-tung, Radovan Karadzic is Ho Chi Minh, Alija Izetbegovic is several of the South Vietnamese leaders, Sarajevo is Saigon, Pale is Hanoi, the Republika Srpska is North Vietnam, and so on.

Indeed, in several interesting senses, Yugoslavia is the Clinton administration's Vietnam. Partly, this is because every administration, to expunge the "shame" of Munich, has to identify an "aggressor" (ideally relatively small and weak) who can be pounded into submission. The George H.W. Bush administration was less belligerent over Yugoslavia than its successor precisely because it had just finished standing up to aggression in Kuwait and did not see any need to do the same again. The Clinton generation, by contrast, had *protested* against the Vietnam War, thus inhibiting America's ability to stand up to aggression at that time and purge the shame of Munich. At the time, this probably seemed a good idea, but it later appeared a considerable political handicap. Thus, the Clinton administration was even more eager than normal to prove itself by looking for aggression to stand up to. Had it not been for the involvement of many of its principals in the antiwar movement in the 1960s, it is likely that U.S. policy toward Bosnia would have been very different, with enthusiasm for a tribunal in The Hague less pronounced.

The story of American policy toward Yugoslavia in the 1990s is of the slow, painful, and incomplete replacement of this model by reality. In 1993, for example, the Vance-Owen Peace Plan, if implemented, would have settled the fighting in Bosnia, much along lines of the Dayton Accords, only several years earlier. It has recently been called "an intelligent and fair-minded attempt to provide a solution to the Bosnian conundrum" and deserved to succeed.[55] Yet as Misha Glenny has remarked, the plan was abused by many who "had either not read it or . . . wilfully misinterpreted its provisions."[56] It could be criticized in the sense that it would have given control of 43 percent of the territory to the Bosnian Serbs (as against 49 percent in Dayton), whereas they were only about 35 percent of the population, albeit mostly in lower density rural areas. But considering that the Bosnian Serbs then controlled about 70 percent of Bosnia, this would have been a major concession on their part. This did not prevent another outing for the increasingly shop-soiled Munich vocabulary, however: a former senior Bush administration official claimed that the plan "amounted to appeasement," and *New York Times* columnist Anthony Lewis warned the administration to "beware of Munich."[57] As Glenny remarks, and as many British officials at the time certainly felt, those in Washington who condemned Vance-Owen had no idea what was in it. But this is not surprising: the document was, symbolically, the Munich agreement, and they did not need to read it to know what it must contain. (If the analogy had been precise, of course, the Munich agreement would have awarded much of southern Germany to the Czechs.) An even more surprising late flowering of the same vocabulary was found after the unsuccessful Rambouillet talks on the future of Kosovo in January 1999. "We walked right up to the edge of appeasement," said one U.S. official of attempts to agree a peace plan with Milosevic.[58] Considering that the NATO demands (effectively nonnegotiable) were for NATO troops to be deployed in a province of Serbia, a referendum probably leading to Kosovar independence after three years, and free passage for NATO forces through Serbia, one is left floundering a little after the precise intent of the analogy here.

Whatever the rights and wrongs of the historical incidents described above, it must be the case that foreign policy cannot be sensibly conducted using a highly simplistic model based on a misreading of history and propelled by shame and the desire for expiation at any price. Whether one believes that U.S. policy in Vietnam or in Bosnia was right or wrong, whether one believes the attack on Serbia in 1999 was justified or not, policy must be made by examining what is actually happening on the ground. If we do not do this, then, at a minimum, we are unlikely to get the right answer. It is particularly dangerous when trying to set up a legal institution, which has precisely to be guided by what actually happened, and what can be proved beyond a reasonable doubt. One of the results of this testosterone-charged verbal escalation is that it will, in practice, be very difficult for the ICTY to present verdicts and findings that will actually satisfy the mood of apocalyptic revenge that has been created, since much of the emotion surrounding events in the former Yugoslavia is actually inherited from earlier episodes. The most dangerous effect of this obsession with stylized views of history is that it blinds Western thinkers to the possibility of other points of view. Some were so obsessed with one tendentious interpretation of World War II, for example, that it never occurred to them that the Serbs might have an equally tendentious one of their own.

Yet politicians do frequently make a virtue of being obsessed with an interpretation of history and see no need to focus less on theory and more on the here-and-now. Madeleine Albright, for example, traded for many years on her own personal experiences of persecution under the Nazis and Soviets, which she believed gave her a universal ability to judge the rights and wrongs of any situation, and actively sought opportunities to stop, as she saw it, similar events occurring in the future. In a well-regulated society, there would be laws to prevent anyone so obsessed by her past from ever having anything to do with foreign policy, which is emphatically not an arena for personal psychodramas to be acted out, especially when lives are involved. The problem with such people (and this is not an *ad feminam* example; they exist everywhere) is that they are incapable of seeing the world as it is and so can never address issues as they are.[59] (Ironically, Albright may have been the right person to deal with the Serbs, similarly obsessed with a stylized view of recent history.)

Lost in Space

In this rather breathless canter, I have tried to make two basic points. First, the vocabulary and concepts of international humanitarian law are not universal; they are culturally specific to the West, albeit the West does not in general wish to have them applied to itself. Second, the West is itself obsessed with a simplified vision of the history of the 1930s and 1940s, as well as the need to avoid repeating it, which means that it is mostly incapable of interpreting major human rights abuses except through this distorting prism. But there is a wider problem also, which is that of the isolation of those in the West who make important decisions from real life as it is lived in countries where these abuses take place. Most educated Westerners live reasonably comfortable lives, in an organized society, where democratic governments more or less work and where they can rely on the police and are fairly secure in everyday life. Most of the world, of course, and especially the kind of places where abuses take place, cannot aspire to this. Sometimes we hear of such societies in the form of a communiqué from a distance. In his introduction to the Polish director Jan Kott's book *Shakespeare Our Contemporary*, Peter Brook remarks that he is "the only writer on Elizabethan matters who assumes without question that every one of his readers will at some point or other have been woken by the police in the middle of the night."[60] Kott certainly does assume this, as he assumes that everyone will understand the mechanics of how to conduct a political assassination, and as he explains *Richard III* in terms of the personal experience his generation had of Nazi and Soviet tyranny. But, of course, Kott is scarcely unique: in all probability, most audiences of Shakespeare's plays and most non–Anglo-Saxon commentators on them have always known exactly what it is like to be woken by the police at 3 A.M. It is we who are unusual. Sometimes we experience such societies firsthand, when we travel on business or holiday: the official who wants a bribe before he will do his job; the cold eyes of the soldier in a state under martial law; the shotgun kept by the bar of the illegal drinking club because the police cannot be trusted; the casual lunchtime conversation about the latest political or business murder and how much it cost. We scuttle gratefully back to the shelter of the embassy or the airplane and do not think what it must be like to live in such a society *all* the time.

Perhaps a Balkan taxi driver or a bar owner in an African town has more actual wisdom about the world than the average journalist, CEO of a large company, or experienced diplomat. They *know* that life is full of shit, that the police are corrupt and brutal, that the government is incapable and not interested. They know, in other words, that you are basically on your own. It is for this reason, perhaps, that even ordinary people who have lived under dictatorships or through civil wars have a kind of natural maturity that few of us in the West ever actually acquire. Thus, Milosevic could often dance rings around foreign visitors, not because he was a political genius but because he was experienced and successful in the world of Balkan politics, with its tools of "deception, corruption, blackmail, demagoguery and violence," in which few Western politicians would have lasted five minutes.[61] So the West has been continuously surprised, in the Balkans and elsewhere, by leaders of factions who tell lies, renege on agreements, and casually switch violence on and off as they feel like it. The West's response is one of pained disbelief and grumpiness that human beings can be so devious. Thus, at the time of the first Markala massacre in Sarajevo in 1994, Madeleine Albright argued that it was "very hard to believe that any country would do this to their own people," and so "although we do not know exactly what the facts are," the Serbs must have done it. It's one thing to make a judgment like this on the basis of evidence (and it is quite possible that she was right about the perpetrators), but it is another to make a virtue of one's own naïveté on the basis of what two recent historians aptly describe as "shaky reasoning."[62] It was typical of the confusions and misunderstandings inherent in U.S. policy at the time that both potential sets of perpetrators were in fact from the same *country* (i.e., Bosnia), although from different ethnic groups.

There is, moreover, a conceptual and personal gulf between even the most empathic Westerner and the kind of person whom they meet in situations of conflict and incipient atrocity. It's not uncommon for Western leaders to meet local politicians who are literally in fear of their lives, from their own side or another side, and who may indeed be dead in weeks or months. Some of us have had personal tragedies in our lives, but how many of us have had to watch our father select which of his children would live and which would die at the hands of the enemy—and be among those who lived? This happened to Budimir Kosutic, one of the extreme Serbs who led the fight against the new Croatian government.[63] How do you even begin to comprehend what dark motivations drive such an individual? This gulf is especially great for those with a strong campaign interest in human rights. Because of their strong attachment to Western liberal norms—admirable in themselves—such individuals come to believe that because the world *should* be like that therefore it *is* like that. The inevitable disappointment at meeting brute reality leads to a kind of psychosis and sometimes to a kind of liberal vigilantism. This happened in South Africa after apartheid. A friend of mine, a former intelligence expert for the ANC's military wing, recalled giving a short and fairly basic presentation on the involvement of the old South African Defence Force in human rights violations to some Truth and Reconciliation Commission investigators from a human rights background. There was a shocked silence at the end, and one of them said,

"You know, for the first time in my life I feel I have been in the presence of pure evil." The commission itself, and its supporting staff, consisted largely of long-term opponents of apartheid, some very brave. Yet with their liberal Western norms, they were completely devastated by what they actually heard. A book like Antje Krog's *Country of My Skull* gives a dire (if unwitting) portrait of how a group of Western liberals (including Krog) had a collective nervous breakdown when confronted with what were, by Bosnian or Rwandan standards, relatively minor atrocities.[64] What kind of country, one has to wonder, did they *think* they had been living in?

To be naive and not to be able to understand is one thing. But here I wish to briefly outline another dangerous Western ideology that greatly complicates the understanding of war crimes and atrocities, because it is confident that it understands when it does not. The dominant theory in international relations is and has been for some time realism. This ideology sees the world made up of states that try rationally to maximize their power and wealth unless restrained by fear of other states or by weakness and political crisis. States, in this view, are ethnically homogeneous and have simple, concrete goals in their relationships with each other, based on self-ish maximization of benefits. Conflict is inherent in any relationship between states unless restrained by the fear engendered through a balance of military power. Like all crude theories, realism has a certain explanatory power for users of small-scale maps, but its weakness is that it utterly fails to explain why states *actually* behave as they do. (It is not a coincidence that realism's first advocates were particularly interested in the period from Bismarck to Hitler when, in a poor light, the theory could be said to correspond loosely with some of the facts.)

What has this to do with war crimes? The important thing about realism is not what it says but what it leaves out. It leaves out all the reasons why conflict between states actually takes place (fear, uncertainty, misunderstanding), as well as all the motives that actually drive politics, such as culture, history, religion, ethnicity, community, and language. It will be seen that realism is a mongrel offspring of our old friends Social Darwinism and the nation-state, with a dash of the Munich myth, which above all is seen as being about *rationally* pursued aggression for realist ends. Realism would explain the fighting in the former Yugoslavia as a simple competition for power in which the Serbs, once they had achieved control of the JNA, made a rational decision to use it to maximize their territory and power. There is an element of truth in that, of course, but such an a priori explanation actually ignores most of the things—fear, paranoia, a warped interpretation of history—that made the Serbs act as they did. It also implies that once Bosnia and Croatia became independent they were full-fledged realist constructs in which, suddenly, there was a complete identity between state and people. Thus, Peter Galbraith, then–U.S. ambassador in Zagreb, reported that the Krajina Serbs in Croatia were "the so-called local Serbs."[65] This probably indicates not bias as such but the stranglehold of realism: after all, there is no Canadian minority in the United States—why should there be a Serb minority in Croatia? In fact, Serbs had lived in the Krajina since the sixteenth century; it would have been as logical to refer to "so-called local whites" in America. Realism is incapable of dealing with a situation where a minority of the population (in Bosnia, arguably a majority), desires, on ethnic or religious grounds, through fear or a warped view of history, to belong to another state.

If realism were confined to an academic ghetto, it would be less of a concern, but it is also dominant in official thinking about foreign policy in the United States. Most of those who guide U.S. foreign policy, and most of those who write about it in the popular media, have probably absorbed the tenets of realism even if they have not formally studied it. And the interchange between government and academic life means a constant new supply into government of people with rigid ideological perceptions of the world and often limited practical experience of it.[66] (It has some influence in the United Kingdom, although to a lesser degree.) So the Clinton administration constructed a notional state, "an idealised multi-ethnic Bosnia."[67] This was a kind of para-Bosnia, full of Good Bosnians, Our Bosnians (like Our Vietnamese and Our Germans), with whom we could identify because they were like us or we thought they were. Most of these people were Muslims (and, indeed, officially and in academic works and journalism "Bosnian" and "Muslim" tend to be used interchangeably), but there were a few Good Serbs and Good Croats as well.[68] Bad Serbs and Bad Croats were simply wished away to be citizens of another country. This led the West (and by no means only Americans) into total confusion between support for "Bosnians" and concern for "Muslim victims," although the two policies were partly irreconcilable, and to confuse Izetbegovic's position as leader of the largest Muslim party with his other job as one member of a seven-man multiethnic rotating presidency.[69] (His mandate expired on December 20, 1992, when a representative of another ethnic group was to take over, but Izetbegovic managed to prevent this from happening.) Thus, the Americans found themselves confronted with such surreal situations as the attendance in Washington, D.C., in early 1993 of the prime minister of the Bosnian government, Mile Akmadzic, who was simultaneously a member of the Bosnian Croat delegation and was therefore negotiating with himself. So like any scheme to impose an ideological pattern upon reality, this one fell apart when applied practically, and there was much puzzlement later about why that should have been so. Even well-informed commentators were so mesmerized by the realist model that they discussed the fighting in Bosnia in terms of "conquest" and "recapture" of territory, as though Serbs,

Croats, and Muslims all lived in separate geographical areas instead of on top of one another.

For many active in the debate about the war in Bosnia (although not necessarily active in attempts to stop it), the real story of the war was therefore about an abstract clash of moral imperatives and Western political psychodramas, not the sufferings of real individuals. Thus, rather than feeling a moral need to bring an end to the suffering, many saw it necessary to *extend* the suffering until a solution that suited their normative framework could be attained. As one Dutch member of parliament said chillingly, when opposing Vance-Owen, what was needed was "an arrangement which will satisfy our sense of justice." The views and desires (and for that matter the welfare) of people in Bosnia themselves were not relevant in this context.[70]

Even more bizarre things have happened with Rwanda. One recent polemical work concludes that the West and the United Nations "betrayed the people of Rwanda" and that "there is nothing the West can now say to the people of Rwanda to compensate for their failure to intervene in their hour of need."[71] One might imagine from this that Rwanda was a Tutsi country, invaded and devastated by forces from outside. In fact, of course, something a little closer to the opposite was true. The "people" of Rwanda were overwhelmingly Hutu (about 85 percent), and the crisis was set off by an invasion of Tutsi political exiles who had been in Uganda since the 1960s. (It is unnecessary to say that this does not for a moment excuse the subsequent killings.) What happened was that Rwanda was reconstructed, in neocolonialist fashion, to be the property of the Tutsi social and political elites. The Hutu lumpenproletariat were simply wished away. In this context, it is instructive, and rather depressing, to note that practically all of the books and articles dealing with the 1994 killings are by non-Africans. Indeed, African students of the episode, until very recently, would probably have gleaned much of what they knew from Internet sites at various Western nongovernmental organizations (NGOs) and universities. This cannot be right, and it is even less acceptable that most of the writing about the episode is not about the Rwandans at all (they are mostly props) but rather about what the West could, should, or might have done, as well as the settling of various internal political scores.

Likewise, the received image of the massacres—carried out by a robotic population organized by ruthless genocidal conspirators with command of the media—is clearly selected to make armed intervention by the West sound more plausibly effective. (It also caters to the neocolonialist desire for clean-limbed Western troops to be sent in to sort out the mess made by savage natives.) But in practice it is doubtful whether any government has ever had such direct control not just over the thoughts of its people but their actions as well, and the reality of any intervention would have been much messier. A moment's thought reveals that, once more, a historical *typos* is at work: the image of the centrally directed Nazi state carrying out its elaborate master-plan for the annihilation of the Jews. In fact, the degree of organization and efficiency of this episode, horrible as it was, has been exaggerated (and the vast majority of Jews who were killed in Germany were Polish and Russian, not German, anyway), but it has left its traces nonetheless on our understanding of later events.[72] Increasingly, experts on the region and investigators and prosecutors are doubtful about the robotic hypothesis and the master plan. Obviously, *some* preplanning went on, since weapons were stockpiled and later handed out, for example, but the simplistic picture of the killings as "simply a conspiracy from above" should perhaps give way to a more sophisticated understanding of how violent political change could make the idea of the extermination of the Tutsi seem widely acceptable.[73]

And there is perhaps another reason for dominant Western perceptions of the Rwandan crisis and its aftermath. As Johan Pottier notes, in discussing the post-1994 era, by "portraying Rwandans as helpless victims in need, the West can cast itself in the role of altruistic saviour, a saviour stripped of ambiguity."[74] Western disinclination to take an interest in the area for thirty years before the catastrophe, followed by heavy-handed financial and political interference late in the day, can therefore be quietly forgotten, and the crisis can thus be redefined as a purely African one that sensible behavior by the West could not then have forestalled.

Such ideological constructs had a powerful influence on the formation of the Hague tribunal (less, to be fair, on its Arusha sibling) and remain powerful today. The main danger lies in the inevitable conflict between this reductive and simplified ideological scheme and the messy, complex picture that comes out in a court of law. At a minimum this explains some of the often poor and misleading commentary there has been on the tribunal's operations from the U.S. media (and the British media, to some extent). More important, the complexities of real life can never measure up to the clarity of an ideology, and ironically, when conclusions reached by the court do not support the constructed view of the conflict, it will be the court, and not the ideology, that will be said to have failed. The ICC will probably suffer from the same difficulties. Speed of communication means that a received version of some atrocity in a remote part of the world may well be available only days after it has happened, with all the imperfections that implies. Sometimes this is performed by the media, but the various relief organizations and NGOs themselves often contribute to the problem as well. As Tony Waters notes, discussing the events that followed the Rwandan crisis, early reports "when unanalyzed, present a fragmented, superficial or incomplete picture," especially when the writers are not themselves from the region, and their reports "are translated unanalysed into emotional donor appeals."[75] This is not only bad for policymaking; it creates a political obstacle to objective investigation and prosecution and may well lead to unrealistic assumptions about what investigations and trials will actually yield.

Conclusion

In this chapter, I have tried to describe the complexity of the political context in which the investigation and prosecution of war crimes take place, as well as the practical problems that can result. In a sense, however, most of these problems are really one: the conflict between idealism and reality or, alternatively, the conflict between the world as it ought to be and the world as it is. On the one side are those who take a strongly normative view of the world and seek to influence events without being prepared to accept responsibility for the consequences. On the other side are those who actually have to make things work and are obliged to take responsibility for events even if they cannot influence them. This is significant for our current purpose, since much thinking about international humanitarian law amounts, in practice, to a normative ideology. I do not mean that its prescriptions are therefore necessarily wrong, but I do argue that they correspond to an ideology: an inductive intellectual construct, complete in itself and not deduced from outside reality. Because this is so, thinking about international humanitarian law proceeds largely in terms of abstract norms; it is unlikely that reality can ever live up to this (although it is reality's duty to try). Thus, the negotiation of the ICC Statute was widely seen more as a theoretical and ideological triumph than as the beginning of a complex and difficult set of practical problems. There is, therefore, a built-in tension between governments and international courts, which have to make things work, and commentators and lobbyists seeking Platonic perfection against rigid ideological criteria.

The authors of the official Dutch Srebrenica report[76] appositely cite Max Weber's distinction between two types of politics: that which is guided by the "ethic of ultimate ends," and that which is guided by the "ethic of responsibility."[77] This is an alternative way of understanding the conflict described above. Governments have no real choice: They have to take responsibility for their actions; and indeed it would be a dangerous and wicked government that pursued abstract ethical policies without consideration for the practical consequences they might have. In war crimes work, this means that governments and courts must adhere to the law, as well as to various internal rules; that they have to respect all sorts of practical limitations on what can be achieved; and that they cannot afford to pursue some abstract idea of "justice" without any consideration at all of the likely practical effects of doing so. Weber recognized very clearly the tension that exists between abstract ethical criteria and real life, and he argued that if "an action of good intent leads to bad results, then in the actor's eye's, not he but the world, or the stupidity of other men . . . is responsible for the evil." Such a person "feels 'responsible' only for seeing to it that the flame of pure intentions is not quelched," and many of his actions will be irrational, at least if we take into account the criteria of probable success, since they are "acts that can and shall have only exemplary value." And Weber saw also that the "ethical" mind-set can be so deeply attached to the pursuit of "ethically good purpose" that it is easily able to contemplate the use even of "morally dubious means . . . with the probability of evil ramifications."[78] And when such exemplary, ethically guided acts have disastrous consequences (like the deployment to Srebrenica), the response is not acceptance of responsibility (since, after all, one's actions were irreproachably ethical in intent) but rather a kind of hysterical denial and a desperate search to identify those who failed to meet the impossible ethical objective. This incompatibility between ethical authoritarianism and messy reality is perhaps the biggest single political obstacle to the successful investigation and punishment of war crimes.

Notes

1. The tangled story of attempts to address alleged human rights violations in Indonesia through a legal mechanism is set out in International Crisis Group Briefing Paper, *Indonesia: Implications of the Timor Trials*, May 8, 2002.
2. See, for example, Gary Jonathan Bass, *Stay the Hand of Vengeance*, pp. 16–20.
3. An interesting, if arguably slightly complacent, discussion of this point is in Michael Ignatieff, *Human Rights as Politics and Ideology* .
4. For an interesting angle on this debate, see Lone Lindholt, *Questioning the Universality of Human Rights*; and Mahmood Mamdani, ed., *Beyond Rights Talk and Culture Talk*.
5. See Mark Aarons, *War Criminals Welcome*.
6. Aaron Haas, *The Aftermath*, pp. 165–169.
7. Nik Gowing, "The One-Eyed King of Real-Time News Coverage," in *New Perspectives Quarterly* 11, no. 4 (available online at www.npq.org).
8. See, for example, Anne Grier Cutter, "Journalists: Must They Remain Neutral in Conflict?" in *United Nations Chronicle*, 36, no. 2 (1999).
9. Martin Bell, "Journalism of Attachment" (available online at http://cci.wmin.ac.uk).
10. Raymond van den Boogaard, cited in Nederlands Instituut vor Oorlogsdocumentatie, *Srebrenica: A "Safe" Area*, pt. 1, chap. 2, sec. 5.
11. Johan Pottier, *Reimagining Rwanda,* p.1.
12. Michael Ignatieff, *The Warrior's Honour,* p. 25.

13. Charles Maier, cited in Peter Novick, *The Holocaust and Collective Memory*, p. 8.

14. Cited by Norman Finkelstein, *The Holocaust Industry*.

15. On women and the Holocaust (see, for example, www.interlog.com/~mighty/: "The prominent analysts of the Holocaust may have erased or ignored gender, but the Holocaust did not."); on gays and the Holocaust (the Gay Holocaust Memorial Site at www.bkeery.homestead.com), and the deaf and the Holocaust ("Hitler's Silent Victims") at deafness.about.com/library.

16. William Blum, *Killing Hope*.

17. For example, online resources are available at www.nativeamerican embassy.net/Holocaust.html; for a discussion of a "Herero Holocaust" see www.namibweb.com; the Waco Holocaust is documented at www.msinc.com/SkyWriter/WacoMusuem.

18. Transcript of *The News Hour with Jim Lehrer*, February 20, 1998, available at http://www.pbs.org/newshour/gergen/february98/chang_2-20.html.

19. Michel Stibon, *Une genocide sur la conscience*.

20. Tadeusz Piotrowski, *Poland's Holocaust*.

21. David E. Stannard, *American Holocaust*.

22. Novick, *The Holocaust*, p. 9.

23. Johan Pottier, "Modern Information Warfare Versus Empirical Knowledge: Framing 'The Crisis' in Eastern Zaire, 1996," paper presented at the Association of Social Anthropologists (ASA) 2000 conference, London, "Participating in Development: Approaches to Indigenous Knowledge" (available online at www.asa2000.anthropology.ac.uk).

24. See Marc Lacey, "Tribunal Says Rwanda Is Stalling Inquiry Into 1994 Killings," *New York Times*, September 7, 2002.

25. Ignatieff, *The Warrior's Honour*, pp. 24–25.

26. Paul Moorcraft, *Reporting Conflict* (the 1999 Vauxhall Lectures) (available online at www.cf.ac.uk/jomec).

27. Maggie O'Kane, review of *Warriors* in *Sight and Sound* (December 1999): 30.

28. John Burns, "The Media as Impartial Observers or Protagonists: Conflict Reporting or Conflict Encouragement in Former Yugoslavia," in James Gow, Richard Paterson, and Alison Preston, eds., *Bosnia by Television*.

29. Cited in *Srebrenica: A "Safe" Area*, pt. 1, chap. 9, sec. 3.

30. Roy Gutman, *Witness to Genocide*. See also an interview with Gutman at http://globetrotter.berkeley.edu/conversations/Gutman/gutman-con6.html.

31. An exhaustive review of this episode and its media coverage is in *Srebrenica: A "Safe" Area*, pt. 1, chap. 6.

32. Something similar happened with the fighting in Kosovo in 1999. The exodus of Albanians, which followed the NATO bombing, was generally described in Washington in the vocabulary of the Holocaust, although when pressed the administration recognized that there was no real parallel. See Roland Paris, "Kosovo and the Metaphor War," *Political Science Quarterly*, vol. 117, no. 3 (Fall 2002): 423–450.

33. Novick, *The Holocaust*, p. 99.

34. Ibid., pp. 247–249.

35. William D. Rubenstein, *The Myth of Rescue*, p. 2; see also Novick, *The Holocaust*, pp. 44–45.

36. Cited by Finkelstein, *The Holocaust Industry*, p. 50.

37. Michael R. Marrus, *The Holocaust in History*, pp. 156–183.

38. Examples are given in Rubenstein, *The Myth of Rescue*, pp. 6–8.

39. Cited in Pottier, *Reimagining Rwanda*, p. 32.

40. Ibid., p. 16.

41. On the futility of plans to bomb Auschwitz, see Novick, *The Holocaust,* pp. 54–58, and Rubenstein, *The Myth of Rescue,* pp. 157–181.

42. David S. Wyman, "What Might Have Been Done," in *The Abandonment of the Jews*, p. 335.

43. Cited by Steven L. Burg and Paul S. Shoup, *The War in Bosnia-Herzegovina*, p. 251.

44. Brendan Sims, *Unfinest Hour*; Linda Melven, *A People Betrayed*; and Francois-Xavier Verschave, *Complicité de genocide*.

45. Vladimir Zerjavic, "It Is Worrisome That Presidential Candidate Stipe Mesic with Haste Declares the Hague Verdict to Be Objective," *Vjesnik*, January 19, 2000. See also Maja Freundlich, "Lies Grow on What's Forgotten," *Vjesnik*, November 23, 1999. Not to be outdone, there is the Serb equivalent in the charges of then–federal information minister Goran Matic about Srebrenica. See M. Galic, "Massacre Near Srebrenica Was Staged by French and Muslim Agents," *Politika*, February 12, 2000.

46. Stibon, *Une genocide sur la conscience*, p. 139.

47. Andjelko Perincic, Radio Croatia, March 5, 2000.

48. Arno Mayer, *Why Did the Heavens Not Darken.*

49. Connor Cruise O'Brien, *United Nations: Sacred Drama.*

50. David Chuter, "Munich or the Blood of Others," in Cyril Buffet and Beatrice Heuser, eds., *Haunted by History.*

51. Eric F. Goldman, *The Tragedy of Lyndon Johnson*, pp. 330–331.

52. See Jonathan Glover, *Humanity*, p. 211.

53. Cited by Jeffrey Record, *Perils of Reasoning by Analogy: Munich, Vietnam, and the American Use of Force Since 1945*, Occasional Paper No. 4, Centre for Strategy and Technology, Air War College, 1998 (available online at www.au.af.mil/au/awc.)

54. Ibid.

55. R. J. Crampton, *The Balkans Since the Second World War*, p. 261.

56. Misha Glenny, *The Fall of Yugoslavia*, p. 224.

57. Cited by Burg and Shoup, *The War in Bosnia-Herzegovina*, pp. 230–231.

58. Thomas W. Lippman, "State Dept. Miscalculated on Kosovo," *Washington Post,* April 7, 1999, page A1.

59. See, for example, Michael Dobbs and John M. Goshko, "Albright's Personal Odyssey Shaped Foreign Policy Beliefs," *Washington Post*, December 6, 1996, p. A25, and, more generally, Thomas W. Lippman, *Madeleine Albright and the New American Diplomacy.*

60. Jan Kott, *Shakespeare Our Contemporary*, p. ix.

61. Glenny, *The Fall of Yugoslavia,* p. 36.

62. Burg and Shoup, *The War in Bosnia-Herzegovina*, p. 169.

63. Glenny, *The Fall of Yugoslavia*, p. 122.

64. Antje Krog, *Country of My Skull.*

65. Apparently in an interview in the Croatian Airlines in-flight magazine. Cited by Robert Fisk in his introduction to Brendan O'Shea, *Crisis at Bihac*, p. x. It is, of course, possible that Galbraith was misquoted.

66. On the inability of American thinking to handle realities of ethnicity, and the political consequences of this, see Walker Connor, *Ethnonationalism.*

67. Burg and Shoup, *The War in Bosnia-Herzegovina*, p. 187.

68. The composition of the ABiH—the official army of Bosnia—was multiethnic in theory and to some extent in practice. The best estimates are that by 1994 the percentage of Serbs was down to about 5 percent. They were mostly conscripts given dangerous duties. See ibid., p. 139.

69. Woodard, *Balkan Tragedy*, pp. 298–299.

70. Cited in *Srebrenica: A "Safe" Area*, pt. 1, chap. 9, sec. 10.

71. Melven, *A People Betrayed*, p. 236. Compare Pottier's comment that "I do not claim to have the right to speak *on behalf of* the people of Rwanda." Pottier, *Re-imagining Rwanda*, p. 5 (emphasis in original).

72. See, for example, Wole Soyinka, "Memory, Truth, and Healing," in Ifi Amadiume and Abdullah An-Na'im, *The Politics of Memory*, p. 23. Soyinka argues that the killings were "apparently" modelled on the extermination of the Jews and that their intellectual organizers may have referred to them as the "Final Solution." No evidence is offered for these contentions, and indeed there appears to be none: it is not even clear that the organizers of the 1994 massacres had *heard* of that episode, or if they had that it would have had any resonance in Rwandan politics. Rather, as I am suggesting, popular understandings of the robotic efficiency of the extermination of the Jews were pressed into service to provide a model for what otherwise would have been a frighteningly chaotic and inexplicable episode.

73. Mamdani, *When Victims Become Killers*, p. 195.

74. Pottier, *Re-imagining Rwanda*, p. 2.

75. Tony Waters, "Conventional Wisdom and Rwanda's Genocide," *African Studies Quarterly* 1, no. 3 (1997).

76. *Srebrenica: A "Safe" Area*, introduction to pt. 1.

77. See Max Weber, "Politics as a Vocation," in *From Max Weber*, p. 120.

78. Ibid., p. 121.

5

The Organization

Once a political decision is made to conduct war crimes trials, it is necessary to set up an organization to make that possible. Even if it is decided that the trials will be conducted in an existing court of law, it is still likely that a special prosecutor will have to be set up in light of the peculiar factors that are often involved. Thus, the Australian government established the Special Investigation Unit in 1987 to examine alleged Nazi war criminals in that country and to see whether any should be prosecuted. It had its own historian and other specialists, reflecting the fact that the alleged crimes mostly happened in obscure parts of Eastern Europe decades earlier.

In this example, as in many others, the alleged crimes took place outside the country, the witnesses did not necessarily speak the language of the investigators, and anyone who would testify had to deal with a completely unfamiliar and complex environment. At least, however, the Australian team—like the British and American teams of the same type—was itself generally homogeneous as regards language and experience. The Nuremberg trials following World War II, although multinational in theory, were run by the four victorious powers in Europe, who were able to decide every important issue among themselves. In the Tokyo trials, the control of the United States was almost total. The trial of Adolf Eichmann, which was conducted during the 1960s in Israel and led to his execution, was conducted in Hebrew and under Israeli law.

Trying to Be Multinational

Truly international trials, blending nationalities in the investigation and prosecution teams as well as national procedures and legal systems, are a very recent idea, that is, since the formation of the two ad hoc tribunals for Yugoslavia and Rwanda under the auspices of the United Nations in the early 1990s. Any international judicial organization of this type, paid for by the taxpayers of UN member states and reporting to the UN Security Council directly, must look and feel like an international organization if it is to have wide legitimacy. This gives rise to a number of problems. First, the organization must be located somewhere that is reasonably accessible, where it will be possible to get good staff to serve, and from where investigators can deploy easily. In the case of the ICTY, The Hague was suitable: it was already a diplomatic and international town with a good quality of life, a large expatriate community, international schools, and locals who spoke various languages. It was close to one of the world's best-connected airports and was convenient for accessing the scenes of the crimes. Given the nature of the Rwandan crimes, the only real option was to have a court somewhere in Africa. The court (although not the Office of the Prosecutor) is in Arusha, a safari town in the mountains of Tanzania with no direct flights from the tiny local airport to Europe or to the United Nations in New York. Beautiful as the environment is, it is inconvenient to get to (the usual method is via Amsterdam and Kilimanjaro); it is desperately difficult to get and retain good staff (many senior positions have been vacant for at least some of the year); and support from the Tanzanian government cannot begin, for understandable reasons, to approach that offered by the Netherlands. It is doubtful whether the envisaged Special Court for Sierra Leone will find things any easier, being in a country with few international air links and that, by some measurements, is currently the poorest in the world.

The International Criminal Court, being based in The Hague as well, will benefit from the same practical advantages that the ICTY does, but this court will suffer from the problem of being based in a rich European country while primarily concerned with investigating crimes committed in poor non-European countries. For practical reasons, moreover, it is unlikely to take up many of the invitations offered to it to investigate the activities of the rich Western states, which will be its primary benefactors, and it will have to work hard if it is to convince the majority of states in the world that it is not just another instrument of Western domination. It is at least possible, though, given the troubles in Africa and the fact that so many African nations have signed the ICC Statute, that a local office of some kind will have to be set up somewhere on that continent.

One way to demonstrate that it is genuinely international is to have a truly international staff, which brings its own practical problems. To begin with, the prosecutor of the ICC, like any prosecutor in other institutions, will have to be acceptable to the West. This means the prosecutor must come from one of a relatively small number of nations whose interests are not seen actively to clash with the West's, enjoy the confidence of Western leaders, and not be subject to pressure to launch or conduct investigations in such a way as to threaten Western interests. At the same time, such an individual must be broadly acceptable to the international community as a whole; this person must also possess the personal qualities needed to deal with powerful individuals around the world. This is a tall order, but not the end of the problem, since the same characteristics have to describe the top half-dozen or so posts in the organization. For practical reasons, moreover, an ICC prosecutor is going to have to speak English or learn it rapidly. This is partly because of the demands likely to be made by the public and media, as well as by the need to engage with national governments in everybody's second language. But this also reflects the fact that it will be difficult for the ICC, or any similar organization, not to use English as its primary language of operation. Again, this is not because all of the staff will necessarily speak English but rather because it is likely to be the only language that many of the staff have in common. A chief investigator from Venezuela, for example, conducting a meeting with a lawyer from Botswana and investigators from Japan, Morocco, and Poland will have no choice but to use English as the medium of communication. Assistance from governments is also likely to have to be offered in one of a very small number of languages. Interpretation during trials and of trial documents will have to be kept to a small number of languages for practical and financial reasons. Judges who speak fluent French can probably manage, but in practice they will probably have to learn English as well. It is hard to imagine permanent staff being taken on without having to pass a language test.

In turn, this has political implications. The fact that English will be the main working language means that documents in English, governments that use English, and English-speaking interlocutors are likely to be the most influential. Journalists who speak English will have the best access, and procedures used by English-speaking organizations will gradually come to dominate. It will be very difficult to appoint or promote non–English speakers to a senior level, irrespective of their ability. In practice, this is bound to limit the pool from which the major players are recruited, and the concept and working methods of the organization will reflect the national traditions from which people come.

International organizations do not usually develop organizational cultures of their own: they take them from the cultures of the organizations that are most influential in their formation. Thus, NATO is largely constructed along an Anglo-American model, the European Union largely along a continental European one. Nations at home with the model in use can work better with it and be more influential in it. The ICTY began as an Anglo-American institution and later moved somewhat in the direction of the continental system. Many would say, indeed, that it still influenced by

U.S. practice, notably in the number of administrative motions that clutter every trial. Yet the ICTY has yet to expand its philosophy to include elements of law and procedure from outside the European and U.S. traditions. It is likely that the ICC will act in much the same way, with the result that defendants from, say, a small Asian nation could find the court operating according to procedures and assumptions totally alien to their experience and that of their lawyer.

There are practical problems in trying to assemble a genuinely multinational staff. The investigators will largely be drawn from the ranks of the police. But police forces vary enormously across cultures, and there are no internationally recognized rank equivalents as there are with the military. Moreover, some societies require police to be graduates of law schools, whereas others prefer practical experience. Some police forces are paramilitary, with military ranks and weapons training, whereas others are purely civilian. Some police forces are used to taking the initiative, opening and conducting investigations by themselves, whereas others are primarily the operational arm of the judiciary in their country. Some police forces emphasize management training; others do not. And so on. Putting all this together and setting up an effective investigations process will be a mammoth challenge. (The ICTY had to establish common criteria for measuring qualifications and experience of policemen since otherwise it was impossible to compare them.) Thus, fundamental decisions must be taken about the structure of the ICC's investigations division and how it can function effectively while preserving a multinational ethos.

There will be similar problems with prosecutors. The management task of coordinating a major trial will be enormous, and few governments provide formal management training even for lawyers working in the public service. Prosecutors themselves, of course, come from many traditions, and have different conceptions of their role and objectives, as well as of their relationships to the police and the judiciary. Some are accustomed to directing prosecutions from the beginning, whereas others receive dossiers already compiled by the police. Some countries employ public prosecutors whose salaries may be comparable to those offered by international courts, whereas others employ prosecutors on a professional fee basis, and the latter may have to take a significant pay cut to work in an international court.

In the past, one way of getting round these problems was for nations to make their nationals available to the organizations sponsored by the United Nations for free—what were known as *gratis secondments*—and even to pay an administrative surcharge on top. This was the only way in which the ICTY and ICTR were able to get up and running promptly, but, of course, secondments are expensive, and only a few nations were able to afford to do so. This worried and upset other nations, which felt that their own nationals were being marginalized; this led to a 1998 UN General

Assembly resolution that put an end to secondments and almost derailed several trials and investigations in The Hague. Irrespective of exact arrangements for the ICC (which is not a UN body but rather a treaty-based entity), this problem will recur as long as some nations can contribute resources and others cannot. Much of the infrastructure of the ICTY, for example, has been contributed by Western governments, including two of the three courtrooms and much technical equipment. This has been essential, but it all adds to the sense of domination by a few states. In the case of the Special Court for Sierra Leone, the fact that the operating costs themselves will come from national contributions will make the position even worse.

What It Will Take

International justice is expensive business. The three courtrooms in The Hague, for example, each have a miniature TV studio so that the proceedings can be filmed by a half-dozen remote-controlled cameras; these may be broadcast outside the courtroom and preserved for posterity. Groups of interpreters ensure that the proceedings can be followed in English, French, and that obscure hybrid Bosanski-Hrvatski-Srpski, known in happier times as Serbo-Croat. Computer terminals give everyone in the courtroom a transcript in one of the languages in nearly real-time: after all, a judge might want to intervene to question a witness and cannot wait until the next day to receive a translation. There are also sophisticated arrangements for showing video footage and projecting onto computer screens and TV monitors images of the numerous documents that are used during a trial. Much of the expense and complexity results from the need to ensure public visibility of the process, notably the Internet site: where this is not possible, sophisticated technology is required to digitize the face and voice of a protected witness, and in extreme cases the events in the courtroom can be protected from public view altogether. And, of course, elaborate precautions need to be taken to prevent the attempted rescue or murder of a defendant, including banning from the vicinity of the courtroom anything that could contain a weapon.

The ICC is likely to be even more expensive, not least because of the extra translation efforts that will be required. The existing ad hoc tribunals work reasonably well at the moment in English, French, and the local languages, and networks of translators and interpreters have been built up. Even now, however, ICTY is expanding into an effective fourth language now that Albanian-speaking witnesses are appearing in trials related to Kosovo. But in a decade's time the ICC could find itself handling trials of perpetrators from Africa, Central Asia, and the Arab world. Arabic may be (reasonably) easy to deal with, but there are languages spoken in Africa that are confined to a small geographical area and that hardly anyone outside that region speaks. Things often go wrong, and it is common to hear complaints of mistranslation or even of the wrong translation attached to a document. It is not too much to suppose that some trials in the future will turn on points of translation: there are a number of Asian languages, for example, that allow considerable flexibility in the meaning of words depending on social context. During the hearings of the Truth and Reconciliation Commission in South Africa, members of the security forces were often confronted with documents written in Afrikaans, and they disputed with the commission the significance of the words used and the English translations of them. Of course, the effort of translation and interpretation required in the trial itself is only the tip of the iceberg. Any kind of investigation in the country, and any exploitation of documents or preparation of witnesses, will need massive translation and interpretation efforts as well. How all this would be arranged is unclear. Machine translation of major languages is now possible, and it may be that seized documents, for example, could be scanned and machine-translated to find out if they are worth exploiting. But actual use of documents or witness statements will probably have to be done the old-fashioned way.

All translation and interpretation contains the possibility not only of error but also conscious or unconscious bias. In Bosnia, for example, the fighting partly took the form of a classic struggle between the sophisticated center and the more conservative, separatist periphery. The Muslims, being more town-dwellers than the others, were more likely to learn English and so provided most of the interpreters for UNPROFOR. There have been accusations that this led to bias, though nothing has ever been proved and it seems unlikely. But it does illustrate the potential pitfalls, which are more likely as the languages involved become more specialized. It is possible, for example, that in a poor African country a few days of working for the ICC could equate to weeks, or even months, of a typical salary, and there may be a long queue of hopeful interpreters making unverifiable promises about the accuracy of their translation. (It is possible, of course, that some of them may be working for local intelligence services.)[1] Such problems may already be occurring in Arusha. Because of the dearth of interpreters between English and Kinyarwanda, interpretation is usually first into French and then into English. In cases of doubt, judges go back to the French text, because it is closer to the original. But virtually all of the interpreters are from Rwanda, and so they will be either Hutu (who might sympathize with the accused) or Tutsi (who might sympathize with the witness). As far as anyone can tell, there has been no deliberate attempt to distort translations or interpretations, but it is impossible to be sure.

As well as investigators, judges, prosecutors, translators, technical experts, and security personnel, an international court will require other disciplines, some of them rare and expensive. Most investigations of war crimes amount, in effect, to the investigation of a type of organized crime. Even if the perpetrators are known, they are unlikely to have been operating on their own initiative, and so any investigation has to go up the political and military command chain that gave the orders. At this level, special skills are required, well beyond those of ordinary police; the most important is intelligence analysis. Good criminal analysts and criminal intelligence specialists, however, are scarce, even in advanced societies, and to recruit enough for the ICC, especially given the need to address very different societies and political cultures at the same time, will be difficult. On the military side, specialized military analysts are also a scarce resource, concentrated in a relatively few nations. But their contribution can be fundamental: in the *Krstic* trial, for example, much of the success of the case depended upon painstaking analysis of captured documents of the army of the Bosnian Serb Republic, as well as other sources, to build up a picture of how the Drina Corps actually conducted operations, as well as the commander's own role. Forensic evidence is becoming increasingly important in war crimes trials, and some disciplines within it have only a handful of practitioners in the world.

The ICC, even more than the ad hoc tribunals, will operate in a political context, and it can be assumed that intelligence services from various countries will try to penetrate the organization. Partly this might be for general interest and to see whether its investigations threaten to embarrass them politically. But the intelligence services of nations under threat of investigation are unlikely to stop at mere collection of information: they will seek to disrupt investigations wherever they can. They may do this by planting agents inside the ICC, by mounting technical attacks, by trying to disrupt investigations in country, or some combination of these. They may seek to bribe or intimidate investigators and potential witnesses and try to find out likely targets of investigation to shield them. Made up of isolated individuals far from home, often with a lifestyle beyond their experience, such an organization is a dream target for intelligence officers. (In 1999, NATO conducted Operation Westar, aimed at breaking up illegal Bosnian Croat intelligence operations in Bosnia, directed against the ICTY and other elements of the international community.)[2] The ICC will therefore need a counterintelligence capability, including the ability to screen potential recruits, mount security investigations on current personnel, and produce its own threat assessments in various countries. Sensitive investigations will require thought and planning in regard to staff. Moreover, in most of the countries in which the ICC is likely to operate, information about useful contacts, potential witnesses, and incriminating documents is likely to be expensive to acquire. The organization will have to have a capability to purchase information (as happens in many domestic jurisdictions anyway) and, in certain cases, use outright bribery.

Many cases will depend on the use of protected witnesses, whose face and voice may be digitized, their identity hidden behind a number. But such witnesses must be contacted in a discreet fashion, then transported, perhaps a long distance, to give evidence. They will then have to be reinserted into their communities without anyone knowing they have been away. Almost by definition such witnesses will be survivors or eyewitnesses of atrocities. They may well be traumatized, and they will be asked to give evidence in an unfamiliar environment, through interpretation, and perhaps be aggressively cross-examined about their experiences. Many such witnesses will never have left their hometown before this, and they will need careful handling and protection by experts to ensure their own welfare as well as their utility in a trial.

The biggest problem the ICC will face is to rapidly develop expertise in the politics and society of areas where it will mount an investigation. The two ad hoc tribunals took several years to develop expertise in their limited geographical areas and are refining it all the time. Moreover, in both cases governments had been studying the problems for some time and were in a position to help. The ICC is unlikely to have the leisure to spend months developing expertise in a country before deciding to open an investigation, and it may do so in an area that is not a priority for major governments, on which there is little hard information that can be used. Almost certainly, it will have to establish some kind of political analysis section to interact with governments, NGOs, and others to identify areas of trouble and develop expertise quickly. But it is simply not practical for the ICC to develop and retain expertise on every potential crisis area: it would require a huge organization, much of which would be without work for nearly all of the time. It seems likely that some kind of modular system will have to be used, including standby arrangements that would allow rapid strengthening of the prosecutor's organization with experts in a particular area. In addition, following the example being set by the Special Court for Sierra Leone, the ICC will rely on formal or informal groups of academic experts, former diplomats, and others who are not employees but will be asked to participate when needed.

Because of the context in which it will operate, the ICC will have to cultivate a good political sense and the ability to withstand massive political pressure. Justice should be blind, but as we have seen, in practice none of us believes that the law can be enforced in an objective fashion, without regard to political factors. There are many groups, as well as individuals in the media and elsewhere, for whom the investigation of a political enemy or popular hate-figure would be an objective in itself, irrespective of an indictment. We can therefore expect attempts to manipulate the court for political reasons, often supported by the media and special interest groups. It can be expected that draft indictments will be prepared and circulated on the Internet, with mass campaigns to persuade the ICC to take them up. Politicians and journalists will bring victims and relatives to The Hague for publicized meetings with the prosecutor; activists will chain themselves to railings and go on hunger strikes until an investigation is opened. The prosecutor will be angrily questioned by aggressive journalists about why so-and-so has yet to be indicted, amid suggestions that political pressure is to blame. Children of victims will be encouraged to cry on cue in front of cameras outside the building while "the ICC does nothing."

Although there are strict limitations on the prosecutor's freedom of action—an investigation requires the approval of judges, for example—the ICTY example suggests that the scope for imaginative abuse of the organization will be significant. Human rights groups will present dossiers for comment and express horror and incredulity when an investigation is not launched straight away. The court's advisory opinion will be sought on contentious trials of political enemies. It may be invited to send observers to a controversial trial or be asked to provide an independent opinion about its propriety. The success of the organization will therefore depend on whether the prosecutor and the senior staff are prepared to face down this kind of pressure and put journalists and special interest groups in their place. If this does not happen, the court will degenerate into a political football, kicked in every direction by political pressure.

What It Will Need

In the general euphoria over the apparent triumph of international criminal law and the signature of the ICC Statute, it is often forgotten that the key to the success of the ICC is the ability to gather evidence, arrest suspects, and gain convictions. If it cannot accomplish these missions, then it is a waste of time and money. The most elaborate organization, the finest staff, and the most perfect procedures will all be pointless unless practical arrangements can be put in place to make these three very difficult things happen. As I have noted, it is indeed surprising how many people seem to see the ICC Statute as an end in itself; they assume that the practical problems will somehow solve themselves.

Life has not been easy for the ad hoc tribunals, even with their narrow focus and considerable political support. The Balkans region was a major foreign policy priority for the major nations of the world for a decade. The ICTY receives massive assistance from states, in The Hague and on the ground, and there are some 12,000 troops in Bosnia with the ability to operate reasonably freely. In Rwanda, the representatives of the victims are now the government, with control of the territory and many of the presumed perpetrators in prison (although the most senior ones generally escaped). Yet enormous practical difficulties in each case have slowed progress considerably.

The ICC will be in a much worse state. Even to begin an investigation, investigators will require access to the sites of alleged atrocities and to potential witnesses. Since it is likely that a conflict will be in progress at the time, this may not be possible at an acceptable degree of risk. (Arranging for the killing of investigators, of course, would be a good way for a state to stop an investigation into its actions.) There may be so many practical constraints—deliberate or otherwise—on the investigator's freedom of action that no useful work can be done. If the conflict is over, or in abeyance, the situation will not necessarily be any easier. All the evidence (e.g., from Kosovo in 1999) suggests that there is no substitute for prompt access to a crime scene by investigators. If a government or controlling faction is being investigated, then it will have every opportunity to delay the issue of visas, for example, while evidence is destroyed and witnesses disappear. A government that wishes to appear cooperative can follow the example of Croatia and raise innumerable obstacles while professing its desire to help. A government that does not care about appearing cooperative could simply refuse investigators entry, and there is not much anyone could do about that. In theory, major governments could put pressure on recalcitrants to cooperate, but this is not the kind of thing that can be done too often, and experience with both Serbia and Croatia suggests that it is not effective anyway. Even if a state formally cooperates and makes no effort to destroy evidence, for example, there are a thousand ways in which an investigation can be slowed down or even halted without it being too obvious.

A more common situation: alleged atrocities may have been committed in an area that is not under immediate government control. It may be impossible for investigators to enter and work there; indeed, the sites may actually be in an area of conflict. Thus, any evidence of atrocities may have vanished by the time the investigators arrive; even if it remains, evidence may have been adulterated by the fighting and be useless. Witnesses may have been killed; maybe they fled or simply vanished. But it is unlikely that investigators, even if they could somehow be inserted and protected while a conflict was in progress, would actually be able to work to a standard that would produce evidence that might convince a court. In the case of exhumations, for example, days may be consumed in finding the exact site and more days consumed in examining and recording the contents of even a small grave.

In Bosnia and Kosovo, the ICTY has been able to carry out investigations and exhumations under the protection of NATO-led troops. In Croatia, protection has, to varying degrees, been provided by local police. But this is not easy or straightforward. Possible graves, for example, must be protected twenty-four hours a day to prevent tampering, and investigators, as well as their vehicles and equipment, must be given round-the-clock protection. It is not just a question of safety: if a grave is left unguarded during the night, it cannot later be proved that something found the next day was not, in fact, planted during the night. But this is a major task, and even a sympathetic government may not have the resources or political will to put its own troops or police in danger for days or weeks to enable foreign experts to work. There are many similar problems.

One answer is for foreign troops to escort investigators to a country. But in practice there are obstacles. Even if a state is willing to assist in this way, it may have little experience; reconnaissance, the selection of entry points, setting up of logistic facilities, and communications would all be necessary preliminaries. Even if the local political authorities were cooperative, and some practical support was provided, a huge amount of baggage would have to be brought along, including ground transportation, recording equipment, and specialist equipment such as heat sensors for locating graves. Interpreters and experts on local conditions would be needed to question any witnesses. Enough troops would have to be sent to completely sanitize an area where investigations were taking place. It is by no means obvious that many states would be prepared to act in this way, or that their parliaments and publics would allow it. There would be an understandable fear that a force of this kind could be attacked or provoked into fighting—with potentially disastrous results. If fighting were actually in progress, it is inconceivable that a force of this kind would be sent, even if the investigators were actually in a position to work.

It is true that some investigation can be carried out without being on the ground. Refugees can be questioned away from the fighting or in another country (as happened in Macedonia in 1999). Aerial photography over a period of time may reveal, for example, where fresh graves have been dug. But a grave is only a grave and indicates only that bodies have been buried. It does not imply that these bodies are the result of an atrocity: they may be battle casualties or civilians caught in the cross fire. But it is doubtful whether any persuasive evidence could be gathered except by being on the ground. Given the tendency of conflicts these days to drag on for years, there may be little of any value by the time investigators actually arrive. In conflicts in those areas bodies may not be buried anyway, and will tend to decay quickly in the heat and humidity.

The ICC will be totally dependent on the cooperation of states if it is to have any clients at all. It will have no enforcement capability of its own and may find that it has indicted, for example, rebel leaders who are hundreds of kilometers from the capital and protected by heavily armed followers; or perhaps they have taken refuge in a neighboring state. Likewise, by the time of trial, witnesses may have been killed or displaced by new fighting, and locating them, in a country where perhaps people do not usually carry much identification, where names may depend on clan and location rather than parentage, and illiteracy is common, could be an impossible task, even if local authorities are cooperative.

Structure and Philosophy

Pursuing criminals is not easy in practical terms, but conceptually it is straightforward. A crime is reported, investigations are made, and a case is built against someone to justify an arrest warrant. There is seldom much argument about whether a crime has been committed or what type of crime it is. But where war crimes are concerned, things are not simple.

The mere fact that the bodies have been found does not mean a crime has been committed. Even bodies of women and children dead in a violent fashion do not show that a crime has been committed, except if there is other evidence suggesting that they were neither combatants nor innocents caught in a cross fire. Thus, a separate investigation must first be carried out to discover even *whether* a crime was committed, since it will be necessary to prove that first. In some cases, the evidence may be conjectural, not the kind that policemen deal with on a daily basis. For example, correspondence and signal logs seized from the headquarters of a militia group may show that reports of atrocities by their own forces were received from time to time. They may also show that instructions were sent back to investigate and punish. Whether a serious investigation should be launched will depend on an assessment of whether the commander concerned carried out his or her duty properly and, if not, whether a court could be convinced that he or she had failed to do so.

There are two basic philosophical approaches to carrying out complex investigations of this type. The first, which is closer to traditional police investigations, is to investigate the circumstances of an alleged crime and to identify the perpetrators. After that, the investigation can continue up the ladder until all of the perpetrators have been accounted for. This does not necessarily mean that all the perpetrators at each level will be indicted and tried, but it does mean that every new investigation has to build on the foundations of a previous one. The difficulty arises near the top of the ladder, since the nature of the crime, and the nature of the individual's involvement in it, will change. At the lowest level, a perpetrator is the one who pulled the trigger. The next level up is the perpetrator who gave the order to fire. After that is the officer who gave the orders to destroy a village, then the person who gave the orders to clean out a whole area, and so forth. At the very top of the ladder, a political figure may simply have been briefed, without objection, in vague terms by a general that something unpleasant was contemplated. Even if a crime occurred on the ground, the form of the indictment will look different in each case. At the lowest level, forensic and identification evidence may be needed. But at the highest level, the prosecution will have to deploy sophisticated political analysis, as well as insiders who can explain how decisions were actually taken. Captured documents may also be of great importance.

An alternative model is to pick targets of investigation and to seek to build cases against them. In practice, this can be done only if there are crimes to which investigators can attempt to link these new targets, and so it would be difficult to begin the operations of a court with an approach like this. However, this strategy acknowledges the fact that no court can pursue every perpetrator and therefore will always concentrate on the most important figures. Taking a more strategic view can reduce the amount of work, but it can also encourage investigators to carry on while getting nowhere in the hope that things will turn up and to justify the time and effort that has already been spent. It can also be criticized as implicitly putting into question the idea that someone is innocent until proven guilty. Finally, there will be enormous interest in individuals whom the ICC is planning to investigate, and leaks and sheer speculation will receive much publicity, making the investigation much more difficult. In practice, the political desire to go after senior figures means that the ICC will probably have to adopt this approach, at least some of the time, which will have practical consequences for the structure and the personnel policy of the organization.

There are two broad approaches to investigating alleged crimes. One is for the police to do the investigation, to assemble a case, and to present it to the lawyers. This is the system traditionally used in Anglo-Saxon countries, and it was the system that the ICTY largely used at first. The other approach is for the lawyers to be involved from the beginning and to direct the course of the investigation at all stages. This approach is closer to that used in Europe, and the ICTY has moved progressively in this direction over the years as a result of experience and complex cases. The current chief of investigations, for example, is for the first time, not a policeman but a French lawyer.

Likewise, there are two possible philosophies of prosecution. One is to set the bar as high as possible on the basis that any charge will be brought if there is a decent chance of proving it. The other is more cautious, bringing only those charges that are highly likely to be proved. These two philosophies have different practical consequences. In the first, trials might take much longer and require more resources. But there are also political consequences: in the first case, a Western hate-figure might be acquitted on a large number of charges and gain much political credibility as a result.

Organizations are both more and less than words and diagrams on paper. They are more because they either work or don't work for reasons of management and organizational culture, and this culture is correspondingly more important than any written procedures or diagrams. They are also less because even what is written may well not be achieved unless the organizational culture makes the system work. This is especially the case with multinational organizations, which are notoriously difficult to manage and operate properly. Moreover, organizations consist of people, and many of the ICC's employees will be carrying out gruesome work under harsh conditions far from their families for weeks and months at a time. They will have to be looked after carefully, or they will leave.

Money and organization are important. Almost everyone who has worked in a large organization knows the inbuilt tensions that exist between the operational and the administrative sides. Both are important, of course, but the operational side of any organization is its justification. The problem is that organizations often don't appreciate this, or at least they act as if they don't. Almost everything about the operation of large organizations comes down to money, even more so with internationally funded organizations, where battles over funding are endless. The two ad hoc tribunals were set up by the United Nations and work within the UN administrative structure. In hindsight, not everybody thinks this was a good idea. One former tribunal official commented that "the good news was that we had an administrative structure when we started. The bad news was that it was the UN's."

When Richard Goldstone was appointed as prosecutor in 1994, most of his early struggles were to do with money, and he relates how he had assumed that the tribunal "which was a suborgan of the Security Council and established by the unanimous vote of its members, would be adequately funded and well supported by the international body. That, unfortunately, turned out to be a naïve assumption."[3] Goldstone even had to pay his own fare to be briefed about the job in New York. This is not a trivial issue. Discontent with pay and allowances, the slow reimbursement of expenses, and difficulty in getting equipment and resources all hurt morale. (It has taken, on average, three months for newly appointed staff in Arusha to be paid.) Niggles about air travel and hotels are important, as anyone who has traveled on business knows; they also have implications for how people perceive the organization as valuing (or not valuing) them. Similarly, since the ICC will be a long-term organization, it will have to attract and retain good people by giving them reasonable career prospects as well as adequate salaries and conditions of service. This will probably be difficult to combine with due attention to diversity at the top, and so there will always be the risk of an exodus of staff at the middle and higher levels. And a truism of organizations is that the best people go first. There will inevitably be institutional tensions between the different functional areas, exacerbated by how they are viewed by the outside world. It still seems strange to many people in The Hague, for example, that most of the early international attention and even government lobbying was focused on the appointment of judges, who had nothing at all to do for several years, rather than on investigations staff, without whom the judges would continue to have nothing to do. Indications are that the ICC may be making the same mistake.

In the Details

Much of the operating system of an international organization is hidden away in its detailed rules and regulations. In the case of the two ad hoc tribunals and the ICC, these are the Rules of Procedure and Evidence (RPE), which govern the way the courts work in terms of the application of the law, as well as in a procedural and administrative sense. Because the ad hoc tribunals were set up quickly, the RPE were left for the organizations to determine, and they have been revised and enlarged by the judges on a number of occasions as new problems were encountered. The RPE of the ICC, by contrast, were negotiated among states in the normal way, and the greater influence of states is reflected in the details. Moreover, the much greater leisure available for negotiation of the ICC Statute means that some of the issues covered in the RPE of the ad hoc tribunals are to be found in the ICC Statute. These are large documents, and much of their content is very technical, but it is worth giving a few examples of the kinds of practical issues they address.

Many of the rules have to do with the administration of trials. They cover, for example, definitions and languages, procedures for amending the rules, how judges are appointed and disqualified, what happens when judges are absent, arrangements for electing the president of the judges, and so forth. They cover the organization of the various parts of the court, the responsibilities and powers of officials, and the bureaucracy that is needed. They also cover more fundamental issues such as the conduct of investigation, the rights of suspects during investigations, arrangements for detention, the issue of indictments, and how suspects are to be arrested. In some cases, rules have been added—especially at The Hague—to reflect experience gained, and the Hague RPE has been amended about two dozens times.

One example is the new ICTY Rule 65, which covers the responsibilities of the pretrial judge. Over the years, the ICTY has tried to shorten trials by managing them better and by disposing of as much detail as possible before the trial starts. Thus, judges now require the defense and prosecution to identify the factual points that are agreed and in dispute. A pretrial judge is appointed for each case and is responsible, for example, for ensuring that the prosecution and defense submit pretrial briefs in good time and that they provide lists of witnesses they intend to call, the time it is envisaged that this will take, and the points each witness will cover, as well as any exhibits and documents they intend to introduce. This kind of arrangement speeds up trials.

Several rules have been introduced to protect the position of governments offering assistance to the tribunal. In theory, article 29 of the ICTY Statute (article 28 in the case of Rwanda), with the force of a Security Council resolution behind it, requires states to cooperate with the tribunals and to provide any assistance that is required. (By contrast, the similar provision in the ICC Statute is a political agreement between states, not a requirement imposed by the Security Council.) But it was clear from the beginning that governments would be reluctant to make information available too freely unless they had adequate assurances about the way in which it would be handled. In this case, the tribunal was very much in the hands of governments, since there were few actual sanctions if states declined to cooperate. In any event, since governments know what information they hold and the tribunal does not, governments will always have the upper hand. The mechanism for resolving this dilemma has been ICTY Rule 70 ("Matters not Subject to Disclosure"); subrule B says in part:

> If the Prosecutor is in possession of information which has been provided . . . on a confidential basis and which has been used solely for the purpose of generating new evidence, that initial information and its origin shall not be disclosed . . . without the consent of the person or entity providing the initial information.

Thus, governments can provide background analytical information to assist with the investigation in the confidence that they control how the prosecutor uses it thereafter and particularly that the prosecutor cannot use the information as evidence without the agreement of the government. This ensures that the prosecutor has access to information that would otherwise not be available and also protects the positions of governments that wish to be helpful. Moreover, Rule 70 also states that if the material is actually used, the trial chamber cannot force either party to produce additional evidence from the same source; nor may it do so on its own behalf or order witnesses to appear to enlarge on it. And if the prosecutor calls a witness to introduce the material in evidence, the judges cannot force the witness to answer questions if that strays into confidential areas. These are limitations on the freedom of the judges to control the trial and do what they want in their own courtroom, but they do allow governments to help the process in ways that would otherwise be impossible. Even though material offered under this rule is not intended for use as evidence, it can still be of great value in helping investigations and making them more effective. The real problems arise as the trial approaches. Although the provision of information under Rule 70 does not mean that it can *never* be used in court, it does mean that the prosecutor can never count on the material being available; therefore the prosecutor never really knows, until the last minute, what the strength of the case might be.

A second example is ICTY Rule 54 as amended ("Orders Directed to States for the Production of Documents"). The original Rule 54 allowed a judge to "issue such orders, summonses, subpoenas, warrants and transfer orders" as necessary. In 1997, the *Blaskic* trial chamber made such an order, at the request of the prosecution, for the Croatian government to produce some material from the archives of the Bosnian Croat forces. The government of Croatia objected to producing this material on the grounds that its national security would be compromised. The trial chamber decided nonetheless that it did have the power to issue subpoenas to states for the production of documents, in spite of security objections.[4] The government of Croatia was uncooperative with The Hague (and ignored the subpoena), but the ruling appeared to give judges the right to issue subpoenas to even the most helpful and cooperative states without giving states the right to be heard in turn. This alarmed many states, and it was doubtful whether this was a good idea. It is unlikely, after all, that any group of judges would have the necessary experience to evaluate the security consequences of producing sensitive material.

The new rule preserved the right of judges to make such an order, but only after a hearing where the state could be represented and analyzing a series of factors. In particular, the judges had to satisfy themselves that every effort had been made to acquire the information in a cooperative fashion. The rule also provides for various safety measures to be used, such as in camera hearings (that is, hearings that are not open to the public) and the production of redacted (edited) documents. The rule specifically does not allow states to be the final arbiters of what will be released to the court, since that would simply enable a noncompliant state to plead national security objections whenever it wished. (In the earlier example, it was generally agreed that the Croats were more concerned about embarrassment to the Tudjman regime than national security.) When the issue came to the ICC negotiations in Rome, however, the result was different, the product of political bargaining. Article 72 of the ICC Statute describes a similar process, but one that ends with the state itself having the final word. Likewise, article 93(4) of the ICC Statute enables a state to "decline a request for assistance . . . if the request concerns the production of any documents or disclosure of evidence which relates to its national security." This approach was supported by the United States, France, and some Asian countries (although not by the United Kingdom). This approach reflected U.S. sensitivity about giving an international institution powers over it, but it also reflected domestic practice in some countries. French officials pointed out, for example, that under French law the state has the final word on such issues.

Conclusion

It cannot be stressed enough that even mundane issues of international justice actually make the difference between success and failure. This applies to any future court, including the ICC, as well as the ad hoc tribunals and special courts set up by the United Nations. There is a temptation to think that the biggest issues facing the ICC have been settled. That may be true to an extent, but the really critical issues have not been resolved. A functioning organization may yet be built, but there is nothing to guarantee that at the moment.

Notes

1. The interpreters who worked for Dutchbat in Srebrenica were observed from time to time visiting the offices of the intelligence branch of the 28th Division, presumably to be debriefed. See Nederlands Instituut vor Oorlogsdocumentatie, *Srebrenica: A "Safe" Area*, pt. 3, chap. 5, sec. 9.

2. See NATO/SFOR Press Release of 17 December 1999, *Operation Westar: Preliminary Results* (at http://www.nato.int/sfor/sfor-at-work/opwestar/t991216a.htm).

3. Richard J. Goldstone, *For Humanity*, p. 77.

4. *Blaskic* (IT-95–14), *Decision on the Objection of the Republic of Croatia to the Issuance of Subpoena Duces Tecum*, July 18, 1997.

6

The Investigation

I n this chapter, I examine the difficulties and complexities surrounding the investigation of war crimes allegations, turning them into specific charges, and then finding evidence to support the charges that will stand up in a court of law. I explain why war crimes investigators must work to a much higher standard of proof than the media and human rights groups, since investigations must be directed toward the production of material that makes the guilt of an accused not likely, or even probable, but rather certain beyond a reasonable doubt.

Obvious Guilt

The first difficulty is political. Where strong emotions are involved (as with atrocities and war crimes), many tend to want justice—or at least revenge—quickly, and some are intolerant of the bureaucratic necessities of uncovering the evidence, issuing warrants, and conducting trials. This problem seems endemic in war crimes trials, because in almost all cases the guilt of the accused is publicly assumed, and the trial itself is seen merely as a way of providing a cloak of legality for the desire to exact revenge. When reality intervenes, as it did in the projected trial of Kaiser Wilhelm II in 1919, the result may be panic and confusion. So it was foreseeable that, as late as May 1945, after months of discussion about the fate of the Nazi leaders, "no real thought had been given to the difficulties of extracting sufficient high-quality evidence . . . to make a conviction look plausible." In turn, this was because earlier discussion had been "based on the assumption of guilt."[1] Indeed, it was universally assumed in the Allied capitals that the German leadership would be put to death: They had better be convicted of serious crimes; there had better be a court; and someone had better find some evidence that would, indeed, make the inevitable convictions seem legitimate. This habit of thought—sentence first, trial later—has continued today and represents the most significant barrier to a fair and objective legal process. But the war crimes judicial process must be conducted in such a way as not to prejudice wider political objectives. Unsafe convictions before courts established for political reasons certainly come in this dangerous category, irrespective of how far they may satisfy the vicarious lust for revenge on the part of foreigners, the desire to use trials for transparently political ends, and the teaching of edifying lessons.

Sometimes, this urge is made explicit. Thus, a distinguished British human rights lawyer apparently thought in early 1999 that the ICTY was intended to "try those guilty of crimes against humanity in the former Yugoslavia." If the guilt of indictees can be taken for granted in advance, it is not surprising that the same figure can advocate, by extension, the immediate arrest of Slobodan Milosevic, against whom there were then no charges, or explain that Milosevic and others would be put on trial "for the crimes they had committed." As a correspondent to *The Independent* protested subsequently, the "point of a trial is to establish whether a person has in fact committed crimes. The point of an investigation is to establish whether there has been a crime and reveal any evidence."[2] Sometimes the connection is less overt. No act of the West during the Rwandan tragedy has been so deplored as the deployment of forces (mostly French) to protect Hutu fleeing into what was then Zaire from the vengeance of the Tutsi. The subtext of these protests is clear: these people were collectively guilty of the appalling massacres of the Tutsi earlier the same year. Western troops should thus have stood by and cheered as they were massacred in their turn. (Those who escaped to Zaire were dismissed as "a cancer" by the former U.S. diplomat Chester Crocker.)[3] When the Hutu fugitives were themselves massacred in 1996, many commentators simply repeated the line from Kigali that "all Hutu refugees are genocidal extremists who collectively deserved their fate."[4] The idea that alleged perpetrators should be arrested, tried, and sentenced only if guilty does not, by and large, enter the picture.

This kind of humanitarian vigilantism is partly understandable when we think of the sheer horror of what is seen, or at least believed, about atrocities, and few people will deny occasionally thinking that death would be too mild a punishment for some reported horror or other. And very often the urge to believe that an individual is guilty—or at least responsible—is overwhelming. It's easy to sit in court in The Hague, for example, and look at some of the defendants—sinister looking middle-aged men with black shirts and sunglasses—and think, *You're obviously guilty.* But you can't run a respectable system of international justice on that basis. Also important, however, is the confusion and ignorance—even on the part of some lawyers—about what needs to be proved in a court and so what kind of investigation needs to be carried out. It is to this issue that I now turn.

Evidence and Evidence

The definition of individual criminal responsibility in the statutes of the two ad hoc tribunals is as follows:

> A person who planned, instigated, ordered, committed or otherwise aided and abetted in the planning, preparation or execution of a crime . . . shall be individually responsible for the crime.[5]
> The fact that any of the acts . . . was committed by a subordinate does not relieve his superior of criminal responsibility if he knew or had reason to know that the subordinate was about to commit such acts or had done so and the superior failed to take the necessary and reasonable measures to prevent such acts or to punish the perpetrators thereof.[6]

This, therefore, is what the prosecutor will be trying to show, and this is what the collection of evidence must be geared toward. The fact that someone is an unpleasant person, or has extreme views, or has publicly praised the commission of atrocities, or advocated them in the past, does not automatically mean that he or she has committed a crime within the meaning of the two statutes. Statements or writings of politicians, especially in a democracy, often seek to appeal to a dominant mood or climb on a passing bandwagon and are not always indicative of their current views, let alone future intentions. What Nuremberg described as crimes against peace are not currently being prosecuted, and we must resist the temptation to assume that states or rulers who we may judge "responsible" for conflicts are necessarily guilty of what are now regarded as crimes, as well. This is especially important since words like *guilt*, *evidence*, and *proof* are thrown around freely in everyday speech; and many organizations, in the media and elsewhere, carry out what they call "investigations." Such language has a wide variety of meanings, but I will concentrate on three areas here that overlap with war crimes investigations to some extent: academic research, the media, and human rights advocacy.

At any level above that of the immediate perpetrator, there will be a political background to the commission of war crimes. And even a thug who murders and tortures may do so out of a desire to revenge a real or imagined wrong from the past. Thus, no trial can take place in a historical vacuum, and courts have often invoked specialist academics and consultants to help them. The *Kordic* trial featured a lively debate about the existence of a Bosnian national consciousness in early modern times. But such debates are unlikely ever to be settled. This is partly because debate is a fundamental part of academic research, but mainly because the sort of questions that academic historians address are complex and multifaceted, and in most cases the evidence—such as it is—is not conclusive. For example, the political history of Rwanda after the 1959 revolution, the rise of the Hutu Power movement, as well as the relationship of the Habyarimana government to that which succeeded him after his murder in 1994 are complex issues that academic experts will grapple with for decades to come—and where much of the evidence is itself ambiguous. Yet attempts to show preplanning and government involvement in the mass killings of Tutsi depend, to some extent, on answers to these questions.

A useful comparator is, again, the intentionalist-functionalist debate about Hitler's role in the Holocaust. The scholarly consensus appears to be settling on the conclusion that there is something to be said on both sides: that ideas for the extermination of the Jews had been around for some time and were held, with varying emphasis, by Hitler and others, but the actual planning and execution were episodic and partly driven by bureaucratic politics. Clearly, if Hitler had ever been put on trial, such a conclusion would have been impossible to use as evidence one way or the other, but it does fairly represent the confused situation at the time as well as the nature of the evidence that remains. (This is why conspiracy featured so heavily in the Nuremberg indictments, since it is then only necessary to prove guilt by association.) The problem is that proof of this kind of scholarly judgment *beyond a reasonable doubt* is almost by definition impossible and, in practice, is never pursued: even the fiercest proponent of a particular historical interpretation will generally concede that there is something to be said against it as well.

But judgments of this kind are important for the resolution of some major war crimes cases. Thus, the *Kosovo* indictment against Milosevic and others alleges that the crimes listed were committed as part of a "joint criminal enterprise"—that is, a conspiracy—that aimed at among others things "the expulsion of a substantial proportion of the Kosovo Albanian population from the territory of the province of Kosovo in an effort to ensure continued Serbian control over the province."[7] Conceptually, it will be clear, this question is very similar to the intentionalist-functionalist controversy described above, and one can imagine it being treated by scholars in much the same way. Some will point to a history of atavistic Serb desires to reconquer the province, note that Milosevic began his political career as a nationalist there, and stress that forced depopulation did in fact occur. Others will argue that the link between public statements and events on the ground is very tenuous and that the deportations themselves were primarily related to combat operations against the Kosovo Liberation Army (KLA). An eventual consensus might emerge that there is some evidence, although not in itself decisive, of a degree of prior planning of the forced depopulations. But judges in The Hague, in this and similar cases, will have to reach firm conclusions on whether such a conspiracy existed and, if so, what its aims were. And they will have to be sure beyond a reasonable doubt of such conclusions.[8]

In principle, therefore, investigators must address issues that are more normally the province of historians. But the opposite is also true: books, whether by academic historians or journalists, are often believed to contain evidence that can be useful in trials. This is sometimes true, but it often amounts to what philosophers call a category error: books might be written to elucidate, to draw attention to problems, or to promote particular agendas, but few are ever written to offer proof of misdeeds beyond a reasonable doubt, and it is not easy to see how they could. Yet several books have been written setting out cases against individuals and effectively demanding an immediate trial of them. Some of these are relatively light-hearted (such as Christopher Hitchens's indictment of Henry Kissinger), but others less so.[9]

The problem is greater with the more evanescent medium of journalism, yet it is surprising how frequently media stories and books by journalists are quoted as evidence of guilt. Journalists sometimes see and hear things that are of interest to investigators, and some have been called to give evidence in trials. But their evidence is usually a small part of a mosaic that is built up to give a court an impression of, say, the degree of control that a warlord exercised in a certain area. It is not a criticism of the media to say that its priorities are different from those of courts and investigators. The rationale of journalists is to get a story and then get that story distributed. Expressing uncertainty about whether atrocities took place, or doubts about who was responsible, do not help. Because of the demands of time and space, strong, simple depictions of events without qualifications or equivocation will be preferred. High casualty figures will be preferred to low ones, even if they are speculative; colorful expressions will be preferred to prosaic or technical ones; and extravagant claims will be preferred to tentative ones. (Thus, the American journalist Roy Gutman claimed in 1992 that *every* woman aged fifteen to twenty-five remaining in Bosnia-Herzegovina had by then been raped.[10]) Every effort will be made to link incidents to names of people the audience may have heard, no matter how tenuous the link, and to personalize issues that might otherwise seem abstract.

In addition, because of the limitations that the media work under, shorthand comparisons are often used to convey what busy and often inexpert journalists want their busy and poorly informed audiences to understand. Partly this is done by the use of the usual shorthand labels: moderate, extremist, terrorist, pro-Western, and so on. But sometimes it is done by the deliberate or unconscious use of historical examples that will resonate with an audience: the Killing Fields, the Holocaust, Concentration Camps, the Gulag, the Butcher of Somewhere. Of all these, it is the imagery of the destruction of European Jewry that is the most powerful, and it is one that journalists often turn to. Journalists are aware that "stories evoking similarities to the World War II holocaust experience are more likely to evoke public interest, political debate—and hence draw a continuing or even expanded focus as newsworthy."[11] Sometimes it is hard to know whether the reference is deliberate or unconscious. Thus, one journalist writing about Kosovo (using "The Killing Fields" as the title of his article) described the scene in Kosovo as "systematic orchestrated evil" carried out by "Slobodan Milosevic's willing executioners."[12] This is, of course, a reference to Goldhagen's book *Hitler's Willing Executioners*. It is not clear whether the journalist (consciously or not) intended this reference to a book that most readers had never heard of. But for those readers who *did* pick up the reference, a legal and moral equivalence was set up that later investigation showed to be unfounded. Sometimes, the analogy is even made with imaginary events rather than real ones. In Kosovo a number of individuals, including Hillary Rodham Clinton, the former first lady and current U.S. senator, individually or collectively decided that scenes reminded them of the film *Schindler's List*. Here, therefore, the comparison is not with a historical incident but with a Hollywood version of a fictional treatment of a historical incident.[13]

It is probably unfair to suggest that journalists always intend such comparisons to be taken literally. To compare the events in Kosovo in 1999 with events in Cambodia under the Khmer Rouge would be the height of bad taste if the comparison were being genuinely made. Rather, human beings cannot bear much atrocity, and they often flounder for words and concepts to describe it. It is natural to turn to what literary critics call *topoi*—standardized comparisons and evocations of events that are generally known. The problem arises, of course, when readers or viewers take the comparisons literally and assume that they are founded upon hard evidence that will in due course lead to a conviction.

Journalists are seldom trained lawyers, and they may obscure legal issues when writing about them, thereby setting up expectations that are disappointed. Thus, the *Wall Street Journal* announced in December 1999 that what had happened in Kosovo earlier that year was "not genocide," apparently because the tally of dead turned out to be much lower than some of the inflated estimates at the time.[14] But recall that the *size* of the butcher's bill has nothing to do with whether genocide has occurred; from a legal standpoint, it is a matter of the perpetrator's intention. *The Independent* in October 2000 claimed that President Vojislav Kostunica of Yugoslavia had "admitted . . . that genocide took place in Kosovo" in an interview with a U.S. TV station. In fact, he did nothing of the kind, as other reports made clear. It appears that the interviewers, unaware that no one had been charged with genocide because of Kosovo, used the word carelessly in a question. According to the BBC, Kostunica replied that he accepted "the guilt for those people who have been killed," although his office later disputed that he had made such a statement.[15] This episode is a useful reminder of the perils of assuming that media reports of personal statements can ever be used as proof. As anyone who has ever briefed the media knows, what goes in is by no means what always comes out.

Much the same applies to the products of human rights groups. It is important to recall that there are no qualifications for being a human rights group or a human rights activist. They are self-selected, and any accountability for what they do is limited. Moreover, the vocabulary of human rights is just that—a vocabulary—and can be abused by the wicked just as easily as it can be used properly by the well-disposed. (Quite a few eyebrows must have been raised after the fighting in Kosovo in 1999 to find that a "Center for Peace and Tolerance" was being set up there by the Serbs.) The fact that a report or set of assertions may be issued by a human rights group does not give such information any special status. Compared to governments, human rights groups have tiny resources and limited analytical capabilities. They also have fewer incentives to tell the truth, since the penalties for governments telling lies are much more severe than any that might be applied to NGOs. There are a number of large and well-funded human rights groups that do good work and seek a high standard of objectivity in their reporting and analysis. And in general, many pass the test for such analysis: they are prepared to admit that they might have been wrong, and they are prepared to cast doubt on reports of atrocities if they think there is insufficient evidence. But most self-styled human rights groups are not like this; they are small and focused on particular areas and often have a political agenda on behalf of their own people or the group they have adopted. Such organizations can do good work: the Serbian and Croatian Helsinki Committees have bravely publicized alleged human rights abuses by their governments, for example. But for the most part, although there may well be capable people and people of integrity in such organizations, the pressures—political, personal, and financial—all tend to reduce the usefulness of the final product for investigation or prosecution. Moreover, if such groups are seeking publicity for a cause, or are competing in an overcrowded market for media attention, they are likely to privilege information that assists these objectives, even if they doubt the authenticity. Such groups can have a symbiotic—indeed parasitic—relationship with human rights abuses, since they depend on them for their very existence.

There are also technical problems. Assembling atrocity reports into a coherent pattern is a process requiring skill and experience, with allowance for bias, confusion, and misrepresentation, as well as for the effects of hearsay and deliberate propaganda. For example, people who have been through traumatic experiences are often vague about exact times and dates, and it is possible that several accounts of atrocities, on different days, are actually the same account. Likewise, a massacre at village A may be the same thing as the massacre "near" village B, the name of which the interviewee cannot remember. Figures for casualties are *always* wrong in first reports and may well be too high or (less often) too low. Ten people who claim to have seen two dead bodies each may in total be reporting two dead or twenty. And few journalists or human rights organizations have their own salaried interpreters: they are therefore dependent on the good faith of locals, whose political bias and language abilities they cannot really evaluate. Sometimes, the consequences of this amateurism can be profound. During the early investigations carried out by the Truth and Reconciliation Commission in South Africa in 1996, largely untrained volunteers took statements through interpreters, which were intended to be included in a database of alleged atrocities. But as one investigator recalled, statements "were coming in with no date of the violations, no names of victims or witnesses, and meanderings in the story . . . they were of very poor quality. I would read the statements, and just want to cry."[16]

Indeed, all attempts to build up evidence of human rights violations by interviews are subject to a crippling weakness: eyewitness evidence is unreliable. While this will not be news to anyone who has served on a jury or been involved in a traffic accident, academic research into perceptual psychology and miscarriages of justice suggests that eyewitness evidence is almost useless for investigative purposes unless it is supported by other material. And testimony from so-called trained observers, such as policemen, is no more worthwhile than that given by ordinary people.[17] Eyewitness testimony has a number of major weaknesses. People are generally bad at estimating when things happened or how long they took. People recall violent incidents less clearly than peaceful ones, and they recall things less well during situations of stress. The presence of weapons can frighten and disorient people and reduce the accuracy of their memories even further. In other words, the kind of experiences undergone by victims and witnesses of atrocities are *exactly* those that make eyewitness testimony especially unreliable.

This happens for a number of reasons. First, memories of what happened depend to some extent on expectations. They may be cultural expectations, they may be based on projections of past experiences, or they may be a result of personal bias or temporary confusion. As time passes, people can remember things that never happened to them but should have. Inexpert interviewers can make these problems worse by inadvertently planting clues in the mind of the interviewee. For example, "tell me about the time the police and soldiers came to your village," or "tell me about the time you were raped," will produce a different response from "tell me what happened to you on April 24." In some cases, different answers can be produced depending on who is asking the questions, as well as whether the interviewer seems sympathetic or is challenging the interviewee's recollection. In some cases, the interviewee looks at the interviewer as a friend and supporter and will tell that person what he or she wants to hear. Some victims and witnesses will retrospectively think that their personal experiences were worse than they really were as a way to increase their own self-importance—assisted by the general Western tendency to regard suffering as a badge of entitlement to sympathy and victim status.

Cultural factors are also important: not every society expects ordinary people to volunteer evidence unless asked. At the ICTR, for example, courts have sometimes been faced with apparent contradictions between statements made to investigators by Hutu witnesses and replies given later in court by the same people. The usual reason is that investigators have not probed thoroughly enough. "Was A in your village" may elicit the answer "Yes," and it may be left at that. In the trial, the witness may add, in answer to further questions, that B, C, and D were there as well, but they would not have volunteered this information earlier unless asked. In almost all cases, interpreters will be required: most of the investigations (as opposed to hearings) of the South African Truth and Reconciliation Commission involved taking testimony, in English, from people whose native language was a local African one, so the statement-takers (generally not professionals) were continuously carrying out mental translations and trying to reorder and synthesize what they heard.

All of this, of course, assumes that the interviewee is the custodian of his or her own memories. But in practice groups of people talk to each other about experiences, and they may also hear them described in the media. After a while, they become unable to distinguish their own memories from the constructed versions of events that they have come to share with others. As a result, relying on personal testimonies, especially well after the event, is extremely dangerous. The Yad Vashem Center in Israel, for example, has an archive of 20,000 personal testimonies. Yet its director has said that most of them are unreliable. "Many were never in the places where they claim to have witnessed atrocities, while others relied on second-hand information given them by friends and passing strangers."[18]

The situation is eased to some extent if the perpetrator is already known to the victim, and so the issue is less one of identification than the easier one of *recognition*. In both Rwanda and the former Yugoslavia, the internecine character of the fighting meant that perpetrators often knew their victims personally and could easily be recognized. Even here, however, there is a strong tendency for people under stress to identify someone who *looks like* a person they know, even if that is incorrect. Two of the

Bosnian Croat defendants in the *Ahmici* trial, Zoran and Mirjan Kupreskic, were originally convicted largely on the evidence of a neighbor who said that she had known them all her life and recognized them without difficulty, even though they were wearing camouflage paint. The court accepted her evidence largely because of the confidence she spoke with and the horrors she had undergone. Yet on appeal the convictions were thrown out. The attack took place in darkness, in poor visibility, and there was no independent corroboration of the involvement of the two defendants in the attack. And this witness's credibility suffered when earlier confident statements she had made turned out to be false. Apparently, the attackers had opened fire from the part of the village where the various members of the Kupreskic family lived, and the victims, in discussion with each other, subsequently convinced themselves that members of the family must, therefore, have participated in the attack.[19]

These problems produce many traps for the amateur and the unwary. For example, when Kosovar Albanian refugees were being interviewed in Macedonia in 1999, a number of them claimed that "Arkan's men" (a reference to the followers of the gangster and paramilitary leader Zjelko Raznatovic, known as "Arkan") had come to their village. This makes a good headline (and there is some hard evidence that the Arkanovici, as well as other Serb paramilitaries, were in Kosovo at the time). But the interviewers, being experienced professionals, asked how the witnesses knew that these were Arkan's men specifically. The reply was that they had been wearing black uniforms, which popular legend held was the usual garb of paramilitaries. This illustrates another paradox of eyewitness evidence: people will introduce things they have only heard about into their testimony to give it more importance. (The situation was further confused by local criminal gangs dressing up as paramilitaries and putting villagers to flight so that they could loot their houses.)

Before any conclusions can be drawn about the value of such material, therefore, analysts must carefully check it against other information, hold it up to the light, and ask whether it makes any sense, even on its own terms. If reports of a massacre are received, then is there any independent evidence that military or police formations were in the area? Is today's massacre report actually the same as yesterday's, only with a different spelling? Does a report that young men from a certain village have disappeared mean that they have been taken away—or that they have left to join the rebels? And after the war is over, is there any evidence that fighting actually took place in such-and-such village? Is there any evidence that exhumed bodies are those of people killed at the time and that they were murdered rather than caught in the cross fire? And if bodies are later discovered in places where there were no reports of violence, are these likely to be additional to the main total, or possibly double-counted?

In what some experts refer to as the Affair of the Twenty Teachers in Kosovo in 1999, we see a case of spectacular failure to apply common sense. The story seems to have originated with Kosovar Albanian propagandists, who circulated reports on the Internet that twenty schoolteachers at the village of Goden had been shot in front of their pupils. This incident was bizarre enough for Western governments to mention it in press conferences, although they stressed that the reports were unconfirmed. They rapidly took on a life of their own, and more and more bizarre and colorful variants emerged, including some in which the teachers were beheaded by grinning paramilitaries. But no one in the media thought to calculate that a village with twenty teachers (and so perhaps 800 children of school age) must be a very large village in Kosovo, and to wonder whether this was actually the case. In fact, the village had a population of only about 200 people: the Serbs were certainly capable of such an atrocity, but it was not carried out at Goden. It seems that the confusion began when reports were received that twenty people had been killed, *one of whom* was a teacher.

It is essentially this process—applying analysis and a bit of common sense to atrocity reports—that distinguishes a genuinely useful investigation from simple propaganda or shock-horror media reporting. One of the few good examples of such work (because it was carried out by professionals) is the study by the Organization for Security and Cooperation in Europe of atrocities in Kosovo in 1998–1999.[20] Another was the UN Housing Damage Survey conducted in July 1999, which examined 206,000 houses in Kosovo—the majority of the stock. Their statistics showed that 42 percent of dwellings were completely untouched, and a further 20 percent needed some repairs. (This can be contrasted with statements by refugees that, if aggregated, would have meant that each village in Kosovo had been destroyed several times over.) The survey also showed that much of the damage was due to fire, which implies that most of the destruction of houses in Kosovo was deliberate rather than a consequence of fighting. Yet a report into refugee flows from Kosovo, although apparently statistically impeccable as regards its main subject, "determined that 10,356 Kosovar Albanians died in the war," which is impossible, since it far exceeds the sum of the number of bodies found and the number of people still missing. The error is explained by the assumption that all of the refugee statements were completely accurate and truthful.[21] As a general rule, no analysis of atrocity reports can produce a result that is more reliable than the reports themselves unless evidence from elsewhere is incorporated. This was the problem with the UN Commission of Experts report on the atrocities committed in the former Yugoslavia. Whatever its other virtues, it was described to me by one investigator as "basically useless" for evidential purposes, since it simply rehashed secondary sources.[22]

The problem is that few organizations outside government and international courts have much interest in carrying out such cross-checking, since the results usually show a murkier and less dramatic picture than initial reports suggested. As a result, people assume that a huge body of compelling evidence exists but is unaccountably not being acted upon. In turn, this produces media stories directly or indirectly demanding action against alleged perpetrators on the basis of nothing more than translations of allegations made to the media by people representing themselves as victims.[23] (You or I would surely insist on a little more proof than that if the police came to arrest us for something they had read about in a newspaper.) Repeated allegations can also lead to unrealistic assumptions about the severity and extent of alleged crimes. Thus, in the *Galic* trial proceedings, it became clear that, while civilians certainly died in the siege of Sarajevo, and crimes were very probably committed, more soldiers than civilians actually died during the fighting. Yet public perceptions, stemming from endless repetitions of the same stock footage, are different.

This is not to say that such reports can never be of any help. As one intelligence analyst put it, "If there's a lot of smoke, the chances are that there is at least some fire." While there are a number of cases in which reports of atrocities are purely imaginary, widespread and credible reports from a reputable organization gathered over a period of time may at least imply that there is something there worth investigating. But that is only the beginning of the process: no interviews, reports, or media stories will ever be more than a trigger for professionals to get involved. (When NATO specialists debriefed Albanian refugees in Kosovo in 1999, there was no expectation that the results would be used as evidence; the purpose was to identify those who might be worth following up with later.) A proper evidence-taking session would normally involve, depending on its importance, a trained investigator (usually a policeman), with a lawyer or an analyst, as well as an independent interpreter. The witness would then make a statement under oath and sign it, and the investigator in turn would make very sure that everything in the statement was the witness's own recollection. This is the only statement of this sort that can be used as evidence in court. Ironically, one of the major obstacles to gathering this kind of evidence these days is what investigators call "contamination," where witnesses have already been questioned by journalists or human rights workers and may now be confused about what happened or have had ideas planted in their head.

This is not just theory. One of the most fascinating and disturbing examples of the limitations of eyewitness testimony in a war crimes trial was the case of John "Ivan" Demjanjuk in Israel in the late 1980s. Demjanjuk, a Ukrainian immigrant to the United States, was sent for trial in Israel when he was identified as a guard at the notorious Treblinka and Sobibor extermination camps in wartime Poland. Demjanjuk fought extradition all the way to the U.S. Supreme Court, but he failed and was extradited, tried, and convicted, largely on the basis of eyewitness evidence. The Israeli court had to grapple with "the tenuous probative value of identification evidence which [was] forty years old," but it concluded nonetheless that "anyone who . . . experienced the terrible reality of the Treblinka extermination camp, cannot forget what his eyes have seen."[24] In other words, suffering created a presumption that the sufferer would tell the truth. Demjanjuk was duly convicted of being a figure known to the U.S. media (although not, apparently, at Treblinka) as "Ivan the Terrible." The case went to the Israeli Supreme Court, with results that might have been anticipated: The defense presented evidence showing that another person had in fact been the Ivan whose crimes were described in the indictment; he did not resemble Demjanjuk at all. The defendant was eventually released.[25] The witnesses had no idea even what Ivan's real name was, but courts in several countries clearly wanted to believe their evidence because of the ordeal they had undergone. The witnesses, in turn, confronted with someone who *might* be Ivan, can perhaps be excused for convincing themselves that, after so many years, their tormentor was within their grasp. Worst of all, the evidence showed that, while Demjanjuk was not Ivan the Terrible, he *was* a camp guard and probably responsible for many deaths. Unfortunately, there was no evidence linking him to any specific incident— unsurprising when we recall that Treblinka was an extermination camp, not a concentration camp, so there would be few witnesses anyway. The whole progress of the trial was steeped in politics: the U.S. authorities had taken action against Demjanjuk partly to ensure continued political support for the U.S. Office of Special Investigations, which was not having much success.[26] They palmed off the case on the Israelis (no one else would take it) because U.S. law did not permit criminal trials under such circumstances, which led to massive political controversy in Israel (Demjanjuk's lawyer had acid thrown in his face). The Ukrainian community in the United States, meanwhile, stood by their man "not because they did not believe he had done what he was accused of doing" but because they believed "he was being attacked by their traditional enemies, the communists and the Jews."[27]

Thus, any attempt to mix politics and atrocity allegations is dangerous. The most famous case is the use of atrocity propaganda by Western ally governments against the Germans in 1914. In spite of what is sometimes thought, the British government was very worried about whether public opinion would support a war on behalf of Belgium. Public opinion was focused on Ireland, where a civil war was anticipated and as a whole was neither pro-Belgian nor anti-German. Elite opinion was divided, and there were large peace demonstrations in many cities. The answer was a successful hate campaign against Germany. The Kaiser (the one German most people had heard of) was selected as the main target, and the media, egged on by the government, portrayed him as a monster, a criminal, a barbarian, and a sadistic mass murderer. A special committee was set up to analyze and publish details of German war crimes, the nature and extent of which were agreed by the British to be unparalleled in the history of modern warfare. The most sickening atrocities, including massacres, rapes, killing of children, and desecration of churches, were presented in salacious, gruesome detail. The incidents described were, in fact, not wholly invented: they were taken from depositions made by some 1,200 refugees made to British barristers through interpreters. No attempt was made to check the accuracy of the reports, nor was there any critical questioning of the supposed witnesses. Nonetheless, the tactic was very successful, as even liberal critics of the war rallied to the cause. As far as historians have been able to discover, virtually none of the incidents described actually happened. Some 5,000 Belgian civilians did die during the invasion of their country—unfortunate but not surprising in a war where millions of soldiers had been provided with unprecedented means of destruction.

The long-term political effects of this episode were generally very negative. British politicians may have convinced themselves that the stories were true—most of the public believed them implicitly—and the anger and disappointment when plans to try the Kaiser had to be abandoned for lack of evidence were correspondingly greater. But in the long term the episode discredited not only atrocity propaganda but also any reports of atrocities; thus, German atrocities, from the 1930s onward, which were much more real this time around, were put into doubt. Although educated people realized that terrible things were happening in Germany, residual skepticism made many wonder whether such reports were exaggerated. But in a wider sense, all atrocity propaganda creates its own reaction. Journalistic excesses at the time of Kosovo (to take the most recent example) certainly produced ridiculous and unsubstantiated figures for the civilian dead. The fact that examination on the ground led to these figures being greatly reduced was, inevitably, taken by some to imply that there had been no atrocities at all, which was equally misguided.

Before we leave the politics of atrocity evidence, it is worth mentioning two episodes that shed some light on why stories are believed and why they may be politically significant. Experience suggests that we believe allegations we read when they fulfill a need. They may correspond to what we fear (or expect) or they may conform to a type of familiar story, or they may justify a course of action or confirm our belief in the rightness of a cause we support. Take, for example, the case of Binjamin Wilkomirski, a Latvian Jewish author whose harrowing memoirs of a childhood during the German occupation were published to massive acclaim and translated into a dozen languages. This book, *Fragments*, was widely praised for its authentic account of the persecution of the Jews at that time. Yet Wilkomirski never existed: the book was written by a Swiss musician and psychiatric patient who suffered from delusions. Its alleged authenticity resulted from the fact that it seems to have been an excellent pastiche: it told its readers, in other words, what they expected to hear.[28] Much the same applies to the bizarre story that arose during the first Gulf War of 1990–1991 that Iraqi soldiers threw premature babies out of incubators in Kuwait so the incubators could be sent back to Iraq. This story—combined with a tearful appearance by a fifteen-year-old girl witness before the U.S. Congress—appears to have had a role in gaining wider sympathy for the war. The story was taken up by many leading Western newspapers and by Amnesty International. It was, of course, a ruse: the teenage witness was the daughter of the Kuwaiti ambassador to Washington. As many observers noted at the time, the story was basically a rehash of the German atrocity stories from 1914. It was widely believed for three reasons that have a wider application. First, there was a natural reluctance to question the testimony of a traumatized child victim (children never tell lies, as we all know). Second, the episode appeared to confirm racial stereotypes of evil Arabs that had been propagated by the media for some time. Third, the story appealed to those who were looking for reasons to believe that the war they wanted to support was not being fought merely to safeguard oil supplies. In other words, the story contained elements that everybody wanted, and in some cases expected, to hear.[29]

Bodies and Evidence

Even when coherent and mutually supporting stories have been obtained by professionals, there is still a need to collect further evidence that will support the anticipated criminal charges. Most war crimes involve violence, if not actual death, and the search for bodily evidence is an important part of any investigation. With obvious exceptions such as amputations, most bodily injuries heal after a while, and so the major source of forensic evidence in investigations is dead bodies. In domestic jurisdictions, to find the body of someone who has died by violence is usually a sign that a crime has been committed. This is not true in a situation of conflict in which killing is a legitimate activity, provided it is done according to the rules of war. Thus, to find a single dead body, or even a group of dead bodies, is not itself a signal that any crime has been committed. This applies even to bodies of women and children. Not only are women and children combatants in certain cases (and so lose their immunity); they may simply have been unlucky enough to be caught in the cross fire. As a result, evidence of dead bodies must be contextualized before it is of any value. Thus, if investigators find a dozen corpses of women, children, and elderly people in a village, much will depend on the general situation. If a large number of corpses in uniform is also found there, then we are probably looking at the aftermath of a battle. If the village is deserted, then it is more likely to be a massacre. If graves containing bodies of soldiers are found outside the village, then it may be different again. Bodies of civilians found in the ruins of a building or village attacked by artillery or airpower may be evidence of a crime. But if a military unit was in the village at the time, or if the village was attacked by mistake, or if a military unit had left only minutes before, then perhaps there has been no crime. But if the village was bombarded without any consideration of whether it was a legitimate military target or not, then dead bodies may be evidence of a crime.

The means of death is always important. The traditional sign of an execution is a bullet in the back of the head, with the corpse in a position indicating that the victim was kneeling down. It is hard to explain this as anything else but deliberate killing, particularly if there are many such bodies. In some cases, however, this situation is not found. In many massacres in the former Yugoslavia, the executioners shot into a crowd to put the victims down, after which survivors would be finished off. This was the situation at Srebrenica in 1995. The killings were done by firing automatic weapons from a distance into groups of men standing upright, and thus the patterns of bullet wounds were basically the same as would be expected in combat. What gave the game away was that a number of the victims had been blindfolded and had their hands tied behind their backs.[30] Had this not been done, or the blindfolds and ligatures removed afterward, then proving the killings would have been much more difficult. Indeed, other alleged killings at the time of the fall of the town were not prosecuted for this reason. There are documented incidents of suicides (often by grenades), as well as of firefights between groups of Muslims, and it would have been immensely laborious to try to prove that any given killing in this town was a deliberate crime. For that reason, charges were confined to what happened several days later, when there was other supporting evidence. Note, by the way, that even if all of the victims were combatants (and many had been), a crime would still have been committed because soldiers who have surrendered or been captured are noncombatants and so deserving of protection.

The situation in Rwanda was more straightforward, since about 40 percent of the killings were done with machetes. It takes at least two or three blows with a machete to be sure of killing someone, and so the deaths must have been deliberately intended and were not acts of war—you don't, in general, fight wars with machetes. When victims are found in situ, things are much easier. Thus, when British soldiers with UNPROFOR entered the village of Ahmici in 1993, they could immediately tell that there had been no battle there, as the Bosnian Croat forces were to claim, but a premeditated massacre. Bodies were found in the same relative positions, with males at the door, women in the interior, and children having hidden wherever they could. Forensic evidence also showed that the fires had been deliberately started, not a by-product of fighting. So if bodies are found together in a charred house, or a group of residents has been killed by a grenade, then the evidence for a crime having been committed is stronger. In Rwanda, many children were killed by being herded together, after which vehicles were driven over them. In many cases, the bodies remained where they fell, and it would be hard for the defense counsel to put forward an innocent interpretation of the evidence.

The fact that bodies have been moved may in itself be suspicious. While military corpses are often reburied at the end of the fighting, it is not obvious why civilians would be, and when there has been an effort to destroy the corpses or make them unrecognizable, then the implication is that someone has something to hide. This happened after the killings at Srebrenica. The army of the Bosnian Serb Republic was concerned that the bodies of the dead Muslims might be found by ICTY investigators and thus had some of them dug up and reburied. Unfortunately, the exhumations were done quickly, with mechanical digging equipment, and many body parts were left in the original graves, which was itself suspicious. Moreover, the reburials were done in a similarly crude fashion, and dirt from the original burial sites was mixed in with the bodies. This meant that investigators were able, by using such techniques as pollen analysis, to reconstruct the process by which bodies had been moved from primary to secondary graves and to produce a complete description for the trial of how this had happened.

Forensic evidence, then, is very important, and no credible investigation can be conducted without it. But as the examples above demonstrate, it cannot answer all questions. Above all, it must be carried out quickly, which is why forensic teams from various countries were deployed to Kosovo in the summer of 1999, just after the entry of the Kosovo Force (KFOR) while the evidence was still fresh and the graves undisturbed. In the future, this may not be so easy. Merely finding such graves could become a problem. In the former Yugoslavia, heat-sensing equipment has been a powerful tool, since decomposing bodies produce signature heat. This is easier in a Bosnian winter than it would be in an African summer, even assuming you can get to the grave in the first place. It is also likely that, as knowledge of forensic techniques become widespread, attempts will be made either to contaminate the evidence (by burying weapons with the victims, for example) or carefully preparing mass graves of one's own people for the investigators to find. One of the best examples of the difficulties of reaching firm conclusions about deaths from forensic evidence is the Racak massacre, which took place in January 1999 in Kosovo during an operation by Serb police to flush out the KLA after the abduction and murder of policemen in the area. It is clear that crimes were committed: some of the dead had been shot at close range, others had apparently been shot while escaping, and some of the bodies had been decapitated. The KLA publicly admitted that twelve of its own people died there but claimed that they were not among the bodies discovered the next day. Some of the others may have been members of village defense teams killed in the fighting.[31] The full truth of the Racak massacre, if it is ever discovered, will have to come from other sources.

However, by and large forensic examinations are not intended to produce the final truth on any incident, nor are they necessarily able to do so. The purpose of forensic examinations is to produce evidence that can be used in court, not to seek some unattainable final truth. Thus, forensic experts will exhume and examine as many bodies as they need to in as many places as is necessary to provide evidence for the charges being brought. In Kosovo, for example, the forensic teams had to produce evidence to show that crimes against humanity allegedly committed by the Serbs were conducted on a "widespread and systematic" basis. This required graves to be examined throughout the region, but it did not require every last body to be traced. (The indictment itself refers to a limited number of incidents and only 500-plus bodies.) By the end of the first year's digging, just under 2,500 bodies had either been disinterred or were identified in other ways, such as photography. More have turned up in later exhumations. But forensic evidence will never tell us either the total number of noncombatants dead or how many were deliberately killed. This is partly because several thousand people are yet unaccounted for, and there is evidence that some bodies were deliberately destroyed. The most we can say is that the figure cannot be *greater* than the number of bodies recovered plus the number of people missing, which would give a figure of some 6,000. If some of those missing are also among the dead who have not been identified, or are in graves not yet found, then that figure will reduce. Likewise, most of the dead bodies are those of young adult males of military age. Some, perhaps the majority, would have been killed on suspicion of being KLA members, or to stop them joining the KLA, or as a warning to others not to do so. But an indeterminate number may also have been killed while members of improvised village defense units, in the cross fire, or even in fighting between Albanian groups. The *total* number of those killed illegally will never be known and is, in any case, not required for trials.

Awareness of these traps means that investigators are generally conservative in counting the number of bodies that have been found. In many cases, bodies have been recovered in parts, and it is hard to know how many complete bodies the parts represent. In general, a rule will be made that one body part, usually a left or right femur, is required before a body is counted. (Counting heads is not so useful, because the cranium fragments easily.) This probably leads to undercounting, but it does mean that evidence introduced at a trial is firm and reliable. Sometimes these counts can lead to important conclusions. The exhumations done around the Srebrenica killing sites, on the same conservative basis, indicate that if the statistics are projected to the number of secondary graves identified, then the total body count is likely to be at the top end of the 6,000–8,000. Few, in other words, got away.

Paper Trails

I have already mentioned the powerful impact that documentary evidence can have on war crimes trials. Although it can be faked, it does not in general decay with time as memories do, it cannot be bribed or intimidated, and it cannot be cross-examined. The search for documentary evidence is therefore a key part of any investigation, especially if the targets are more senior figures who were nowhere near the scene of the crime.

A surprising amount of evidence is available from open sources. Constitutions and laws often provide the basic building blocks for an analysis of how a regime operated. Lists of government ministers, promotions and transfers in the armed forces, and details of command appointments all add to the picture. A general who has been publicly promoted or praised for his or her success in an operation cannot later disclaim any knowledge of it. Military magazines and newspapers, official gazettes, official reports, government communiqués, and statements in parliament are all potentially useful sources and have the advantage that they are productions of governments. While media reports of what people have said are often inaccurate, they can have their uses. A politician whose defense is partly that he or she was a political moderate can be discomfited by the production of media material documenting extreme views. Likewise, on a number of occasions in The Hague, defense witnesses have been confronted with their own public record of extremism, and experts called by the defense have been shown to be less expert than advertised. The great advantage of this kind of evidence is that it is much easier to use in court than almost any other type.

A second important area is captured or acquired documents. The Nuremberg war crimes trials were probably the first in which documentary evidence was used on a large scale, and this was possible because Nazi Germany, although a chaotic state in terms of policymaking, inherited a developed administrative tradition that kept detailed records. So the operational orders issued by the Wehrmacht in 1941, with their rhetoric of racial struggle and annihilation, and their unashamed injunctions that all means were to be used, would make a respectable foundation by themselves for charges that the Nazis planned what we would now call genocide against the population of the Soviet Union. This tradition (shared with most other European countries) required all decisions of government to be justified by reference to a law or decree and all decisions to be formally issued in writing. This tradition extended to the former Yugoslavia, and it means that, even in the chaotic early days of the fighting, there was often a paper trail that would later help to establish who was giving the orders. Thus, the Bosnian Croat militia may have been a scratch military organization, but from the earliest days its commanders, like Tihomir Blaskic, sent out a stream of numbered and detailed orders to military units under their command. The army of the Bosnian Serb Republic was somewhat better organized, and while no paper record seems to exist of the orders for the killings at Srebrenica, much of the planning that surrounded them was documented with great precision. When these documents were captured, they were of great use in the *Krstic* trial; investigators were able to produce logs for the vehicles that had reconnoitered the killing sites, as well as orders for the requisition of buses and 500 liters of petrol.

A very important type of document is represented by various publications on doctrine and tactics. Doctrine sets out a series of rules for military forces about how to fight, and a great deal can be deduced by experts who study such publications. Many armies—especially those influenced by the Soviet model—have a prescriptive doctrine that gives even senior commanders little latitude about how they conduct operations. This was true of the old Yugoslav army, as well as the elements into which it disintegrated (and, for different reasons, of a number of Asian armies, including that of Indonesia). The Serb-dominated Yugoslav Armed Forces (Vojska Yugoslavije, VJ) and the Bosnian Serb army were the most obvious inheritors of this doctrine; but the Croatian Army (Hrvatska Vojska, HV) and Croatian Defense Council (of Bosnia—Hrvatsko Vijece Obrane, HVO) and the mainly Muslim Army of Bosnia and Herzegovina (Armija Bosne i Hercegovine, ABiH) had a leavening of professionals, who were more likely to have used a familiar existing model than to devote time to thinking up a new one in the middle of a war. For this reason, pleas by military defendants in a number of trials in The Hague (e.g., that units for which they were responsible were somehow out of control) have not been found convincing by the judges. This is particularly helpful in establishing high-level involvement. If doctrine calls for even small and local attacks to be approved by senior commanders, then you don't need copies of *every* order to argue convincingly that the orders for an attack where atrocities have been committed would have been handled in the same way.

There are limitations, of course. Few military or political organizations deliberately write down and distribute orders for gross violation of human rights, whether or not they believe that one day such orders could be used against them. But this does not necessarily matter. Documentary evidence of this kind is often used not so much to establish guilt for a specific incident (although this may be possible) but rather to build up a picture of the functioning of a military and political command system. If, for example, a particular militia commander can be shown to have frequently sent orders to a unit, and received reports from it, then a command relationship with that unit can be established. If that unit can independently be shown to have carried out atrocities, then there is a powerful argument that the commander has a responsibility of some kind. At a minimum, it would be possible to argue that the commander's duty to investigate and punish alleged abuses has not been carried out. But it may be possible to argue further that if the unit was routinely under the commander's responsibility, then it would be strange indeed if it just happened to commit atrocities on a whim without permission and without reporting what had been done. Likewise, if captured records show that, in a given formation, minor violations of military law were investigated and punished, then it is much harder for a defendant to argue that major violations somehow could not be. These records do not even have to be purely military ones. Documents show that elements in both Belgrade and, to a lesser extent, Zagreb were providing financial and manpower assistance to their protégés in Bosnia, and it would surely be an inattentive government that was not aware of this at the highest level.

A more serious problem is the tendency to read too much into documentary evidence or simply to misunderstand it. This can happen if the reader is actively looking for evidence against someone he or she dislikes, or because of sheer unfamiliarity with the subject matter, or perhaps a mixture of both. It is what is often known as the smoking-gun phenomenon: the desire to find a single piece of incriminating evidence that will fix the guilt of the accused once and for all. In real life, such documents seldom turn up. Consider, for example, the document known, rather grandly, as the "Protocol of the Wannsee Conference"; on examination it proves to be a rather ordinary set of minutes—a record of discussion—of a short meeting that took place near Berlin early in 1942. When the minutes of the meeting were first discovered in 1947, they were immediately seen by U.S. prosecutors as "perhaps the most shameful document of modern history," even as the "Rosetta stone of Nazi murder."[32] In fact, the minutes largely consist of a briefing given by Reinhard Heydrich, the chief of the Reich Security Main Office, to a group of Nazi functionaries, as well as an appeal for help with a plan to "solve the Jewish problem" by deporting Jews to the East. The able-bodied would be put to work on construction tasks, the others killed. No decisions were taken at the meeting, and if we had only this document to go on, it would be impossible to predict accurately the nature and course of the actual process of extermination that was already under way.

We do not even know whether the minutes are accurate and complete (as anyone who has attended official meetings knows, much depends on who is writing the minutes). Prosecutors at the time, and historians since, have searched feverishly for the Rosetta Stone, the single document that will say, in effect, "Annihilate all the Jews of Europe, Signed A. Hitler." Given the way governments work, especially the Nazi state, it is likely that there never was such a document, and there was probably no simple decision to carry out the course of action either. But as Mark Roseman remarks, "Our need for precise answers is greater than that of the documents to supply them," which is something that often happens when responsibility for atrocities is an issue.[33]

Documents can be incomplete, misinformed, or deliberately evasive. They may have been composed for reasons different from those that prosecutors want to use them for. If I go to a meeting where dubious plans are discussed and do not object as strongly as I should have done, I might go back to my office and write a self-exculpatory piece of paper to others, claiming that I made much stronger protests than I actually did. There are numerous captured Bosnian Serb documents from the time of the 1995 Srebrenica offensive, including some signed by Radovan Karadzic, which order the troops involved to respect the laws of war. Do we then assume that the perpetrators of the Srebrenica massacres ignored these orders? At the other extreme, the "Instructions to the Muslim Fighter," distributed to the units of III Corps of the ABiH, in addition to allowing units to loot property and keep four-fifths of what they could steal, explicitly gave the commander of a unit the right to declare the normal rules of war suspended and to attack civilian targets if "the situation and the general interest demand." Under such circumstances, the soldiers are to obey their leaders rather than the rules of law. Yet it is not clear exactly what effect this order was designed to have or how widely it was obeyed.[34]

Problems also arise when those who uncover allegedly secret documents have strong views on the subject matter. Alleged leaked and secret documents are not new: the so-called Protocols of the Elders of Zion, for example, of the early twentieth century were supposed to be leaked documents from the International Jewish Conspiracy headquarters, and such figures as Adolf Hitler and Philippe Pétain believed implicitly in their accuracy because they wanted to believe. More recently, an entire Internet subculture has grown up around the so-called Majestic-12 documents, apparently dating from the late 1940s and detailing an agreement between the U.S. government and aliens from Zeta Reticuli who offered new technologies in exchange for basing facilities in the United States. These documents are presumably fakes, but they are very good fakes, and many intelligent people have accepted them as true.[35] Various scientists and engineers who claim to have worked on the alien spacecraft have appeared at UFO conferences around the world. More recently, Richard Tomlinson, formerly of the British Secret Intelligence Service, has claimed to have evidence that that organization was responsible for the death of Princess Diana, and a worryingly large number of people appear to believe him. Documents are becoming easier to forge all the time (there are doubts about a number that have surfaced in The Hague), and these days your local computer super-store contains everything needed to produce them at negligible cost. Anyone who can obtain copies of some genuine documents and scan them into a computer can then produce any variation. There are forensic techniques that can be used to discover, for example, if a document was digitized, but these are expensive and likely to be used only in trials. All sorts of rubbish is therefore likely to appear on the Internet and will be believed by those who want to believe them.

Even when documents are authentic, they need to be interpreted carefully. Historians must be wary of such traps (they often forget that a politician who has signed a document has not necessarily read it). But historians do have professional training and knowledge of the context to help them. Amateurs frequently misunderstand things totally. To take the Srebrenica example again, various allegedly secret documents have appeared on the Internet claiming to show Western culpability or even involvement in the massacres. Thus, an order from New York to the commander of the Dutch battalion is described on one Internet site as being to "defend the town." It actually instructs the commander to defend himself and his headquarters, which is different. On one occasion, Yasushi Akashi, the UN Secretary-General's special representative in Bosnia, was interviewed—interrogated, really—by a Dutch journalist about his time there. The journalist asked whether it was true that there were secret negotiations between the French and the Serbs offering the release of French hostages in return for a halt to air strikes. Akashi replied that there was no truth in this. Then how, asked the journalist triumphantly, did he explain his own leaked memo of June 19, which says that Milosevic had been notified by French president Jacques Chirac of President Bill Clinton's approval that no air strikes would be launched if they were unacceptable to Chirac. Akashi replied that one shouldn't take statements like that seriously. You mean, says the journalist, pose of sneering aggression suddenly slipping, that Milosevic cannot be trusted?[36]

In other contexts, the idea that anyone could believe that Milosevic, to whom lying came as easily as breathing, *could* be trusted would seem comical. Here, the impulse to believe in Western conspiracy and complicity is evidently so strong that it overpowers common sense. This illustrates another point: the distinction between fact and comment, often ignored in the media, is fundamental in all diplomatic reporting. Diplomats are obliged to record what an interlocutor actually says, even if it is rubbish.

Yet even if it is evidence of what was said, it is not evidence of what actually happened.

Even when documents are authentic, it may not be clear what they mean. Technical terms and circumlocutions can always be a problem, even without the disruptive necessity of translation. Thus, most military forces employ terms like *mopping up* to describe the business of overcoming the last few points of resistance when the main battle has been won. In some contexts, and in some languages, it might mean no more than that. In other contexts, however, it may mean something closer to ethnic cleansing. The use of the word *special* in a military context generally means something unorthodox is under way. In some societies the word may designate only the operations of elite forces; in others it might imply anything up to the so-called special units of Jews who operated the gas chambers in Nazi extermination camps. In the old Warsaw Pact (and in the former Yugoslavia), units known as diversionary brigades were special forces–type units used for sabotage and intelligence-gathering. In the fighting in the former Yugoslavia, such units (like Drazen Erdemovic's 10th Sabotage Detachment) were in fact often used for messy and usually illegal tasks because they were judged reliable.

Insiders and Experts

In addition to documents, eyewitness testimony, and forensic evidence, investigators will often pursue other types of evidence that may also be useful. The most useful, if it is available, is insider information, especially if the insider is close to a major political or military leader. Such people can play a valuable role in explaining to a court, for example, how decisions were made within a military or political leadership chain, and they can have more credibility than any amount of seized material. For this reason, courts will always seek insider testimony if possible. Yet it is not easy to obtain. Unless a regime has been completely destroyed, giving evidence against its leadership can be very dangerous, so special measures will need to be taken to ensure that the witness is safe. These may include giving testimony in closed session and anonymously, as well as spiriting away the witness from home without anyone knowing. In some cases, they may never be able to return home and will have to be settled elsewhere.

The use of such witnesses creates problems for a court, and the judges may be reluctant to accept all of the evidence without looking for corroboration elsewhere. If the inside witness is also a perpetrator, or a colleague of one, then the situation can be more difficult. In general, the motivation for one perpetrator to give evidence against another will be selfish: hoping to offload the guilt on to another, and, with luck, receive a more lenient sentence. An insider may cooperate fully with the prosecutor and give evidence against the accused, hoping for leniency, but this outcome will not necessarily be automatic. The sort of plea-bargaining practiced in U.S. courts has not been employed in the ad hoc tribunals, and the judges are not forced to take account of the insider's behavior in determining a sentence.

Another useful tool is the expert witness. Expert testimony can cover such abstruse issues as the historical background to a conflict, the interpretation of constitutions, or the doctrine and capability of various military forces. Archaeologists and anthropologists, as well as experts on language and psychology, have all been used as witnesses. Military officers often make very good expert witnesses, particularly by explaining to judges how the military system works and how military units are commanded and controlled. Major General Richard Dannatt from the United Kingdom gave evidence of this kind in the trial of General Radislav Krstic, for example. More junior officers and soldiers are often excellent witnesses about the military situation in which they were deployed or about the organization of the various parties. Likewise, diplomats and aid officials can explain how the political system in which they worked operated, and how, for example, one might be able to solve a problem by going to see an individual who was very close to the president.

A final type of evidence—although not one that needs to be actively searched for—comes from interviews and interrogations of suspects. This may happen before an arrest (and suspects can be interviewed under caution to protect their interests), or it can happen when they are in custody. While their rights—including their right to silence—need protection, voluntary statements may provide valuable evidence later. The statement made by General Krstic before his trial, for example, contained admissions that he was told about massacres alleged to have been carried out by his troops but did nothing to investigate them because he was afraid.

Help from Governments

The investigative resources of any war crimes court will always be limited, not only in numbers but also in capability. A court will certainly have investigators, and it should also have criminal and military analysts and probably a few political experts and technical specialists as well. But such people will not be able to cover everything, and there are many technical disciplines in which a court cannot realistically expect to develop expertise of its own.

We have already seen how important outside forensic help is, but there are all sorts of scientific and technical capabilities that are expensive to maintain and that exist in very few places in the world. Much of this extra assistance must be provided by governments. Some of it is mundane yet critical to investigations. Courts will need assistance in locating and approaching potential witnesses. Military officers and diplomats move around, and courts will need help tracking them down. Even when technical experts work outside governments—in universities, for example—courts will often want to approach them via official government channels. There are also other individuals who may never give evidence but whose insight into a particular regime—as an accredited diplomat, for example—can be useful in helping investigators understand the background. Government experts have also provided advice, and sometimes evidence, on such subjects as ballistics and shell impacts, the reliability of voice recordings and printed documents, radio wave propagation, and sniping weapons and tactics. No court could conceivably develop this kind of expertise without assistance.

In principle, states have an obligation to cooperate with the two ad hoc tribunals, and they in fact promised to cooperate with the ICC if they signed the ICC Statute. But there must be some kind of agreement about how such cooperation will work in practice; no one seriously thinks that the issue of peremptory orders would be a good idea. Indeed, one of the problems is that courts are unlikely to know what governments know, or what they can provide, until informed about it. This element of circularity can be addressed only if there is a determined effort to build up good working relationships with governments at a personal, informal level. Informal help is thus one of the most important things that governments can supply. They can guide investigators toward promising lines of inquiry and away from nugatory ones; they can suggest what might be possible if investigators ask; and they can warn where the cupboard is likely to be bare.

The provision of assistance by states is both the secret weapon and the Achilles' heel of war crimes courts. Precisely because it is so fundamental, there is enormous scope for states to frustrate investigations. This is most easily done not by outright opposition but by quiet obstructionism—sorry, we don't know where those people are; no, we have no information on that issue; unfortunately that person has left the military and we can't find him. Since the court will not know the truth, it is difficult to challenge misleading assertions, even if they may be wrong. It is not an exaggeration to say that the ICC will have to solve this problem if it is to conduct investigations successfully. Because the ICC's remit is so wide, and because the interests of far more states are involved than was the case with the ad hoc tribunals, the scope for manipulating the court by furnishing or withholding information is enormous. The scope for manipulating investigations by making false or misleading and incomplete evidence available is just as large.

Governments do have legitimate concerns, of course, and they may reasonably fear that investigators with no experience in government, and perhaps little knowledge of the complexities of a situation, might blunder around, causing trouble for everyone. There are many types of experts employed by governments who could never be expected to give evidence in public, as well as information that could do enormous damage in the wrong hands. The Anglo-Saxon procedures of the ad hoc tribunals have not helped either. Some European nations, with no tradition of cross-examination of witnesses, have been reluctant to allow personnel to give evidence for fear of being exposed to politically inspired attacks by the defense—what a former French defense minister called *la justice spectacle*.[37] To some extent, these worries have been overcome with experience, and in fact there are probably few areas of concern by governments that ultimately cannot be satisfied through careful thought. Yet there is much that courts can do to help themselves in their relationships with governments. The latter do not usually respond well to blanket requests for evidence. Busy and over-worked bureaucrats are unlikely to be very happy about spending time unearthing large amounts of material that might then turn out to be irrelevant. It is important, therefore, that investigators have a proper strategy in mind before starting and that they approach governments—and, for that matter, international agencies—in a coordinated way so that these organizations have confidence in them and are more likely to want to help.

Intelligence and Evidence

One of the things that, almost by definition, governments possess and courts do not is intelligence. So much confusion has been caused by the application of intelligence to war crimes investigations, and so much sheer rubbish written about intelligence in general, that we need to take a step back to examine what intelligence is and how and why it is collected.

In essence, intelligence is an aid to government decisionmaking and for assessing what might happen in the future. Governments need information to make decisions, and much of that is available from open sources or from the normal process of interaction among governments. When the needed information is not available in any other way, it must be obtained surreptitiously. Intelligence, in other words, is the process of acquiring information that another government, entity, or individual does not want to divulge without them knowing you have it. It is the process, rather than the source, and certainly not the reliability, of intelligence that distinguishes it from ordinary information. In some societies, information might be freely or easily available, but in others it may be hidden and must be dug out through the use of intelligence.

Intelligence is collected because it is expected to be *useful* for making policy or for judging future behavior. Because intelligence is expensive and often difficult and dangerous to collect, it is only collected if there is a perceived need that cannot be filled in any other way. In a properly organized intelligence community, intelligence is collected only against prescribed requirements, according to priorities set by policymakers. This means that the purposes for which intelligence is gathered, and the uses to which it is usually put, are generally different from the kind of persuasive evidence required for a criminal trial.

Even indications that atrocities *may* be committed, which could provoke diplomatic action, for example, seldom approach any kind of level of proof. Moreover, in most cases intelligence on suspected atrocities will not be a high priority unless there is something one can actually *do* with the information received. For most of World War II, for example, the British and the Americans had some idea, from intelligence sources, of the horrors being perpetrated in the East by the Nazis. But there was nothing they could do, and there was little to be gained by diverting intelligence assets from winning the war. The same information was easily available in the open media. It is also true that "intelligence was and is meant to be used," but in the opposite sense from that which Richard Breitman imagines. It is not that a use must be found for all intelligence (most of it indeed is never used at all); rather, intelligence should not be collected, much less analyzed, unless it is likely to be useful.[38]

Above all, we need to realize, contrary to what Breitman and many others believe, that governments do not "know" anything from intelligence sources. Because of its fragmentary nature, intelligence never provides anything more than indications, and much of it is useless until fit into a context. For this reason, analysts often use similes such as a mosaic or a jigsaw puzzle to represent the need to carefully fit apparently unconnected fragments together in the hope that a coherent picture will appear. And when intelligence is obtained from human beings, they may have personal reasons for blurring, suppressing, or expanding on the truth. Analysts, struggling to provide guidance for policymakers from a collection of material that may be contradictory in places, will therefore use expressions like *assess* to indicate they are making the best judgment they can without claiming to be completely sure of their conclusions. Any intelligence assessment can be upset at any moment by a piece of new information. But governments have to make decisions, and that means using the information and the assessments that they have available. Most laypersons who write about these issues have never seen a piece of intelligence. Thus, many journalists covering these issues lack the background to evaluate the questionable nature of a given piece of intelligence, let alone its probative value as evidence in a court of law. A small example may help. For obvious reasons it cannot be a real one, but it follows the kind of format in use in various countries and is based on some declassified examples. Let us assume that a western government is interested in the prospects for peace in an area where there is fighting against ethnic rebels, and has targeted some of its collection assets accordingly. Something like this may come in.

In late June, a senior member of the president's military staff said that the president and the chief of the army had recently discussed the need for a possible operation to finally defeat the rebels in the east of the country. The president asked for a detailed plan to be presented within two weeks and indicated that he would then take a decision about whether to proceed or not. He was, however, worried about foreign reaction to a sustained campaign and wanted the operation carried out as quickly and firmly as possible. The attorney general, who was present at the meeting, mentioned the need for any operation to avoid violations of the laws of war.

Most intelligence services would append comments to this summary, including an estimate of how reliable and well-placed the source is, and whether it is confirmed or put in doubt by other material ("collateral"). So there might be a comment saying "shortly after the meeting, the President left on an extended foreign trip. There is no independent reporting to suggest that an operation is under way, or has even yet been planned." Six months later, the Army does launch a campaign, although it is limited in scope to an attempt to capture several key towns. Accusations are made of atrocities committed by the Army, and the ICC is called on to investigate after the state concerned has refused to do so. (If the report above is ever leaked, of course, it will be said that the government concerned "knew" of plans to commit atrocities and "covered up" the knowledge.) What relevance does a report of the kind mentioned above have to an investigation? Although the text above (deliberately) gives no clue about who the actual intelligence source may have been, it would not be too difficult to work out, especially using the kind of investigative techniques customarily employed by dictatorships, and it is doubtful whether any editing could improve the situation. The most that could be said informally to the ICC was that there were various indications that an attack was being considered at some earlier stage. Even if there were some political miracle like a change in government, and somehow the text could be used in a truncated form in court, it would probably not be very helpful. Who was the source? Can't tell you. Who was the member of the military staff? Can't tell you. Can we speak to the agent? No. What lawyers call the "probative value" of such a piece of paper would be very small indeed. And most intelligence reports are like this. They contain things that may be wrong or incomplete, they may contain speculation disguised as fact, and they may be contradicted by an equally plausible report that arrives the next day. It is not uncommon for reports to predict the future correctly based on faulty information, and vice versa. Above all, reports generated in a highly charged political environment may be inherently untrustworthy, and the information passed on by a source may actually be intended to deceive, or even to manipulate, rather than to inform. This is likely to be an increasing trend, as sophisticated groups realize that a good way to influence foreign governments is to work out who might be an intelligence officer and to pass likely candidates information about atrocities that is actually false, but corresponds, perhaps, to what the government concerned wants to hear.

A good example of questionable information is represented by the reports of Nazi extermination camps during World War II. Some of these reports turned out to be accurate, whereas some were completely wrong. *At the time*, it was impossible to tell which was which. Thus, a report sent to British intelligence from a Polish resistance worker who had been in Auschwitz claimed firsthand knowledge of the means of killing in the camp. Among much accurate information was the assertion that the Germans were killing inmates both by high-voltage electricity somehow projected into metal-walled chambers, as well as by some use of air at very high pressure. Thus, in 1943 the British "knew" these things (which they unaccountably failed to publicize), although they were completely imaginary.[39] This illustrates a fundamental principle of weighing evidence— whether by an analyst or a journalist—that a single piece of information, no matter how attractive and compelling, must never be allowed to dictate conclusions unless there is collateral for it elsewhere.

Thus far, I have been discussing what technicians refer to as "human intelligence." At first sight, intelligence gathered by technical means should be easier to use, since it is a passive process and therefore doesn't involve the same sensitivities in regard to its sources. But as various histories of World War II code-breaking have demonstrated, there are dangers in allowing another state to know that you can read what it is writing. In any event, such information is fragmentary and makes little sense unless one can put it into a larger context. A signal from headquarters that says "move to point X-Ray and prepare to conduct Operation Hercules if criteria identified in Plan Gorgon are met" is not going to thrill a court as it stands. In some cases one may not even know who is speaking. A signal from PANORAMA to ZLATAR means more if one knows who or what the code names represent—the VRS Main Staff Command Post and the Drina Corps HQ in 1995 respectively. But even if one knows who is speaking and about the subject matter, the fragmentary nature of such material can make it useless. Wisdom after the fact is, of course, easy to acquire.[40]

Part of the problem is that the public's and elites' understanding of intelligence is hopelessly distorted by journalism, popular fiction, and Hollywood. Thus, the usual criterion for accepting assertions about intelligence is not whether they are logical and sensible but whether they correspond to received ideas from popular culture. Popular culture has a fundamentally romantic view of intelligence, which sees the agencies of the world as all-seeing, all-knowing, and all-capable. When agencies claim to have no coverage on a particular subject, therefore, they are by definition lying and must be covering up something. The reality is usually more mundane, and thus the help that technical intelligence can provide is correspondingly limited, apart, perhaps, from a nudge in this or that direction.

In practice, use of this kind of information in court is difficult. An intercept, after all, is only words on a piece of paper, with no guarantee about the origin, the accuracy of the translation, or even completeness. Few states would agree to give the technical details of collection or to make the operator or the translator available. And even if one did, the defense could argue still that, for all the court knew, the government concerned had made up the whole thing. Governments are even less likely to want to do this in the future given that irresponsible political charges of "knowing" about and "covering up" things will certainly be made on the basis of a few scraps of misunderstood material.

In one case, that of General Krstic, intelligence material was of value. The Sarajevo government handed over large numbers of tapes and transcriptions of intercepts that it claimed to have carried out in the summer of 1995. The political importance that they attached to the Krstic trial was such that the Sarajevo government was prepared to give full details of how and where the intercepts were carried out, to provide copies of the original tapes made at the time, as well as to allow the operators to give evidence. It was necessary to get these tapes technically examined and to provide evidence that the voices were correctly identified. Even then, some of the intercepts were indecipherable, some were rejected by the court, and even those that were accepted were not given much weight unless corroborated by other evidence. And there will be very few cases in the future where such high-quality material will be available.

A final area of intelligence work that has attracted much interest is overhead surveillance. This can be collected by satellite or by aircraft carrying various types of sensors. The latter category, which is much less sensitive, has been used successfully in a number of trials. The classic use of such material is in before-and-after pictures of residential areas. If the first photograph shows the town intact, and the second shows roofs missing, it usually means that the houses have been burned, and then it is clear that an attack must have taken place on the town between the dates of the two photographs. Satellite imagery, for all its security problems, has been used successfully on a number of occasions. One example, again from the *Krstic* trial, included imagery of prisoners on the football field at Nova Kasaba on July 13, just before they were killed.[41] By itself, of course, such imagery is largely useless; out of context, the photo could depict a group of footballers at a training session. Imagery alone will never be decisive (in spite of popular fantasies about it, which are drawn less from real life than from

Hollywood films like *Goldeneye*) and will probably always be of more value in triggering investigations than in proving matters in court.

Strategy

A war crimes investigation is a mammoth undertaking, involving many types of specialist expertise and assistance from outside. Keeping all of the threads together, developing the investigation, and ensuring that it results in useful evidence are major tasks. It is easy for an investigation to lose its way and to waste huge amounts of time and money without achieving any results. For this reason, an *investigation strategy* is essential. This covers how the resources of the investigators and analysts are to be deployed, as well as the structure and underlying philosophy of a given investigation. It also includes the collection of information as such, the analytical processes that it undergoes, and what is done with the final product. Confronted with a pattern of alleged widespread human rights violations, investigators could opt to follow up each and every lead and no doubt waste time interviewing the same witnesses several times for different purposes. In the case of Rwanda, for example, the sheer number of victims, perpetrators, and incidents could have kept investigators occupied for decades had they attempted to cover everything. As a result, senior managers must learn to target investigations toward particular incidents, which may be egregious, large-scale, or merely typical of the atrocities committed.

When the ICTY began investigating, for example, it decided to examine four areas first. The first was Vukovar, scene of some of the worst alleged atrocities by Serbs against Croats during the early months of the fighting; the second was the alleged killings in the Lasva Valley by Bosnian Croat forces; the third was allegations of murder and torture at the Muslim-run Celebici prison camp; and the fourth was the widespread allegations of murder and torture at concentration camps run by Bosnian Serbs near Prijedor. All of these led, in due course, to indictments, and some defendants have already been convicted. When reports began to surface of the scale of the alleged massacres at Srebrenica, it was immediately clear that investigating them would be a major new commitment.

How should an investigation be structured? Essentially, it should be built from the ground up. Any investigation has to start from indications that a crime has been committed. However, attention should quickly shift, once the criminal basis has been established, to the *linkages* that would help identify the actual perpetrators, and this is more an issue of analysis than of simple investigation. Unless the sole target of the investigation is the immediate perpetrators themselves (which would make little sense), some estimate also needs to be made of the involvement of higher-level military and political leaders, provided something like a chain of command actually exists. At that point, the scope of the investigation, including its targets, will become clear. Its objective, of course, is not the fine-grained establishment of truth but rather finding compelling evidence to build cases against individuals. At that point, the investigation proper can begin, the results analyzed, more investigations undertaken to fill gaps, and so on until enough evidence has been gained to indict an alleged perpetrator or perpetrators.

The evidence needed, and thus the strategy, will vary depending on the type of perpetrator being investigated. For a low-level perpetrator, who is alleged to have carried out the atrocities himself or herself, the kind of evidence required is straightforward. To begin, evidence must establish that crimes actually took place on the ground. Next, eyewitnesses able to identify or recognize alleged perpetrators, and victims who have survived, will be sought out. Any video, photo, or forensic evidence that the crimes actually took place will be important. It will also be useful to know where the low-level perpetrator fits into the chain of command (if there is one), since an investigation against higher-level perpetrators may well be possible. Inquiries into higher-level perpetrators must begin from the same set of facts—to establish that a crime has been committed—but will involve other factors as well. For a medium-level perpetrator, there is also the need for evidence to prove where the person fits into the chain of command, whom he or she commanded and reported to, and what legal or practical command authority that person had over the forces alleged to have carried out the atrocity. Operational documents and plans and background expert witnesses will be more valuable at this level. In the case of high-level perpetrators, such evidence as books, official speeches and interviews, as well as government documents will also be needed. Some help may come from intelligence sources, since intelligence assets are most likely to be directed at high-level targets.

As investigators and prosecutors know, the evidence they need to build a case extends far. Almost any information gathered by investigators, supplied by witnesses, or furnished by governments will come in handy: orders of battle and organizational charts; locations and strengths of units; uniforms worn; communications equipment and practices; commanders and other personalities; movements of units observed by witnesses; documents and manuals; information about political structures and state organization; information on how political regimes function in practice; locations of headquarters; the organization; structure and personnel of the police; links between the police and the military; and the structure of local organized crime. Much of this material will never be used in court, but it will be critical to guide investigators and analysts and to identify possible targets for indictment.

On the Ground

Everything to this point has been premised upon the idea that an investigation into alleged crimes is actually possible. This will sometimes be the case. It is possible, at least to an extent, in Sierra Leone, where foreign troops and government forces have effective control of the country. It is possible in Rwanda (although not without difficulty), since the victims now control the country. It was easy in Kosovo, where NATO forces control the terrain. But very little was actually possible on the ground in Bosnia before the entry of NATO-led peacekeepers in early 1996, and it was considerably longer before any useful work could be done in Croatia and Serbia. One has to wonder whether the euphoria over the ICC Statute should be tempered by skepticism about the chances of actually being able to conduct useful investigations. Much depends on chance. If the ICC's first investigation is a result of a reference by the Security Council, and an international force is present on the ground, then the chances of an investigation are good. But just as likely, some of the first investigations carried out will be in hostile territory. Take, for example, the Democratic Republic of the Congo, where some 2 million have died in confused fighting between a half-dozen armies and twenty-odd paramilitary factions, including complete lunatics like the Lord's Resistance Army and the Mayi-Mayi who have little that anyone would recognize as a command system at all. The DRC, a country of some 50 million people, is sometimes described as Europe without roads. It is the size of Western Europe but with virtually no infrastructure. It is alleged to take three months to drive from Kinshasa to the eastern borders, should you be rash enough to attempt it, and that is where the fighting has largely occurred. There is no possible way in which the DRC government could provide protection or logistical support to an investigation; parts of the country are not under its control anyway, and there has been little central administration since the late Joseph Mobutu seized power in 1965. As a result, an investigation team would probably have to enter from Rwanda or Uganda, which would have its own problems, as both of those nations have had troops in the DRC. Even then, journeys of hundreds of miles over rough terrain would be necessary, in search of witnesses who spoke no English and probably no French either. (There are five major languages spoken in the DRC, about two hundred altogether.) Local interpreters and helpers would have to be hired, largely on trust. Even if there were no fighting, such an operation would be extremely dangerous, and it is not clear that an ethical organization would actually risk its people in some circumstances. (There would, of course, be many nonmilitary hazards to face, notably some of the mysterious and fatal infectious diseases that are springing up in that part of the world, for which there is currently no known cure, and in some cases not even a name.)

In such circumstances, the general consensus is that an investigation team would probably need military protection, although it is not clear who would provide it. A company-sized unit (say, 100 men) would probably be needed to provide basic protection, communications, and transportation. Such a force would need at least lightly armored vehicles and would probably have to be supplied, and perhaps inserted, by helicopter. The investigators would need a secure rear base, itself probably served by regular flights by transport aircraft. Medical teams, satellite communications, sophisticated maps (largely nonexistent), and considerable logistical support would be necessary. And all of this would occur to insert perhaps six or eight investigators into a country for a few weeks. If the intention is to conduct forensic examinations or to search and seize material, the requirement could be much greater.

Conclusion

Such are the problems that will be facing the International Criminal Court. Perhaps investigations will not, on average, be as difficult as this, but they will certainly be much more difficult than anything attempted thus far. In most cases, reports of atrocities will appear before the fighting is over, when it may be too dangerous, or simply impossible, to get to the area where the crimes are supposed to have occurred. The political consequences of this are likely to be profound. There will be pressure to send in investigators anyway, perhaps with a token protection force, only to find that all the witnesses have fled hundreds of kilometers before an advancing army. And after the inevitable casualties, there will be recriminations and suggestions that the ICC is not working and should be closed down. Unless the ICC is lucky, it will be pushed to do much in the way of investigation at all.

Notes

1. Richard Overy, *Interrogations*, p. 12.
2. ABC, *Foreign Correspondent*, Interview with Geoffrey Robertson, March 30, 1999; Geoffrey Robertson QC, "Only Sanctions Will Force Out Milosevic's Gang," *The Independent,* June 20, 1999; letter to *The Independent,* June 27. 1999.
3. Roy Gutman, "Rwanda Chief's Vision Sets African Agenda," *Newsday,* November 28, 1996.
4. Johan Pottier, *Re-imaging Rwanda*, p. 57. Pottier is especially critical of the American journalist Philip Gourevitch, who has written widely on Rwanda.
5. ICTY Statute, art. 7.
6. ICTR Statute, art. 6.
7. *Kosovo* (IT-99–37), Second Amended Indictment, October 16, 2001, para. 16.

8. Christopher Browning, *Ordinary Men*; Daniel Jonah Goldhagen, *Hitler's Willing Executioners*.

9. Christopher Hitchens, *The Trial of Henry Kissinger*.

10. Cited in Nederlands Instituut vor Oorlogsdocumentatie, *Srebrenica: A "Safe" Area*, pt. 1, chap. 9, sec. 2.

11. Frederic A. Moritz, *Is This Another Nazi Kind of Thing* available online at www.worldlymind.org/watershed.htm).

12. John Sweeney, "The Killing Fields," *The Observer*, June 20, 1999.

13. Kosovo refugee exodus "straight out of Schindler's List," *CNN*, April 2, 1999; Robert Fisk, "Truth Is Dying in the Ruins of Silent Capital," *The Independent*, April 9, 1999; "Reality Check: Genocide," *Mojowire*, May 14, 1999 (available online at http://www.motherjones.com).

14. Daniel Pearl and Robert Block, "War in Kosovo Was Cruel, Bitter, Savage; Genocide It Wasn't," *Wall Street Journal*, December 31, 1999.

15. Stephen Castle, "Leader Owns up to Kosovo Genocide," *The Independent*, October 25, 2000; "Kostunica Admits Kosovo Guilt," BBC News, October 24, 2000; "Kostunica Disputes CBS Broadcast," *Online Journalism Review*, October 27, 2000.

16. Richard A. Wilson, *The Politics of Truth and Reconciliation in South Africa*, p. 43.

17. See, for example, Elizabeth F. Loftus, *Eyewitness Testimony*.

18. Peter Novick, *The Holocaust and Collective Memory*, p. 275.

19. *Ahmici* (IT-95–16), Appeals Chamber Judgment, October 23, 2001.

20. Organization for Security and Cooperation in Europe, *Kosovo/Kosova: As Seen as Told: The Human Rights Findings of the OSCE Verification Mission*, 1999 (available online at www.osce.org/kosovo/documents/reports).

21. Patrick Ball, *Policy or Panic: The Flight of Ethnic Albanians from Kosovo, March–May 1999*, American Academy for the Advancement of Science, 2000; "How Coder Cornered Milosevic," *Wired*, March 19, 2002.

22. *Final Report of the Commission of Experts Established Pursuant to Security Council Resolution 780*, 1992 (S/25274).

23. See, for example, Felix Blake, "Nusreta Survived the Rape Camp, but Her Torture Is Unending," *The Independent*, November 23, 2002.

24. Jonathan M. Wenig, "Enforcing the Lessons of History," in Timothy L.H. McCormack and Gerry J. Simpson, eds., *The Law of War Crimes*, p. 116.

25. A good summary of the case and its implications is at the Nikzor Project's website (www.nikzor.org).

26. The U.S. Office of Special Investigations was set up in the 1980s to investigate accusations against naturalized U.S. citizens of involvement in Nazi crimes from World War II. Like its analogues in Australia and the UK, it found the job very difficult.

27. Gitta Sereny, *The German Trauma*, p. 309.

28. On Wilkomirski, see Stefan Maechler, *The Wilkomirski Affair*. Maechler was the historian appointed by the publishers to examine the allegations of fraud made against the author.

29. See, for example, Gavin Esler, "My Greatest Mistake," *The Independent*, September 10, 2002.

30. See *Srebrenica Investigation: Summary of Forensic Evidence—Execution Points and Mass Graves*, Prosecutor's Exhibit 140, May 16, 2000.

31. *Milosevic*, testimony of Shukri Buja, June 5, 2002 (transcript pp. 6318–6326).

32. Mark Roseman, *The Villa, the Lake, the Meeting,* p. 4.

33. Ibid., p. 34.

34. *Hadzihasanovic and Others* (IT-01–47), Amended Indictment, January 11, 2002.

35. See the collection of documents at www.majesticdocuments.com.

36. Yasushi Akashi interviewed by Robert van der Roer, (available online at www.bosnet.org/archive; http://www.bosnet.org/archive for 1998).

37. "Bosnie: aucun officier français ne témoignera devant le TPI," *Le Monde,* December 10, 1997.

38. Richard Breitman, *Official Secrets,* p. 9.

39. Ibid., p. 117.

40. The recent claim that the Australians (inevitably) "knew" about plans for massacres in East Timor illustrates the point. Mike Head, "Leaked Spy Intercepts Prove Australian Complicity in Timor Massacre," *Sydney Morning Herald,* March 25, 2002.

41. *Krstic* (IT-98–33), Prosecution Exhibit 12/3.

7

The Arrest

N o criminal justice system can be regarded as credible or effective, or
as a deterrent to further offending, or a vehicle for vicarious revenge
by the public, unless it is able to round up those it believes are guilty of
crimes and put them on trial. Indeed, a criminal justice system that *cannot*
do these things is scarcely worthy of the name. In most Western societies,
arresting wanted criminals, if not always easy, is at least straightforward.
Western police forces work in organized societies in which information
about citizens is freely available. They can usually rely on the help of the
public and, in serious cases, on the public taking the initiative to contact the
authorities. They can usually count on the support of other government
departments and even other governments. Most criminals in the West submit fairly quietly, and even dangerous and violent criminals can usually be
arrested at a time when they are inattentive, unarmed, or asleep. Even in the
United States, armed shootouts between police and criminals are not common, and there are few cases in which the criminals have more firepower
than the police.

A Question of Identity

With occasional exceptions, the above scarcely applies to fugitives from
international justice. To begin with, it may not be obvious who to look for.
Almost by definition, war crimes take place in circumstances of confusion
and dislocation. In some cases, targets for investigation and arrest may
have official positions, and if investigators can get to official files, some
details may be available. But even then, investigators may have no better
idea who to look for. Consider the following hypothetical description of a

fugitive: "Believed to be middle-ranking officer in government forces, probably major or lieutenant colonel. Known as the 'Angel of Death' or 'Angel.' Blond hair, medium build, age between thirty-five and forty-five. Speaks with pronounced northern accent. No distinguishing marks." Here is a typical description of a lower-level perpetrator, such as those responsible for the Serb camps in Bosnia: "First name Dusan or Dragan, also known as 'Duso' or 'The Electrician' (comment: his reputed method of torturing inmates). Second name unknown. Heavy build, aged between forty and fifty, sometimes wears moustache. Serbian flag tattooed on one forearm. Believed to come from Foca. Drinks heavily."

Even if there is credible evidence linking such people to atrocities, witnesses are unlikely to have the kind of details that make an arrest possible. Few perpetrators will give their full name and date of birth when opening fire, and although low-level perpetrators will often be known to their victims, the ambiguous outcome of the *Ahmici* trial shows that this method of identification cannot always be trusted. Trying to estimate age, for example, is often not easy, especially in conditions of stress. Balkan males tend to age rapidly, while by comparison those in Africa and Asia often appear to age rather slowly. In most cases, especially for lower-level perpetrators, there will be no photograph available. Identities can be confused or even merged. For a long time, a character known only as "Gruban" was featured on the ICTY indictment list. There was no photograph or description, and eventually the indictment was withdrawn because the individual probably did not exist but had been confused with another indictee.

Even higher-level perpetrators may not always be captured on film, especially if they are engaged in questionable activities. One of the coconspirators (but not, it should be said, indictees) on the Milosevic Kosovo indictments is Franko "Frenki" Simatovic, the head of the State Security Department (Resor Drzavne Bezbednosti, RDB) Operations and link to Serb paramilitary groups. But as newspapers have noted, there are no photographs of him in existence and only the vaguest of physical descriptions. If he were ever indicted, therefore, the first task would be to find out what he looked like.[1] And some fugitives have been unsporting enough to change appearances. In 1998 Louise Arbour, the prosecutor of the ICTY and ICTR, publicly drew attention to the practice of the government of the Republika Srpska in "issuing false identification papers to those persons indicted by the Tribunal in an attempt to shield them from the Tribunal's jurisdiction."[2] It can be assumed that any reasonably alert government or intelligence service would do the same in the future if it wanted to protect indictees.

Even when a full name is available, it may not get investigators very far. Many societies have what seem to be unusual naming conventions, with several names depending on the context. Some names are really clan names (about one-third of Korea is called Kim), and others depend on locality, parents' names, or even profession. Muhammad the metalworker, son of Aziz the bricklayer, in the village a few kilometers from here may be all the identification investigators can find. A real-life example of confusion over names occurred in 1996, when a Bosnian Serb called Goran Lajic was arrested in Germany. When asked to confirm his identity upon his initial appearance at The Hague, he said that he was indeed Goran Lajic but not *the* Goran Lajic they were seeking: he was someone else of the same name. After some considerable confusion, this person was eventually released.[3] In June 1999, British SFOR forces detained (or so they thought) one Dragan Kulundzija, another member of the Bosnian Serb war crimes fraternity. Sitting in court a few days later, I almost had a heart attack when the detainee denied that that was his name. Eventually, it became clear what he meant: He was Dragan *Kolundzija*; his name had been mistransliterated from the Cyrillic alphabet, not a difficult mistake to make. (His date of birth was also wrong.)[4]

In some cases, the only information about an alleged perpetrator may be that he or she is an officer of some kind. Yet even then, it might be hard to use evidence of this sort: few witnesses would be able to tell a major from a major general unless they had military experience themselves. Finally, many perpetrators these days will be foreign, or at least from another clan or ethnic group, and their words might not be intelligible anyway. Any plan for the arrest of someone in these circumstances has to begin with a careful and probably time-consuming effort to work out exactly who is being sought and what that person looks like.

The Short Arm of International Law

Even if there is a confident identification of a high-level miscreant and a recent photograph and biography, that is only the beginning of the problem. Many Bosnian and Rwandan indictees appear to have sought refuge abroad, where they have protectors. Bosnian indictees have found it easy to slip across the borders into Croatia or Serbia. For a long time those two states had no intention of cooperating with the ICTY, and indictees there were basically safe. Even with more compliant governments in those two states, the practical problems of tracing and arresting such people remain very great. Moreover, popular sentiment is often strongly behind them, since they tend to be seen as heroes rather than criminals, and it might be politically difficult to arrest them, even if the court concerned believes it has discovered their location. (In early 2003 the Croatian government was struggling with the order to hand over General Janko Bobetko, seen by most Croats as a war hero—although their position was eased when the

ICTY indicated that because of Bobetko's poor health, they would not press too hard for his transfer.) There are, of course, cases in which indictees are found to be in their own country, and in theory a government should then be obliged to arrest them. But if a government simply refuses, or argues that it is too difficult (as the government of the Republika Srpska did), then there is not much investigators can do. It's hard to argue for sanctions against a state that claims to be trying without success.

Sometimes governments can be genuine in their protests. The fugitive may be hiding in a distant part of a country with poor communications and ineffective security forces. He or she may be protected by organized crime, or by elements of the state which are out of control, such as the military or the intelligence services. The fugitive may be extremely rich and powerful, able to afford protection sufficient to make an operation too risky. He or she may have sympathizers within the state apparatus able to warn of impending arrest efforts or able to issue threats of reprisals if any action is taken against them. It is easy to imagine, for example, a situation in which the ICC indicts the leader of a vicious militia group in an impoverished African state whose forces are then put to flight and retreat to their power base in a distant part of the country. In theory, the government should then go after and arrest the person. But there are many African countries where the writ of government scarcely runs in distant parts, even in the best of times, and there may be no chance of taking the indictee until the war is won. Even that will not necessarily be the end of the matter. Some indictees may have secrets that others do not want revealed and may be killed before being handed over. Others may be killed out of revenge when captured. Borders in Africa are sufficiently permeable that the indictee may simply disappear to a neighboring country.

The lack of an enforcement mechanism may well prove to be the Achilles' heel of the ICC. It is almost certain that many of its indictments will be along the lines just described, and it may be years before indictees are brought in, if ever. Brave talk of ending the culture of impunity and the dawn of a new age of justice may have some merit but will be ineffective if efforts at arrest prove unsuccessful. Indeed, unless the first ICC indictees are brought in fairly promptly, the organization may suffer credibility problems that it could not overcome. If a state refuses to hand over a high-profile ICC indictee, for whatever reason, then ultimately it will be the court, rather than the state, that will feel the venom of the media and popular opinionmakers. "The Failure of the ICC" may be the title of a report that is almost certain to be written around 2007. After all, although the parade of indictees into The Hague and Arusha is impressive, given the size of the problems those two institutions have faced, it has not saved the courts from accusations of failure as soon as they started issuing indictments that did not instantly lead to arrests.

Due Process

Even when a state is fully cooperative and able to arrest an indictee, procedures must be followed to ensure all that is done is legal and proper. In
ordinary criminal cases, a fugitive from one country arrested in another
country will be handed back only if there is an extradition treaty between
the two countries. While such treaties are common, they are certainly not
universal; states are by convention unhappy about extraditing suspects for
purely political offenses, and political and human rights concerns may prevent even conventional criminals from being handed over. (The European
Union, for example, is legally prohibited from handing over criminals
whose actions might lead to the death penalty in any of the states that retain
capital punishment.) For national prosecutions of war criminals, these are
the mechanisms that must be relied upon, and thus war criminals have tended to flee to countries that have no extradition treaty with the state that pursues them. There is not much a state can do in such circumstances unless it
is prepared to break the law itself, as Israel did in kidnapping Adolf
Eichmann in 1960. Even for two friendly states there are procedural rituals
to endure. If all this seems a little bureaucratic, consider whether anyone
would want to be pulled off the streets and transported unwillingly to
another country for prosecution without any checks of identity or evidence
of involvement in crime.

The situation of the two ad hoc tribunals is easier, at least at first
glance. Under the tribunals' statutes, states have an obligation to transfer
any indictees on their territory to The Hague or Arusha. (The word *transfer* is used here rather than *extradition* because neither the ICTY nor the
ICTR are states. The ICC Statute has an entire section (article 102, "Use of
Terms") devoted to this difference). This obligation is far-reaching (much
more so than its analogue in the ICC Statute) and can include a requirement to hand over indictees who are on trial, or even in prison, in another
country, since the tribunals can exert what is called "prior jurisdiction" in
such cases. An extreme example is that of Zoran Zigic, a Bosnian Serb
who was taken out of the military prison in Banja Luka in 1998, where he
was serving a sentence for murder, and transferred to The Hague.
However, where states are cooperative, the transfer must be carried out
legally and properly. Among the provisions of the respective statutes are
those requiring states to pass laws that make transfers to The Hague legal.
In most cases, this was done quickly, but until the laws were in place it
was not possible for some states to transfer indictees. Thus, the transfer of
Dusko Tadic, the first person tried at the ICTY, was delayed for months
until the German government had passed an appropriate law, that government having previously pleaded in The Hague "its inability to comply
immediately with the provisions of any formal order for deferral that may

be issued by the International Tribunal, due to a conflict with the munici-
pal laws and the Constitution of the Federal Republic of Germany."[5] In the
Federal Republic of Yugoslavia in 2001, the same problem arose over the
transfer of Slobodan Milosevic, although in this situation it was judged not
to matter.

Some European states, while still passing laws of this kind, have
attempted to put unilateral limitations on their cooperation with the tribunals and have effectively taken it upon themselves to judge the competence of the tribunal to judge individual cases.[6] Likewise, some courts have
refused to accept that the statutes of the ad hoc tribunals take precedence
over national laws and policy. The U.S. government was deeply embar-
rassed in December 1997 when a Texas magistrate refused to permit the
transfer of Elizaphan Ntakirutimana, a Rwandan genocide indictee resident
in the United States, to the ICTR. His argument—reflecting similar arguments made in Balkan states—was that the enabling law passed by
Congress was contrary to the provisions of the U.S. Constitution. This ruling was reversed by a District Court judge in August 1998. Eventually, the
U.S. Supreme Court rejected an appeal against that decision by
Ntakirutimana in January 2000, although he was not actually transferred to
Arusha until March 2000.

The provisions of the ICC Statute are largely along the same lines,
with the proviso that the ICC is *not* a subsidiary organ of the UN
Security Council, and so the requirement to arrest and transfer indictees
to The Hague is only a political commitment by virtue of signing the
statute. While in theory some disciplinary process could be invoked in
case of constant obstruction, the ICC prosecutor will not have the personal right of access to the Security Council that the ICTY/ICTR prosecutor enjoys, and discussion of sanctions would be a bit academic. If the
ICC has been asked by the Security Council to take an interest in a particular case, it can refer instances of noncompliance back to the council
for whatever use that may be. Otherwise, it simply reports noncompliance back to the ICC Assembly of State Parties, which has no coercive
powers whatever. Although the statute specifically bars states from questioning the decision by the ICC to seek an arrest, it does allow (indeed, it
requires) states to make sure that the proper procedures have been followed domestically. An inventive state, by deliberately making procedural mistakes, could hold up the extradition of a suspect for some time.
Likewise, the warrant for arrest has to contain "a concise statement of
the facts which are alleged to constitute the crime" pursuant to article
58(7)(d), which may give the government concerned some unpleasant
options, for example, in disposing of witnesses or anyone who knows too
much about the facts.

Guns Blazing

There will be many cases, of course, where indictees are being sheltered by states or entities that have no interest in handing them over and where indictees are for the most part secure. Alternatively, as mentioned above, they may be beyond the reach of a government that genuinely desires to help. In such a situation, outside governments will be under great pressure, once more, to *do something*. What are the options? The options of external actors against a noncompliant state are limited to threats and bribery. Of these, there is a natural limitation to the threats that can be employed. A country that is prepared to shelter an international war criminal is likely to be at odds with the international community anyway, and sanctions and other coercive measures might already be in place. Moreover, such measures need broad international support if they are to be effective, and the country concerned may have political or economic friends or have other ways of weakening the effect. The biggest problem, however, is that sanctions and similar measures can be applied only once. What do you do when the same country decides to shelter a second indictee? And as experience with Serbia and Croatia has shown, there will always be those who argue for a relaxation of sanctions once the country concerned has made a gesture in the right direction. Maintaining support for a sanctions regime is never easy, and it will often run afoul of other priorities that might argue for closer engagement with the same regime.

If the stick is hard to use, the carrot is not necessarily more effective. The noncompliant state has to be offered an inducement that will make it worth its while to hand the indictee over, and often this will not be possible. In practice, some form of bribery will be required. Generally, bribery is at the collective level and may involve approval of an aid or debt-reduction package or trading concessions. This can work on occasion—the transfer of Slobodan Milosevic is one case where it seems to have had an influence—but the repertoire is limited, and most aid and trade packages are multinational, which means that they take time and effort to put together. Bribery of individuals is not necessarily to be excluded, although it is difficult to be sure the money is well spent, and there are obvious legal difficulties if the idea is pressed too far. In certain countries it may be possible to bribe a dissident faction of the security forces if the job is within its capability. In any event, such tactics would have to be acceptable to the judges of the ICC. The ICTY judges, in a continuing series of complex rulings, have made it clear that certain methods (e.g., luring) are acceptable ways of snagging the wanted, but it is still unclear where the line is ultimately to be drawn.[7]

Such difficulties inevitably lead to agitation for more muscular methods to be employed, and there is seldom any shortage of hare-brained proposals for international snatch squads from militaristic human rights activists who have never in their lives held anything more lethal than a staple gun. Since these ideas are likely to resurface, it is probably worth explaining some of the practical problems. Many have arisen in the context of the successful attempts of the NATO-led Stabilization Force troops in Bosnia to apprehend indictees. The details of these operations are confidential and should remain so, but I will refer from time to time in this discussion to publicly known problems. I will not deal with criticism of SFOR activity in the war crimes area as such, except to say that much of it is fatuous and poorly informed.

The first major point is the need for governments to be legal in their actions. In the British system, for example, the military is not allowed to carry out illegal activities under any circumstances, or even to assist with them, and anyone who tries to use military forces in this way commits a crime. This limitation—and it is not unique to the United Kingdom—inevitably limits what can be done. Mounting an invasion of another country is hard to justify under international law, no matter how pure the motivation might be, without the explicit support of the UN Security Council; and obtaining this support would pose severe problems of its own. Likewise, there are many legal limitations on the methods that can be used, even if one is in a country with the blessing of its government. British soldiers are subject to British law wherever they happen to be in the world, and the position of most countries is similar. In any event, governments have a moral and political responsibility to uphold international norms and standards: one does not enhance international respect for the rule of law by violating it. The problem is that all of these fundamental arguments do not respond to the public appetite for action and vengeance. (Indeed, I have heard the need for British soldiers to obey the law dismissed as a "technicality." At a conference a few years ago I enlarged on some of the above in explaining why certain crackpot ideas indeed fell in that category: most would have violated international law. "This is far too important to worry about international law," a professor of international law sitting next to me said.)

A second problem is that attempts to arrest war criminals are unlikely to take place in a political vacuum. In almost all cases, there will be a strategy of justice and reconciliation as part of the attempt to rebuild the political structures of a state and to remove the problems that could lead to another outbreak of violence. Thus, any policy for targeting war criminals has to support long-term international political objectives or, at a minimum, not obstruct them. In practice, and whatever they may say, even the most extreme advocate of indiscriminate action would not suggest that such action should be pursued irrespective of the practical consequences. Thus, to take a slightly fanciful example, it would no doubt be possible to pressure war crimes indictees to surrender by arresting their families and threatening to execute them one by one until they did so. Even if such techniques were morally and legally acceptable, they would cause far greater damage to overall political objectives than the benefits they could possibly provide. The reason that the many operations conducted against indictees in Bosnia have not produced political disasters is only partly because of the skill and professionalism of those involved; it is also partly because of the elaborate thought given to ways of ensuring that bad consequences do not result.

In other words, there must be political as well as legal limitations on what is sensible. A spectacular failure was the botched attempt to arrest several lieutenants of the Somali warlord General Mohammed Aideed in October 1993. The basics of the story are well known, but the world has tended to concentrate on the effects on the United States rather than on Somalia. A minimum of 500 Somalis died during the operation, many of whom were civilians, and twice that number were wounded. The operation led eventually to the withdrawal of the U.S. contingent and the collapse of the UN mission to, and the country of, Somalia.[8] It is hard to believe that even the most extreme human rights activist would seriously regard the destruction of an entire country as a fair price to pay for the arrest of two figures, even had the operation been successful. Yet governments are under enormous political pressure to rush in with guns blazing—and damn the consequences. Journalists in Bosnia, for a few euros, will be told stories about the famous war criminal Thugovan Slobovic, who drinks every day in a café near an SFOR post. (Of course, the more euros paid, the better the story.) It is easy to see how such pressure could lead to stupid and dangerous situations. Imagine a group of non-KiSwahili-speaking peacekeeping troops passing a cafe in some East African country one day and saying to themselves, "Gosh, that looks a bit like the famous war criminal Abdul Aziz in there. Although this is a country where weapons are very common, let's nonetheless rush into the cafe, guns at the ready, shouting 'United Nations' and drag him out. We won't ask for reinforcements, we won't get a good quality photograph, we won't get some intelligence people to track his movements, and we will ignore the police car down the road because this guy is about to finish his coffee, and we'll be criticized by human rights activists if we let him go."

All this is rather discouraging. So what is the likelihood that future ICC indictees will find themselves physically in the dock at The Hague? First, the main determinants will be practical ones rather than nebulous issues of "will" and "commitment." But human rights activists and their media supporters will tend to take morally one-dimensional positions that arresting war criminals is an overriding moral obligation and that issues of practicality, and even legality, are secondary. There is thus the potential for conflict between governments and their opponents, as well as for the repetition of Somalia-style disasters. If such disasters *do* occur, of course, governments will be abandoned by those who were urging them to act just the day before.

The most likely circumstance is that a peacekeeping force under UN or regional auspices will be deployed into a country that has just suffered major human rights abuses during a war at a time when ICC indictments are being issued or pending. Once such indictments are formally issued, there will be enormous pressure on the United Nations to use its forces to detain some of the indictees, with angry media stories complaining that these individuals are free while the United Nations "does nothing." There are major drawbacks to precipitate action. The first is political. Assuming that the country concerned has signed the ICC Statute, then it has an obligation to arrest and transfer indictees to The Hague. That process is likely to be part of a larger process of compliance with international norms, as well as political and institutional reforms in the country. The assumption that international forces will be available to do all the difficult and unpopular tasks may well obstruct this larger political process. Governments can decide not to do things that are desirable for political rehabilitation, secure in the knowledge that others will act instead and attract any criticism that might be coming. This has happened in Bosnia, where authorities of the Republika Srpska have declined to arrest and transfer ICTY indictees, thus preserving their political position and leaving others to do the dirty work.

Another basic problem is that arresting criminals is not a military function, nor should it be. Few military forces in the world possess such skills, even in their military police components, much less soldiers sent on peacekeeping missions. Moreover, the mix of nations in an international force means that capabilities, training standards, and even sympathies can vary greatly. In any event, a peacekeeping force will be structured to achieve its own purpose and will seldom be suited for conventional military operations, as Bosnia and other similar experiences have shown. Peacekeeping forces are supposed to act in a transparent and overt fashion to develop trust and promote cooperation and reconciliation between factions. They have not historically been expected to gather intelligence (by definition a covert act), although the need for such a capability is increasingly being recognized. It is unlikely, in any event, that a multinational force could actually deploy with the specialist capabilities that would be required for a successful detention operation. If a peacekeeping force *did* act against ICC indictees, then it would compromise the very objectivity that made it acceptable to all sides in the first place.

Because arresting criminals is generally not a military function, it is unlikely that the mandate or rules of engagement would explicitly cover such a situation. Mandates and rules of engagement are highly political documents and represent limitations that the Security Council (acting as an effective surrogate for world opinion) wishes to put on the freedom of the commander. It is easy to get the idea, reading polemical treatments of the atrocities of the 1990s, that the Security Council somehow overlooked the need to give warfighting powers to UN forces in Bosnia and Rwanda. In fact, the mandate, the force structure, and the rules of engagement are designed to reflect the political objectives that the wider international community has, as well as the limitations under which nations are prepared to offer contingents. Moreover, as I have already noted, there are fundamental differences between the structure of forces that are intended to keep the peace and those that are intended to fight a war. Thus, the UN force in Rwanda in 1994, sent to monitor the 1992 Arusha Accords, was "hampered by serious shortcomings in equipment, personnel, training, intelligence and planning"; in addition,

> [The commander] was sent half battalions from Bangladesh and Belgium and a battalion from Ghana. This meant a command and control structure which was totally inefficient; far too few troops were available for operations.... The Ghanaian battalion had to be deployed for two months without their equipment. The Bangladeshi transport company was short of trucks ... they did not even have a kitchen. The Bangladeshis were unable to move themselves, let alone the Tunisian company attached to them.... There were no spare parts, manuals or mechanics to service [armored personnel carriers] and the crews had never fired their main weapons.[9]

This force, in other words, was fairly ineffective even in the low-intensity world of peacekeeping. Faced with the need to confront large numbers of machete-wielding Hutu women and children, it would probably have disintegrated at once. (I have spoken to a number of African officers whose units have returned, shaken and traumatized, from combat against child soldiers in different parts of Africa.) In these circumstances, it stretches belief that anyone could seriously think it, or any similar force, was capable of detaining those subsequently indicted.

In addition, the characteristic de facto command arrangements of UN forces—where a commander cannot (as in Bosnia) do very much without the consent of the contributing governments—would make it effectively impossible to carry out detention operations, with the attendant risk of violence, even with a genuinely capable force. In turn, this reflects the limitations placed by states on the freedom of action of contingents they send on operations of this kind. In most cases, the approval of parliaments is needed for troops to be sent overseas. Public opinion is often suspicious of such deployments and expects real limitations on the troops' actions. It is simply not realistic—or acceptable in a democracy—to suppose that a nation that deployed an infantry battalion to a cease-fire monitoring mission will learn from the media one morning that two dozen of its troops have died in an ill-conceived plan to snatch an ICC indictee. Indeed, such initiatives, especially if there are casualties, could do a great deal to destabilize the mission and threaten its political objectives.

A preparedness to take casualties is not all that common among nations sending troops on missions overseas. The gung-ho Anglo-Saxon mentality (shared to some extent by the French) is not shared, or even necessarily understood, by much of the rest of the world. Most countries, especially those who retain conscription, see their military forces as defenders of the country. In some cases, this extends to peacekeeping in the traditional sense and, perhaps, to participation in regional security operations. But supporting the idea of troops going into action in someone else's country, and killing and being killed, is not exactly universal, and many troop-contributing nations make it clear they will furnish troops provided they have assurances that they will not be committed to combat. As an example, public support for Dutchbat III diminished when it took its first and only casualty (ironically from the Muslims) on July 8, 1995, at Srebrenica. Most Dutch people, according to opinion polls, then wanted to bring the boys home.[10] In the future, it is hard to imagine easy public acceptance of deaths in, say, an Asian UN contingent resulting from an operation to detain black men indicted by white men for the murder of other black men. Indeed, while public support for NATO detention operations in Bosnia has held up well, this is partly due to the low level of violence involved. If every operation had resulted in casualties to the detaining forces, it is unlikely that public opinion would have allowed the operations to continue.

And such operations are not without risk. In the very first detention operation in Bosnia, carried out by British SFOR troops in July 1997, they attempted to detain Simo Drljaca, the Prijedor police chief and head of the wartime crisis staff. According to official statements, Drljaca pulled a gun and began shooting, wounding one of the soldiers. He was then shot dead.[11] During the next operation, conducted by Dutch SFOR troops in December 1997, there was another exchange of fire. Vlatko Kupreskic, one of the *Ahmici* indictees, was wounded as a result.[12] In October 2001, the appeals chamber freed Kupreskic, and had he died four years previously, it is now clear that an innocent man would have been killed.[13] In January 1999, Dragan Gagovic was shot dead by French SFOR troops near Foca after he had tried to drive at them to avoid detention.[14] Gagovic was a karate teacher, and in the back of his car there were five children, whom he was bringing back from a karate tournament in Montenegro. By great good fortune, none was hurt. Had there been casualties among the children, it is likely that detention operations would have had to be suspended, at least for a while. Finally, in October 2000 German SFOR troops attempted to detain Janko Janjic. Allegedly screaming "You'll never catch me alive! I'll never surrender! Fuck you!" Janjic detonated a grenade, killing himself and wounding four German soldiers. Relatives of Janjic in the same house were also injured.[15] Operations can go wrong in other ways as well. In 1998, British SFOR troops detained, or so they thought, the identical twins Pedrag and Nenad Banovic in Prijedor. Only later did it become apparent that another set of identical twins of the same age had been picked up—the Vukovics—and they were speedily returned home. Fortunately, there was no violence on that occasion.[16]

There are, in other words, only modest prizes for getting it right and potentially horrendous penalties for getting it wrong. In most situations in most countries, the practical judgment would have to be that no individual's arrest, no matter how high-profile, is worth hazarding the success of the mission as a whole and the political objectives of the international community. This puts a premium on getting the timing right and is another component in the careful planning that operations must have if they are to be successful.

A theoretical option with a noncompliant state is for an outside state or states to use military force to extract the indictee. This is not a serious option for two reasons and so merits only the briefest mention. First, such an operation would be illegal unless approved by the UN Security Council, and that would amount to a public announcement that an operation would take place, forfeiting the element of surprise. Second, such an operation—effectively, the invasion of a sovereign state—would require massive and complex resources, time, and luck.

Conclusion

The chances of the ICC rapidly putting its hand on everyone it indicts are limited. Many indictees will be in foreign countries where the governments may or may not be willing to hand them over, and many others will be beyond the reach of military forces in the area. Media and critics will look for someone to blame. While the United Nations will attract some of the criticism, much of it is likely to land on the ICC, simply because there is no one else to blame. It is not obvious why it should be the ICC's fault that a state refuses to hand over an indictee, but in practice that is how critics of the organization will decide to interpret it.

What can be done to help? The most obvious mechanism, and one that has been used by the ICTY with some success, is the sealed indictment, whereby the indictee does not know of the indictment until the knock comes on the door. It was introduced by Louise Arbour, the second prosecutor. She made it clear publicly that she was introducing the system essentially as an operational tactic to improve the chances of SFOR and states to carry out arrests. The ploy was successful, and a number of individuals who might have fled if they had known they were indicted have remained within reach. Most of them were in Bosnia, where SFOR was able to collect them, but an important exception was General Momir Talic, who was detained in Vienna in 1999 by the Austrian authorities.

It is hard to argue with this logic. Some fastidious academic lawyers have deplored it, presumably because sportsmanship requires the quarry to be given a head start. But this is not a game; it is a deadly serious enterprise in which people get killed, and no government would willingly forego an option that safeguarded its own people and made the task easier to accomplish. Other complaints come from the local political authorities (usually Serbs) and can be automatically disregarded. After all, there are few jurisdictions where police publicly announce that they intend to arrest a particular criminal within a few hours. Although the ICC Statute is silent on this point, we can assume that one of the few mechanisms open to the ICC to increase its success will be some variant of the sealed indictment. This will, of course, place a premium on knowledge of the likely movements of an indictee, as well as close cooperation between the ICC and the state that is asked to carry out the operation.

Notes

1. See "Franko Simatovic Frenki: The Croat Who Heads Milosevic's Secret Police," *Vijesti,* September 5–7, 2000.
2. ICTY, "False Identifications," press release, CC/PIU/336-E, July 24, 1998.
3. See *Sikirica and Others* (IT-95–8-T), Order for the Withdrawal of Charges Against the Person Named Goran Lajic and for His Release, June 17, 1996.
4. ICTY, "Kolundzija Case (Keraterm Camp): Initial Appearance—Hearing Suspended; Evidentiary Hearing on the Accused's Identity on 24 June 1999," press release, CC/PIS/410-E, June 15, 1999.
5. *Tadic* (IT-94–1-D), In the Matter of a Proposal for a Formal Request for Deferral to the Competence of the International Tribunal Decision of the Trial Chamber on the Application by the Prosecutor for a Formal Request for Deferral to the Competence of the International Criminal Tribunal for the Former Yugoslavia, Judgment of November 8, 1994.
6. See Axel Marschik, "European National Approaches to War Crimes," in Timothy L.H. McCormack and Gerry J. Simpson, eds., *The Law of War Crimes*, pp. 95–99.
7. In the case of Slavko Dokmanovic, a sealed indictee who was lured into eastern Slavonia and detained by UN authorities there, the Trial Chamber decided that the method of arrest was acceptable. See ICTY, "Dokmanovic Case—Trial Chamber Denies the Motion for Release by the Accused," press release CC/PIO/251-E, October 27, 1997.
8. For a good analysis of military blunders in the planning and conduct of the operation, see Sean J. Edwards, *Mars Unmasked: The Changing Face of Urban Operations* (Santa Monica, CA: Rand Corporation, 2000), pp. 11–18.

9. William Shawcross, *Deliver Us from Evil*, p. 108.

10. Nederlands Instituut vor Oorlogsdocumentatie, *Srebrenica: A "Safe" Area*, pt. 3, chap. 6, sec. 8. The soldier was Sergeant Raviv Van Renssen, who was killed by either a shotgun blast or a grenade (accounts differ) while withdrawing from an observation position. See ibid., pt. 3, chap. 6, sec. 7.

11. *Hansard,* House of Commons, July 10, 1997, cols. 1072–1073

12. SFOR, Joint Press Conference, Sarajevo, December 18, 1997.

13. *Kupreskic and Others* (IT-95–16), Judgment of October 23, 2001.

14. "Statement by the Secretary General of NATO ... on SFOR's Action Against an Indicted War Criminal," press release 99(002), January 9, 1999.

15. D. Dardic and I. Gajic, "Death Rather Than Extradition," *Reporter*, October 18, 2000.

16. ICTY, "Release of Two Persons Believed to Be Indicted by the Tribunal," press release, CC/PIU/335-E, July 23, 1998.

8

The Trial

Most people, and that includes those who make decisions about war and peace, have absorbed the majority of ideas about trials from TV and film. Even the depressing and banal experience of being a juror does not banish these ideas altogether. From *The Merchant of Venice* to *Perry Mason*, the trial has been a powerful narrative device and a symbol of much wider attempts to arrive at the truth, or at least some form of justice. In Christian tradition, the Last Judgment was in many ways the culmination of all of history, when God would judge the living and the dead and send each human to the place merited by their conduct or by the solidity of their faith.

A political problem with international justice is that it must meet the requirements of a largely secular society that still seeks what are essentially divine attributes in international organizations. Just as intervention is the wrath and omnipotence of God, and intelligence is the omniscience of God, so international justice is a poor substitute for the swiftness and certainty of the justice of God. That justice, to be feared and admired, was never constrained by rules of evidence, never hamstrung by procedural maneuvers, and never subject to appeal to a higher authority. And the justice of God, being terrible, swift, and certain, based on omnipotence and unchallenged virtue, combined moral with legal judgments; indeed, it was primarily about morality rather than law in its bureaucratic sense.

Side by side with the exaggerated hopes for the law in Western society, there has always been an undercurrent of cynicism about how the law works in practice, and lawyers have had, and continue to have, a status within Anglo-Saxon societies that few other trades would envy. But the impulse to believe in the effectiveness of the rule of law, and in the organization of the world along just and moral lines, is very strong, and it is stronger still in non–Anglo-Saxon cultures in which the law is seen less as a rich man's toy and more as a guarantor of basic rights. (Recall that Nelson Mandela studied law in the hope of improving the lot of black people in South Africa, rather than his own prospects, which would be more typical of an Anglo-Saxon society.)

While any legal system will inevitably produce practical compromises and organizational inefficiencies, they matter less when someone is accused of crimes against property than when they are accused of crimes against humanity. Moreover, the Nuremberg trials remain as a kind of moral dramatic pageant, preserved on film (the interesting bits, anyway) as a constant reminder of what such trials are expected to be like. It is not a criticism of those responsible for trials in The Hague and Arusha to say that they seldom, in practice, live up to the requirement for drama and spectacle that this precedent would imply. This is inevitable, since the process of proving a case against a higher-level perpetrator is a complex and bureaucratic one: the prosecution list of exhibits in the *Krstic* trial runs to 150 pages, every document translated into two other languages. Likewise, the defense has to patiently worry about the evidence in an attempt to undermine it: there will be no surprise witness or dramatic courtroom confession five minutes before the final hour.

As a result, major war crimes trials often give the impression of being held in slow motion. Simultaneous interpretation, no matter how good, always slows things down, and when, as in Arusha, witness evidence must be translated first into French and then into English, and questions put into the reverse order, it is surprising how little ground actually seems to be covered in perhaps an hour of court time. Then there are the inevitable inefficiencies: documents get lost or have the wrong translation appended; technical equipment malfunctions, witnesses, defendants, or judges are ill; the courts have days off for UN holidays; or a witness simply fails to show up. Then there are the rules against leading witnesses, which means that testimony must be extracted piece by piece in slow motion. Among other things, a trial is a complex administrative exercise, and a surprising amount of time is taken up with issues such as the timing of hearings, the admissibility of evidence, and argument over the numerous administrative motions that make up a large part of the business of any trial. On a slow day in The Hague or Arusha, nothing much seems to be happening.

Yet criticism of the slow pace of justice in these two courts, while partly highlighting unquestioned management inefficiencies, is the product of exaggerated expectations, as well as inevitable disappointment in the actions of fallible human beings. Moreover, any large organization has its own internal politics—its own struggles for power and fame—that are bound to get in the way. The struggle between those who want the Rwanda tribunal to be genuinely international, and those who want it to be more African, has not improved its speed and effectiveness. The ICC is likely to have similar problems, not least because much of its management will be Western, whereas almost all of its defendants will be non-Western.

In addition, many believe that the purpose of these courts is to convict people. They reject the arguments of others who were involved with national prosecutions of war criminals in the 1980s that, in the British and Australian cases, for example, the process was partly successful, since investigations and some trials were actually carried out. If, at the end of the day, there was inadequate evidence to secure a prosecution, or even bring one, that does not mean that the system failed; it simply means that the evidence was not there. The idea that a justice system has failed unless it produces a string of successful prosecutions irrespective of the quality of the evidence is a dangerous idea for any society claiming to be based on the rule of law. In this sense, therefore, the acquittal of various Bosnian Croats for the *Ahmici* killings is an example of the system of justice working as it should, not of its failure.

Whose Justice, Whose Court?

Despite the slow pace and level of detail at which these courts work, their atmosphere owes a great deal to their Anglo-Saxon origins. It is curious, in the indolent heat of a Tanzanian summer, to sit in a stuffy courtroom in Arusha and listen to a British-educated black barrister, sporting a wig, begin the day with a customary African greeting: "good morning witness GEH, and how are you today?" ("I'm fine sir, how are you?") Yet the cultural difference is probably much greater for the witness than it is for any spectator.

The problems of language and security mean that the atmosphere in the courtrooms in The Hague and Arusha is high-tech and intimidating. Unless the witness is protected, cameras are trained on the stand at all times; interpreters whisper testimony in two other languages; and dozens of computers record a transcript in three languages and show the shots from the other cameras. Security guards with guns and radios are noticeable, and everyone, including the witness, wears headphones, through which all communications are received. In Arusha, the atmosphere is a little less intimidating, but then so is the society; at least most Yugoslav witnesses will have seen a TV set before.

The simple process of traveling to a court and giving evidence carries its own cultural dissonance. Victims and many of the nonvictim witnesses often come from small and enclosed rural communities. The sense of dislocation—of being the center of a frightening amount of attention—can be off-putting. For many Yugoslav witnesses, the trip to The Hague was the first time they had boarded an airplane. For many Rwandan witnesses, the trip to Arusha was the first time they had ever *seen* an airplane. Many witnesses are protected and fear for their own safety if anyone finds out where they are. They are isolated and may well be in a metropolis for the first time in their lives. It is for these reasons that the two ad hoc tribunals have victim and witness protection teams, which try to take care of the psychological, as well as the physical, protection of witnesses. Grave as these problems now are, they are bound to be much worse in the ICC, where witnesses may have to travel many thousands of kilometers to an utterly unfamiliar culture where nobody speaks their language, and they may have to be away from home for a week or more, even if their appearance in court is brief.

Much of the excitement of a trial in the Anglo-Saxon tradition comes, at least notionally, from the interaction between the judge, the defense, and the prosecution. An Anglo-Saxon, if called to give evidence, would have at least some idea of what to expect. Yet most of the world does not operate this system and has difficulty understanding it. A number of Yugoslav witnesses in the early days, for example, started to get up and leave the court when the prosecution had finished with them. They were startled, and in some cases upset, to find that their testimony was going to be put in public question by the defense. The experience of cross-examination can be unnerving; for a traumatized victim, it may be much worse. Ironically, the tradition of cross-examination was so little understood in Yugoslavia that many of the early defense attorneys did a poor job in attacking the credibility of the prosecution witnesses.

Not every tradition finds it easy to grasp the idea of independent evidence presented on one's own behalf. Authoritarian political cultures, or cultures where there are strong social and hierarchical pressures, may make this concept harder to understand. And there will be many cases, of course, in which a witness's duty to tell the truth will be at odds with his or her wider political objectives. It might be tempting to exaggerate guilt, consoled by the thought that everybody in the community back home *knows* that the accused is guilty. At a minimum, the ICC will be dealing with cultures in which concepts of law (inasmuch as they even exist), as well as concepts of individual and collective rights and duties, will be different from those that the most judges, prosecutors, defense lawyers, and investigators have learned.

There are, of course, some things that can be done to improve the situation. Witnesses must be carefully selected and briefed about what to expect. People they know and trust can travel with them, and they can be looked after by people from their own country, or at least people who speak their language. The Rwanda tribunal has gone especially far in this respect: in a country where about half the population is illiterate, witnesses get an illustrated booklet in Kinyarwanda that explains, in everyday terms, what they are going to be asked to do and takes them through the various stages of traveling to Arusha and giving testimony. As in many other cases, the ICC will confront an extreme version of this problem: it may find itself producing a half-dozen such booklets for witnesses from different cultural backgrounds before a sensible trial can take place.

Unlike trials in a domestic jurisdiction, where language is less commonly an issue, the fairness and reasonableness of trials in international courts will depend greatly on getting the language aspects right. Simultaneous interpretation is essential if a trial is to run at any speed at all, but simultaneous interpreters are highly skilled professionals who earn a great deal of money, and they are often in short supply, even for the major languages. The work is mentally exhausting, and interpreters will generally have to rest every thirty minutes or so. A seven-hour day in court, therefore, will mean having two, or possibly three, interpreters available all the time. ICTY was able to draw on a sizeable pool of Serbo-Croat interpreters into French and English (though not without some security concerns). The ICTR has not been so fortunate—there are very few Kinyarwanda interpreters into English—and the ICC can expect language problems as well.

Any court conducts its administrative affairs according to a series of rules that are set by negotiation and tradition. Visitors to the ad hoc tribunals are surprised by the complex way in which practices have developed there, drawing on several traditions. One obvious variation is the presence or absence of a jury. Anyone who has served on an Anglo-Saxon jury will recall being told something like "the facts, ladies and gentlemen, are for you to determine." The judge is primarily a kind of super-referee and expert on matters of law. Most countries do not have this tradition, although some have lay assessors in place of jurors. In some systems with juries, the judge will sit in on their deliberations. For obvious reasons, it was not remotely feasible for the two ad hoc tribunals to operate with juries, and so the three judges have become the "triers of fact" as well as legal experts, and not all of them were prepared.

The absence of a jury has other practical consequences. It enables much more work to be done on paper and in advance of the trial (e.g., by requiring the defense and prosecution to produce preliminary submissions and to agree between them which factual points are agreed and which are in dispute). But the absence of a jury affects the entire tone of a trial. To some extent, the tactics that the two sides employ in a jury trial will be psychological in origin, that is, they will target the emotions of the jury as much as their rational faculties and hope to sway jurors even if the evidence does not point in their favor. While such tactics will work with any human being, especially where atrocious crimes are concerned, they are much less likely to work with experienced criminal judges. But not all judges at the two tribunals are from this background. Surprisingly, many of the judges were academic scholars or legal administrators who never had been inside a courtroom in their lives. The slow progress of some of the early trials can partly be explained by the difficulties certain judges had in managing an unfamiliar process.

Another feature of the Anglo-Saxon system that seems normal is that resources are heavily weighted toward the prosecution. This is acceptable; after all, the prosecution assumes the burden of proof (in effect, the defense need not respond at all). Yet this pattern, and the associated need for the prosecution to prove its case beyond a reasonable doubt, is based on specific assumptions. The main one is that the prosecution may rely upon the resources of the state if needed. (The ad hoc tribunals can only call on the resources of states, which is a very different matter.) Although the bar is set as high in war crimes courts, the courts themselves do not have the same resources. And the defense itself may have significant resources available that a typical defendant does not have. In the *Blaskic* trial, for example, the defense was being funded by the Croatian government (odd, at first sight, since Blaskic was a Bosnian).[1] And the resources of that government were being devoted to get an acquittal. This imbalance, with a handicapped prosecution and an unexpectedly powerful defense, is likely to be a feature of trials of high-level political or military leaders in the future.

One characteristic of the Anglo-Saxon tradition that *is* helpful in this context, perhaps, is the relatively transparent nature. Evidence that the prosecution introduces is set out in detail in the court, can be challenged by the defense and queried by the judges, and leaves an audit trail for anyone who watches or reads the record of the trial. This takes longer and is subject to many qualifications, but it does expose the workings of the system to inquiry and enables challenges to be mounted. In the inquisitorial system (used throughout much of the world), much depends on a general faith that the examining magistrate has done a competent job and is unbiased. It is difficult to see how that system could ever work very well in a war crimes court, since accusations of bias and political machinations are, and will be, standard criticisms. The lack of visibility and accountability in the inquisitorial system, and the degree of trust it requires, would make the credibility of the court much harder to establish.

The absence of a jury also means that some of the rules of evidence can be relaxed. The judges, after all, are considered mature and balanced enough not to be swayed by factors that would confuse a jury of laypersons. Thus, prior publicity about an accused, which might have derailed a trial in some national jurisdictions, is thought not to apply: the judges in the *Milosevic* trial are assumed to be uninfluenced by the tidal wave of negative publicity about that individual which has been a feature of the last decade or so. Similarly, evidence that would be inadmissible in certain national courts is admitted. Hearsay evidence—that is, evidence of an indirect nature—is often admitted in the ad hoc tribunals. A good example is, again, from the *Milosevic* case, where the judges allowed a British politician, Paddy Ashdown, to recount an episode in which the late Franjo Tudjman, after he became president of Croatia, told him that he and Milosevic had done a deal to carve up Bosnia between them. Thus, the judges were admitting evidence from Ashdown about what Tudjman told him Milosevic told *him*, which is several levels removed from direct evidence. In a case like this, the judges are presumed to be skilled enough to weigh such evidence and give it the right importance; that is not a task that a jury of laypersons could be expected to perform.

Finally, the courts conduct a sizeable percentage of work in secrecy. It would be nice if this were not so, and it is right, in theory, that international justice should be as open as possible. But we have to remember that the courts are, for much of the time, confronting indictees who have considerable resources and are unlikely to be very scrupulous about interfering with, threatening, bribing, or even murdering witnesses if will help their case. All of these things have happened at one time or another. A particularly gross example occurred during the *Blaskic* trial at the ICTY, where Stipe Mesic (now president of Croatia) gave evidence about the Croatian government's support for the Bosnian Croat secessionists in 1993. Although the court was cleared for the occasion, and Mesic gave evidence anonymously, somehow news leaked, and the fact of his testimony was announced in Zagreb by the Tudjman regime. To no one's surprise, unidentified "patriots" ambushed Mesic outside his house and beat him severely, no doubt as a warning to others. How the regime in Zagreb learned what had happened, given that so few people knew Mesic was in The Hague, remains a mystery. The Rwanda tribunal makes even greater use of protected witnesses, and the ICC will likely have to do so as well. In addition, some documentary evidence has been presented in secret session, and some government and other witnesses have had their identities protected. There are even provisions for issues to be raised with the judges (or even one judge) directly, without the defense knowing what is going on. None of this is ideal, of course, but there is little alternative.

The merging of various traditions, as modified by the needs of practicality and security, have produced an odd environment in the ad hoc tribunals, and no doubt the ICC will be different again. Anglo-Saxons generally find themselves more at home with the system, since it is recognizably based on their traditions. How defendants and their lawyers in the ICC will react is an interesting question, but clearly the court, if it is to have credibility and be any kind of deterrent at all must look and feel like a court in which the majority of the legal traditions of the world can be discerned in some fashion. Belief in the integrity of the court, and thus in the force of its verdicts, will depend partly on those who will watch and report on the trials; there must be some air of familiarity to the proceedings.

Criminal trials, by their very nature, cannot present a complete picture. A trial can be compared to a military operation, in which the prosecution aims, by the use of clever tactics and various means at its disposal, to achieve the objective, which is the conviction of the accused (who also has plans to evade conviction). Thus, it is the result that counts, not the material that might incidentally become available. (Some information may become available as part of the prosecutor's duty to hand over exculpatory material.) For this reason, the prosecution may well decide to drop charges it might not be able to prove or omit witnesses that will provide redundant testimony. In the *Milosevic* case, for example, only a small part of the allegations made about the behavior of the Yugoslav forces in 1999 actually made its way into the charges, and so witnesses were called only if their evidence related to incidents covered in the indictment. Therefore, only a small portion of the suffering was covered in court, and only an insignificant proportion of the victims ever testified. And the decision of the judges in April 2002 to restrict the number of prosecution witnesses "will give the victims in the courtroom in which Milosevic speaks less time to be heard— or no time at all."[2]

One may ask, "So what?" The purpose of a trial is to establish whether the accused is innocent or guilty, not to act as a therapeutic psychodrama for those who believe they have suffered. Even if it were thought wise to use trials for this purpose, there are obvious cost and logistic impossibilities in giving, say, 800,000 Kosovar Albanians or 300,000 Croatian Serbs the time and space to recount their stories. Even with unthinkable levels of resources and unimaginable commitments of time, the vast majority would have to be left out. In any event, we should not let the modern cult of the victim blind us to the fact that alleged victims appear in court not as victims but as witnesses, and we have already seen that it is quite possible for such people to be innocently mistaken about what occurred, or even deliberately lying. Indeed, in one sense a criminal trial is implicitly intended to show *whether* those claiming victim status are actually victims or not, depending on whether the charges are actually proved. This is bound to contrast with the modern consensus that anybody can be a victim if they think they are.

Moreover, this approach tends to obscure what courts are actually intended to accomplish. In domestic jurisdictions, the court and an organized system of justice replaced the blood feud. In the new dispensation, the accused was alleged not to have harmed another individual as much as violated a law passed by the community to prevent harm. The difference is significant. The self-styled victim is a witness to whether laws have been violated, not an individual seeking personal redress. As soon as we turn the court into a theater for confrontations between alleged victims and alleged perpetrators, we stop trying to establish truth and turn in the direction of politics and show business.

Facts to Be Proved

In a domestic criminal case, even a serious one, the elements that the prosecution must prove are modest, usually touching the immediate circumstances of the alleged crime. In war crimes trials, even of low-level perpetrators, this is often not so, and the range and depth of factual material is much greater. If we examine the judgment in the *Krstic* case, for example, which is probably the most complex that the ad hoc tribunals have completed, we see the number of issues. They include: the breakup of the former Yugoslavia; the origins of the Srebrenica conflict; the UN Safe Areas policy; the plans drawn up by the Bosnian Serb Army; the various meetings that took place among Bosnian Serb generals after the fall of the town; the escape of an armed column toward Tuzla; the chain of command of the Drina Corps; and the standard of proof required for a genocide conviction. All this, of course, is in addition to evidence about the facts of the killings and who was responsible. Even in more mundane cases, some of the argument at the trial has little to do with the circumstances of the crime. As we have seen, the law of war crimes is complex, and some alleged offenses can be described in a number of different ways. A mass killing and deportation incident, for example, can be described as a crime against humanity as well as genocide. The facts of the case will be the same, but a mass of evidence may have to be produced to try to prove that the intent of the perpetrator was genocide.

This was the case in the early days of the courts, when there were few precedents to go by, and it partly accounts for the extreme slowness of some of the early trials in The Hague and Rwanda. For example, the first trial at the ICTY was of Dusko Tadic, a Bosnian Serb official in Prijedor, where some of the earliest atrocities in the fighting in Bosnia were committed. Tadic was what is referred to as a low-level perpetrator (he would probably not even be indicted today), but his case raised a number of issues that had to be settled at that time, because it was the court's first opportunity to address them. One was whether the individuals in the camps in Prijedor were "protected persons" within the meaning of the Geneva Conventions. This required proof of the existence of an international armed conflict at the time and that the individuals were in the hands of a "foreign power." The situation was complicated by the fact that the forces of the rump Yugoslavia (which did not recognize Bosnian independence) were in

Bosnia for part of the time. No one was suggesting that the circumstances of the crimes *themselves* amounted to an international armed conflict. Tadic was a Bosnian, as was the hierarchy of people (including Drljaca and Kovacevic) to whom he reported. His victims were Bosnians as well, albeit of different ethnic groups. But the court eventually decided that the involvement of the rump Yugoslavia in the fighting in Bosnia, especially the involvement of the Yugoslav army and the help provided by Belgrade to Bosnian Serb separatists, effectively made the conflict international, at least in certain places and times. But it also decided that the Bosnian Serb authorities in Prijedor, while linked to Belgrade, were not so closely controlled as to amount to a foreign occupation force, and so the Geneva Conventions did not apply. Eleven of the counts were dismissed as a result.[3] The offenses themselves, and the suffering of the victims, did not change. A similar process occurred in the trial of Tihomir Blaskic, who was convicted of grave breaches of the Geneva Conventions because of the involvement of Croatia in the fighting in central Bosnia the following year. Although some precedents had by then been established, the argument was still complex and difficult.[4]

A similar case arose when the *Tadic* trial chamber (and ultimately the appeals chamber) had to define "armed conflict." Under the ICTY Statute, it is necessary to demonstrate the existence of an armed conflict before crimes against humanity can be proved. Because this was the first time that the issue had arisen, there was no existing definition, and the court had to produce one before considering whether or not Tadic's acts had been committed in the context of an armed conflict. All of this—as with the separate debate on the existence of an international armed conflict—was distinct from the issue of whether Tadic had actually committed the offenses. Also, the Rwanda tribunal had to grapple with the question of genocide in the *Akayesu* trial. As we have seen, it is unlikely that the framers of the Genocide Convention expected it to be used operationally, and until then it had never been done. The court in Arusha was obliged to confront many of these issues for the first time in the case of a low-level perpetrator. This created its own problems, since the assumption had always been that genocide trials, if there were any, would be of high-level perpetrators, whose clear intent was to destroy ethnic groups. But Jean-Paul Akayesu was only a regional official carrying out orders and clearly unable, as a matter of practicality, to kill more than a small proportion of the Tutsi in Rwanda. So the court had to decide what the phrase "in whole or in part" meant, then decide whether the part of the Tutsi population allegedly killed on Akayesu's orders was big enough to qualify. It decided that it was. But all of this was in addition to (and, in a sense, irrelevant to) whether Akayesu had actually committed the acts of which he was accused.[5] Similarly, a significant part of the trial of General Krstic, including a great deal of written learned legal argument, was taken up not with what he did but what his intentions were when he did it. The effect of all these debates is that the guilt or innocence of the individual tends, for a while, to be a lesser issue, and the accused sits for days, or even weeks, in the court as ethereal arguments take place around and above them.

The ICC will face the same problems, since it will not be bound by the jurisprudence of the two ad hoc tribunals. As with those tribunals, things will improve and trials will become shorter as the court gains more experience. But it is also true that the ICC will be handling, almost from the beginning, complex and difficult cases against senior or other important figures. As experience in The Hague and Arusha has shown, there is a level of precision beyond which texts, no matter how elaborate, cannot go; some things cannot be clarified until there is a real trial. The statute calls for the ICC to concern itself with "the most serious crimes of international concern," but it also requires the court to determine that the case is inadmissible where it "is not of sufficient gravity to justify further action by the Court."[6] Elsewhere in the same article, the court is required to declare the case inadmissible if it is being investigated or prosecuted by a state with jurisdiction over it, or if the state has investigated and decided not to prosecute, unless, in either case, the state is unwilling or unable to do so properly. (It is not clear what happens if a state places an individual on trial, finds him or her guilty, then rapidly pardons the person or commutes the sentence. This has happened on several occasions, most famously when President Richard Nixon pardoned Lieutenant William Calley.)

Judges, therefore, may be called upon to measure the gravity of a crime against some kind of standard. Some crimes that the ICC will prosecute—such as genocide—should be straightforward to determine. But it is not clear that looting—even though a war crime under article 8 of the ICC Statute—necessarily counts, at least unless it is practiced on a massive scale. Judges may also have to decide whether domestic investigations or trials are being properly conducted. At a minimum, this can mean that they will be making intensely political judgments about a country's judicial system. More worrisome, they may have to judge whether or not national authorities are conducting an investigation or trial in good faith. This will be especially difficult when a state—like Croatia under Franjo Tudjman—is making every effort on the surface to behave properly but in practice everyone knows that a cynical policy is being pursued. So we can assume that the first trials at the ICC will feature, as did the trials at the ad hoc tribunals, complex and time-consuming debates about the jurisdiction of the court and the admissibility of the case itself.

Finally, perhaps, it is worth emphasizing that war crimes trials, now and in the future, take so long because the prosecution is seeking to prove something that is inherently complex. The most common type of trial at the

ICC will be of a major political or military leader who was far removed from the incidents that took place. The first matter is to prove that the incidents actually occurred. This cannot be achieved only by statements from victims. In some cases (as in the Srebrenica killings) there may be few or no direct witnesses anyway. Rather, extensive forensic, photographic, and other technical evidence may have to be deployed to demonstrate, for example, that a mass grave does not contain bodies of soldiers killed in action or civilians caught in the cross fire. Independent witnesses and observers, perhaps from a UN mission, may be called to corroborate statements by survivors. Next, the prosecution will have to produce evidence about who carried out the killings. In many African conflicts, the sides are scarcely distinguishable from each other and may in fact join together at some point, as in Sierra Leone. Demonstrating which units carried out an attack may be difficult and could require technical analytical evidence to do with known deployments or appearances by foreign military observers present at the time. Witnesses who served in the units concerned may give evidence about who was involved.

All of this is necessary, but it is hardly sufficient. The prosecution then needs to show that the accused was actually responsible for what went on or, at a minimum, had the power to prevent or punish and failed to use it. This can be difficult enough even with a conventional army. Experts on Indonesia, for example, have suggested that there were no less than four separate lines of command between Jakarta and East Timor in 1999–2000: the formal ones of unit subordination and district command, the informal one operated by the special forces, and the very informal one that relied on the patron-client relationship common in the Indonesian Army, among others. Likewise, there are political systems—even democracies—where the minister of defense and the chief of defense have less actual power over the armed forces than the president and his or her military adviser, and where the latter can personally deploy forces for operations. In many African conflicts, militias operate with no clear command hierarchy and often show loyalty only to individuals on a personal basis. Trying to establish effective control of a militia unit by a politician in a city hundreds of kilometers away would be a painstaking and complex task that would take time. Much of the evidence in such a case would be indirect, and the court would have to accept the analytical inferences that the prosecution drew from it.

Even if it were established that the crimes were committed and that the accused had some responsibility, the crimes would have to conform to the definitions laid down in the statute of the court. Thus, to demonstrate that crimes against humanity have been committed, the ICTY prosecutor must show that an armed conflict was in progress at the time. This requirement has been dropped in the ICC Statute, which will enhance the chances of prosecuting militia leaders in Africa, for example. But the other requirement for the proof of crimes against humanity is that the atrocities should be "widespread and systematic," which is to say that random atrocities, even conducted on a large scale and very brutally, would not qualify unless there were an underlying plan of some kind. Proving this controlling intelligence, which will be difficult in some Third World conflicts, will require evidence to be collected and produced for the court.

The Trial Itself

After all these preliminaries, what will a trial at the ICC look like? The ICC begins its life with a much more elaborate statute, and much longer rules of procedure and evidence, than did the ad hoc tribunals, and it has benefited from their experience. But many things will become clear only when a trial starts, mainly because the issues raised in the early trials will be peculiar to the circumstances of the indictment, and there is no way that the judges can prepare for everything in advance.

The first point is that international justice is moving toward enhancing pretrial procedures. In The Hague this has meant a change of procedure to appoint a pretrial judge, who is in effect the business manager for the trial. Within seven days of the accused appearing in court to have the charges put to them, the judge is selected to coordinate the preparation of the trial and to "take any necessary measure to prepare the case for a fair and expeditious trial."[7] Part of the judge's role is to ensure that the prosecutor presents a pretrial brief, containing a summary of the evidence that the prosecutor intends to bring, as well as a statement of points in dispute. The prosecutor must also present a witness list, a summary of testimony, and a list of exhibits. After this is completed, the judge will also order the defense to file a witness list and a list of exhibits. In general, this change has speeded the process, and it is not surprising that the ICC will operate in much the same way: indeed, the ICC Statute specifically foresees a pretrial chamber, which will handle the legal and procedural issues that arise between the investigation and the opening of trial. In particular, it is responsible for issuing arrest warrants[8] and confirming the charges before trial.[9]

One important effect might be that evidence about the crimes is never presented in court. The majority of the defendants before the ICC will be from the senior management level, and they are unlikely to have taken part in the crimes themselves. A typical defense, therefore, will be that, although the crimes were no doubt committed, they had no knowledge of them, did not order them, and could not have prevented them. (Many people at the time thought this would have been a sensible defense in the *Krstic* trial, but the defendant decided otherwise.) As a result, the crime base evidence may go largely unchallenged, and the defense will concentrate instead on the linkage evidence, which purports to connect the accused to the crimes. There are good and bad consequences of such a development. It will, of course, reduce the length of the trial, possibly substantially. It will also reduce the need to bring witnesses from the region to give evidence about the circumstances of the crimes and thereby save money and time. But this also means that the trial becomes an increasingly technical matter, in which patterns of political control and the minutiae of military command systems will come to dominate the proceedings.

For those who see such trials as a form of political theater for teaching moral lessons, or as a chance for the voices of victims to be heard, this is unwelcome. But it is also likely to have political consequences. The media will find it much more difficult to produce newsworthy reports about constitutional provisions on control of the armed forces, or arguments about military reporting chains, and so, in the end, may not report much at all. And while the eventual judgment will record the factual elements of the crimes, even if they are not disputed, the effect will be much less than if the evidence about the crimes themselves were presented in court. This could be a special problem when, as will often happen, initial reports of the crimes in the media are massively exaggerated. Thus, the trial of a general whose troops have been accused of genocide by the media may in fact open only with charges of crimes against humanity, but the public record might never be corrected.

In Arusha and The Hague there has been a gap of some months between the arrival of an indictee at the court and the start of trial. This is not surprising. There is no way in which trial teams, let alone witnesses and technical experts, can be available at any moment to drop everything and start a trial. Judges and prosecutors may be busy with other trials (unless the ICC is far more generously staffed than seems likely), and courtrooms may well be booked for other matters. Moreover, good management of court resources often means that it is sensible to wait for a critical mass of defendants to be assembled to avoid having to have the same trial, with the same evidence and the same witnesses, on numerous occasions. Where large numbers of individuals are indicted for the same group of offenses (such as the Bosnian Croats for the Lasva Valley, or the Bosnian Serbs for the Prijedor camps), the sensible course would be to try them all together. This was not possible because of delays in arrests and administrative problems, and so there has been an awkward compromise resulting in numerous delays and multiple trials. The most extreme case is that of the Banovic twins, Nenad and Pedrag, two camp guards who would probably not even be indicted today. Problems in tracking them down meant that by the time they eventually appeared in The Hague they could not be joined to any other trial, and so there will probably have to be a separate trial. The ICC will face problems at least as severe as this.

In addition—and most important—the defense must be given time to prepare properly, to look through the prosecution evidence, to conduct counterinvestigations, to ready its own witnesses, and to consider how to respond to the prosecution's pretrial brief. There is provision for the accused to represent himself or herself, and this has occasionally happened. In the Rwanda tribunal, Jean-Paul Akayesu sacked his defense counsel after the verdict and represented himself in the sentencing phase. More recently, Slobodan Milosevic has elected to represent himself. In that case (and the same will be true of the ICC), the court has appointed so-called amici curiae (friends of the court) to ensure that justice is done. Appointing defense lawyers will be nowhere near as straightforward in an international court as in a domestic one, and it tends to add delays. (Some people in The Hague and Arusha have worried from time to time about the quality of defense lawyers there, arguing that it does the cause of justice no good if things slip through that should have been queried in court.) In The Hague, there was a particular problem finding lawyers from the region who could operate successfully in an adversarial system. Most of the early Bosnian Serb defendants had counsel from the region, generally Serbs themselves, so that they could confer in their own language, although Western co-counsel were sometimes employed as well. These individuals were of variable quality: the best that can be said of some is that they tried hard. The ad hoc tribunals have now tried to lay down some criteria for the selection of defense counsel, insisting that he or she is "admitted to the practice of law in a State, or is a University professor of law," and speaks English or French.[10] The ICC equivalent provisions are rather stricter, requiring defense counsel to have "established competence in international or criminal law and procedure, as well as the necessary relevant experience" and "have an excellent working knowledge of and be fluent in at least one of the working languages of the Court."[11] It is not clear how this is to be reconciled with the right of the accused to "conduct the defence . . . through legal assistance of the accused's choosing."[12] Nor is it clear who is responsible for assessing the qualifications of defense counsel, especially where language is concerned. There have been recent moves to set up an international criminal bar to defend putative ICC indictees, following a conference held in Montreal in June 2002.[13] If this increases the quality of the defense in international criminal trials, it can only be a good thing; it is in no one's interest, in the end, for the accused not to have a proper defense.

Language, once again, is likely to be a major complicating factor in the ICC. Although the court will have two working languages, English and French, it will also have to publish judgments, as well as other decisions "resolving fundamental issues before the Court," in Arabic, Chinese, Russian, and Spanish.[14] It is not clear that anyone has given much thought to the practical implications of this decision. The ad hoc tribunals struggle to meet the demands of bilingualism, and it is common for judgments to appear in one language months before they appear in another. This may be less of a problem with final judgments, but it will be much more important with the mass of judgments on issues such as admissibility, which are time-sensitive. At the ICC, it is possible that such judgments will not actually be available in, say, Chinese, until the trial is actually over, especially given the formidable problems of translating material that is at once legally and conceptually complex and full of detailed military vocabulary.

In addition to the two working languages, the ad hoc tribunals have in effect elected to operate a third: that of the region itself. In practice, it is hard to see how the ICC can avoid doing this, often in several languages. Article 67 of the ICC Statute gives the accused the right to an interpreter to follow the course of the trial. In practice, it is likely that, as at the ad hoc tribunals, all documents will have to be translated into the language of the accused, with constant simultaneous interpretation being provided. If an accused speaks English or French to an acceptable standard this would be less of a problem, but the article requires that he or she should "fully understand and speak" the language, and this will often not be the case. There will be a lot of room to argue after the fact that a given trial was unfair because the defendant did not completely understand some of what was going on, and it is unlikely that an alert defense counsel would overlook the chance to create mischief by requiring the court to work in a third language, knowing the problems that would cause for the prosecution. It is true that the ICC Statute does not require interpretation into the accused's mother tongue, still less any language that the accused happens to like. But while it is true that at The Hague judges in the *Celebici* trial refused an application for interpretation into "Croatian," rather than Bosnian/Croatian/Serb, this request was a flagrant piece of politicking, rather like a defendant requesting interpretation into the dialect of Yorkshire, Provence, or Texas. In practice, the ICC will almost certainly have to conduct a trial in the mother tongue of an accused as well, if that is not English or French. Not only will this be a massive administrative burden; there will also be problems for some languages in finding simultaneous interpreters, as well as translators capable of rendering, say, captured military documents from Africa or Asia into English and French.

One of the significant ways in which the ICC will resemble a common law court is that the defendant must be present. This has led to many of the problems noted above, where trials have had to be split in order that those in custody could be tried. In many systems of law, especially those that make large use of documents, trials in absentia are common and are not thought to be unfair. The ad hoc tribunals did not have this practice, and the ICC has followed this example, although not without some debate in Rome. In some ways this is odd, because it is hard to see that a trial of a major indictee who is not present is in any way unfair: it is the choice of the individual, after all, not to be there. Moreover, such didactic and deterrent potential as the ICC might have could be reduced if there were some trials that were never actually conducted because of the absence of a defendant. But this argument has been lost and seems unlikely now to be reopened.

One way in which the ICC follows the continental model more closely is the extent of evidence that is admitted, and in this respect it follows the example of the ad hoc tribunals, where hearsay evidence is introduced from time to time. The rules of procedure say that the evidence must be "relevant" and "necessary."[15] Much of the evidence will come from witnesses, and it is assumed that they will generally be present in court. Some witnesses have given evidence by video in The Hague, but this is not common and has disadvantages. There is provision for this in the ICC Statute, as there is for evidence to be given in camera.[16] In the ICC Statute, these measures are indicated for "a victim of sexual violence or a child," although in practice it is more likely that these measures will be used, as they have been in the ad hoc tribunals, to protect witnesses generally who are in danger of victimization.

One of the most valuable types of evidence at trial is information in the possession of national governments. Although the Hollywood effect is present here as well, and assumptions about what governments know and possess are often wildly exaggerated, the resources of national governments are much greater than those of any court, and so in principle they should be capable of providing valuable help. The problem is that much government information is, by definition, sensitive and confidential. It does not necessarily have to be intelligence-related: many government officials have friends in other governments who will tell them things, or show them things, which strictly they should not, perhaps because they are worried about the policies of their own government. This information is usually reported back with a caveat, something like "please protect." Sometimes there will be a stronger caveat if the source is opening himself or herself to dismissal or even prosecution by speaking so frankly. Information of this kind must be protected, as must information given officially, but in confidence, by other governments, as well as information obtained in criminal investigations.

This problem first arose in The Hague, where the *Blaskic* prosecution tried to get hold of material that it believed would help the case. It was actually material of Bosnian origin that Bosnian Croats had prudently sent to Zagreb, where it was beyond easy reach. The court ordered the Croatian government to hand over the material, but it refused, claiming national security, although there was no such defense. In October 1997, the trial chamber produced a ruling that appeared to give the judges the right to be the final arbiters of whether or not a state should provide the information requested in any similar case. The problem is that it is difficult to see how a rule can be written that protects the interests of states that genuinely want to be helpful yet that does not allow states that are trying to obstruct the proceedings an easy exit. On the one hand, a state could presumably define anything it found embarrassing to disclose as "national security" information and thus protect the guilty from the full weight of the evidence. On the other hand, a defense team could apply to have categories of sensitive government material made available in open court in the hope of finding something that could be used in its favor, or simply to embarrass the government concerned. Some governments might be cynical enough to sponsor motions of this kind before the court purely as intelligence-gathering exercises. Sanitization of texts and hearings in camera can help to some extent but are not complete answers.

If there is an answer, it must be that a state with genuine security concerns should find it possible to articulate those concerns in some way that will be convincing. It is not necessary to produce the material itself (or perhaps produce it only for a single judge) to provide a convincing explanation why the information cannot be used in court. (Interestingly, the Croats failed to even try this tactic.) The issue was controversial during the ICC negotiations (reflecting national practices that varied widely), and what emerged was a long and complicated provision (article 72), which, while continuing the idea of negotiations and attempts to find a practical solution, eventually enables a state to refuse to obey an order from the court to produce material. The only sanctions are referral to the Assembly of States Parties or the UN Security Council, which are no doubt terrifying punishments but which might not be wholly effective. While we should not fall into the trap of romantically exaggerating the importance of this kind of material for trials, the way this article was settled represents a modest, but useful, victory for the ungodly.

Verdict and Sentence

In Anglo-Saxon common law systems, much of the drama of the trial lies in the verdict, usually to be delivered after a suspenseful wait of hours or, in extreme cases, days. But in war crimes trials, juries do not deliver verdicts; judges deliver judgments—and fairly substantial ones at that. A verdict of 100 pages in The Hague or Arusha is common (even a press summary may take several pages), and so a wait of months for the judgment is normal. Majority verdicts are fairly common—the appeals chamber split 3-2 in the *Erdemovic* case—and the judgments often contain energetically argued dissenting judgments. There are several practical reasons for these differences.

To begin with, most war crimes trials are complex, involving a collection of incidents over a period of months or even years, difficult issues of responsibility and control, and often more than one defendant. New points of law arise all the time and need to be settled, and most of the factual matters on which the judges have to pronounce are themselves highly complex. Judges are professionals and experienced and so are thought capable of, and accustomed to, setting out their thoughts in an organized way, something a lay jury could not be expected to do. Moreover, the very absence of a jury requires courts to give verdicts in a way that is transparent and for permanent record. For this reason, judgments are a summary of the case and trial: the judges will generally rehash the background of the case, the details of the accused, the main arguments made by the prosecution and defense, the main conclusions of fact, as well as the legal issues to be settled. The fact that there has been disagreement between judges is important, especially since the appeals chamber may ultimately support the minority point of view. Again, most war crimes trials have multiple counts in each indictment (some can take nearly an hour to read at the initial appearance), and in some cases separate charges are brought on the same set of facts, each of which must be considered separately.

After the verdict (sometimes immediately after) comes the sentence. One of the first decisions made about the ad hoc tribunals was that they would not be able to apply the death penalty, and this has been carried forward into the ICC. There are several reasons: apart from general abhorrence of state-sanctioned killing among civilized nations, it is improbable that any state that retained the death penalty would actually be available, and acceptable, to carry it out. But the most important reason, perhaps, is practical. I was once sitting in a courtroom watching a British officer giving evidence, and next to me was sitting an American military lawyer. He asked me whether the ICTY could impose the death penalty and seemed rather surprised when I said that it could not. I then asked him what he thought the political consequences would be of an international, but Western-dominated, court putting to death a Bosnian (in this case, a Bosnian Serb) in a foreign country. After some thought, he conceded that this might create the odd martyr or two.

But there is no doubt that the absence of the death penalty creates disturbing anomalies. For example, since 1994 the Tutsi government of Rwanda has been keen to execute Hutu it holds responsible for the mass killings in that year. Yet these are generally the less important perpetrators. Those most responsible for the killings, those who are being tried in Arusha, will not face the death penalty if convicted. In another irony, they are likely to be extremely well looked after, since prisons that house convicted criminals indicted by the ad hoc tribunals have to meet minimum UN standards, and these standards are often higher than average Africans would expect in their private homes. Indeed, it is likely that African states that agree to taking convicted Rwandan criminals from Arusha will have to build expensive new jails, much more luxurious than any they have for domestic criminals. And finally, convicted war criminals will get an excellent level of health care in a continent where it is usually limited or nonexistent. In particular, a percentage of the indictees (some believe it could ultimately be as many as 50 percent) are or will be HIV-positive and will therefore have to be given expensive medical care to keep them alive, something those they have persecuted will never be able to afford. A high proportion of future ICC indictees are likely to come from Africa, but it seems unlikely that they could serve their sentences there given that conditions must "be consistent with widely accepted international treaty standards governing treatment of prisoners" and that they must be no "more or less favourable" than those for prisoners convicted of the same offenses in that state.[17]

Even if punishment is to exclude the death penalty, there remains the question of what kind of punishment is appropriate for such crimes if charges are proved. Here again, the tendency for reactions to atrocities to be logarithmic rather than arithmetical is obvious. If murder is appropriately punished by life imprisonment, with release on bail after ten years, and if the punishment for the murder of several people is life with no remission, then what punishment is appropriate for the murder of scores of people, or hundreds, or even thousands? There is no answer to this question, because human life is not long enough, even if it were thought that the death of 100 people should be punished a hundred times (or even ten) times as severely as the death of one. What can certainly be said is that the ad hoc tribunals have taken a markedly harsh line in the sentences they have awarded so far. Thus, Tihomir Blaskic, the Bosnian Croat military leader, was sentenced to forty-five years in prison for the horrifying events in the Lasva Valley. General Radislav Krstic, the hero of Srebrenica, was later sentenced to forty-six years for that crime. It is generally thought, rightly or wrongly, that life imprisonment is being considered for Milosevic should he be found guilty, since after that, evidently, no escalation is possible. The issue of punishment was, naturally enough, hotly debated in the Rome negotiations, and there is a curious provision that limits prison sentences to a maximum of thirty years or, alternatively, life imprisonment "when justified by the extreme gravity of the crime and the individual circumstances of the convicted person."[18] This is odd, since the court should really, according to its statute, only be trying extremely grave crimes anyway.

The severity of punishment has to do with the punitive function of courts, if indeed punishment serves any practical purpose at all. In theory, punishment is supposed to act as a deterrent, although it is doubtful whether it does that (see Chapter 9). Punishments are also, as in domestic jurisdictions, intended to express a sanctioned revenge on the part of the victim and society and to attempt to redress, as it were, the moral balance.

The situation is further complicated by the fact that the judges seem unsure and divided about the purpose of the punishments they are handing out.[19] Societies have often grappled with this question when trying to devise punishments for offenses thought heinous, such as religious offenses or treason against an anointed monarch. The attempts they made—hanging, drawing and quartering—are best understood as a fairly desperate attempt to somehow mark out, in theatrical fashion, the fact that these offenses were seen as *really bad* and so somehow had to dictate a punishment that was, symbolically at least, worse than death. But we have become more civilized since then, and perhaps the only form of moral statement open to courts is to pile up the years on the sentence, hoping this will be taken as an expression of disgust and horror at what the perpetrator has done. The absence of the death penalty means that a perpetrator can never experience what the victims experienced, and this is one reason why even the strictest sentence fails to appease victims or members of the same community, who generally claim that the sentence, whatever its length, is hopelessly inadequate. (Meanwhile, the perpetrator's supporters are horrified at the severity of the sentence and question how a court could possibly convict individuals merely for defending their own people.) Sentences, no matter how severe, are never going appease victims—indeed, they are probably fundamentally incapable of doing so—and will always leave a residue of disappointment on one side and resentment on the other.

The conviction and sentence are not, of course, completely the end of the story. Both the ad hoc tribunals and the ICC have separate appeals chambers (shared in the case of The Hague and Rwanda), and both prosecution and defense can approach them not only on the verdict and sentence but also on many other issues from different stages of the trial. (In the common law system, the prosecution generally cannot appeal an acquittal.) It has seemed odd to some that there is no court beyond the ad hoc tribunals to which an appeal can be made, but this is more understandable when we recall that the two tribunals are subsidiary organs of the UN Security Council and thus above any other court. In theory, the Security Council might be able to overrule the courts in certain cases, but this has never been tried and seems unlikely. In the case of the ICC, there was a deliberate decision, following the ad hoc model, to have trial and appeals chambers in the same organization.

Assuming a conviction, and that the appeals chamber upholds the verdict and sentence at least in part, then the criminal goes off to serve the sentence. In the case of the ICC, this is in a country decided by the court under a complex series of rules set out in article 103 of the ICC Statute. And that will probably be the last anyone sees of them for some time. There has never been a provision for parole in the ad hoc tribunals, and, given the context in which they work, it is hard to see how there could be. The ICC has provisions for release under certain circumstances, but not for parole as such. Even if it were technically possible to release someone with the sure knowledge that he or she could be collected later and reincarcerated should he or she misbehave (however defined), it is doubtful whether the political reaction, which might include attempted murder, would be worth the notional gain in fairness. The issue of whether a major war criminal could ever be accepted back into society once more is complex and difficult. Fortunately, for practical reasons, the issue seems unlikely to arise soon.

*   *   *

Although investigations, arrests, and the preparation of cases all consume huge resources and raise profound legal, practical, and ethical issues, it is the trial itself that is both the justification and the test of the whole process. If trials are unconvincing, end equivocally, or fail to end at all, then the organization that conducts them will, understandably, be written off as a failure. But whether the necessarily complex and bureaucratic process of conducting war crimes trials will actually produce results that are politically acceptable enough to guarantee the longevity of the ICC and similar institutions is something only time will reveal.

Notes

1. Blaskic was born of Bosnian Croat parents in Kiseljak, a hard-line, largely Croat town outside Sarajevo.
2. Mirko Klarin, "Milosevic Prosecution 'Emasculated,'" *Tribunal Report,* April 23, 2002 (available online at www.iwpr.net).
3. *Tadic* (IT-94–1), Judgment of July 14, 1997.
4. *Blaskic* (IT-95–14), Judgment of March 3, 2000.
5. *Akayesu* (ICTR-96–4-T), Judgment of September 2, 1998.
6. *Rome Statute of the International Criminal Court* (hereinafter ICC Statute), art. 17(d).
7. ICTY, IT(32), *Rules of Procedure and Evidence* (hereinafter ICTY RPE), 21st revision, rule 65 *ter* (B).
8. ICC Statute, art. 58.
9. Ibid., art. 61.
10. ICTY RPE, Rule 44(A).
11. ICC, *Rules of Procedure and Evidence*, (hereafter ICC RPE), Rule 22.1.
12. ICC Statute, art. 67(d)1.
13. Elisabeth Kalbfuss, "A New World Watchdog: Lawyers' Group Would Play Key Role in Cases Before ICC," *Montreal Gazette*, June 14, 2002.
14. ICC RPE, Rule 40.
15. ICC Statute, art. 69.2.
16. Ibid., art. 68.2.
17. Ibid., art. 106.
18. Ibid., art. 77.1.
19. See Schabbas, *An Introduction to the ICC*, pp. 137–141.

9

The Truth?

At some point in our lives, all of us were probably taught to differentiate between various forms of truth. There was scientific truth: the hypothesis that best fit the results of experiments and observations and that was subject to modification and change in the light of both. There was, conversely, religious truth, which accepts certain assertions because of their origin, rather than their content; and its ally, political and ideological truth, which must be accepted by followers whether it corresponds to the facts or not. Political truths are especially dangerous, since their wide acceptance makes them almost into facts, and in politics one often confronts shadow rather than substance. The establishment of truth commissions, such as the Truth and Reconciliation Commission formed in South Africa following apartheid, leads to other kinds of truth.

Ye Shall Know the Truth

In theory, and to some extent in practice, legal truth is closer to scientific truth than any other type. It is what can be proved in a court of law, and in criminal cases such proof must be beyond a reasonable doubt. Yet fundamentally legal truth is much more subjective compared to scientific truth, because it depends on the weighing of arguments within a process that contains no scientific methodology. It is always possible, especially in finely balanced cases, that one jury or another or a different set of judges would come to another conclusion about guilt and innocence. Thus, the Bosnian Serb Goran Jelisic was acquitted on the charge of genocide in Brcko in Bosnia, and the truth, for the time being at least, is that genocide did not take place there. Given the complex and slippery nature of the evidence,

225

however, as well as the scope for arguing intent, another set of judges could have reached a different conclusion, and genocide in Brcko would now be a proven fact. Or consider the Bosnian Croat Vlatko Kupreskic. When he was detained by Dutch SFOR troops in 1997, he was accused of complicity in one of the most horrendous crimes of the Bosnian conflict, although technically he was innocent until proven guilty. He was found guilty, and the truth of the Ahmici incident included his participation. Yet that truth had to be rewritten once more when he was freed on appeal, without a stain on his character. Now in spite of the impressive record of acquittals in this case, it is clear that *someone* carried out the Ahmici massacre, and the court cannot state whether or not Kupreskic was one of the perpetrators; the most it can say is that the evidence for his participation is not strong enough to secure a conviction. Whether the acquitted defendants in the *Ahmici* case were involved is known only to them and a few others, and the process of law is unable to help us.

Although war crimes prosecutors often hope to arrive at the truth as a by-product of trials, they are usually modest about what can be expected, and the kind of truth they seek is often at a high level of generality. For example, no one who is prepared to be convinced by evidence can now doubt that a massacre took place near Srebrenica in July 1995, or that the vast majority, and perhaps all, of the missing males are dead. Likewise, trials in The Hague have thrown light on such issues as the true story of the background to the Srebrenica killings as well as Bosnian Croat political objectives in 1991–1992. At the time of writing, it looks as though the Milosevic trial will produce the best account we are ever likely to have of the fighting and the killings in Kosovo in 1998–1999.

But these are partial and pragmatic truths and do not bring absolute certainty. Unfortunately, the demands made on war crimes trials go much farther than that: they often include a search for a kind of transcendent truth, which in turn is expected to have all sorts of healing effects subsequently. "Ye shall know the truth," according to the Bible, "and the truth shall make ye free." But it is obvious that that truth is not truth as discovered by fallible human beings but rather a transcendental truth that announces itself in unmistakable terms and is obvious and convincing to all. The kind of questions that people hope courts can address are sometimes at a high level (Is X guilty of Y?) and sometimes at a detailed level (What happened to my husband, brother, and son?). Back on earth the ability to answer these questions is limited.

There are many reasons for this. Some questions, especially those of moral or political responsibility, are not addressable by a court anyway, but unfortunately these are the questions of most interest. Likewise, the mechanics of mounting a trial often militate against attempts to find the full truth of everything. Prosecutors will often choose to present only that set of facts that will lead to a conviction. The full story of what happened in a particular village at a given time may never be known, because it does not form part of the prosecution case, and so it is not examined in court. Often, in turn, this is because the truth of what happened is probably unknowable, and so the court could not be expected to reach a verdict on the evidence available. In a future trial, the International Criminal Court may debate whether to bring a charge of genocide against an individual, in a climate of excited speculation about the existence of a genocidal episode. It may eventually be decided not to bring that charge because the evidence alleging genocide is not strong enough, and so a safer charge, probably crimes against humanity, would be brought instead. This does not mean that genocide did not take place in that locality, but it does mean that the law will never be able to shed any light on whether or not it did.

Similarly, truth is often not available at the tactical level of personal experience. Sometimes, by DNA testing, it will be possible to show at least that a certain person is unambiguously dead. It may also be possible to show, because of the type of wound, or the presence of a blindfold, that the person did not die in combat or was murdered. But often this will not be possible, and there will never be a finding of fact that an individual was murdered as opposed to dying in battle or being caught in the cross fire. And in many cases the victims will not form the subject of trials anyway. No one actually knows, even approximately, the actual death toll from the fighting in the former Yugoslavia. And in Rwanda the *difference* between the highest and the lowest estimates is probably greater than the total of all Yugoslav deaths. No conceivable program of trials could ever shed light on the precise total of these casualties or who was responsible for the events that led to them. Yet it is precisely at the tactical level, of course, that the greatest interest lies. People want justice, revenge, or at least understanding on a personal level.

At best, war crimes trials can address only some elements of a complex and confusing picture. In some cases, incidents may be too inconsequential, from a practical standpoint, to merit the complexity and expense of a trial. There is much controversy, for example, about the extent of the killings of Croats by Muslims before the attacks on Ahmici and elsewhere in 1993. There is much disagreement about how many Serbs were killed by Muslim forces under Naser Oric around Srebrenica in the years before the fall of that town.[1] These incidents have probably been inflated for political reasons and have been used in trials in defense of Croats and Serbs to justify the atrocities carried out by each. It would therefore be helpful to the cause of truth if the alleged miscreants were put on trial, but lack of resources will probably prevent that from happening. But even when the cases are significant enough to be worth investigating by any standards, the information may not be there, there may be no witnesses, or the accused themselves may be dead. So the full story of Zagreb's role in the breakup of Bosnia, and the expulsion of hundreds of thousands of Serbs from Croatia in 1995, may never be told in court because the main architects—President Franjo Tudjman and Defense Minister Goijko Susak—are now both dead (and beyond the reach of the law).

Thus, the contribution of war crimes trials to the establishment of *the truth* about large and complex episodes of violence is likely to be limited and patchy, because trials are actually intended for other purposes than the writing of history. But there are also important limits to what trials can discover, even about the incidents they address, because of how they are conducted. Many see the adversarial Anglo-Saxon tradition as unsuitable for establishing the truth. By definition, what is proved cannot be more than what is alleged, and what is alleged will often be what prosecutors think can be proved. And facts must be proved beyond a reasonable doubt. While this is the minimum standard by which we all would hope to be judged, it does mean that convincing theories about what happened in a particular context cannot be considered true because they fail to meet this criterion. Other kinds of trials and other traditions, of course, come to a conclusion on the basis of the relative strength of the evidence. Thus, to take an example from Anglo-Saxon legal tradition, in 2000 the revisionist historian David Irving sued American academic Deborah Lipstadt and Penguin Books, her publisher, for libel for calling him a "Holocaust denier." The resulting trial, although technically on this point, amounted to a full critical appraisal of various revisionist theories casting doubt on the existence of attempts to exterminate the Jews of Europe—and refuted them. It is hard to read the judgment without feeling that some issues, at least, have now been definitively settled, although no one was on trial, and proof beyond reasonable doubt was not required (the standard of proof in civil trials is lower).[2]

This episode illustrates that the function of a court in establishing truth may lie in areas incidental to individual guilt or innocence. Much of the enduring impact of the Nuremberg trials, after all, was due to the documentary evidence presented, even if our recollection of exactly who was found guilty of what has faded. Likewise, much of the background material that has been recounted in trials in The Hague and Arusha will be of great value in the future to demonstrate what happened. The evidence introduced by the prosecution in the *Krstic* trial about the origins of the Srebrenica crisis, not challenged by the defense, will remain an excellent summary of the background to the massacre. Similarly, the *Blaskic* trial threw up a lot of interesting material about the involvement of Croatian forces in the fighting in Bosnia, as well as Zagreb's plans to join the Croat-dominated areas of Bosnia to Croatia. Experts had always assumed that the vote of the Bosnian Croats for independence in the 1992 referendum was tactically inspired, so that the eventual separation of Herzegovina and its fusion with Croatia proper would be easier. The introduction of some Bosnian Croat documents—although intended to prove only the existence of an international armed conflict and so the relevance of the Geneva Conventions—throws interesting light on that episode. For example, Mate Boban, then president of the regional crisis staff for Herzegovina, and Dario Kordic, then president of the HVO in Travnik, cochaired a meeting in Travnik on December 12, 1991 (i.e., some months before the referendum on Bosnian independence). The meeting concluded that "the Croatian people of this region, and all of Bosnia and Herzegovina still support the unanimously accepted orientation and conclusions adopted in agreements with President Dr Franjo Tudjman on 13 and 20 June 1991 in Zagreb." These principles were that "the Croatian people in Bosnia and Herzegovina must finally embrace a determined and active policy which will realise our eternal dream—a common Croatian state." A referendum to approve this objective should soon be put in hand. The meeting accepted that there were still "forces in a segment of the HDZ BH leadership which oppose the historic interests of the Croatian people in BH," and it favored "a non-existent sovereign BH in which the Croatian people would be condemned to genocide, and would disappear from history."[3]

It is likely that the main bequest of the ad hoc tribunals to the cause of truth will be the huge volume of documentary material collected (though not always used) during the trials. These include tens of thousands of pages of witness statements, as well as photographs, technical reports and analyses, and, most important, official documents of the parties to the conflict. This will be a major source for any attempt to write a definitive history of the conflicts. As one analyst put it, the material in The Hague will fundamentally change our view of the Yugoslav conflict. And this, perhaps, is the problem. Any serious use of these archives will be a long and complex task, subject to all the frustrations, inconsistencies, and contradictions familiar to anyone who has ever worked with original source documents. The picture they yield will be complicated and messy, and it will not recommend itself to anyone looking for good propaganda material. This is why, perhaps, trials to date have had so little real effect on the way in which the conflicts are generally perceived: the same tired oversimplifications continue to circulate and even gain strength from elements of the trial judgments that can be made to seem consistent with them. In many ways, this is not surprising. All sorts of journalists, pundits, and even historians committed themselves to extreme views at the time, on the basis of inaccurate and sometimes biased reporting, and much of what was written then is in need of revision today. But experience suggests that people find it difficult to modify their views in such circumstances, especially when they have made a moral and political commitment to one particular hypothesis in the past. As a result, there is likely to be an expanding reality gap, as the years pass, between what is shown in court and what is believed outside, and this is scarcely going to help the process of disseminating the truth.

Popular perceptions of events are often established quickly after they happen, and it takes a generation or more for serious scholarship to find its way into the public consciousness. In the case of trials, which are usually long and complex, this is a special problem. There is no way in which a careful, 300-page judgment, no matter how sound, can ever compete for public attention with a thirty-minute TV documentary, no matter how shoddy, that provides viewers with gripping images. So if the ad hoc tribunals are ever to disseminate their version of the truth, the task will be a long one. This situation will improve only if those who demand that courts be set up to establish the truth are prepared to accept the truth when it appears, even if they dislike it. So far, there is little sign of this happening. The situation is much more difficult when politics is directly involved, since the issues that war crimes courts address are usually inflammatory. The material that emerged in the *Blaskic* trial hit the Croatian government in such a sensitive spot that the latter instantly denounced the prosecution and demanded a right of reply before the court. But the revelations were also a blow for those, in the Balkans and elsewhere, who persisted in seeing the 1992 Bosnian referendum as a genuine expression of majority popular sentiment for independence (although there were many voters who did feel this way). All factions in the Yugoslav fighting, and their foreign apologists, are going to find uncomfortable truths coming out of the trials in The Hague, and it will be a measure of their own integrity how they allow it to affect them. The omens are not good: it may be said that the truth will make you free, but the Bible equally points out in another place that "wisdom crieth out in the streets and no man regardeth it."

Part of the problem lies in the different understandings of what constitutes truth and how it relates to events in a court of law. As we saw earlier, for many cultures, individual rights, as well as individual guilt or innocence, are less significant than their collective equivalents. Just as many in the United States argued that O. J. Simpson was a representative of a minority that had suffered and was therefore innocent (or, conversely, that he was a member of a dangerous minority and therefore guilty), so in the Balkans and in Rwanda those involved tended to judge along collective rather than individual lines. For the Croats, the truth of the Lasva Valley killings was that the Bosnian Croats were a small minority in a country whose independence had produced a Muslim-dominated government and who therefore had to carve out areas for themselves that they could defend, with help from Croatia proper. Exactly who did what to whom and where is a relatively trivial issue, when the *real* story is about desperate attempts to prevent the annihilation of the Bosnian Croats as a people. Similarly in Rwanda, there are, as one prosecutor put it, "two truths: a Hutu truth and a

Tutsi truth." The Tutsi truth is better known (and better founded), but it is not accepted by the Hutu, who see themselves as responding to an exterminatory invasion from abroad by a former ruling group who oppressed them until 1959 and murdered hundreds of thousands of Hutu in Burundi twenty years previously. In these charged interpretations, where each party considers itself a victim in danger of annihilation, there is little interest in individual misdeeds by one's own side. Indeed, intones a chorus of Serbs, Croats, Muslims, Hutu, and Tutsi, so-and-so cannot be guilty of a crime because he was "only defending his people."

It is for this reason that the truths of the verdicts handed down in The Hague and Arusha are generally not accepted in the regions in which they operate. There is a rather naive idea that, once the full horrors of what was done are known, citizens of what was Yugoslavia will experience a Damascene conversion and approve of the punishment of their own people. This is about as likely as the British people rejecting Winston Churchill and Bomber Command for the destruction of Dresden, or Americans turning in disgust from Harry Truman because of revelations about what happened at Hiroshima. Not only do we make excuses for the behavior of our own people; we take criticism, let alone attempts to address such issues juridically, as an insult to ourselves. Every time British TV broadcasts a mildly critical program about Bomber Command, the station is flooded with complaints claiming that heroes are being libeled and insulted—and what about the Germans? Thus, in the Balkans the conviction of an accused is generally represented as an insult to all Serbs, Croats, and Muslims and an assertion of their collective guilt.

Much depends, of course, on whether one thinks that courts are capable of arriving at the truth in the first place or even seek to do so. In the Anglo-Saxon world we tend to think this is possible in theory, although in practice we often dismiss findings by courts when they do not satisfy emotionally. But in many societies, where courts have always been instruments of social control, the very concept that a court would naturally arrive at the truth would seem naive. This certainly was the case in the former Yugoslavia, and it is asking a great deal of people in the region to credit that a court largely set up, funded, and staffed by Western powers that have intervened militarily in the Balkans can ever deliver verdicts that represent the truth or even would seek to do that. Against this background, issues such as the strength of the evidence are secondary; after all, it could always have been faked by Western intelligence services. For these reasons, few in the Balkans can accept that the ICTY reaches, or is even interested in, the truth.[4] There are groups that believe this, but they are not numerous. Individual political leaders—Stipe Mesic of Croatia is a notable example—certainly do take this view, and Mesic and others have argued that trials can actually be valuable in moving guilt from a collective to an individual level. Some antigovernment publications in various countries have been prepared to concede that the ICTY might have gotten it right: Croatian newspapers like *Nacional* and *Feral Tribune* have an honorable record, and some Muslim and even Serb media outlets have been prepared to consider that their own people have committed atrocities and have been, or might be, fairly found guilty. But these are the views of a small minority, as are those of the English-speaking students whom Western journalists are always meeting in cafés.

It is true, of course, that these are early days, and we should not yet despair of the truth, as established by the court, eventually making its way into the consciousness of the Balkans (or, for that matter, parts of the Western media). History, though, is not encouraging. The most that can be expected, perhaps, is a kind of sullen acceptance that such verdicts must be respected, with lip service being paid to the truth of the story that has emerged. This is starting to happen in the states of the former Yugoslavia: the "moderates" are not those who are horrified by the crimes of the Milosevic regime, for example, but rather those who accept the reality of the tribunal in terms of power politics and recognize that they have to say accommodating things about it to get money and favors from the West. As they say in the Balkans, "Kiss the hand you cannot bite." So the kind of truth that emerges from trials, or even from nonjudicial inquiries, is unlikely to be widely persuasive on its own merits. Even if trials are in principle capable of getting at the truth, that truth is likely to be rejected or ignored by people who have already made up their minds what the truth is that they want to hear. So truth, unfortunately, often must be imposed, as it was in Yugoslavia after World War II. Trials by themselves are not enough. Few Germans at the time, preoccupied with survival, seem to have paid much attention to the Nuremberg trials. As in Japan—where the Tokyo trials are still widely perceived as a travesty of justice—it was the detailed political control that the victors had over the society of the vanquished that made the imposition of a certain concept of truth possible. Even if—as in the case of Germany—the truth was, indeed, largely true, its success in molding the views of future generations was achieved only through coercion. Sometimes attempts to find the truth through trials fail anyway, as with France after World War II. Trials of Vichy collaborators were divisive and went nowhere, because many of the accused claimed that they themselves had actually been part of the resistance, subverting the Vichy regime from within. Far from establishing the truth, this led many people to think that the truth was unattainable.

This does not mean, of course, that all attempts to arrive at the truth in criminal trials are doomed, much less that we should abandon them. It means rather that we must stop loading onto the shoulders of justice requirements it is not suited to meet and that we should be modest in our expectations of what incidental clarifications justice can achieve. The most likely way in which the truth will emerge is in the patient work of specialists in law and history, which in time will make its way into the public domain. It may therefore be of interest if I offer a hypothetical situation of how this might happen and what the result would look like. I am going to use the example of Srebrenica because it is the best-known atrocity of modern times, as well as the one that has attracted the wildest speculation and polemic. There is also an unprecedented amount of documentary material available.[5]

When fighting broke out in Bosnia after the declaration of independence in 1992, the Bosnian Serbs, some 37 percent of the population, and who had boycotted the independence referendum, attempted to secede from the new state and join with what remained of the Serb-dominated Federal Republic of Yugoslavia. They were assisted in this by the Federal Army (JNA), which was by then heavily dominated by Serb and Bosnian Serb officers, until it withdrew from Bosnia after May 15, 1992. At this point, JNA personnel who were Bosnian Serbs remained behind to set up the new Army of the Serb Republic (the VRS), with help and assistance from Belgrade. The objective of the Bosnian Serbs (and of Belgrade) was to carve out an area of Bosnia that they could control, then join this area to Serbia proper and to the areas of Croatia where Serbs lived. However, few areas in Bosnia were entirely Serb, and this plan required that non-Serb populations be driven out. Srebrenica was only about fifteen kilometers from the border with Serbia and was part of an area of great strategic importance for both sides. The prewar population of the town was some 37,000, of whom about three-quarters were Muslim, the rest Serb. In May 1992, when fighting broke out, Serb paramilitaries captured the town and held it for several weeks. Shortly afterward, Muslim forces headed by Naser Oric, from nearby Potocari, recaptured the town and then held it until its fall in July 1995. The Muslims pressed on, capturing and burning villages and expelling Serb populations, at one point expanding the size of the area they controlled to some 900 square kilometers. A counterattack by the VRS, however, pushed them back and reduced the size of the pocket. Refugees from areas recaptured by the VRS crowded into Srebrenica, increasing the population of the town to about 50,000–60,000.

The situation of the Muslim population in Srebrenica was untenable in the longer term, and the sensible thing would have been to evacuate it. But the town had enormous significance for the Sarajevo government, and it criticized the evacuation of about 8,000–9,000 refugees by the UN High Commission for Refugees as ethnic cleansing. On April 16, 1993, the UN Security Council responded by passing a resolution urging that "all parties and others treat Srebrenica and its surroundings as a 'safe area' that should be free from armed attack or any other hostile act." At the same time, the

Security Council created two other UN-protected enclaves, Zepa and Gorazde.[6] In retrospect, this policy seems fatally flawed and appears to have been adopted on the basis of sensationalist reporting of conditions inside the enclaves. UN commanders negotiated a deal whereby the enclave was to be demilitarized under the supervision of UN troops, but the two sides could not agree on how much of the enclave would be demilitarized. In practice, the decisions by the United Nations changed nothing. The enclave was not demilitarized, and the Sarajevo government had no intention of letting that happen. General Sefer Halilovic, the Muslims' overall commander at the time, testified that he had ordered that no serviceable weapons should be handed over to the United Nations. Muslims frequently attacked Serbs from the safe area, and helicopters brought ammunition into the enclave in violation of the no-fly zone that had been agreed. To the Serbs, it evidently seemed that the "Bosnian Muslim forces in Srebrenica were using the 'safe area' as a convenient base from which to launch offensives against the VRS and that UNPROFOR was failing to take any action to prevent it."[7] For their part, the Bosnian Serbs had not given up their intention to capture the enclave, and they did everything possible to prevent aid from arriving and to weaken the morale of its inhabitants, defenders, and the tiny number of UN troops stationed there. The situation remained stable for several years.

From 1993 onwards VRS soldiers from the Drina Corps besieged the town; their number probably fluctuated between 1,000 and 2,000. They were heavily outnumbered by the Muslim 28th Division in the town. The strength of this unit is unclear: Serb intelligence estimates at the time suggested a strength of some 15,000, although Halilovic himself claimed that it was only one-third that size. The lower figure is probably closer in terms of actual combat power: in some cases ABiH soldiers did not have weapons. The Muslims continued to launch attacks on surrounding villages and to build up their strength, with the intention of tying down Serb troops. On July 26, 1994, Oric wrote to Sarajevo, following up discussions with II Corps there and forwarding a "list of material-technical means required for operations" against the Serbs, including mortars, recoilless rifles, howitzers, and large quantities of ammunition."[8] In November 1994, the 283rd East Bosnian Light Brigade in Srebrenica drew up a plan to attack and disarm UN Protection Force troops at the "Vezionica camp" in the town. The UN troops would be given five minutes to surrender and hand over their equipment, after which they would be fired upon. It is not clear why the operation, which had been planned in great detail, did not go forward.[9]

The situation changed in early 1995, when it was clear that the end of the fighting was now in sight. The Bosnian Serbs began to reinforce the area with larger and better quality forces and to intensify their efforts to undermine the enclave by restricting the food and other aid that could enter.

Apparently a decision was made at the end of March 1995 to attack the enclave. It seems that, while the Bosnian Serbs hoped eventually to capture the town in some way, their immediate objectives were more modest, limited to severing communications between Srebrenica and Zepa and reducing the safe area to the town itself.[10] They were worried about the size of the Muslim garrison and concerned that NATO would seize the opportunity to attack them, possibly by dropping in paratroops to fight on the side of the Muslims.[11] (They were not concerned about the presence of the UN forces, which were, in any event, incidental to the action, except insofar as they were expected to act in "support" of the Muslims.)[12] At that point there was no suggestion that large-scale deliberate killings would follow the eventual fall of the town.

The commander of the Drina Corps, General Milenko Zivanovic, signed the order for the operation to attack the enclave—known as KRIVA-JA 95—on July 2, and the attack itself began in earnest on July 6. The forces that advanced on Srebrenica were relatively small: a two-battalion tactical group, together with a platoon of tanks, a platoon of armored personnel carriers, and an artillery battery, as well as other small units. The operation made much faster progress than had been anticipated, and by late on July 9 the Serbs found themselves, to their surprise, four kilometers from their starting point and only one kilometer from the town itself. The decision was then taken to press ahead and to capture the town, "with the goal of finally disarming the Muslim 'terrorists' and demilitarising Srebrenica."[13]

Frantic calls from the defenders of the town to Sarajevo for reinforcements went unacknowledged, and NATO aircraft failed to appear. By July 11, the Serbs were able to mount a victory parade through the town, led by General Ratko Mladic. In panic, some 20,000–25,000 refugees from Srebrenica fled to the UN headquarters at Potocari: almost all of them were women, children, and elderly men, although there were perhaps 1,000 men of military age. The killings, as well as burning of houses in the enclave, began almost immediately, although these acts seem to have been largely spontaneous rather than part of any plan. On July 12 and 13, the women, children, and the elderly were bused out of Potocari and returned to Muslim-held territory. They were naturally eager to escape the appalling conditions there, although it is equally clear that the VRS was keen to be rid of them. The unexpected fall of the town meant that the VRS had no plans to deal with the inhabitants, and so VRS commanders were reduced to desperate measures to find the buses and the petrol. At the same time, the few men of military age in Potocari were rounded up and either killed or taken away to Bratunac.

At the same time, Muslim 28th Division forces were making plans to break out from the town toward Muslim-held territory to the north. The column that formed up consisted of perhaps 5,000 soldiers and 5,000–10,000 male civilians (i.e., the vast majority of the males in the enclave). A small number of women, children, and elderly were with the column: most were subsequently captured by the Serbs and put on buses out of the area. The departure of the column ("brigade by brigade and in a fairly organised manner") took the Serbs by surprise, and they scrambled to mount attacks against it.[14] They were unable to stop thousands of men in the column from fighting their way through to Muslim-held territory, but the majority were either captured or killed in the fighting. The captured men from the column were then taken to Bratunac to join those who had been captured in Potocari. (Almost all of those eventually murdered had been with the column and were not among those separated out at Potocari.) It is not clear when the idea of killing the prisoners first occurred to the VRS commanders, although it clearly cannot have been until they had large numbers on their hands. It seems likely that the decision was taken late on July 11 or early on July 12. Certainly, the previously requisitioned buses were being used to transport male prisoners to Bratunac on the evening of July 13, although to what fate we cannot be sure. (All sides in the *Krstic* trial agreed that neither the attack on the armed column, nor the transport of the prisoners, was itself a crime, but the prisoners, whether soldiers or civilians, were then entitled to be properly treated by their captors.)

However, captured VRS records showed that on July 13 a car belonging to the Zvornik Brigade was used on a long series of trips to Bratunac, as well as to a number of sites where the executions subsequently took place. Although there is no direct proof that the occupants of the car (three military policemen) were reconnoitering possible killing sites, it is hard to see what innocent explanation there could be for these trips. The first executions began in the late afternoon of July 13, and they continued until July 16. The executions were meticulously planned and carried out, and special digging equipment, including excavators and bulldozers, was used to prepare the graves. Fourteen primary gravesites were identified and exhumed by investigators, as well as a smaller number of sites where bodies were reburied once world attention began to learn what had happened. (All of these execution sites were some considerable distance from Srebrenica-Potocari, and there is no way that the United Nations could have known what was happening.) Exactly how many died is uncertain, and it was not the function of the trial court to determine that, but just over 2,000 bodies were exhumed from a representative sample of graves. Many bodies had documents showing that they came from the Srebrenica area, and others had copies of the Koran, indicating their Muslim affiliation. Many had been blindfolded or were tied with ligatures. It is likely, therefore, that few, if any, of the missing 7,500 Muslim males from the area survived, and it is

clear that the vast majority who died were murdered rather than being battle casualties or innocent victims.

The material produced for the *Krstic* trial probably represents the best
chance we have of understanding what happened in July 1995: few atrocities have ever been documented as well. But the trial was concerned essentially with issues of personal criminal guilt and did not shed much light on
the two most interesting questions that remain to be settled: Why did the
town fall effectively without a fight? And why did the VRS, after capturing
the town, decide to execute so many prisoners? The materials from the trial
document do, however, give a few clues.

It is clear that by July 1995 the VRS and the Drina Corps were worn
out. Many of Drina Corps' component units were "ill-equipped and unsuit-
ed for offensive combat operations," and many of the troops were physically unfit for combat; the Zvornik Brigade seems to have been the only capable fighting force and provided most of the troops for the attack.[15] The
attack was anticipated with some trepidation by an army that was over-
stretched and contained many reluctant conscripts who wanted to go home.
The VRS had always been short of manpower and was reluctant to take
more casualties if that could be avoided. Given that the Muslims were monitoring VRS communications, it seems unlikely that they had no idea of the
parlous state of morale in the attacking forces. Although it was always
accepted that the Srebrenica enclave, with its huge refugee population, was
not defensible in the final analysis, the consensus among analysts is that it
would have been possible to hold up the Serb advance for some time and to
inflict enough casualties on the attackers that they would have settled for
their initial objectives rather than capture the town. It would also have
given time to make a fighting withdrawal from the town. Moreover, there
was only one approach, up a road that, according to one military expert,
"three men with a bad attitude" could have held for some time.

Yet no serious resistance was offered (the highest figure offered for
Muslim casualties is twenty dead in five days of intense fighting between
sizeable forces).[16] And no sustained attempt was made to evacuate the town
until after it had fallen. Why? Morale in the enclave was low, with most
people simply wanting to get out. According to an intelligence report from
the enclave written in August 1994, the biggest problem was that "members
of the Army of the Republic of BH are increasingly abandoning the [demil-
itarized zone]." Some in the 284th Brigade had already fled toward Tuzla,
and some who were recaptured apparently said that they left because they
"were separated from their families, did not have enough food, and lacked
many other things."[17] The fact that the Sarajevo government had effectively
kept them prisoners in Srebrenica for political purposes may have made
them less keen to fight to defend the town; in any event many of them were

not from Srebrenica. Yet according to captured Serb intelligence reports the column that escaped to the north fought ferociously, "overwhelming" the defenders, and appeared to have inflicted casualties on the Serbs as they passed through.[18] Moreover, although Sarajevo appears to have known of the attack almost straight away, no attempt was made to send a relieving force (in spite of the enclave's alleged importance), or even to launch a diversionary attack elsewhere, until early on July 10, by which time organized resistance had more or less collapsed. At that point, elements of three divisions were told to carry out diversionary attacks. Little is known about these attacks, or even if they took place, but they were "far away from Srebrenica and it was almost certain that, whatever effort they put in at that stage, it was simply too little, too late."[19]

As for the quick fall of the town, the most likely explanation is that a deal was arranged between senior political figures on the two sides. Certainly, the idea of swapping the enclaves for areas around Sarajevo had been in the air for some time. According to the report by the UN Secretary-General, it was discussed between Izetbegovic and the leaders of the Srebrenica community in Sarajevo in 1993. Some of those present at the meeting also claimed that Izetbegovic told them that a NATO intervention was possible, but only if the Serbs were to capture Srebrenica and kill at least 5,000 Muslims. (Izetbegovic subsequently denied that he had said this.) Discussions between Serbs and Muslims about ceding control of the enclaves apparently continued for some time.[20] A number of Muslim politicians have subsequently accused the Sarajevo government of deliberately sacrificing the town and its inhabitants in pursuit of a peace settlement. Ibran Mustafic, the founder of the Srebrenica branch of the SDA, claimed in an interview in 1996 that Sarajevo had ordered attacks to be carried out on the Serbs to provoke them into attacking the town and that the "scenario for the betrayal of Srebrenica was consciously prepared" by the leadership in Sarajevo.[21] Another Srebrenica politician, Hakija Meholjic, who was present at the 1993 Sarajevo talks, has made similar accusations.[22] No serious peace plan presented during the fighting envisaged that the enclaves would remain in the area controlled by the Sarajevo government.

Materials produced during the trial certainly support the strong presumption that the town was allowed to fall as part of an explicit or implied bargain, which recognized that, with the end of the war in sight, the safe areas no longer served a political or military purpose and that it would be difficult to imagine them continuing as isolated enclaves in an area overwhelmingly held by the Serbs. It would have been difficult to negotiate a detailed plan to hand over the enclave (and if there was one, the Drina Corps seems not to have known about it). It is more likely that there was an understanding that the Sarajevo government would allow the enclave to fall by neglect, as much more could have been done to organize and arm the troops there. Certainly, the facts that Naser Oric was taken from the town in April 1995 and not allowed back; that the Serbs, in spite of their fears encountered little resistance and suffered few casualties; that the forces in the enclave were nonetheless motivated to mount a mass breakout attempt; and that they were clearly heavily armed and fought well at that stage—all tend to support the view that something odd happened in this place in July 1995. The evidence does not, however, support the view that the massacres were desired, or even expected, by the government in Sarajevo. The VRS hierarchy itself seems to have been unprepared for the town's capture, and there is no evidence that there was any preparation for the massacres, or even any thought given to the possibility, until after the town had fallen. For its part, the Sarajevo government seemed as puzzled as anyone about where the missing men might be.

This leads finally to the question: Why did the massacres take place at all? The trial documents make it clear that this was a late improvisation and that frantic efforts had to be made to assemble the necessary equipment. Yet politically it was a stupid move (and there is no evidence that Radovan Karadzic, for example, knew about it), since it was bound to inflame international opinion against the Serbs when it was discovered and would provide NATO with exactly the pretext to attack that the Serbs had feared. Moreover, it ruled out what might have otherwise been a useful exchange of prisoners.

The most likely single reason for the massacre was revenge. It is known that the Serbs entered Srebrenica with a list of 387 Muslim men they suspected of war crimes—essentially of being behind the attacks on Serb villages in the area.[23] There is plenty of anecdotal evidence of VRS officers stalking the town demanding, "Where's Naser?" But Naser wasn't there, nor were the commanders of the 28th Division, who had by then left, nor, so far as we can tell, the vast majority of the 387 individuals on the list. It is possible that this disappointment, coming so soon after the town's "liberation," was the catalyst for the massacres. It is also possible that the deal, if there was a deal, included the peaceful surrender of the garrison, which did not happen. (There have been allegations that senior Muslim commanders tried to persuade the fleeing troops to return to Srebrenica.)[24] It does seem, however, that the idea of committing the massacre was that of Mladic (who claimed that his parents had been murdered by Muslims in World War II) rather than Krstic. There are several pieces of evidence, including intercepts, showing that Krstic was giving orders that civilians were not to be harmed as late as July 12.[25] From the material presented in his trial, Krstic appears as a weak man, rather than an evil one, who went along with illegal orders rather than originating them.

The Truth Shall Make Ye Free

There has been a proliferation of criminal proceedings against alleged violators of human rights. Along with that has come an increasing interest in nonjudicial options aimed at finding out the truth about an incident through more amorphous and less rigorous modes of inquiry. The best-known example of this process is the South African Truth and Reconciliation Commission, but in fact the idea originated some years before in Latin America, when countries that had previously been under military rule became democracies.[26] At the beginning of the process, objectives were limited and were, to varying extents, accomplished. Since the 1980s, however, the process has become much more ambitious, and grandiose claims have been made for the efficacy of truth commissions not only in discovering the truth but also in promoting reconciliation, healing, and even nation-building. It is fair to say that these wider objectives remain a matter of hope and assertion: there are no actual examples where this can be shown to have happened.

This is not surprising when we consider the vague and ambitious claims that are made for the process or rather the group of processes. The metaphor in widest use—the healing effect of facing up to the past—is ultimately drawn from psychoanalytic theory, in which the patient, with the help of a skilled professional therapist, gradually uncovers repressed incidents from the past and comes to terms with them. In practice, though, much of the vocabulary and concepts used in writing about truth processes are drawn more immediately from contemporary works of popular psychology and self-help found in the local bookshop. At a minimum, it will be clear that there are substantial differences between an approach aimed at healing an individual and one aimed at healing an entire society. The first, of course, arises from that distinction: people vary enormously, and it is a matter of experience that some people respond well to psychoanalysis and others do not. Moreover, it is not clear, even as a matter of principle, that approaches aimed at healing individuals, conducted over many years by skilled therapists in a private and secure environment, can be extended to cover a transformative process conducted in public, over a short period, with a huge number of disparate individuals. Second, a society that is to be healed will by definition contain victims and perpetrators, participants and bystanders, supporters and opponents of various acts. Indeed, there is no reason why an individual cannot be part of more than one category; and everyone's personal experience will be a mixture of some of these experiences and, perhaps, others as well. Seeking to heal a society made up of such disparate groups is, at best, an immensely complex undertaking. Third, whether one makes a long-term commitment to psychoanalysis, or whether one merely purchases *How to Deal with the Past and Heal Your*

Life in Five Easy Steps, that person is making a commitment to change and beginning that process voluntarily. Little therapeutic value can ever be gained by forcing people to accept treatment, and if this is true of individuals, then how much more must it be true of societies, where victims and perpetrators are mixed together and may even be the same people?

This reminds us of the essentially political nature of most truth processes, which are generally involuntary, at least in part, rather than voluntary. Facing up to the past is not easy for any group or society, and so it is normal for the small, the weak, the defeated, or those who are politically marginalized to be invited to take this step. Certainly, we are generally much quicker to invite others to face up to their pasts than we are to volunteer to face up to our own. To suggest that the British should face up to their responsibility for bombing civilians in World War II, or that the Americans should face up to Hiroshima, would invite furious condemnation—and "they started it anyway." Yet these countries are among the first to recommend a therapeutic process to others. Unsurprisingly, therefore, it seems that there is no actual example of an entire population or group voluntarily deciding, as a matter of collective therapy, to begin a search for the truth. More normally, it is the result of a political deal, domestic power politics, or, increasingly, pressure from abroad.

Truth cannot be confronted unless it can be known, and there are at least three criteria that must be met before this is possible. First, the truth must be knowable, at least in principle. Second, when known the truth must be accepted by all as the truth, and not propaganda. Third, the truth must be disseminated and acted upon by all parts of the community jointly. In practice, this has never happened, usually because it is impossible, or nearly so, to meet the first two criteria. It is naive to expect final and transcendental truth from legal processes, given their inbuilt limitations. But such processes do at least have some advantages: They are rigorous and objective in their methodology; and their evidence and conclusions must undergo public testing. Few truth processes can expect to do this. If the intention is to illuminate specific human rights violations, then there is little alternative but to rely on the statements of alleged victims or relatives or friends of victims. Yet such evidence is almost always unreliable even in the objective setting of a courtroom. In a nonjudicial inquiry, with no opportunity to test the evidence, it is unlikely to produce much of lasting value. Official records can and do provide helpful material, although there are obvious incentives for perpetrators to destroy such material; confessions can help also, even if the motives of confessors are sometimes dubious. But it would be dangerous to expect too much reliable truth from such processes.

These problems are magnified as the truth being sought becomes increasingly large-scale and more general, because the first questions that must be answered are definitional. Where most large-scale violations of human rights are concerned, a concept of truth must first be established before individuals can accept it, and they will seldom do so if the concept violates their own impression of what the truth was at the time. In much of Latin America, for example, military rule was welcomed, or at least tolerated, by large sections of the populations whose own concept of truth was that human rights violations, if they were accepted to have occurred, were necessary to protect against the communist revolution that was being attempted; in their view, killings and bombings by alleged terrorists were the real cause for concern. Even if compelling documentary evidence of wide-scale human rights abuses is produced and accepted, the context will always be personal and even ideological, whatever the recommended truth may be. One of the strangest things about truth processes is how uncannily they mimic the destructive habits of ethnonationalism: they are essentially accusations of collective responsibility for the past and sired by ethnic determinism out of racial guilt. So today the Japanese (albeit for political reasons) are often condemned for not having faced up to the truth of the Pacific War and for not rewriting their textbooks to make their guilt over it, and the related atrocities, more manifest. But even leaving aside the controversy about the origins of the war, the fact is that the personal experiences of Japanese people have almost no point of connection with these concepts at all. While official Japanese presentations of the war to their own people are not necessarily more reliable than Western ones to theirs, they are somewhat closer to popular Japanese experiences than Western ones are. For the Japanese who lived through it, the war was an incomprehensible catastrophe, caused by a dictatorial and inept government, bringing enormous suffering and destruction to the Japanese people, and ultimately the bombing and occupation of their country. Every Japanese after the war had an Uncle Hiroshi who came home from the war with his health ruined, and perhaps an Uncle Ichiro who never came home at all and is buried somewhere in Manchuria. The truth in terms of lived experience of the war simply has no connection with Western and Asian political pressure to recognize certain political interpretations as true; and it is surely the crudest type of genetic determinism to expect constant and permanent repentance and expiation from a group of people whose only connection with the perpetrators of the undoubted atrocities is the fact that they were born in the same country at a much later date.

In general, factual documentation of atrocities is meaningless, politically and even morally, when taken out of context. The kinds of excuses we have seen continue to apply even when the truth of a particular incident is revealed. But at some level, perhaps, these are not excuses but represent the way in which even atrocious acts can take on a different complexion depending upon the circumstances and the intent of the perpetrator. Most of us (perhaps even Germans) would resist simple comparisons between the bombing of German cities and the extermination of European Jewry, even if the intent of the organizers of each episode was the same: a speedier end to the war. Further and darker revelations about the horrors of Dresden, for example, are unlikely to change this view. As a result, the idea that revelations of the truth of atrocious episodes *by themselves* can result in facing up to things is not persuasive, since an exculpatory context can always be found, and there are usually charges of "you're another" that can be made as well. Indeed, experience suggests that persistent attempts to *force* people to face the truth about historical episodes are no more effective than trying to persuade people to drink less by telling them how much harm they are doing to themselves, especially when one is known to be partial to the odd drink or two.

Healing the Nation

The more ambitious the objectives of truth processes, the more problems they encounter. I want to devote the rest of this chapter to the South African Truth and Reconciliation Commission and its work, because it is the most ambitious, the best known, and in some ways the most problematic of all of these attempts, yet it is increasingly seen as a model for elsewhere. There is already a huge literature on the TRC.[27] Here, after some preliminary remarks, I will focus on two issues: what kind of truth was found; and whether any reconciliation has occurred.

The origins of the TRC were political, although this has been obscured somewhat by the attitude of religious awe that surrounded the commission from its earliest days. Essentially, the TRC was the outcome of a compromise between the desire to do as much as possible and the fear of doing too much. Many in the liberation movement wished to put on trial the luminaries of the apartheid regime, who themselves sought a blanket pardon. Even if trials had actually been feasible—and those that were attempted ran into huge problems—the political consequences would have been potentially destabilizing. Yet the sins of apartheid could not be left unaddressed altogether. The result was a context-specific compromise, which could (and, some would argue, should) have turned out differently. The remit of the TRC was to "promote national unity and reconciliation in a spirit of understanding which transcends the conflicts and divisions of the past," by "establishing as complete a picture as possible of the causes, nature and extent of the gross violations of human rights which were committed during the period from 1 March 1960" to April 1994, including "the antecedents, circumstances, factors and context of such violations, as well as the perspectives of the victims and the motives and perspectives of the persons responsible for the commission of the violations, by conducting investigations and holding hearings." It was also responsible for facilitating "the granting of amnesty to persons who make full disclosure of all the relevant facts relating to acts associated with a political objective and comply with the requirements of this Act," as well as "establishing and making known the fate or whereabouts of victims and by restoring the human and civil dignity of such victims by granting them an opportunity to relate their own accounts of the violations of which they are the victims, and by recommending reparation measures in respect of them."[28]

This was an ambitious agenda, especially since its full achievement would rely on the extent to which a series of untested hypotheses proved to be true. In particular, the idea that the truth would actually promote unity and reconciliation was a matter of faith at that stage. The TRC was also asked to focus on one element of the story of the apartheid years—the serious violations of the human rights of individuals. This had several practical consequences. First, the vast majority of those who suffered under apartheid did so institutionally and collectively, through political and economic subjugation, denial of basic legal rights, compulsory resettlement, and blighting of personal and family lives. Many also suffered institutional violence and arbitrary arrest. They did not suffer murder, assault, rape, and torture, and so they were not invited to tell their own stories. Instead, the TRC concentrated on individual atrocities, although, given the numbers, it had to be selective even there. As a result, many have argued, like Mahmood Mamdani, that only "a diminished truth" was sought, one "crafted to reflect the experience of a tiny minority: on the one hand, perpetrators, being state-agents; and, on the other hand, victims, being political activists."[29] Second, the hearings tended to concentrate on well-known and controversial incidents. In pure numerical terms, the majority of the deaths took place in the period between the un-banning of the African National Congress in 1990 and the election in 1994, and most of them were the result of armed clashes between the ANC and the Inkatha (albeit prompted to some extent by shadowy government forces). Yet it would have seemed very strange indeed if the TRC had spent its time looking at these events alone. Third, by focusing on individual incidents of violence, the TRC was naturally required to consider acts committed by the liberation movement as well, irrespective of the fact that the political background was very different. Finally, by presenting a thematic rather than historical survey, the TRC's report took all of the crimes out of context and made them, in effect, the work of a series of individual bad apples rather than evidence of systemic violence. As many observers have noted, this narrowing of the focus to the perpetrator alone makes the whole task of nation-building and reconciliation much easier.[30]

The TRC was aware that it was dealing with a difficult and complex issue that resisted a simple approach. Indeed, the final report included a methodological section that explicitly addressed the issues of "what truth—and whose truth?" The report identified four categories of truth: "factual or forensic truth; personal or narrative truth; social or 'dialogue' truth and healing and restorative truth."[31] The report went on to discuss several of these truths in more detail. It argued that

> by providing the environment in which victims could tell their own stories in their own languages, the [TRC] not only helped to uncover existing facts about past abuses, but also assisted in the creation of a "narrative truth." In so doing, it also sought to contribute to the process of reconciliation by ensuring that the truth about the past included the validation of the individual subjective experiences of people who had previously been silenced or voiceless.[32]

"Healing truth" was defined as "the kind of truth that places facts and what they mean within the context of human relationships—both amongst citizens and between the state and its citizens. This kind of truth was central to the [TRC]."[33]

Even with repeated readings, it is not clear what statements like this are supposed to mean. In principle, they probably mean that facts objectively determined could, and perhaps should, be put in a wider context of how people felt about the abuses and how those fit into some larger context. There is nothing wrong with this, and it is probably the result of an almost impossibly wide remit, including the determination of findings of fact and a version of those findings that would somehow assist reconciliation. But in practice such principles continue the worship of the victim (or the self-identified victim) by treating subjective experiences and recollections as though they were always objectively true. They also lead to the disquieting thought that if "individual subjective experiences" are to be recognized as a kind of truth, then in theory the subjective experiences of perpetrators must be taken into account also, since for the individuals concerned they were no less real.

The TRC was supposed to make findings of fact only on the basis of material analogous to that presented in a court of law. In practice, this was not always possible, since corroboration, in the form of amnesty applications or seized documents, was often not available, and in some cases findings about important incidents were made on the basis of witness recollections alone. This would have mattered less if the exercise had been intended to recover subjective impressions of persecution and to give those who considered themselves victims a chance to tell their stories. But the TRC was expected to do much more than that: to present the truth about a series of infamous incidents, and to identify those responsible. The problem is that most victims and survivors saw only their immediate tormentors. But unless they were themselves to confess and to identify their commanders, then the interesting questions—who ordered the atrocities and why?—would never be solved. Although the TRC did make findings about high-level perpetrators, largely on the balance of probability, it is still not clear whether the findings have any meaningful legal status.

One perverse result was that crimes that had appeared simple in the past took on a more complex and dubious appearance before the TRC. Given the use by the authorities of black informers and agents provocateurs, the ANC and its allies were inclined to see treason everywhere, and alleged collaborators were sometimes murdered on what proved to be very flimsy evidence. It sometimes turned out, therefore, that presumed victims of apartheid had actually been executed by their own side. In some cases it became clear that they had indeed been traitors, in some cases not, and in still others culpability never became clear. For a number of families, the TRC hearings brought not certainty but permanent confusion about the deaths of children and husbands that will never be resolved.

A complex and interesting case is that of the so-called Pebco Three, who were activists with the Port Elizabeth Black Civic Organisation and who disappeared in May 1985.[34] It was clear that they were murdered by the security police, but black and white policemen gave sharply different accounts of how they had died. More disturbingly, however, a black policeman applying for amnesty alleged that, under torture, one of the activists had claimed to be a paid informer for another intelligence service and that, upon further checking, this proved to be the case; he was killed anyway. There seems to be no prospect of actually finding out what the truth was.

Yet no one will deny that important things did emerge from the TRC process. Much that was previously secret became known, not least from the mouths of the perpetrators themselves. And in some cases it can be said that the nearest approach to the truth that was actually possible has been achieved. The sight of senior police and military commanders and political leaders admitting what had previously been denied, and even apologizing for it, was interesting and valuable. But this leads us to the second question about the TRC. Did it achieve its stated goal of reconciliation and healing? The report set out its expectations for healing in a long and elaborate mixed metaphor:

> There can be little doubt that gross violations of human rights and other similar abuses during the past few decades left indelible scars on the collective South African consciousness. These scars often concealed festering wounds that needed to be opened up to allow for the cleansing and eventual healing of the body politic. This does not mean, however, that it was sufficient simply to open old wounds and then sit back and wait for the light of exposure to do the cleansing.[35]

The actual meaning of this is obscure, which often happens when metaphor is allowed to guide thought rather than the other way around. The analogy is of wounds to a body, generally inflicted by an outsider, that for some reason are not treated. In practice, of course, this rarely happens, and few of us would deliberately conceal physical wounds we had suffered. Most bodily wounds heal naturally and are covered up to make them heal faster. Probably, the intended analogy is to *mental* wounds, which indeed can get worse if untreated. But the problem with the situation the TRC was enquiring into is that there was a state—a body politic, if you will—divided against itself, inflicting wounds on itself. The idea that the country was "ill" for a single reason or could be "cured" by a single process is therefore not convincing. In particular, many of the alleged perpetrators and their supporters did not accept that view of themselves: indeed, for them the roles were reversed. Moreover, as Mahmood Mamdani warned, the TRC process did not involve most ordinary people. Many whites, as far as one can judge, considered that the evils that it brought to light had been committed by a tiny number of security force personnel, probably beyond anyone's control. For that reason, few whites attended the hearings or even paid much attention to them. Most seem to have been "genuinely shocked when they learned of the activities of the death squads and other atrocities, but they believed them to be no more than one part of the picture . . . The more shocking the disclosures became, the more they felt able to distance themselves from them."[36]

Something can be said about the effects of the TRC at the individual level. At least some of those who gave evidence at the hearings found psychological relief from doing so, and a few of the perpetrators sought forgiveness. Some of these impromptu pairs did undergo tearful reconciliations in public, and some of them seem to have been genuine. But it is hard to be sure, given the intimidating atmosphere of religiosity surrounding the process, and the aching desire of Desmond Tutu and his colleagues to have examples of reconciliation, how deep and genuine some of them really were. But it is also clear that for some of those who spoke before the TRC the process was itself traumatic and left them worse off than before—yet without any follow-up help.[37] The problem in many cases was not that those who appeared before the TRC had repressed their memories but that they could not forget them. Individuals, therefore, were not necessarily healed by their participation, and the expectation that they would be is perhaps another consequence of constructing a process like the TRC on the basis of metaphors. Many people approached the TRC out of a belief that they would receive practical help, financial compensation, or even because, as one of the early witnesses put it, "I just want the commission to have sympathy with me, to understand what I went through when these things happened."[38]

For practical reasons, those who applied to the TRC for amnesty were not expected to demonstrate repentance, or even regret, for what they had done, and few did so. This caused considerable anger among friends and relatives of victims, who often attended the hearings and did not make reconciliation any easier. But this attitude is not surprising, since, once again, context is everything despite the apolitical and moralistic tone of the TRC report. Perpetrators generally argued that they had been following the orders of a legitimate government and had done what was necessary to protect the country at the time. Legally, *and even morally*, therefore, few of them felt the need to apologize.

The effects of the TRC at the general level are hard to gauge since most of the evidence is impressionistic and anecdotal. On the one hand, it is as rare to meet unashamed apologists for apartheid today as it no doubt was to meet convinced Nazis in Germany in 1950. Most people who have visited the country regularly will recall having been told, even by Afrikaners, that "I always knew the system was wrong," or "it was obvious that things would have to change" even before the 1994 election. By the same token, spontaneous personal acknowledgements of guilt or responsibility are equally rare. There are some relatively objective studies telling us what people at least *say* they think about the past. For example, in 1996, the Centre for the Study of Violence and Reconciliation in Johannesburg carried out a major study into the feelings of white South Africans about their past. Some of the conclusions are startling. Asked whether "the majority of white South Africans have always been in opposition to apartheid," no less than 30 percent of white respondents strongly or largely agreed, and another 16 percent were unsure. Not much more than 50 percent thought that the statement was wrong. Yet throughout the National Party era, whites voted overwhelmingly for parties that supported apartheid, and when that party lost votes in the 1980s, it did so to more hard-line parties. These statements were made only two years after the 1994 election, and before the TRC had properly begun work, at a time when it was possible to deny the full extent of the atrocities committed by the previous regime. Separate questioning showed that 56 percent of whites thought the system of apartheid was unjust (only 25 percent thought it was not), and 41 percent would do "everything" to prevent the system returning (only 9 percent would welcome it).[39]

These attitudes can be interpreted in different ways, but it is possible that they are an early sign of a relatively common process, whereby people reconfigure their memories of the past to make themselves feel more comfortable in the present. In certain types of societies, where there is a clear, shared interest in living together, these reconfigured memories eventually combine to form a single national myth. In countries where the need or desire to live together is not strong, then the myths drift apart and are themselves a catalyst for future conflict. In the case of South Africa, it was clear to all except a few extremists that the different groups would simply have to learn to live with each other, or they had no collective future. (The opposite happened in the former Yugoslavia, where separate myths persisted because ethnic solidarity was valued more than a collective future.) Learning to live with each other means evolving a view of the past that is sufficiently common that it would not constitute a source of friction in the future. This collective view, if it comes to pass, will *not* necessarily be the same as the conclusions of the TRC. It may be a question of what Sarah Nuttall and Carli Coetzee have called "negotiating the past," with the complication that the elites may not, in the long run, be in charge of the negotiations.[40]

Indeed, it can be argued that there is an elite authoritarian streak to trials and truth commissions. In the case of trials, this is less of a problem, since if one accepts the legitimacy and honesty of the court the verdict should not be controversial, even if it is not what some people are hoping for. But a truth commission with ambitious objectives, a huge area to cover, modest means, and relaxed rules of evidence is bound to have to select one interpretation, or set of interpretations, from among the many possible ones it could have chosen, and official sponsorship of this interpretation effectively forecloses all others. Truth commissions—notably the TRC—are often, in fact, elite political bargains in which individuals and groups are symbolically purged by a public wrist-slapping; a myth agreed between elites is then regarded as *the* truth. As Brandon Hamber and Richard Wilson have argued, a process like the TRC can become "an ideology for subordinating diverse individual needs to the exigencies of national unity and reconciliation. Truth commissions aim to construct memory as a unified static and collective *object*, not as a political process," and thus prevent further debate.[41] Yet it looks very much as though popular perceptions and myths—which is how reconciliation develops—do not necessarily tie in with what the TRC has pronounced and may diverge from it much more in future.

An example of reconciliation through myth occurred in France after World War II. France was divided by occupation and, effectively, civil war between 1940 and 1944, and the forces of liberation, which triumphed after the Allied invasion and probably represented the majority of the population, put collaborationists on trial and sought to impose their version of truth on the country as a whole. It did not work because there were powerful forces in the country whose view of the recent past was different. Collaborationists saw themselves as the real patriots, carrying out a prudent policy in the best interests of the country and defending it against the attacks of communist terrorists beholden to Moscow. Especially in the early days of the Cold War, when the power of the former collaborationists was greatly strengthened, there was no way in which the forces of the resistance could ever impose a single view of the past on the country. After Charles de Gaulle's accession to power in 1958, the result of what amounted to a coup by the forces that had supported collaboration, he rapidly realized that some form of compromise on the past was required. So was born the idea of *40 million résistants*: the concept that France, as a whole, had resisted German occupation in various ways, some internally and some externally. This is not actually true—and new books are published in France detailing some new gruesome allegation from the period of the occupation—but its official adoption did enable a picture of the wartime period to be developed that pleased most people, and it has contributed greatly to the unity of France in modern times. Perhaps the same will happen in South Africa. In a generation, it may be accepted that most people opposed apartheid, some openly, some by trying to undermine it from within, and that their collective efforts were rewarded with the huge political changes that took place between 1990 and 1994. This will not be true either, but it may be an effective way to promote national unity and, in a sense, reconciliation as well. It's easier to forgive people if you believe that you were, if not on the same side, then at least moving in broadly the same direction.

Perhaps the problem is that we have allowed analogies to become masters rather than servants. A better set of analogies may be found in the psychology of interpersonal relationships, where any kind of harmonious existence has to result from compromise on all sides, as well as a willingness to overlook faults, turn the page, and start again. Expecting reconciliation from trials and truth commissions is surely about as logical as expecting reconciliation from divorce hearings and custody battles. If we do think this way, then a rather different set of policy imperatives results. Partly, also, it is a question of process and objectives. In the early days of truth commissions, the two were linked, in the sense that investigations could lead to more clarity about the fates of individuals. But as objectives became more complex and ambitious, the relationship between the process and the outcome became more speculative and harder to assess. If, however, the concentration is on outcome—a society largely at peace with itself—then we should accept that trials and truth commissions, whatever their other benefits, may well not achieve this, and to be prepared to contemplate the use of other processes instead or in addition.

Moreover, the use of truth commissions in the future may lead to unanticipated problems. It is generally assumed that such commissions are of value in exposing the earlier lies of state authorities about violations of human rights. But this is unlikely to be the pattern in the future, as they are increasingly held in postconflict societies in which all sides have committed atrocities. Indeed, the reports they issue may well turn out to be uncomfortable reading for journalists and NGOs who for professional or political reasons presented the situation at the time in a particular light. Truth commissions investigating, say, the atrocities in Rwanda or Sierra Leone are bound to produce a version of events very different from that presented at the time, not necessarily any nicer, but usually much more complex and nuanced. As the old saying goes, "Be careful what you ask for—you might just get it."

As an experiment, I once asked a group of about thirty military and civilian officials from ten African countries to consider some of these issues. This was in the context of a training course on peace missions held in Johannesburg, where students were being asked to do practical exercises on a scenario I had devised. At a certain point in the scenario, I asked them to examine proposals for trials and truth commissions in a fictitious African state in light of experience elsewhere in Africa. After an evening's deliberation, they doubted the utility of such institutions in building nations and promoting reconciliation, and they pointed to a number of cases in Africa where it had been decided to close the books on the past and concentrate on the future. Namibia and Mozambique were often mentioned, as was Angola, where peace had just been achieved and where the parliament had just unanimously voted—to the apparent fury of Western NGOs—to grant an amnesty to UNITA rebels who surrendered. They saw no necessary connection between justice and peace: if anything, it was the opposite.

One reason for this is the different approach to the effects of war in African societies. Traditional African medicine sees health, including mental health, as an aspect of relationships with the spirit world, and war is especially disruptive because so many people die away from their homes and their ancestors. Healing is therefore a collective process anyway, one in which individuals are healed by a process of purification and reintegration. Thus "while modern psychotherapeutic practices emphasize verbal exteriorization of the affliction, here through symbolic meanings the past is locked away. . . . To talk and recall the past is not necessarily seen as a prelude to healing or diminishing pain. Indeed, it is often believed to open the space for malevolent forces to intervene."[42] The success of this model in war-traumatized societies like Angola and Mozambique may perhaps give us pause for thought.

Conclusion

This chapter has addressed peace, justice, truth, and reconciliation—all rather fuzzy and disputed concepts, which are to be found in opposition to each other as often as they complement each other. As Frederik Van Zyl Slabbert asks, "Can there be reconciliation without truth? Of course there can. Often truth is the first victim of reconciliation."[43] It is difficult to have all of them, and societies will often have to decide to sacrifice one to achieve others. Both trials and truth processes have important jobs to do, but it is unreasonable to expect them to carry out what are basically magical, transformative functions and produce healing or reconciliation as a result. Indeed, justice and truth may themselves conflict with each other. It is likely that, for some time at least, every conflict brought to a conclusion will spawn external proposals for a truth commission of some sort, possibly while an ICC investigation is ongoing. The two processes are not complementary and proceed in different ways. A truth process may create an impression of guilt that a court cannot sustain but that will put enormous pressure on the ICC to investigate and prosecute nonetheless. And by the time the ICC gets to taking testimony, witnesses may have been so involved in a truth process that they are effectively useless in court. This has been very much the pattern with the ad hoc tribunals and is a risk now facing the Special Court for Sierra Leone. It is likely to be the pattern in the future as well.

There is a difference between repressing the past and agreeing to let it alone or to limit either trials or inquiries in some way. Since a completely common view of the past is intellectually and practically impossible, attempts to impose one will generate opposition and conflict. Any single interpretation will classify some groups and their descendants as victims and others as perpetrators. While in theory this need not obstruct a process of reconciliation, in practice it will often encourage people to look back in conflict rather than forward in cooperation. Political leaders of the official victim group are likely to exploit this status for their own benefit, whereas political leaders of the official perpetrator group will exploit the sense of resentment that is likely to arise. As the exiled Croat philosopher and journalist Boris Buden put it, "What victims really need is to move beyond being only victims."[44] And Wole Soyinka has pointed out the risk that a society "may lose itself in the labyrinths of the past," and never move beyond it, if it looks back too much.[45] History suggests that we might profitably twist George Santayana's famous dictum: "Those who cannot forget the past are condemned to repeat it."

Notes

1. All estimates are somewhat speculative. The official Dutch Srebrenica report, Nederlands Instituut vor Oorlogsdocumentatie, *Srebrenica: A "Safe" Area* (pt. 2, chap. 2, sec. 4), suggests that there were "at least a thousand" Serb casualties.

2. *The Irving Judgment: David Irving v. Penguin Books and Professor Deborah Lipstadt.*

3. "Conclusions of a Joint Meeting of the Herzegovina Regional Community

and the Travnik Regional Community," *Grude*, November 12, 1991. Prosecutor's Exhibit 406/2. The document, and others that help to shed light on Croatian policy at the time, are also discussed in the *Kordic and Cerzek* Judgment (IT-95-14/2), para. 472.

4. See, for example, Refik Hodzic, "Balkan Media Undermine Hague," *Balkan Crisis Report*, no. 390, December 12, 2002.

5. In what follows, I have relied primarily upon the following documents from the *Krstic* trial in 2000: the Prosecutor's Pre-Trial Brief, February 25, 2000; the Defence Pre-Trial Brief, February 29, 2000; the *VRS Corps Command Responsibility Report*, April 5, 2000 (Prosecution Exhibit 401/a); the *Srebrenica Military Narrative: Operation Krivaja 95*, May 15, 2000 (Prosecutor's Exhibit 403/A); *Statement of Major General FR Dannatt CBE MC*, June 27, 2000 (Prosecutor's Exhibit 385/A); and the Judgment of August 2, 2001. Other specific documents are referenced where used.

6. UN Security Council Resolutions 829 and 834 (1993).

7. *Krstic* Judgment, para. 24.

8. *Krstic*, Exhibit D27A.

9. *Krstic*, Exhibit D39A.

10. See, for example, Exhibit OTP 428A, an order dated July 2 to the subordinate units of the corps, which describes the main purpose of the attack as being to "split apart the enclaves of Srebrenica and Zepa and to reduce them to their urban areas."

11. See ibid., sec. 9.

12. *Srebrenica Military Narrative*, para. 3.6.

13. Ibid., para. 3.12.

14. Interim combat report from Lieutenant Colonel Pandurevic, Zvornik Brigade Commander, July 18, 1995, Prosecutors' Exhibit 675A.

15. *Srebrenica Military Narrative*, paras 3.1–3.2.

16. *Srebrenica: A "Safe" Area*, pt. 3, chap. 6, sec. 21.

17. *Krstic*, Exhibit D29A.

18. Interim combat report, July 18, 1995.

19. *Srebrenica: A "Safe" Area*, pt. 3, chap. 6, sec. 8.

20. *Report of the Secretary-General pursuant to General Assembly resolution 53/35: The Fall of Srebrenica* (A/54/549), November 15, 1999, paras. 115–116. See also *Srebrenica: A "Safe" Area*, pt. 1, chap. 10, sec. 9.

21. "President and Army Command Sacrificed Srebrenica," *Slobodna Bosna*, July 14, 1996.

22. Hasan Hadzic, "5000 Muslim Lives for Military Intervention," *Dani*, June 22, 1998.

23. *Srebrenica Military Narrative*, para. 5.19.

24. Interim combat report, July 18, 1995.

25. *Krstic* Judgment, paras. 358–359.

26. For a good history of truth commissions, as well as a discussion of their achievements and problems, see Priscilla B. Hayner, *Unspeakable Truths.*

27. Full-length memoirs of the TRC include Alex Boraine, *A Country Unmasked*, and Piet Meiring, *Chronicle of the Truth Commission*. A good narrative history is Martin Meredith, *Coming to Terms*. Critical books about the TRC have come from the left (Terry Bell, *Unfinished Business*) and from the right (Anthea Jeffrey, *The Truth About the Truth Commission*). The latter's close identification with the Inkatha Freedom Party has itself attracted criticism. A wide-ranging critique of the methodology and process of the TRC is Richard A. Wilson, *The Politics of Truth and Reconciliation in South Africa.*

28. *Promotion of National Unity and Reconciliation Act*, No. 34 of 1995, chap. 2, art. 3(1).

29. Mahmood Mamdani, "A Diminished Truth," in James and Van de Vijer, eds., *After the TRC*, p. 59.

30. See, for example, Wilson, *The Politics of Truth and Reconciliation*, p. 55.

31. South African Truth and Reconciliation Commission, *Final Report*, October 29, 1998, vol. 1, chap. 5, para. 29.

32. Ibid., para. 39.

33. Ibid., para. 43.

34. Ibid., vol. 2, chap. 3, paras. 240–244. See also Janet Cherry, "Historical Truth: Something to Fight For," in Charles Villa-Vicencio and Wilhelm Verwoerd, *Looking Back Reaching Forward*, pp. 137–138.

35. Ibid., vol. 1, chap. 5, para. 47.

36. Meredith, *Coming to Terms*, p. 313.

37. Hayner, *Unspeakable Truths*, pp. 141–144.

38. Cited by Meredith, *Coming to Terms*, p. 5.

39. Gunnar Theissen, *Between Acknowledgement and Ignorance: How White South Africans Have Dealt With the Apartheid Past*, Centre for the Study of Violence and Reconciliation, September 1997 (available online at www.wits.ac.za/csvr/papers)

40. Sarah Nuttall and Carli Coetzee, eds., *Negotiating the Past*.

41. Brandon Hamber and Richard Wilson, "Symbolic Closure Through Memory, Reparation and Revenge in Post-Conflict Societies," paper presented at the conference "Traumatic Stress in South Africa," Johannesburg, January 1999 (available online at www.wits.ac.za/csvr/papers).

42. Edward C. Green and Alcinda Honwana, "Indigenous Healing of War-Affected Children in Africa," World Bank, *IK Notes*, no. 10 (July 1999): p. 3. See also Alcinda Honwana, "Sealing the Past, Facing the Future: Trauma Healing in Mozambique," in *Accord*, no. 3 (1998): 75–80 (available online at www.c-r.org).

43. Frederik Van Zyl Slabbert, "Truth Without Reconciliation, Reconciliation Without Truth," in Wilmot James and Linda Van De Vijer, eds., *After the TRC*, p. 70.

44. Boris Buden, "Truth and reconciliation? No, Thanks!" Lecture given in Belgrade, March 2002, with extracts published in *Reporter*, April 2, 2002.

45. Wole Soyinka, "Memory, Truth, and Healing," in Ifi Amadiume and Abdullah An-Na'im, eds., *The Politics of Memory*, p.21.

10

The Future: Never Again?

N o reasonable human being, if given the chance, would oppose the idea of trying to prevent large-scale violations of human rights in the future, and most people would agree that it is worth spending time, money, and effort to try to bring this about. When we consider the resources that will be put into this general objective—from full-scale courts to relatively minor truth processes—we can agree that the objective seems to be a priority for the international community.

At first sight, it may seem curious that this is so—not in absolute terms (since good is always worth doing) but in relative terms. After all, the vast majority of avoidable suffering in the world in recent times does not come from violations of international humanitarian law, or even from violence. As has been the case for decades, the largest killers, especially of children and the weak, are hunger, malnutrition, exposure to the elements, and preventable diseases caused by the absence of cheap medicines and clean drinking water. Moreover, while the link between courts/truth commissions and the prevention of further atrocities is tenuous, the major plagues that afflict humanity are easy to tackle in principle. After all, there is no lack of food or cheap medicines in the world (they are just in the wrong places), and clean supplies of drinking water can be provided easily. Yet while programs to alleviate all of these evils do exist, the world seems curiously reluctant to display the kind of determined attitude actually required, or to give them the political visibility—through UN Security Council resolutions, for example—that would ensure that governments spent as much time and attention on them as they do, for example, on Balkan politics. And so I have been harangued a number of times by Africans demanding to know why the West does not take more seriously the situation in the eastern Democratic Republic of the Congo, where the death toll since 1998 is approaching some 3 million, even if the majority of the deaths are from good old-fashioned starvation and disease.

Indeed, we do seem to have placed deaths associated with atrocities on a different moral plane than deaths from other causes. The widow of someone killed in a massacre or murdered in a concentration camp will have her tears covered prolifically, her muffled desire for revenge discreetly reinforced, when her sufferings are portrayed in the media. Yet the same widow who loses a husband as a soldier in a battle, or as the innocent victim in a cross fire, must be presumed, from the way media coverage is organized, not to have suffered so much. Why is this so? A cynic might suggest a mixture of three reasons. First, politics is often the art of *not* doing things: solving small problems rather than big ones, addressing popular causes rather than unpopular ones. While ending world hunger, for example, is conceptually easy, it is politically difficult, since it requires changes of policy on finance and trade that the starving are not able to require of the well-fed and that well-fed governments view as politically suicidal anyway. By this argument, a concentration on atrocities diverts attention away from unmanageable issues to manageable ones. It might also be argued that the norms that are being violated when atrocities take place, if not the sole preserve of the West, are often the result of Western initiatives and are key components of the foreign policies of many of their governments. Western governments and informed opinion react strongly to violations of norms with which they feel a particular connection, especially when they take place near their borders. And finally, of course, any sustained discussion of poverty and hunger puts Western aid and trade policies under scrutiny, whereas a discourse of human rights tends to involve the West holding other countries to account for their imperfections.

If these assertions appear too cynical, there are other, more practical explanations of the special place we assign atrocities. They are easy to visualize and conceptualize. Large-scale human misery is difficult to comprehend: a group of bodies in a ditch means much more than claims of tens of thousands starving to death. And starvation is a process that kills very slowly and that is not dramatic to describe if one is a survivor. Starvation, like poverty or access to medical care, is in addition such an *immense* problem that it produces feelings of helplessness and despair. Even if the will and money were there, where does one start? And finally, crimes have perpetrators, and it is satisfying to be able to hate them, feel superior to them, and call for revenge and punishment. By contrast, part of our despair when faced with mass suffering of other kinds is that our impulse for revenge and punishment cannot easily find a target.

All of this is true, at least in part. But the real issue is: Does it matter? What difference would it make to what we were going to do anyway? There are basically two answers to this question. First, even if all these assertions were true, that is no reason not to do good where we can. It would be absurd, after all, to leave serious violations of human rights unaddressed simply because there are other problems left to one side as being too difficult. We have to start somewhere. Second, while it is indeed true that we have to start somewhere, exactly where is a significant political issue, and the things we fail to do are probably of more significance than the things we decide to address. Accepting that all politics is about suboptimal choices, it is hard to agree with the second argument. It is, in effect, a warrant for immobility, an argument that nothing should be done until everything is done. Since everything cannot be performed at the same time, then in effect nothing is done at all. It is also an argument fatally reminiscent of that found in the Balkans: Why are Westerners investigating and prosecuting *our* people when Westerners are not pursuing the *other* side as fiercely? Political complexities notwithstanding, it is hard to argue that we should not do good when we have the power to do so.

If We Can, How Should We?

Accepting that the prevention of atrocities in the future is a sensible objective, how should it be done? There are a number of possibilities. We could try preventative diplomacy before anything serious has happened. We could try military intervention at a later stage. We could try some kind of truth commission. Or we could try education and exhortation. We could hope that the mere existence of the International Criminal Court will have a deterrent effect.

Preventative diplomacy can certainly work, but its greatest champions would agree that it is unlikely to be able to prevent atrocities from occurring if the situation has already deteriorated into violence. Its real strength lies in finding ways to resolve problems before they reach the stage of violence. The classic modern examples include Burundi, which nearly, but not quite, followed Rwanda down the slippery slope.[1] Macedonia is another, as it teetered on the edge of the abyss for some time. Yet the more we examine these examples, the more they demonstrate the demanding nature of the conditions that have to exist before preventative diplomacy can work. For a start, the powers that are intervening must have a clear idea of what they want to achieve, or at least what they are trying to stop. And their objectives must be reasonable in domestic and international terms. Preventative diplomacy failed early on in the former Yugoslavia because the West sought to impose, or at least encourage, a theoretical and normative solution, whereas the only outcome that might have prevented the violence— delaying independence for Croatia and Bosnia so that minority rights could be guaranteed—was not acceptable to Western political opinion. In

Rwanda, by contrast, it can be argued that foreign interventions that led to the 1993 Arusha Accords actually destabilized the situation and made violence more likely. Likewise, the 1999 Lomé Agreement on Sierra Leone left many points (including accountability for atrocities) unaddressed and had no lasting impact. Not all diplomatic intervention is useful, whatever the motives. It helps if the state concerned is small and weak and if the state and other actors are actually amenable to pressure: if these conditions are not met, intervention can make things worse. Indeed, there are going to be cases in which the arrival of foreign diplomats will in and of itself destabilize the situation, perhaps by convincing one side that it is about to be betrayed and that it should therefore strike first. It also helps if the problem is soluble, or at least amenable to management, and if a compromise is actually possible. Preventative diplomacy works best when outside agents can identify solutions that the contestants themselves, often trapped in a dead end by the logic of their own conflict, cannot see. Outside political, technical, financial, and even military assistance can help to stabilize a situation and, ideally, provide some kind of neutral authority in which all sides can have confidence.

Given that conflict and atrocity generally result from situations of tension and insecurity, it is logical that one of the best contributions outside states can make is to increase the security and prosperity of states in which underlying problems make internal conflicts possible. It is unfortunate that this rarely happens. Indeed, the complex of ideologies and developments of globalization, whatever its merits, is likely to increase economic and social insecurity in many parts of the world and so indirectly encourage the development of situations in which atrocities are likely to occur. It has been argued that in Africa, for example, various moves to launch economic and political rebirth, with their neoliberal economic components, will in practice create the conditions for war and atrocity to flourish. Indeed, "the war in the DRC may well offer a prophetic vision of what rapid liberalisation may have in store for areas of the globe that remain peripheral to the interests of the great powers."[2]

What about the military possibilities? First, we must distinguish between post-Brahimi militarist fantasies and what is actually likely to happen in real life. In practice, human rights violations seldom, if ever, take place in front of the helpless gaze of foreign troops who are powerless to intervene. In general, perpetrators are not stupid and will wait until they are unobserved before starting. But are there real possibilities for using military forces to stop atrocities from happening? Here again, it is helpful to distinguish between the use of military force to stabilize a situation of inherent tension and conflict, and so perhaps indirectly prevent atrocities, and ideas of somehow preventing individual atrocities from occurring. The problem with the second idea—seductive as it may be in theory—is that it tends to confuse two quite different policies. There is practically no modern example of intercommunal violence where atrocities are not committed by all sides at some stage, although it is true that some actors may be more willing or more able to commit crimes, and some sets of circumstances may make them easier to commit or to conceal. In the case of state-sponsored atrocity the argument will be somewhat different, but even then there are many cases in which the forces opposing the government (as in South Africa and certain parts of Latin America) themselves resort to violence that may target, or at least hurt, civilians. One option is simply to ignore this fact and intervene on the side believed to have committed the fewest atrocities or the side that, in any event, should win. In practice, this means conniving at, and perhaps even indirectly encouraging, atrocities committed by the side one favors.

Moreover, the balance of atrocities frequently changes as a conflict endures. Atrocities committed by side A as it advanced may have stirred the conscience of the world to intervene, but by the time the troops arrive, side B may be attacking in its turn and committing atrocities all its own. The alternative policy is to declare zero tolerance for atrocities wherever they may be committed, which will immediately offend and alienate all parties to the conflict and pose great problems of definition and consistency. Because the chances of intervention troops actually witnessing atrocities in progress are infinitesimal, there will be immense scope for the parties to manipulate the intervention troops in an attempt to discredit the operation. We have seen that many war crimes involve issues of proportionality and may involve acts that, in other circumstances, would be legal. One can imagine, for example, a platoon of foreign troops being invited to take action to protect a village under mortar fire from the hills, then being told by one side that the village is a military headquarters and by the other side that it is occupied by civilians alone. It is hard to imagine what sensible instructions could be given to troops in such circumstances or what good they could possibly be expected to accomplish.

It is more likely that military forces can help to avoid, rather than prevent, atrocities if they can stabilize a situation, stop the fighting, and separate the combatants. But this is a demanding set of objectives even for expert, heavily armed forces, especially since atrocities are very frequently conducted at a smaller scale and are completed quickly. Thus, when KFOR entered Kosovo in 1999, it had a strength of some 50,000 troops and was probably the greatest concentration of firepower ever assembled in an area of such size (that of Greater London) since World War II. But it proved completely incapable, although it tried hard, of preventing Albanian extremists from murdering hundreds of Serbs and expelling thousands more from the province. And it is unlikely that the average UN peace mission, for example, would be able to do as much as even KFOR. Such forces may in practice be able to do no more than postpone or, with luck, prevent atrocities taking place on a large scale or in an organized way.

Knowing About It

Even the limited role that political or military intervention might play in preventing or limiting atrocities depends absolutely on having some idea that atrocities are in fact going to occur. While this is sometimes possible, such conclusions (they will probably never amount to "knowledge") are often too vague and general to be useful. Although much work has gone on into atrocity-forecasting models, they do not yet offer much more than common wisdom could otherwise predict. There are plenty of countries with ethnic divisions, a failed political system, poverty and hardship, and a collection of extremist politicians. The interesting thing is why atrocities sometimes take place in this situation and sometimes don't. The reasons— or at least the triggers—are often impossible to predict because they are contingent and, to some extent, random. An example is the assassination of an extremist politician, which could actually calm or inflame the situation, depending on when it happened. The opposite is also true: we do not know which factors prevent atrocities from happening. A very slightly different outcome to the negotiations among Bosnian political parties in 1992, for example, could well have staved off a war that everyone recognized would be brutal if it had occurred.

It may simply be a matter of tweaking existing systems. Thus, work that governments already do to predict where crises might occur could in theory be extended to assess whether large-scale atrocities are likely. Analysts already tasked to answer questions such as What are the chances of the current political crisis leading to violent conflict? could in theory also ask, basically drawing on the same body of material, Is there the possibility of large-scale ethnic violence and atrocities? The U.S. government reportedly had some success with this approach in the late 1990s. But even if the material exists, such assessments, by their nature, can only be indicators. They are not going to tell you *where* or *when* atrocities are going to take place, and they cannot account for circumstances in which—as happened in Macedonia in 2001—all the ingredients for atrocity were in place but nothing happens. As Barnett R. Rubin has noted, such techniques are always a "blunt instrument" and cannot cope with the proliferation of motives and actors in a real situation.[3] And one might add that such models seldom try to include fear as a variable—critical in many circumstances, but hard to measure. Moreover, whether such judgments are readily available or come from classified sources, the conclusions must be believed if they are to have any impact. It required no special inside knowledge, for example, to see in 1991–1992 that Bosnian independence and recognition of that country would probably lead to widespread violence and atrocity, but partisans of recognition could not afford to believe these conclusions when they were offered.

Yet there are strident demands today for much more ambitious schemes, based in turn on some bizarre and unrealistic ideas about what governments are capable of accomplishing. Thus, a group of doctors calling themselves Physicians for Human Rights urged, before a subcommittee of the U.S. Congress, that "the United States and others should devote significant resources to gathering intelligence in situations where preparations for mass ethnic killing appear to be underway so that they can quickly intervene to stop the killing." This was easy to do, the doctors argued, because

> quantities of information so vast as to be unusable are collected through satellite photography, radio and telephone intercepts, etc. The key to using this material effectively to inform a response to burgeoning genocide is in 1) telling the intelligence gatherers what to look for in a specific area of search and to focus the inquiry on indicators of trouble ahead (such as troop movements, flow of weapons, positioning of vehicles, orders given, received, and acknowledged, etc.) 2) ordering that the material be analyzed and evaluated specifically for purposes of information about the possibility of mass killing; and 3) making that information available to policy makers both in the U.S., the U.N., and other foreign capitals so that it can be acted upon.[4]

This is a small masterpiece of self-delusion and naïveté, owing its inspiration not to real capacities of intelligence organizations but to Tom Clancy novels and James Bond films. But it is dangerous, because it reflects, and also helps to reinforce, common misperceptions about what governments can do. And once governments are assumed to have these capabilities, then it follows that *any* massacre could have been prevented because governments must have known about it in advance. It also perpetuates an inaccurate and anachronistic view of how atrocities are planned and carried out: few people believe that massacres in Sierra Leone or the DRC could have been known about, let alone prevented, in this way. (In any case, the territory in those countries is obscured by clouds much of the time, making the collection of overhead imagery much more difficult.)

There are two points to be made about attempts even to *collect* information that supposedly would predict atrocities and that are as relevant to human rights NGOs and to media organizations as they are to governments. The first is about priorities. Governments collect information only if it is likely to be useful. In spite of what some doctors may think, the capacity to collect information by intelligence means is limited. It is also complex, expensive, and in some cases dangerous, so strict priorities must be enforced to ensure that a country's intelligence assets are deployed in the most effective way. It is not just that there is no point in using scarce assets unwisely; resources directed at one place cannot be directed at another. Just like media organizations, governments would be criticized if they targeted their assets at, say, human rights violations in Tajikistan while ignoring a potential nuclear conflict between India and Pakistan. And in practice it is often impossible to do both. There is a great deal of difference between making opportunistic use of material collected in the course of things and actively scouring the world for human rights violations, a task that would probably absorb the energies of the major intelligence organizations of the world for a long time. And we must not forget, of course, that much intelligence information is incomplete, misleading, contradictory, or just downright wrong.

The second issue is language. Learning a language to the point one can interpret material takes an average of three years, plus time to gain experience and learn specialized vocabulary. So any organization that thinks it might need linguists must plan at least five years in advance and train and recruit people for what it thinks it might need rather than what it needs today. Moreover, once people have cultivated specializations, they tend to stay with them: one can't simply switch linguists from, say, Chinese to an African language overnight. It's unclear how many analysts fluent in Kinyarwanda Western governments had in 1994, but the answer is probably very few, perhaps none at all. But before we criticize, we should ask ourselves whether it was realistic to assume, in the mid-1980s, that Rwanda was going to blow up ten years later and so ask people to learn a difficult and little-used language despite the pressing need for Arabic, Russian, and Serbo-Croat linguists. Some intelligence organizations do not view language as a high priority anyway. Already, it is clear that one reason for the failure of U.S. intelligence services to predict the September 11, 2001, terrorist strikes was a shortage of qualified Arabic interpreters. A report by the U.S. General Accounting Office revealed that thousands of hours of recordings collected before that date had still not been translated months afterward. In addition, the U.S. government appeared to be seeking speakers only of standard official Arabic, useless for understanding regional dialects and even normal conversations.[5] Unfortunately, foreigners do not always discuss these issues in English, at least not among themselves.

The same problems arose in practice with the intelligence intercepts made available by the Sarajevo government to the ICTY for use in the trial of General Radislav Krstic. The listeners had many advantages: They spoke the same language as the targets; they had had years to learn to recognize voices; they knew all the specialized vocabulary; and the work was technically straightforward. Yet results were often mediocre. Sometimes the conversations were inaudible, sometimes speakers could not be identified, and sometimes they used code phrases, nicknames, or private colloquialisms.

And the results of analysis were not always very useful either. In many cases, far from helping to predict events, the intercepts are so fragmentary that it is possible to make sense of them only if one knows what followed. It is interesting that the Sarajevo government, with all this intelligence at its disposal, never claimed to have been able to predict the attack on Srebrenica, let alone the decision to carry out massacres.

So the idea that there are huge amounts of information out there just waiting to be swept up to predict atrocities is a fantasy, and this applies to great events and smaller ones. It is true, for example, that the UN commander in Rwanda sent a fax to New York in January 1994 reporting allegations that massacres of Tutsi were contemplated, and this was passed along to the UN Security Council. But even if by some miracle immense practical problems of intervention could have been wished away, the fact remains that nations receive allegations like this more or less every day, and almost all of them turn out to be wrong: they cannot all be acted on even if the capability exists. In neighboring Burundi, meanwhile, Ahmedou Ould-Abdallah had a different problem. UN staff members, untrained in military affairs and intelligence analysis, were sending back alarmist reports of large-scale violence to New York, even mistaking claps of thunder for intense combat. Fortunately, large intervention forces were not dispatched there on a daily basis, so no harm was done.[6] In principle, of course, better-trained people could discriminate between credible reports and incredible ones, but that process itself is far from foolproof, and any group of analysts—especially international ones—will frequently disagree about which is which.

Another complicating factor is seen in the different objectives of the actors. Many human rights organizations are small and depend for their existence on a single funder who needs to be convinced that there is actually a human rights problem that their funding will fix. They thus have every incentive to spread alarmist reports in an attempt to retain support in the global atrocity marketplace. Likewise, journalists know that reporting impending conflict is a sure way to get a story printed, and even the most scrupulous, sent out to cover an incipient war, will feel unenthusiastic about not sending a report back if there is nothing to say. But these alarmist reports often get fed back into the country itself, becoming a further complication and even an incitement to violence. NGOs as well as the media played a very destabilizing role in Burundi, for example.[7]

Moreover, international intervention, if it happens, is by definition never neutral. It will always benefit one side more than another, and it will always be more attractive to some groups than to others. For that reason, and with the examples of East Timor and Kosovo in mind, we can assume that various groups, as well as their media and political supporters, will actively try to provoke intervention in the future through a sustained propaganda campaign; indeed, there is likely to be greater competition to secure intervention in an area because interventions are going to be few and difficult.

Trying to make sense of the information coming in, and trying to sort the genuine from the fake—or the simple mistake—is an enormous problem even for large governments. It is likely to be beyond the United Nations for some time. And national governments, less influenced by propaganda, often have a better and less alarmist idea of what is happening from their own sources.

Finally, we might pause for a moment and ask, once more, why all this effort is devoted to preventing serious human rights violations. A major political crisis took place between India and Pakistan in 2001–2002; at one stage it looked as if there might be another war. No special skills of analysis are required to predict that war between nuclear states means millions will die, and yet the response was limited to diplomatic pressure: there was no suggestion that the world should intervene militarily to stop millions from dying. So is the message we want to convey that it is all right for people to die in nuclear explosions but not all right for them to be massacred in intercommunal violence? If not, we had better attend to our rhetoric.

Teaching Tolerance

Since almost by definition crisis interventions come too late, it is natural to wonder whether there are longer-term things that can be done to limit crises or prevent them in the first place. Given the role played by propaganda and political extremism in the buildup to crises, many have wondered whether education, and especially teaching people the truth about the past, is not a useful way of preventing atrocities in the future. *Never again!* in other words, because we have been educated about the possibilities of extremism, and we recoil from following that path in the future. There is something in this notion: tolerance is never a bad thing, and it is surely worth teaching. But the idea that education, the pursuit of the truth, the conduct of war crimes trials, and the erection of museums will somehow reduce future atrocities depends on a connection between intolerance, ignorance, and atrocities. And there is no real evidence to support such a view.

We have to distinguish between crises, which sometimes but not always generate atrocities, and atrocities per se. The world came close to war in October 1962 during the Cuban missile crisis, but the quarrel was one between political elites: ethnic Cubans and Russians were not targeted by American mobs in the streets. Yet politicians can and do exploit and exacerbate ethnic or other tensions for their benefit, and sometimes atrocities result, but these are separate issues and so must be considered as such.

Extremists often garner support from voters for reasons not connected to their intentions, such as they may be, to do harm to other groups. This is especially the case with the most celebrated example of the twentieth century: the Nazis in Germany. There is nothing to suggest that the millions who voted for the National Socialists in 1932 and 1933 had any special feelings of hostility toward the Jews, or other alleged racial enemies, who were scarcely mentioned in the campaigns. (Indeed, the Jews were well integrated into German society at the time.) The 1920 Nazi program (deemed "unalterable" by Hitler) had a single bland reference to the Jews, and there is no indication that anyone beyond a few fanatics actually thought the subject was at all important. The Jews were not a particular target for the regime in its earlier years, and most of Germany's relatively small Jewish community had been rescued by 1939. It was only the conquest of Poland, and then of the Soviet Union, that allowed the extermination of the Jews to begin in earnest. Although there were anti-Semitic fanatics throughout the top echelons of the Nazi state, racial intolerance was rarer among those who actually did the dirty work of killing. They were driven much more by such factors as fear, the desire for revenge, and loyalty to their comrades, as well, of course, as the brutalizing effect of war itself. Indeed, many of the leaders of the infamous "Task Groups" (*Einsatzgruppen*), who conducted mass executions of Jews and others in Poland and the Soviet Union had nervous breakdowns, and eventually the *Einsatzgruppen* themselves were replaced by industrial-style killing at extermination camps.[8] As far as possible non-Germans—such as Demjanjuk (whom we met in Chapter 6)—were used in the running of the camps, and the most appalling jobs were left to the Jewish "Special Detachments." Moreover, many of the worst atrocities of the war were committed not by Germans but by foreigners in their service. About two dozen nations, from Norway to Bosnia, provided SS contingents of different sizes, and the German Army itself used hundreds of thousands of locally recruited auxiliaries. It was, for example, a Ukrainian SS unit that suppressed the 1944 Warsaw Rising.[9]

The primary motivation for atrocities is usually *fear*, and in the case of the Germans this was fear of the notional Jewish conspiracy to destroy them, but also fear of what the Red Army could do if it won. Although there was much less regime propaganda about the inferiority of the Russians, typical German behavior toward the average Russian soldier was probably worse. This reflected not only the army elites' fear of communism but also centuries of fear and contempt for barbaric Asiatic hordes across the borders, as well as folk memories of earlier conflicts, in particular the behavior of the czarist army in World War I.[10] It was this combination of fear and inherited prejudice that led to the large-scale massacres of Soviet troops early in the war. About 5.7 million Soviet troops were listed as captured between 1941 and 1945, of whom perhaps only a million survived. (An unknown number were also shot out of hand.) Most of these deaths (primarily from disease and starvation, although perhaps half a million were executed) took place early in the war, after the great encirclement battles of 1941, and it is hard to think of another modern example of sheer brutality on the same scale. Moreover, these deaths were the result of written orders from the German High Command, which specifically instructed its soldiers that Soviet prisoners were not entitled to the protection of the Geneva Convention.[11]

So although negative stereotypes of enemies certainly make atrocities more likely, on their own they do not make them inevitable, or even probable, and generally require another component—usually fear. The Pacific War was a particularly gruesome example of what competing stereotypes can accomplish, but once again actual motivations for atrocities varied, and in any event it shows less the creation of stereotypes as much as fear engendered by their recollection. For example, Allied troops were often told that the Japanese were so fanatical that they never surrendered and that any offers to surrender should be ignored. And there *were* occasions when Japanese troops did commit suicide with hand grenades in an attempt to take Allied troops with them. Likewise, military regimes in South America, albeit strongly anticommunist, appear to have acted as they did out of fear of a communist takeover rather than any desire to persecute for the sake of it. The same was true in South Africa, where the regime saw itself as desperately defending white Christian civilization against the barbarian hordes. As apartheid assassin Dirk Coetzee told an American journalist in 1994, "I didn't run up and down the country killing people for the fun of it. It was either them or us."[12]

So indoctrination can perhaps make this kind of behavior more likely, but whether it happens or not depends on other criteria. As we have seen, the major one, ironically, is history or, in this context, Truth with a capital *T*. Demagogues almost never try to stir up hatred and division from nothing, because it is not worth it. There always must be some element of truth in what they say, and there always must be real fears. Ironically, these are often exacerbated by harping on real historical incidents from the past.

The atrocities against Serbs that took place in World War II were real enough, even if they were later exaggerated, and many Serbs in Bosnia and Croatia had experienced them personally and were prepared to exact retribution against those they held responsible. The simple answer to the problem of how to prevent a group that inflicted atrocities in the past from doing so in the future is not necessarily the promotion of truth and mutual understanding; rather, it may be to destroy that group so it cannot pose a threat any longer. Why take the risk? As one Bosnian Serb politician put it in 1991 (the fiftieth anniversary, as it happened, of the German invasion of

Yugoslavia), "The Serbs will not let themselves be surprised again as they had done in 1941."[13] *Never again!* Conversely, the recovery of buried truth (or "truth") can also be destabilizing. The Croatian leader Franjo Tudjman famously traced his rebirth as an extreme nationalist to discovering that official figures for Serbs killed in World War II had been exaggerated, and so Croat guilt correspondingly inflated. Attempts to promote understanding and tolerance, important as they are, can never compete with the strength of these kinds of emotions and experiences. Even where, as in the former Yugoslavia, mutual niceness was legally compulsory and enforced with violence, it never affects people's behavior at a basic level and will fall apart under stress.

Some of the same is true of Rwanda. Popular journalistic accounts of the killings (which was all that were available at first) often suggested that the Hutu-Tutsi distinction was simply invented by the Belgian colonists and that precolonial Rwanda was a place of idyllic mutual tolerance and civilization. Now that serious works of academic scholarship have begun to appear, it is clear that specialists have known for decades that this distinction was not invented by the Belgians but had existed since the time of the Tutsi King Rawbugiri (1850–1895), who created a centralized state in which the distinction was institutionalized through various forms of labor service and, in the process, solidified Tutsi domination and Hutu subordination. By the time the first German colonists arrived in 1898, tensions, and even hatreds, between the two groups were already well established. The Belgians, when they took over the country, certainly institutionalized these differences according to current European racialist ideas, but they did not invent them.[14] And for thirty years before the 1994 killings, Hutu-Tutsi relations in the Great Lakes had been marked by mutual hostility and occasional large-scale violence.

It follows from this that we probably pay too much attention to demagogues compared to the backgrounds against which they work. The commendable desire to avoid lazy and incurious journalistic clichés about fighting breaking out spontaneously because of ethnic hatreds should not lead us to assume that hatreds (and fears) do not exist or that they are not sometimes solidly based in the lives of ordinary people. In general, it must be, as Barnett Rubin suggests, that while "leaders manipulate symbols and identities in times of crisis . . . culture is not an infinitely malleable political tool. Demagogic leaders cannot manipulate cultural values or fears that do not exist."[15] Just as protests in Western colonies in the past were explained by the imperial powers as troublemaking by a few hotheads, we now tend to see ordinary people in similar countries merely as the helpless puppets of extremist Svengalis. We would do well to recall, once more, that political crises favor those who take advantage of them. Nationalist extremism was not invented by Milosevic and Tudjman, and had it not been them, it would have been someone else. Research into the history of Srebrenica, before and during the war, for example, makes it clear that relationships between Serbs and Muslims in the area were bad from the late 1980s onward and that there were a number of acts of violence. There is no indication that this tension or these acts were orchestrated by outsiders.[16]

The same applies to the media, a current favorite target (sometimes literally) for those seeking an explanation for atrocities. It is not the case that the media can by themselves, or even with others, provoke atrocities. Recent academic research on the role of the state-controlled media in Rwanda, for example, has shown that, while it certainly increased the sense of crisis and siege in the country and presented the Arusha settlement as a surrender to the Tutsi, it did not incite the killings, which would have gone ahead anyway.[17] And this is typical: control of the media can sow dissent and increase fear and paranoia, but in general it does not seem to induce people to go out and spontaneously murder their neighbors. Indeed, those who listened to the broadcasts of the infamous Radio Télévision Libre des Milles Collines at the time found its output generally so ridiculous that it is hard to believe anyone took it seriously at all.[18]

The question remains though whether museums, exhibitions, books, trials, and films can ever teach lessons and help to prevent atrocities in the future. It is hard to believe they will, for three reasons. First, context is everything. If one is seeking to introduce someone to a negative part of history, one will, almost certainly, find excuses and justifications of the type we have seen, because implicitly one is attacking that person's group and that person. When the Smithsonian Museum in Washington planned to mount an exhibition around the *Enola Gay,* the B-29 bomber that dropped the first atomic weapon on the Japanese city of Hiroshima, it intended to devote part of the exhibit to the human and material damage. The project was submerged by a tidal wave of criticism from retired Air Force officers and right-wing politicians who claimed that the museum was behaving in an unpatriotic fashion and supporting left-wing propaganda. The debate was not over the effects of the bombing—they were hard to dispute—as much as the context. Critics wanted the exhibition to support their contention that the bombing had shortened the war and so saved American lives, with the inevitable corollary that it did not matter very much whether innocent Japanese civilians had died to make that possible. As it happens, Japanese museums in Hiroshima and Nagasaki do the reverse: they fail to mention anything of the wider background at all, taking their context merely from the sufferings of the Japanese people and drawing conclusions from the incidents in favor of peace and general disarmament. It is a commonplace of international humanitarian law texts and literature that there are certain incidents that are objectively so bad that they warrant immediate condemnation by all. Thus, the preamble to the ICC Statute refers to "unimaginable atrocities that deeply shock the conscience of humanity," as though humanity were a single entity that thought the same about everything. In fact, moves toward international justice will always be hampered by the universal tendency to measure the gravity of crimes essentially by who committed them and who the target was.

The context, in fact, tends to dominate the facts, even when all are known. Vietnam has been written about more than almost any other war, and killings and bombings of civilians have been well documented and are in the public domain. Yet the overall impression, from the shelves of books in American bookstores and the parade of Hollywood films, is not only to deemphasize this element of the story but actually to portray the United States itself as the victim, and the war as something inflicted on the American people by the Vietnamese, rather than the other way around.[19] It is for this reason, presumably, that (as far as one can tell from experience in Hanoi and Saigon), the Vietnamese people have now forgiven the Americans; but the Americans have yet to forgive the Vietnamese. A powerful state with a strong culture can, indeed, so reframe a disreputable part of its own history that it can bury the event itself in a self-justifying context.

This brings us to the second problem: all museums, memorials, trials, exhibitions, and even books to an extent are manifestations of power relationships. They take money, and they need organization and permission, and which narrative is told depends upon who has these things. Thus, in the former East Germany, any mention of the atrocities committed by the Red Army in the last stages of World War II was simply forbidden for political reasons, and the role of the German Communist Party was correspondingly glorified. But even where the situation is reversed, information is accurate, and the overall impression is truthful, the result will be, in political terms, a gain for some and a loss for others.

The dominant narrative of the Pacific War, developed by Western states, identifies the Japanese as villains and requires them, their descendants, and their descendants in turn to seek continual forgiveness and demonstrate continual remorse—in principle, forever. This is a situation brought about by a power relationship, and it likewise contributes to the maintenance of one. The narrative is a constructed narrative even if all of the events described are actually true: the trick is one of selectivity and, yet again, context. So it's not surprising that many younger Japanese now feel that the time for ritual obeisance is over and are becoming bored with the whole thing, and political figures in Japan are rethinking that period of history and want it to be presented more favorably. These calls are often dismissed in the West as the product of extreme nationalism, and some of them are, but mostly they represent the political law that for every action there is *always* a reaction.

Thus, the Tito era, with its partisan roots, tended to calumnify the Croats for their cooperation with the Nazis. By the 1960s, it was thought that tempers might have cooled a little, and a museum was opened in Jasenovac to tell the story of the camp there. By all accounts it was as sober and accurate a narrative as one could hope for in a one-party state, but soon after the Croatian declaration of independence in 1991 it was completely destroyed. Visiting the site a little later, Michael Ignatieff noted

> Every book in the library has been ripped up and tossed on the floor. Every glass exhibit case has been smashed. Every photograph has been defaced. Every file has been pulled out of every drawer. . . . Some quite amazing hatred of the past has taken hold of the people who did this. As if by destroying the museum, they hoped to destroy the memory of what was done here.[20]

Yet this is not hard to understand. A younger generation, tired of being seen as perpetrators, wanted a positive image of the history of their own group and reacted intolerantly against negative ones. This mood helped to produce the dangerous and irresponsible attempts by Tudjman's HDZ party to rehabilitate the Ustasha years and the wartime leader and collaborationist Ante Pavelic, which put understandable fear into the hearts of Serbs, Jews, Gypsies, and others and helped convince many that the Serb separatists in Croatia deserved support. Any attempt at the imposition of a historical narrative, no matter how accurate, is likely to set off a political reaction at some stage in the future.

Finally, there must be some logical connection between the educational or didactic event itself and the effect it is trying to create, which in turn requires some clear idea of what one wants to achieve. But this seldom seems to happen in practice. Teaching people about the extermination of the Jews in Europe is one thing, but expecting this to help prevent atrocities in the future depends on there having been lacking something in the perpetrators or the population as a whole in the 1940s that, had it been supplied, could have prevented the atrocities. It is not clear what that is. As we have seen, ignorance and intolerance tend not to be major causes of atrocities. It is often argued that trials or truth commissions can establish facts that are then seen to be incontrovertible and accepted by all, thus making repetition less likely in the future. But while various processes can produce reasonably accurate accounts of what has gone on, there is little sign that their products will actually change the mind of anyone who does not wish to be persuaded. When we consider that tens of millions of Americans say they believe that the earth was created a few thousand years ago, or that millions more believe that aliens have been abducting people for decades, or that the Apollo moon landings were faked in a studio, then we might pause and wonder just how powerful the effects of evidence and logic actually are. It is likely, in fact, that only the fair-minded will actually allow themselves to be convinced by trials or exhibitions, and it is not the fair-minded who are usually the problem.

Trying to teach didactic lessons from the past is fraught with problems unless one knows what one is trying to accomplish. The continued use of the extermination of European Jewry, in particular, as a touchstone and point of reference with a single interpretation is hard to understand. As with any sufficiently complex historical episode, it contains episodes that could be used to justify practically any point of view, and in practice this appears to be what happens. The U.S. National Holocaust Museum, for example, is a decent attempt to tell a complex story, even if controversial issues, like the extent of Jewish collaboration and the involvement of non-Germans in the killings, are glossed over. But in many ways it is also pointless, situated as it is in a country where violent ethnic prejudice has not resulted in massacres in recent years. For this reason, perhaps, its sponsors could hope only that visitors would be inspired to work for a "deepening of [the quality] of American civil and political life and enrichment of the moral fibre of this nation." In fact, it appears that the lessons people draw from the exhibit are very much those they want to draw: antiabortionists compare the Germans who did not help the Jews to those who do not protest against abortion today. One teacher told her students that if the Jews had converted to Christianity, God would have saved them.[21] There is probably no position or prejudice that cannot be supported by reference to the Holocaust: I have heard it offered as the clinching argument for the unrestricted right of individuals to own guns.

The Law as Deterrent

Finally, what about the argument that the existence of courts capable of trying violators of human rights could act as a deterrent in the future? Could this happen? The answer is a qualified "maybe." Any criminal justice system is capable of acting as a deterrent, and most in practice do to some extent. But all empirical studies agree that the existence of courts and penalties is of little value if the offender does not believe he will be caught or, if caught, convicted. The same is likely to be true at the international level. The ICTY certainly had little deterrent effect in the years immediately after its establishment, because it was regarded as a largely impotent organization that could not conduct field investigations and had little capacity to require anyone it indicted to come to The Hague. It has gained in status and influence as it operates more easily and is able to bring in the miscreants. It is this issue of capacity, rather than more abstract questions of the clarity of the law, the skill of the judges, or even the strength of the case, that will determine whether the ICC succeeds. It will be a deterrent only if potential miscreants believe first that it will act objectively and fairly in its investigations, second that it will actually be able to conduct investigations and bring charges, and third that it will have the capacity to apprehend fugitives and put them on trial. The first of these conditions should be met objectively by any reasonable selection of staff for the ICC. But it will be a far harder task to convince non-Western nations that it will actually act in this way. Paradoxically, the greatest problem may be if potential indictees believe that it is not their actual conduct that will determine whether or not they are indicted but whether they retain the support of those they believe control the court politically.

The other two conditions are essentially practical and can be met only if states (including the state of the indictee) actually cooperate. Some states will cooperate, of course, because they take their duties as signatories seriously, although their capacity to act in a practical fashion may be limited. But other states, including those who might be sheltering fugitives, will have to be leaned on in some fashion, possibly bribed and threatened to cooperate. This is never easy, and it may be difficult to accomplish on a regular basis. There is a risk that prospective violators of human rights will have learned lessons from the problems of the ad hoc tribunals and that we are inadvertently creating a collection of wiser and cleverer war criminals. It will be clear that records should be destroyed (and witnesses too, if possible); that nothing should be written down, said over the telephone, or committed to computer; that guilt and responsibility should deliberately be widely diffused; that every effort must be made to penetrate and disrupt investigations; and, most important, that there is a need to find a major international state as a protector that can effectively insulate miscreants from unwelcome attention.

The other problem with the deterrence theory is that, like all such theories, it relies on the target being a rational actor who makes a cost-effectiveness decision to use atrocious means rather than staying within the law. The climate of fear in which most atrocities arise makes this the unlikely case, even assuming that militia leaders and warlords in remote African countries have an understanding of the complexities of international humanitarian law. (My own contacts with African militaries suggest that even professionals do not always understand these things.) It also needs to be remembered that atrocities often give one a powerful military advantage, and a leader may be reluctant to give up that advantage—and perhaps lose an important battle—just to stay within certain legal parameters. In any event, much will depend on how the threat of legal action compares to all the other threats that a leader may face. Defeat may mean, at best, exile and poverty and, at worst, imprisonment, torture, and death. Victory may mean the survival of an ethnic or religious group, as well as substantial personal rewards. The possibility of being put before an international court at some stage in the future may not mean much to a potential perpetrator. There is a good historical precedent for this: the announcement by the Allied powers in 1943 that the Nazi leadership would be put on trial does not seem to have affected German behavior at all, except to make the Nazis more determined to fight on. Partly, this was because the regime was far more concerned about the *non*-judicial treatment it could expect from the Soviet Union if it lost.

However, it is possible that a deterrent process of some sort could work, but in unexpected and indirect ways. In the past, international law has effectively been unenforceable, except against small poor nations for brief periods of time, because there is no powerful overarching authority that can compel compliance. For this reason, it is probably fair to see it less as a body of law as such and more as a system of declaratory norms or even an ideology.[22] This does not mean it has no effect, and states will indeed generally try to abide by international law when they can and will normally defend even egregious actions by reference to international legal norms. But states are not generally obliged to produce legal justifications for their behavior before a court, and if they are, judgments against it are hard to enforce.

The situation in international humanitarian law is different, because human beings, not states, are the subject of any action. Psychologically, this makes an enormous difference, since human beings are prone to fear and uncertainty in ways that states are not. Just as we behave irrationally when we are offered the small chance of winning a large amount of money, so we are equally irrational at the small chance of a large penalty. Lying awake at night, we may think to ourselves, that, rationally, the ICC will surely not bother with us, but on the other hand. . . .

While such a perception is not going to produce moral conversions, or radically affect the policies of governments, at an incremental level it is possible that it will be quietly effective. Henry Kissinger, taxed recently over alleged involvement in war crimes in Indochina, commented that "the decisions made in high office are usually 51-49 decisions, so it is quite possible that mistakes were made."[23] In the future, it is likely that even large states may be influenced a little toward caution by the perception of personal vulnerability, and some of these decisions may be 49-51 decisions instead. It is also possible that individual commanders and officials, again made uneasy by a sense of personal vulnerability, may be less inclined to carry out illegal or dubious acts, and this may slow down or even disrupt atrocities. There is some anecdotal evidence that individual Serb commanders were bothered by a personal sense of vulnerability during the 1999 Kosovo crisis, as were Indonesian military officers when the East Timor crisis began later that year.

Never **Again?**

Much of this book has been devoted to pointing out the difficulties, uncertainties, and hypocrisies involved in the stumbling and preliminary attempts of the world to deal with serious violations of international humanitarian law. It is appropriate to end, therefore, on a more positive note, to examine what can be attempted to prevent these violations in the future—what actually stands a chance of working.

The first thing to recall is that we are not dealing with one thing but several. The circumstances that produced the atrocities of the Khmer Rouge in Cambodia are not the same as those that produced the human rights violations of the apartheid regime or the Chilean junta, and both in turn are different from the circumstances that produced mass atrocities in the former Yugoslavia. Likewise, the actions of the perpetrators are very different. The Khmer Rouge deliberately set out to destroy the educated classes and the urban dwellers, whereas the apartheid regime, once the blacks were safely in their place, was content to drink beer and watch rugby. It was only when people started protesting that the regime became violent. In some cases, atrocities are linked to political objectives, in some cases they are pathological, and in still others they are generated from steadily rising tension and violence. So it follows that whatever prophylactic measures we can identify will not be relevant in all cases; indeed it is as pointless to talk about "the war criminal" as it is to talk about "the terrorist." Like that of terrorist, the status of war criminal is not one that people seek voluntarily, and in some senses labeling someone a war criminal (or terrorist) is a value judgment made with hostile political intent. Recall the ease with which ordinary decent men and women have become war criminals in extreme circumstances; ultimately, we are them, and they are us.

The nearest thing to a general rule is that war crimes tend to occur in circumstances of tension and crisis. This may be because individuals in crises do strange and sometimes violent things, it may be because crises provide room and opportunities for strange and violent people, or it may be a mixture of the two. Thus, moves to enhance the stability and prosperity of states, as well as being desirable in themselves, can do a great deal to prevent the situations in which atrocities happen. It was the political crisis in Cambodia following the 1970 invasion by the United States that turned the Khmer Rouge from an obscure group of fanatics into a homicidal government. It was an economic crisis, followed by a political one, that brought an obscure German political party from 2 percent of the popular vote in 1928 to control of the government in 1933. And political and economic crises propelled extremists in the former Yugoslavia from obscurity into positions of power. Trying to deal with the consequences of such crises without dealing with their causes will not achieve very much. If we are serious about tackling atrocities, then we need to invest in macroeconomic and political stability: full employment, social justice, and economic egalitarianism.

Lack of these characteristics not only creates the space for extremists to flourish; it also causes ordinary people to rally to them. The two basic questions we all ask are, Who will protect me? and Who will look after my interests? When a central authority is incapable of carrying out these tasks, or there is no central authority, people organize themselves, or are organized by others, for their own protection. When the state does not function objectively and fairly, people organize themselves into groups for their own advancement, to lobby the state for privileges for their own group. And because there are few societies without internal tensions of some sort, and because group security and group interests can very easily conflict with each other, tension and violence will easily result. Even when tensions between groups are not profound, there will be a temptation to throw in with local warlords, militia leaders, even criminals if they promise security and protection. The absence of central government control and administrative structures makes it easy for such groups to proliferate but also difficult for them to control territory, except by violence and intimidation: few of them have the capacity to set up administrative structures. It also creates a climate in which organized crime can flourish, adding to the insecurity.

We can try to prevent these things by strengthening states and their capacity to provide the security that people need. Strong states are out of fashion at the moment, but it will be clear that, as the state retreats, some other organizing principle will take over, since no political vacuum endures for long. It may be that the organizing principle will be based on regional or religious differences, on economic power (often foreign), or simply on who can control an area by brute force. In all of these situations, we can expect less respect for human rights. But a strong state is not in itself always a guarantee of stability. One of the reasons why the Soviet Union endured so long was that its state apparatus essentially dealt with all threats to its preeminence equally. Although it was a far weaker state than many in the West thought (it vanished like an ice-cream cone in the sunshine in the space of a couple of years), it was not the preserve of any particular group and treated all nationalist agitation, for example, with equal ferocity. The same was true of the former Yugoslavia, although it was much more complicated.

Where a strong state is identified with a particular ethnic, religious, or national group, it tends to be a source of instability. Groups excluded from power may resent their subordinate status, especially if the security forces of the state are used against them. They may equally desire to capture the resources of the state for their own use, as the incumbents have done. This kind of situation can institutionalize conflict and encourage violations of human rights. What will help prevent this is a state that is capable, in general terms, of reconciling differences among its peoples as much as possible without resort to violence. This means putting the emphasis on representative participation and on state- and institution-building so that good intentions can actually be put into practice. It means a legal system perceived as fair and trustworthy. It does not necessarily mean the imposition of Western-style competitive representative democracy. Indeed, it may imply a form of institutionalized power sharing, in which the tyranny of the majority is not allowed to hold sway. The imposition of democracy actually encourages the abuse of human rights, in the hope of ensuring that one's community is able to vote and others are not. It is for this reason that Ahmedou Ould-Abdallah believed that majority democracy simply would not have worked in Burundi and would probably have destabilized the country, as Rwanda was destabilized by the same process.[24] The West may have to put some of its cherished political norms on hold in the interests of the security and safety of people.

By the time we get to actual intervention, we are almost always too late. (Both Burundi and Macedonia have special factors that are well worth studying.) In particular, one should not trust technocratic solutions. Intervention forces, satellite photography, signals intelligence, and so forth are not going to help, and intervention by military forces, as in Somalia, is almost always a recipe for making a bad situation worse. However, when military forces are preparing to enter a country, perhaps as peacekeepers, perhaps to clean up the mess afterward, then there are things that can be done. If fighting is still continuing, then the very presence of trained and disciplined troops can help reduce it. This happened on many occasions in Bosnia, especially when British battalions were patrolling, although it requires careful judgment to patrol aggressively and yet still maintain the impartiality of the peacekeeper. While peacekeepers cannot, and should not, be investigators, they can nonetheless provide the leaders and commanders of various factions with frank advice, and even warnings, about where their conduct might lead. Records of these meetings, and of all dealings with commanders and leaders, could be priceless in building cases in the future. Personnel should be encouraged to keep diaries, to take photographs and video images, and to preserve official records. These will often cover political and military command structures and issues of control and subordination rather than first-hand evidence of crimes as such, although these will also be important. In all of this, of course, the peacekeepers will have to be careful not to compromise the overall objectives of the mission by being seen as policemen snooping around for evidence. Much of what peacekeepers can do comes under the headings of keeping the eyes open and hanging onto records.

Even after the fighting there is much that can be done. Peacekeepers may be needed to physically escort and protect investigators and offer logistic support and transport. They may also be used to provide security for exhumations and to secure captured evidence, sometimes actively seeking it out. They may be able to help with spiriting witnesses out of the country to give evidence or to safe environments where they can be questioned. Possibly they may be able to assist with tracking down and arresting fugitives. All of these tasks, even the simplest, are outside the general run of peacekeeping. Troops will need to be specially trained and prepared for these tasks, and governments, as well as parliaments and the public, will have to be prepared for casualties if things go wrong.

There is much that governments can do that does not depend on the presence of troops. Some of this is basic and involves direct financial support, as well as political support in the United Nations and elsewhere, especially when things get difficult. Governments can ensure that records are kept, allow and encourage their own employees to give statements and evidence, and encourage good quality people to apply to join the ICC and similar organizations. Governments can provide background briefings on complex subjects, facilitate visits to areas in which they have an interest, and maintain a dialogue with the ICC in an attempt to ensure that its efforts are directed where they will do the most good. They can also refrain from playing political games with the court and trying to sabotage or undermine if it starts investigating areas that for them are sensitive. It is not too much to say that the ICC will stand or fall partly by the assistance it gets from governments. But the other element is public opinion or, rather, elite opinion, as represented in the media and by groups that comment on such things. The media and NGOs have an enormous role to play in helping the ICC to survive its first few years. The more realistic their expectations, the more they encourage people to understand the problems the court will face; this will help the court succeed in the long run. It is imperative that they resist the easy temptation to criticize and dismiss the ICC after a short time to garner headlines and publicity.

Finally, we need to find some way to address the problems of the extremism of lived experience. In the comfortable West, we are inclined to forget how much of the violence of recent years represents personal revenge, direct and vicarious, by people who have suffered things that we cannot begin to visualize. Trying to blame everything on the media, or on a few extremist politicians, is just as much an intellectual copout as blaming ancient ethnic hatreds.

While atrocities certainly proceed from malicious inclination, from warped history and psychological disturbance, they also—as W. H. Auden famously pointed out—arise from the consciousness of evil done by others in the past and the need to seek revenge for it. If Auden's solution in "September 1, 1939"—universal love—eventually seemed unrealistic even to him, and led him to suppress the poem, it does not mean that the underlying analysis was incorrect.

Nothing can change the world overnight. Anyone who thinks that the ICC represents the end of impunity and a new dawn for humanity has a serious misconception. But progress has been made, albeit haltingly and in the face of furious opposition and endless derogatory accusations. Provided we keep our expectations to what can reasonably be accomplished, there is every reason to think that more useful progress will be made. *A bit less in the future!* does not have the same ring as *Never again!* but it is a realistic target.

Notes

1. On Burundi, see Ahmedou Ould-Abdallah, *Burundi on the Brink.*

2. Ian Taylor and Paul Williams, "South African Foreign Policy and the Great Lakes Crisis: African Renaissance Meets *Vagabondage Politique,*" in *African Affairs*, no. 100 (2001): 285.

3. Barnett R. Rubin, *Blood on the Doorstep*, p. 146.

4. "The 1994 Rwandan Genocide and US Policy: Testimony of Holly Burkhalter, Physicians for Human Rights, Subcommittee on Human Rights and International Operations" May 5, 1998 (available online at www.phrusa.org/research/warcrimes/wargenocide.html).

5. A. Brownfield, "Homeland Security Needs More Arabists," *Jane's Intelligence Review* 14, no. 7 (July 2002): 6.

6. Ould-Abdallah, *Burundi on the Brink*, p. 117.

7. Ibid., pp. 60, 83.

8. Heinz Höhne, *The Order of the Death's Head: The Story of Hitler's SS*, tr. Richard Barry (London: Penguin Books, 2000), pp. 363–369.

9. An exhaustive survey of non-Germans who fought with the Nazis is David Littlejohn, *Foreign Legions of the Third Reich*. See also Gerald Reitlinger, *The SS: Alibi of a Nation,* pp. 152–160 and 190–206, and Höhne, *Order of the Death's Head,* 457–460.

10. See Michael Burleigh, *The Third Reich,* p. 490.

11. See Hans-Adolf Jacobsen, "The *Kommissarbefehl* and Mass Executions of Soviet Russian Prisoners of War" in Hans-Adolf Jacobsen, Hans Bucheim, and Martin Broszat, *Anatomy of the SS State*; and Omer Bartov, *Hitler's Army,* pp. 83–89.

12. Bill Berkeley, *The Graves Are Not Yet Full,* p. 174.

13. Cited in Nederlands Instituut vor Oorlogsdocumentatie, *Srebrenica: A "Safe" Area,* pt. 1, chap. 3, sec. 6.

14. This scholarship is reviewed in Johan Pottier, *Re-imagining Rwanda,* esp. pp. 109–129.

15. Rubin, *Blood on the Doorstep*, p. 27.

16. See, for example, *Srebrenica: A Safe Area,* pt. 1, chap. 10, sec. 7; and pt. 2, chap. 2, sec. 2.

17. Mel NcNulty, "Media Ethnicisation and the International Response to War and Genocide in Rwanda," in Tim Allen and Jean Seaton, eds., *The Media of Conflict,* pp. 174–175.

18. John Pender, "Understanding Central Africa's Crisis," paper presented at Africa Direct conference "Rwanda: The Great Genocide Debate," London, July 27, 1997 (available online at www.udayton.edu/~rwanda/articles/genocide/understanding.html).

19. One of many examples is David Kaiser, *American Tragedy*.

20. Michael Ignatieff, *Blood and Belonging*, p. 22.

21. Peter Novick, *The Holocaust and Collective Memory*, p. 260.

22. For international law as ideology, see Shirley V. Scott, "International Law as Ideology: Theorizing the Relationship between International Law and International Politics," in *European Journal of International Law* 5, no. 3 (1994): 313–325. The idea that law is not law unless it can be enforced is associated with the "command theory" of English legal theorist John Austin (1790–1859).

23. Jamie Wilson and Giles Tremlett, "Kissinger Admits Possible Errors on Vietnam," *The Guardian*, April 25, 2002.

24. Ould-Abdallah, *Burundi on the Brink*, pp. 71–72.

Bibliography

Aarons, Mark. *War Criminals Welcome: Australia, a Sanctuary for Fugitive War Criminals Since 1945*. Melbourne: Black, 2001.

Alexievich, Svetlana. *Zinky Boys: Soviet Voices from a Forgotten War*. London: Chatto and Windus, 1992.

Allen, Tim, and Jean Seaton, eds. *The Media of Conflict: War Reporting and Representation of Ethnic Violence*. London: Zed Books, 1999.

Amadiume, Ifi, and Abdullah An-Na'im, eds. *The Politics of Memory: Truth, Healing, Social Justice*. London: Zed Books, 2000.

Auriol, Vincent. *Journal du Septannat, 1947–1954* (Journal of a Seven-Year Term, 1947–1954). Paris: Armand Colin, 1970.

Aussaresses, Paul. *Services Speciaux: Algerie, 1955–1957* (Special Services, Algeria 1955–1957). Paris: Perrin, 2001.

Bass, Gary Jonathan. *Stay the Hand of Vengeance: The Politics of War Crimes Tribunals*. Princeton, NJ: Princeton University Press, 2000.

Bauman, Zygmunt. *Modernity and the Holocaust*. Cambridge, UK: Polity, 1991.

Beigbeder, Yves. *Judging War Criminals: The Politics of International Justice*. London: Macmillan, 1999.

Bell, Terry, and Dumisa Buhle Ntsebaza. *Unfinished Business: South Africa, Apartheid, and Truth*. Johannesburg: Red Works, 2001.

Berkeley, Bill. *The Graves Are Not Yet Full: Race, Tribe, and Power in the Heart of Africa*. New York: Basic Books, 2001.

Best, Geoffrey. *War and Law Since 1945*. Oxford, UK: Oxford University Press, 1994.

Blum, William. *Killing Hope: US Military and CIA Interventions Since World War II*. Monroe, ME: Common Courage, 1995.

Boraine, Alex. *A Country Unmasked: Inside South Africa's Truth and Reconciliation Commission*. Johannesburg: Oxford University Press South Africa, 2001.

Bourke, Joanna. *An Intimate History of Killing: Face to Face Killing in Twentieth Century Warfare*. London: Granta Books, 2000.

Breitman, Richard. *Official Secrets: What the Nazis Planned, What the British and Americans Knew*. London: Allen Lane, 1998.

Browning, Christopher R. *Ordinary Men: Reserve Police Battalion 101 and the Final Solution in Poland.* Rev ed. London: Penguin Books, 2001.

Burg, Stephen L. and Paul S. Shoup. *The War in Herzegovina: Ethnic Conflict and International Intervention.* Armonk, NY: M. E. Sharpe, 1999.

Burleigh, Michael. *The Third Reich: A New History.* London: Macmillan, 2000.

Carlton, Eric. *Massacres: An Historical Perspective.* London: Scolar, 1994.

Cawthra, Gavin. *Policing Apartheid: The SAP and the Transition from Apartheid.* London: Zed Books, 1993.

Celan, Paul. *Selected Poems.* London: Penguin Books, 1993.

Clarke, I. F. *Voices Prophesying War, 1789–1945.* Oxford, UK: Oxford University Press, 1966.

———. *The Pattern of Expectation.* London: Jonathan Cape, 1979.

Conan, Eric, and Henry Rousso. *Vichy: Un Passé qui ne passe pas* (Vichy: A Past Which Does Not Pass). Paris: Fayard, 1994.

Connor, Walker. *Ethnonationalism: The Quest for Understanding.* Princeton, NJ: Princeton University Press, 1994.

Conroy, John. *Unspeakable Acts, Ordinary People: The Dynamics of Torture.* London: Vision Books, 2000.

Crampton, R. J. *The Balkans Since the Second World War.* London: Longmans, 2002.

Davidson, Eugene. *The Nuremberg Fallacy.* 2nd ed. Columbia: University of Missouri Press, 1998.

Davis, Mike. *Ecology of Fear: Los Angeles and the Imagination of Disaster.* London: Picador, 1999.

De Kock, Eugene. *A Long Night's Damage: Working for the Apartheid State.* Johannesburg: Contra, 1998.

Denitch, Bogdan. *Ethnic Nationalism: The Tragic Death of Yugoslavia.* Rev ed. Minneapolis: University of Minnesota Press, 1996.

Detter, Ingrid. *The Law of War.* 2nd ed. Cambridge: Cambridge University Press, 2000.

De Waal, Alex, ed. *Who Fights? Who Cares? Warfare and Humanitarian Action in Africa.* Asmara, Ethiopia: African World, 2000.

Dicks, Henry V. *Licensed Mass Murder: A Socio-Psychological Study of Some SS Killers.* London: Chatto, Heinemann for Sussex University Press, 1972.

Douhet, Giulio. *The Command of the Air.* Trans. Dino Ferrari. New York: Coward-McCann, 1942.

Dower, John. *War Without Mercy: Race and Power in the Pacific War.* London: Faber and Faber, 1986.

Du Preez, Peter. *Genocide: The Psychology of Mass Murder.* London: Boyars/Bowerdean, 1994.

Ellis, Stephen. *The Mask of Anarchy: The Destruction of Liberia and the Religious Dimension of an African Civil War.* New York: New York University Press, 1999.

Felsteiner, John. *Paul Celan: Poet, Survivor, Jew.* New Haven: Yale University Press, 1995.

Finkelstein, Norman G. *The Holocaust Industry: Reflections on the Exploitation of Jewish Suffering.* London: Verso, 2000.

Friedlander, Saul. *Probing the Limits of Representation: Nazism and the "Final Solution."* Cambridge, MA: Harvard University Press, 1992.

Garrett, Stephen A. *Ethics and Airpower in World War II: The British Bombing of German Cities.* New York: St. Martin's Press, 1993.

Gay, Peter. *The Cultivation of Hatred: The Bourgeois Experience: Victoria to Freud.* Vol. 3. London: W. W. Norton, 1993.

Gellner, E. *Nations and Nationalism.* Oxford, UK: Basil Blackwell, 1993.

Girardet, Raoul. *La Crise militaire francaise, 1945–1962: Aspects sociologiques et politiques* (The French Military Crisis, 1945–1962: Political and Sociological Aspects). Paris: Armand Colin, 1964.

Glenny, Misha. *The Fall of Yugoslavia: The Third Balkan War.* 3rd ed. London: Penguin Books, 1996.

Glover, Jonathan. *Humanity: A Moral History of the Twentieth Century.* London: Pimlico, 2001.

Goldhagen, Daniel Joshua. *Hitler's Willing Executioners: Ordinary Germans and the Holocaust.* London: Little, Brown, 1996.

Goldman, Eric F. *The Tragedy of Lyndon Johnson.* New York: Knopf, 1969.

Goldstone, Richard. *For Humanity: Reflections of a War Crimes Investigator.* Johannesburg: Witwatersrand University Press, 2000.

Gow, James, Richard Paterson, and Alison Preston, eds. *Bosnia by Television.* London: BFI Publications, 1996.

Groves, Leslie R. *Now It Can Be Told: The Story of the Manhattan Project.* London: Andre Deutsch, 1963.

Gutman, Roy. *Witness to Genocide.* New York: Macmillan, 1993.

Haas, Aaron. *The Aftermath: Living with the Holocaust.* Cambridge, UK: Cambridge University Press, 1995.

Hartmann, Anja J., and Beatrice Heuser, eds. *War, Peace, and World Order in European History.* London: Routledge, 2001.

Hayner, Priscilla B. *Unspeakable Truths: Confronting State Terror and Atrocity.* New York: Routledge, 2001.

Herr, Michael. *Dispatches.* London: Picador, 1978.

Heuser, Beatrice. *The Bomb: Nuclear Weapons in Their Historical, Strategic, and Ethical Context.* London: Longmans, 2000.

Hilton, Hamann. *Days of the Generals: The Untold Story of South Africa's Apartheid-Era Military Generals.* Cape Town: Zebra, 2001.

Hitchens, Christopher. *The Trial of Henry Kissinger.* London: Verso, 2001.

Hochschild, Adam. *King Leopold's Ghost: A Story of Greed, Terror, and Heroism in Colonial Africa.* London: Macmillan, 1999.

Höhne, Heinz. *The Order of the Death's Head: The Story of Hitler's SS.* tr. Richard Barry. London: Penguin Books, 2000.

Ignatieff, Michael. *Blood and Belonging: Journeys into the New Nationalism.* London: Vintage Books, 1994.

———. *The Warrior's Honour: Ethics, War, and the Modern Conscience.* London: Vintage Books, 1999.

Ignatieff, Michael, et al. *Human Rights as Politics and Ideology.* Princeton, NJ: Princeton University Press, 2001.

Irving, David. *The Destruction of Dresden.* London: Macmillan, 1963.

The Irving Judgment: David Irving v. Penguin Books and Professor Deborah Lipstadt. London: Penguin Books, 2000.

Jacobsen, Hans-Adolf, Hans Bucheim, and Martin Broszat. *Anatomy of the SS State.* London: Collins, 1968.

Jeffrey, Anthea. *The Truth About the Truth Commission.* Johannesburg: South African Institute of Race Relations, 1999.

Judah, Tim. *The Serbs: History, Myth, and the Destruction of Yugoslavia.* London: Yale University Press, 1997.

Kaiser, David. *American Tragedy: Kennedy, Johnson, and the Origins of the Vietnam War.* Cambridge, MA: Harvard University Press, 2000.

Kaldor, Mary, and Basker Vashee, eds. *New Wars: Restructuring the Global Military Sector.* London: Pinter, 1997.

Kelman, Herbert C., and V. Lee Hamilton. *Crimes of Obedience: Towards a Social Psychology of Authority and Responsibility.* New Haven, CT: Yale University Press, 1989.

Kershaw, Ian. *The Nazi Dictatorship: Problems and Perspectives of Interpretation.* 4th ed. London: Arnold, 2000.

———. *Hitler, 1936–1945: Nemesis.* London: Penguin, 2000.

Knightley, Philip. *The First Casualty: The War Correspondent as Hero and Myth-Maker from the Crimea to Kosovo.* London: Prion Books, 2000.

Kott, Jan. *Shakespeare Our Contemporary.* 2nd ed. Trans. Roleslaw Taborski, with a preface by Peter Brook. London: Routledge, 1966.

Krog, Antje. *Country of My Skull.* London: Jonathan Cape, 1999.

Levi, Primo. *If This Is a Man* and *The Truce.* Trans. Stuart Woolf. London: Abacus, 1987.

Lindholt, Lone. *Questioning the Universality of Human Rights: The African Charter on Human and Peoples' Rights in Botswana, Malawi, and Mozambique.* Aldershot, England: Ashgate Publishing Company, 1997.

Lindquist, Sven. *Exterminate All the Brutes.* Trans. Joan Tate. London: Granta Books, 1998.

Lippman, Thomas W. *Madeline Albright and the New American Diplomacy.* Boulder: Westview, 2000.

Littlejohn, David. *Foreign Legions of the Third Reich* (4 vols.). San Jose, CA: R. J. Bender, 1987.

Lloyd, Anthony. *My War Gone By I Miss It So.* London: Doubleday, 1999.

Loftus, Elizabeth F. *Eyewitness Testimony.* Reprinted with a new preface. Cambridge, MA: Harvard University Press, 1996.

Longmate, Norman. *The Bombers: The RAF Offensive Against Germany, 1939–1945.* London: Hutchinson, 1983.

Maechler, Stefan. *The Wilkomirski Affair: A Study in Biographical Truth.* Trans. John. E. Woods. New York: Schocken Books, 2001.

Maier, Charles S. *The Unmasterable Past: History, Holocaust, and German National Identity.* Cambridge, MA: Harvard University Press, 1988.

Mamdani, Mahmood. *When Victims Become Killers: Colonialism, Nativism, and the Genocide in Rwanda.* Princeton, NJ: Princeton University Press, 2001.

Marrus, Michael R. *The Holocaust in History.* London: Penguin Books, 1989.

Mayer, Arno. *Why Did the Heavens Not Darken? The Final Solution in History.* New York: Pantheon Books, 1988.

Mazower, Mark. *The Balkans.* London: Weidenfeld and Nicolson, 2000.

McCormack, Timothy L.H., and Jerry J. Simpson, eds. *The Law of War Crimes: National and International Approaches.* The Hague: Kulwer Law International, 1997.

McCullough, David. *Truman.* New York: Simon and Schuster, 1992.

Meiring, Piet. *Chronicle of the Truth Commission.* Vanderbijlpark, South Africa: Carpe Diem Books, 1999.

Melven, Linda. *A People Betrayed: The Role of the West in Rwanda's Genocide.* London: Zed Books, 2000.

Meredith, Martin. *Coming to Terms: South Africa's Search for Truth.* Oxford, UK: Public Affairs, 1999.

Nederlands Instituut vor Oorlogsdocumentatie. *Srebrenica: A "Safe" Area.* Amsterdam: Nederlands Instituut vor Oorlogsdocumentatie, 2002.

Norwich, John Julius. *A History of Venice.* London: Penguin Books, 1983.

Novick, Peter. *The Holocaust and Collective Memory: The American Experience.* London: Bloomsbury, 2000.

Nuttall, Sarah, and Carli Coetzee, eds. *Negotiating the Past: The Making of Memory in South Africa.* Oxford, UK: Oxford University Press, 1998.

O'Brien, Connor Cruise. *United Nations: Sacred Drama.* London: Hutchinson, 1968.

Orwell, George. *Complete Works.* 20 vols. Ed. Peter Davison. London: Secker and Warburg.

O'Shea, Brendan. *Crisis at Bihac: Bosnia's Bloody Battlefield.* Stroud, UK: Sutton Publishing, 1998.

Osiel, Mark J. *Obeying Orders: Atrocity, Discipline, and the Laws of War.* New Brunswick, NJ: Transaction Publishers, 1999.

Ould-Abdallah, Ahmedou. *Burundi on the Brink, 1993–95: A UN Special Envoy Reflects on Preventive Diplomacy.* Washington, DC: United States Institute of Peace, 2000.

Overy, Richard. *Interrogations: The Nazi Elite in Allied Hands, 1945.* London: Allen Lane/Penguin Press, 2001.

Pauw, Jacques. *Into the Heart of Darkness: Confessions of Apartheid's Assassins.* Johannesburg: Jonathan Ball, 1997.

Pick, Daniel. *War Machine: The Rationalisation of Slaughter in the Modern Age.* London: Yale University Press, 1993.

Piotrowski, Tadeusz. *Poland's Holocaust: Ethnic Strife, Collaboration with Occupying Forces, and Genocide in the Second Republic, 1918–1947.* London: McFarland, 1998.

Plato. *Protagoras and Meno.* Trans. W.K.C. Guthrie. London: Penguin Books, 1956.

Pottier, Johan. *Re-imagining Rwanda: Conflict, Survival, and Disinformation in the Late Twentieth Century.* Cambridge, UK: Cambridge University Press, 2002.

Pouillot, Henri. *La Villa Sursini: Tortures en Algérie. Un appele parle; juin 1961–mars 1962* (The Villa Sursuni: Torture in Algeria. A Conscript Speaks Out; June 1961–March 1962). Paris: Editions Tirésias, 2001.

Ratner, Stephen, and Jonas A. Abrams. *Accountability for Human Rights Atrocities in International Law: Beyond the Nuremberg Legacy.* 2nd ed. Oxford, UK: Oxford University Press, 2001.

Reitlinger, Gerald. *The SS: Alibi of a Nation, 1922–1945.* London: Heinemann, 1956.

Reno, William. *Warlord Politics and African States.* Boulder: Lynne Rienner Publishers, 1999.

Richards, Paul. *Fighting for the Rain Forest: War, Youth, and Resources in Sierra Leone.* Oxford, UK: James Currey, 1999.

Roberts, Adam, and Richard Guelff, eds. *Documents on the Laws of War.* 3rd ed. Oxford, UK: Oxford University Press, 2000.

Roseman, Mark. *The Villa, the Lake, the Meeting: Wannsee and the Final Solution.* London: Allen Lane, 2002.

Rubenstein, William D. *The Myth of Rescue: Why the Democracies Could Not Have Saved More Jews from the Nazis.* 2nd ed. London: Routledge, 2000.

Rubin, Barnett R. *Blood on the Doorstep: The Politics of Preventive Action.* New York: Century Foundation Press, 2002.

Schabas, William. *An Introduction to the International Criminal Court*. Cambridge, UK: Cambridge University Press, 2001.

———. *Genocide in International Law*. Cambridge, UK: Cambridge University Press, 2000.

Schell, Jonathan. *The Time of Illusions*. New York: Alfred A. Knopf, 1976.

Sereny, Gitta. *The German Trauma: Experiences and Reflections, 1938–2001*. London: Allen Lane, 2001.

Shawcross, William. *Deliver Us from Evil: Warlords and Peacekeepers in a World of Endless Conflict*. London: Bloomsbury, 2000.

Sheehan, Neil. *A Bright Shining Lie: John Paul Vann and America in Vietnam*. London: Picador, 1990.

Sims, Brendan. *Unfinest Hour: Britain and the Destruction of Bosnia*. London: Allen Lane, 2001.

Stannard, David E. *American Holocaust: Columbus and the Conquest of the New World*. Oxford, UK: Oxford University Press, 1992.

Stibon, Michel. *Une genocide sur la conscience*. (A Genocide of the Conscience.) Paris: L'Espirit Frappeur, 1998.

Taylor, Telford. *The Anatomy of the Nuremberg Trials: A Personal Memoir*. London: Bloomsbury, 1993.

Todorov, Tristan. *Nous et les autres: La rélexion francaise sur la diversité humaine* (We and Others: French Thinking About Human Diversity). Paris: Seuil, 1985.

Verschave, Francois-Xavier. *Complicité de génocide? La politique de la France au rwanda* (Complicity in Genocide? French Policy in Rwanda). Paris: La Découverte, 1994.

Villa-Vicencio, Charles, and Wilhelm Verwoerd, eds. *Looking Backward, Reaching Forward: Reflections on the Truth and Reconciliation Commission of South Africa*. Cape Town: University of Cape Town Press, 2000.

Weber, Max. *From Max Weber: Essays in Sociology*. Edited and with an introduction by H. H. Gerth and C. Wright Mills; with a new preface by Bryan S. Turner. London: Routledge, 1991.

Webster, Sir Charles, and Noble Frankland. *The Strategic Air Offensive Against Germany, 1939–1945*. London: Her Majesty's Stationery Office, 1961.

White, Hayden. *The Content of the Form: Narrative Discourse and Historical Representation*. Baltimore: Johns Hopkins University Press, 1987.

Wilson, Richard A. *The Politics of Truth and Reconciliation in South Africa: Legitimizing the Post-Apartheid State*. Cambridge, UK: Cambridge University Press, 2001.

Woodward, Susan L. *Balkan Tragedy: Chaos and Dissolution After the Cold War*. Washington, DC: Brookings Institution, 1995.

Wyman, David S. *The Abandonment of the Jews: America and the Holocaust, 1941–1945*. New York: The New Press, 1984.

Yeros, Paris, ed. *Ethnicity and Nationalism in Africa: Constructivist Reflections and Contemporary Politics*. London: Macmillan, 1999.

Index

About the Book

W ar crimes typically are discussed in sensational terms or in the dry language of international law. In contrast, David Chuter brings clarity to this complex subject, exploring why atrocities occur and what can be done to identify perpetrators and bring them to justice.

Chuter confronts the real horror of the murder, rape, and torture that are subsumed under the dispassionate phrase "serious violations of international humanitarian law." But his discerning analysis also situates war crimes in their historical and cultural context—acknowledging the social and cultural mind-sets that allow them to happen—and discusses the political and policy issues surrounding them. Offering a nuanced typology of war crimes and a thoughtful discussion of the laws relating to them, *War Crimes* also grapples with such troubling questions as whether the outcomes of tribunals can come close to "the truth"—and whether they can help to prevent atrocities in the future.

Working for the British Ministry of Defence, **David Chuter** has had responsibility for Balkans war crimes issues and support to the International Criminal Tribunal in the Hague. He is author of *Humanity's Soldier: France and International Security, 1919–2001*, and *Defence Transformation: A Short Guide to the Issues*.

Due Date	Date Returned
T/Aug. 21, 07	SEP 0 5 2007
T/DEc 01,09	APR 3 0 2010
www.library.humber.ca	